W9-CLM-832

CONTEMPORARY SPIRITUALITY

Contemporary SPIRITUALITY

Current Problems in Religious Life

Edited by

ROBERT W. GLEASON, S.J.

The Macmillan Company, New York

Nihil Obstat: John A. Goodwine, J.C.D.
Censor Librorum

Imprimatur: ✠ Terence J. Cooke, D.D.
Auxiliary Bishop of New York

New York, New York—December 27, 1967

The nihil obstat and imprimatur are official declarations that a book or pamphlet is free of doctrinal or moral error. No implication is contained therein that those who have granted the nihil obstat and imprimatur agree with the contents, opinions, or statements expressed.

Library of Congress Catalog Card Number: 68-15937

First Printing

The Macmillan Company, New York

Collier-Macmillan Canada Ltd., Toronto, Ontario

PRINTED IN THE UNITED STATES OF AMERICA

ACKNOWLEDGMENTS

THE author gratefully acknowledges permission from the following publishers and individuals to reproduce copyrighted material: Guild Press, America Press, Association Press and Herder and Herder who published *The Documents of Vatican II,* from which the translation of The Decree on the Appropriate Renewal of the Religious Life is taken, Copyright © 1966 by The America Press. Used by permission; *Gregorianum* for "Transformatio Mundi et fuga mundi" by Charles Truhlar, 1957, translated by James Byrne, S.J.; *Vie Spirituelle* for "La Priere Evangelique" by Louis Lochet, June 1960 issue; and for "Enfance Spirituelle et Infantilisme" by Louis Beirnaert, July 1951 issue, translated by Michael L. Mazzarese; *Vie Spirituelle Supplement* for "Principles of Maturity" by Albert Ple, which appeared in 1958; *Theology Digest* for "The Meaning of Christian Hope" by Bernard Olivier, Spring 1955; "Contemplative in Action" by Emerich Coreth, Winter 1955, used also with the permission of *Zeitschrift für Katholische Theologie,* 1954; "St. Paul: Liberty and Law" by Stanislas Lyonnet, Spring 1963; and for "Love and Celibacy" by Bernard Haring, Winter 1955; *Christus* for "Dieu est fidele" by Henri Holstein, 1965, translated by Michael L. Mazzarese; *Doctrine and Life* for "Work and the Christian Life" by Nivard Kinsella, May 1961; *Spiritual Life* for "The Loss that is Gain" by Barnabas Ahern, December 1959; *Sponsa Regis* for "The Problem of Poverty," "The Motives of Poverty," "Poverty in the Modern World," and "The Challenge of Poverty" by Karl Rahner, 1962; *Cross Currents Quarterly* for "A Basic Ignatian Concept: Some Reflections on Obedience" by Karl Rahner; *The Catholic Biblical Quarterly* for "Authority and Power in the New Testament" by John L. McKenzie and also reprinted with permission of The Macmillan Company from *A Theology Reader,* edited by Robert W. Gleason, S.J., Copyright © Robert W. Gleason, S.J., 1966; *Revue de l'Universite d'Ottawa* for "Respect for the Individual as an Expression of God's Will" by John Navone, 1963; *Review for Religious* for "The Psychological Possibility of Intellectual Obedience" by Thomas Dubay, March 1960; and for "The Church's Holiness and Religious Life" by Gustave Martelet, also used by permission from *Editions Priere et Vie; The Way* for "If We Endure With Him" by William Lawson; *National Catholic Guidance Conference Journal* for "Psychiatric Concepts of Maturity" by Alfred R. Joyce.

Contents

1

Saint Paul: Liberty and Law

STANISLAS LYONNET, S.J.*

St. Paul's assertion admits no compromise: The Christian vocation is a vocation to liberty. The Christian is a son, not a hireling, not a slave. "You have been called to liberty, brethren," he writes to the Galatians. And again, "If you are led by the Spirit, you are not under the Law" (5:13, 18). These proclamations, and others like them, were a source of scandal not only to the Jews but even to some of the first Christians. That St. Paul found himself the object of latent hostility, or at least of a painful lack of understanding, from the very beginning of his missionary activity to his last days, was mainly due to his attitude toward the Law and to his preaching of Christian liberty. St. Paul was unyielding whenever the principle of Christian liberty was at stake. For him it was no secondary doctrine, no side issue; the whole religion of Christ was in the balance.

Although the doctrine of Christian liberty which he preached was worked out in his controversies with the Judaizers, and hence in very particular circumstances, still a doctrine can be found in St. Paul's arguments that has undeniable validity and importance for our own day. His doctrine can be summed up as follows: The Christian who is led by the Spirit finds himself freed, in Christ, from the Law of Moses; he is freed from it not only as the Law of Moses, but as law. He is delivered from any law that constrains or coerces (I do not say *binds*) him from without; yet, this in no way makes him an amoral being, outside the realm of good and evil.

* Stanislas Lyonnett, S.J.G., is coauthor with I. LaPotterie, S.J., of *Life According to the Spirit,* soon to be published by Alba House.

DELIVERANCE FROM LAW

When he speaks of law, St. Paul obviously has in mind especially that Law which for him and for his Jewish contemporaries was uniquely worthy of the title, the legislation given on Mount Sinai. To measure the offense his statements must have given to his fellow Jews, we only have to recall how they venerated and honored the Torah. The Law was the word of God, the water that slakes all thirst, the life-giving bread, the vine laden with fruit; in it were hidden the treasures of wisdom and knowledge. In short, the Law held the place St. John and St. Paul were rightly to announce as that of the Christ.

But from this Law the Christian has been delivered. St. Paul declares: "You are not under the Law but under grace" (Rom. 6:14). A wife is bound to her husband as long as he is alive, but, when he dies, is completely free from the law that bound her to him, so that she is not an adulteress if she marries another. In like manner the Christian, united to Christ dead and risen, is dead to the Law, delivered from it, no longer its subject (Rom. 7:1-6). But had not the Law played a role in the history of the chosen people? Indeed, but it was the thankless one of a jailer, or of a pedagogue, the slave whose task it was, not to teach the children, but to lead them to their teacher (Gal. 3:23-24). Beyond this, St. Paul paradoxically asserts that the Law, which the Jews revere as the source of life, has been imposed by God on man to bring him death. The economy of the Law was not that of a blessing but of a curse (Gal. 3:10).

LAW PROVOKED TRANGRESSION

"What then was the Law?" he asks in the Epistle to the Galatians (3:19), and his answer is that it was given to provoke transgression. This was a shocking statement, even for Christian readers; and well-meaning copyists very soon tried to soften it harshness. But there is no way out—the text is concerned with provoking transgressions, not with repressing them.

Is this a witticism? Is it a paradox? Not at all! In fact, the Epistle to the Romans brings out St. Paul's idea with even greater precision. Emancipation from the Law is one of the key links, indeed, the final one, of his argument. Freed from sin, from death, and from the flesh, the Christian cannot be saved unless he is also freed from the Law; only this final liberation will strip sin of its power, its dominion over man: "Sin shall not have dominion over you, since you are not under the Law, but under grace" (Rom. 6:14). To be under the Law, then, is the same as to be under the rule of sin. Never before had St. Paul been so incisive.

A source of scandal for the Jews, such assertions run the opposite risk of leaving the modern Christian reader quite indifferent. He has never felt any strong attachment to the Law of Moses. He finds it quite normal not to be obliged to observe its complicated ritual or its many observances—as circumcision, the minue prescriptions for keeping the Sabbath, for preparing food, or for contacts with the pagan world. These, as far as he can see, have no real religious value. As a matter of fact, had St. Paul intended no more than the Christian's deliverance from these obligations, his statements would hardly raise problems. Nor would they offer any great interest for the man of today. But so understood, they would be a caricature of his true teaching.

Under the term "law," St. Paul certainly includes that part of the Mosaic legislation which concerns the moral life in the strict sense; in fact, the Epistle to the Romans speaks of no other aspect of the Law but the moral one. As for the seventh chapter, where the question is expressly treated, everyone must at least see with Father Huby that, if St. Paul has the Law of Moses in mind, it is "not in its ritual and ceremonial positions" that he considers it, "but in its permanent moral content." In other words, he is concerned with the Law of Moses as a positive expression of the natural law. Besides, St. Paul is explicit: The "law of sin and of death"—that is, the Law that provokes sin and leads to death—from which he proclaims we are free, is clearly designated by means of one precept of the Decalogue: "I did not know sin save through the Law. For I had not known lust unless the Law had said: 'Thou shalt not lust' " (Rom. 7:7).

PRECEPT EPITOMIZES LAW

Let us press this passage further. The English translation "Thou shalt not lust," may suggest that the Apostle had a particular commandment in mind, the one that prohibits carnal desires. This would be a serious mistake. Not only is the context of Exodus 20:17 or

Deuteronomy 5:21, from which this prohibition is taken, utterly opposed to such an interpretation, but in the Septuagint, the Greek word *epithumein,* whether in its verbal or substantive form, hardly ever evokes the idea of carnal desire. What the commandment forbids, in the most general sense, is the craving for what belongs to another, whether it be his house, his wife, his slave, his ox or ass, or anything else that he owns. In much the same way, Ecclesiasticus sums up the whole Jewish Law in the one precept: "Avoid all evil" (17:22). For Ben Sirach, this precept seems to epitomize not only the legislation of Sinai but all the expressions of God's will that have ever been given to man, expressions that have their synthesis in a unique law and covenant.

It is not surprising, then, that St. Paul in turn should choose an all-embracing formula, one that could be applied to every divine command, even the prohibition imposed upon our first parents, the prototype of all others. In his desire to describe how man becomes conscious of sin, to describe, too, the essential role played by law in this process, Paul thinks of the biblical description of sin that became the pattern of all our sins; all succeeding generations of men unfailingly share in it and reproduce it again and again in their own lives. Many have noticed that more than one detail in chapter seven of Romans is in some way reminiscent of the third chapter of Genesis. In any case, keeping in mind the narrative of Genesis may help throw light on and clarify a passage that is at first sight enigmatic.

Adam and Eve are living in a state of familiarity with God when the serpent comes and persuades them that they will be like gods if they taste of the tree of knowledge of good and evil. Immediately, the fruit, which has become the means of securing this divine privilege, seems to Eve an unknown delight. The Bible brings this out emphatically: "The woman saw that the tree was good for food, pleasing to the eyes, and desirable for the knowledge it would give" (Gen. 3:6). But as soon as Adam and Eve break God's command, they find themselves reduced to nakedness, stripped of everything that previously constituted their happiness. Cast out of the garden, they are deprived forever of God's friendship. Unless God Himself mercifully intervenes, the gate that leads to the tree of life—of that life which belongs to God alone, and to those who are united to him—is forever shut. Now God's command was unquestionably good, spiritual, divine. It is not the command but the serpent who is responsible for all the world's ills. And yet, according to the biblical account, the command did play a role; the serpent used it to induce our first parents to disobey. Though it was supposed to preserve life in them, in reality it became a cause, or at least an occasion, of death.

LAW BRINGS DEATH

This is the point St. Paul is trying to make in the much discussed passage of his Epistle to the Romans. There is only one change in the cast of characters: Sin, personified, plays the part of the serpent. "What shall we say then? Is the Law sin? By no means! Yet I did not know sin save through the Law. For I had not known lust unless the Law had said: 'Thou shalt not lust.' But sin, having thus found an occasion, worked in me by means of the commandment all manner of lust, for without the Law, sin was dead" (Rom. 7:7-8). Sin was a powerless corpse.

"But," St. Paul continues, "when the commandment came, sin revived (*anezēsen*)"; heretofore a lifeless body (*nekros*), it rose up (*ana*) a living thing (*ezēsen*), "and I died," this is, I lost that eminently divine privilege of life. "And the commandment that was unto life was discovered in my case to be unto death. For sin having taken occasion from the commandment deceived me" (as the serpent deceived Eve) "and through it killed me" (7:8-11). Hence, for St. Paul, just as for the authors of Gen. 3 and Wis. 2:24, the one responsible for death is neither the Law nor its author, but the serpent or the devil or sin.

But if "the Law is holy and the commandment holy and just and good," (7:12), how then are we to explain God's strange conduct? If He desires nothing but life, why give man a law that, in fact, will lead him to death? St. Paul provides the answer: "Did then that which is good become death to me? By no means! But sin, that it might be manifested as sin, worked death for me through that which is good, in order that sin by reason of the commandment might become immeasurably sinful" (7:13), in other words, that sin might exercise its full power as sin by means of the commandment.

According to the Jews, the Law gave life. However, a law as such, even if it proposed the highest ideal, could not change a creature of flesh into a spiritual being, alive with the very life of God. If this were possible, it would mean that man has no need of being saved, that he can actually save himself! Far from giving life, far from destroying or even curbing the death-bearing power of sin in man, the purpose of the Law is, as it were, to permit sin to exercise all its virulence, but in so doing, to bring sin itself out into the open and unmask it. The Law does not take sin away, rather it reveals to man his sinful state.

LAW UNMASKS SIN

Let us note that, properly speaking, law does no provoke sin, but transgression. St. Paul looks upon transgression as the outward expression of a far more deeply rooted evil, *hamartia:* not merely carnal concupiscence, but an evil power personified, corresponding to that deeply rooted egoism by which man, since original sin, orientates everything to himself instead of opening himself to God and to others. It is this "sin" that must be destroyed in us; and, left to itself, law is incapable of the task. But by permitting "transgression," law makes sin unfold itself and helps man, through his painful experience, to seek his Savior. This is the way St. Paul understands the role of law, a role that is indispensable, ultimately beneficent and salutary. But this role is associated with any law that is truly law, to any rule that is imposed on man's conscience from without. It is from the "rule of law" as such that St. Paul declares the Christian freed.

LAW OF THE SPIRIT

Is the Christian, then, a man without law, a creature beyond the realm of good and evil? St. Paul issues a flat *no* to this objection. "What then? Are we to sin because we are not under the Law but under grace? By no means!" (Rom. 6:15). The eighth chapter of the Epistle to the Romans contains his solution. Chapters five, six, and seven of the Epistle set forth the conditions necessary for the Christian to be saved: deliverance from sin, from death, from the flesh, and the final deliverance, that from the Law. They show that each successive deliverance is secured for the Christian in Christ, and in Him alone. Then, chapter eight begins with a cry of triumph: "There is therefore now no condemnation for those who are in Christ Jesus!"

St. Paul states the reason precisely: "For the law of the Spirit, (giving) life in Christ Jesus, has delivered me from the law of sin and death" (8:1-2). So man is delivered from that Law which, according to the incontestable testimony of the Bible, had been the instrument of sin and death, by something that St. Paul also calls a law: the law of the life-giving Spirit.

What does this mean? Can Christ have been satisfied with substituting for the Law of Moses another code, more perfect or less complicated perhaps, but of the same nature, which would thereby keep the Christian under legal rule? This would contradict all that has gone before. St. Paul had just opposed to the Law of Moses, not another law, but grace: If sin no longer exercises its dominion over you, he explains, it is because "you are not under the Law but under grace" (Rom. 6:14). Has he changed his mind? Not at all! His choice of expression has changed, but not his thinking.

NEW LAW DIFFERS RADICALLY

The "Law of the Spirit," then, does not differ from the Law of Moses—and a fortiori from all non-revealed law—merely because it sets up a loftier ideal and makes greater demands. Nor does it differ because if offers salvation at a bargain, as if Christ had replaced the unbearable yoke of the Law of Sinai with an "easy morality." No, the law of the Spirit is radically different. It is not just a code, not even one "given by the Holy Spirit," but a law "produced in us by the Holy Spirit"; not a simple rule of action outside us, but something that no legal code as such can possibly be—a new, inner source of spiritual energy.

If St. Paul applies the term "law" to this spiritual energy, rather than the term "grace" that he uses elsewhere (Rom. 6:14), he probably does so because of Jeremia's prophecy announcing a new covenant, the "New Testament." For the prophet, too, speaks of law: "This is the covenant which I will make with the house of Israel. . . . I will place my law within them, and write it upon their hearts" (31:33). The Christian who receives the Holy Spirit as an active force within him, becomes capable of "walking according to the spirit," that is, walking in conformity with what the Old Law, "spiritual" though it was, demanded of him in vain. This is why St. Paul, after setting forth man's deliverance by the law of the Spirit, thanks to the redemptive work of Christ, can attribute to that work the following aim: "that the justification of the Law"—that justification which the Law wished but could not obtain from us creatures of flesh—"might be fulfilled in us" (Rom. 8:4).

From this basic teaching flows notably the fact that Christian morality is of necessity founded on love, as St. Paul teaches: "The whole Law is fulfilled in one word: Thou shalt love thy neighbor as thyself" (Gal. 5:14, Rom. 13:8-10). The reason is that love is not first of all a standard of conduct, but a dynamic force—it is precisely because the Law, as a law, was not love that it could not justify man.

Under these conditions, it is easy to see that a Christian, a man led by the Holy Spirit, can at the same time be freed from every external law—"not be under the Law"—and yet lead a perfect moral and virtuous life. Having reduced the whole Law to love, St. Paul adds: "Walk in the Spirit, and you will not fulfill the lusts of the flesh" (Gal. 5:16). Nothing could be more obvious, he explains, since these are two antagonistic principles: If you follow one, you must oppose the other.

"If you are led by the Spirit, you are not under the Law." In fact, what need would you have of law? A spiritual man knows perfectly well what is carnal and, because he is spiritual, he will fly from it as by instinct. Since he has no need, then, for a law to constrain him from without, the Christian, led by the Spirit, fulfills every law in the full liberty of the sons of God.

THE CODE OF CHRISTIAN LAWS

Why, then, does the religion of Christ still require a code of laws? Why should there be kept alongside the chief unwritten element that justifies, another written element that does not justify? If this state of affairs was strange in the old economy, does it not become unintelligible in the economy of grace? Not at all!

The Pauline principle remains: "The Law is not made for the just, but for the unjust" (I Tim. 1:9). If all Christians were just, there would be no need to restrain them by laws. Law, as a rule, does not enter upon the scene except to arrest disorder. For example, as long as Christians received Communion frequently, the Church never thought of obligating them under pain of mortal sin to do so at least once a year. But when fervor declined, she promulgated the precept of Easter Communion to remind her faithful that it is impossible to have divine life without being nourished by the flesh of Christ. Even though all are subject to this law, it is really not directed to the fervent Christian who continues to receive Communion during the paschal season not because of the Lord's command, but because of that inner need which prompts him to communicate every Sunday or even every day of the year. This does not imply that he is no longer bound by the precept but that as long as he experiences this inner need—which is a fruit of the Holy Spirit leading him—he will in fact fulfill the precept, without even adverting to the fact. On the other hand, as soon as that inner need no longer makes itself felt, the law is there to constrain him and to warn him that he is no longer being led by the Spirit.

HELPS RECOGNITION

In the latter case this law will play the same role for the Christian that the Law of Moses did for the Jew. As a pedagogue to lead him to the Christ, it will not only act as a sort of substitute for the light no longer supplied by the Holy Spirit, but will, above all, help him to recognize his condition as a sinner—one who is no longer led by the Holy Spirit. And since such a recognition is for St. Paul the first requirement for man's cure, it becomes evident that the law was made for sinners.

But the law is set down even for the just. Although he is in the state of grace, that is, led by the Holy Spirit, the Christian, as long as he remains on earth, possesses the Spirit only imperfectly, as a sort of pledge (Rom. 8:23; II Cor. 1:22). As long as he lives in a mortal body, he is never so completely freed from sin and from the flesh that he cannot at any moment fall back under their sway. Now in this unstable position, the law—the external, written, objective norm of man's conduct—will guide him in distinguishing the works of the flesh from the fruit of the Spirit and keep him from confusing the inclinations of his sin-wounded nature with the inner promptings of the Spirit. Until the Christian acquires full spiritualization in heaven, there will remain alongside grace (the chief element of spiritualization, alone able to justify) a secondary element, no more able to justify than was the Old Law, but still indispensable for sinners, and by no means superfluous for the just who are still imperfect.

MUST REMAIN SECONDARY

Still it is necessary that this secondary element remain secondary, and that it not tend imperceptibly to assume the role of the principal element, as happened to the Jewish Law in St. Paul's time. To ward off this ever-threatening danger, it is well to recall a basic principle, a corollary of the foregoing doctrine: The external law can be only the expression of the interior law. Works can be commanded only because they bear a necessary relation to the inner grace of the Holy Spirit.

Either they will be works that put us in contact with the humanity of Christ from whom all grace flows, and are therefore necessary to produce in us the inner dynamism that is faith working through charity. Or they will be works that translate and give concrete expression to this inner law of love.

As a consequence, any purely external violation of law, an "involuntary sin," a violation which by definition is unrelated to the interior law, cannot be a genuine violation. On the other hand, an observance devoid of love is also devoid of meaning. Anyone who attaches an independent value to mere observance will try to keep it up at any cost; he may even imagine that he is still obeying the law when in fact he is dodging or "outwitting" it (cf. Mark 7:9-13). But for the man who sees in the outward observance nothing but an expression of the inner law, such an attitude is unthinkable. Since the sole aim of the external law is to safeguard the Christian's inner dynamism, it derives all its value from the latter, not the other way around.

OFFERS NEW NORM

Another consequence of the relationship between love and law is that ordinarily the outward law will not provide the Christian with an ideal, the attainment of which could possibly satisfy him, but simply with a minimum below which the dynamism that constitutes him as a Christian will inevitably fail him. For this reason the code of the New Law, while including a series of positive commands and prohibitions, before all else offers the Christian a completely different norm: the imitation of the person of Christ, particularly of his love, which in turn is a reflection of the love of the Father.

St. Paul hardly knows another norm. Following the example of Christ, who commanded his disciples to be perfect as their heavenly Father is perfect, St. Paul can only repeat to his faithful that they should contemplate Christ and imitate him. "Be you, therefore, imitators of God, as very dear children, and walk in love, as Christ also loved us and delivered himself up for us" (Eph. 4:32-5:2, 24-26).

The pious Jew, so zealous in his devotion to the Law, strove to know it better and better, so that he might observe its most minute details. For a Christian, the Person of Christ is the whole law, not only with regard to its principal element, the Spirit of Christ imparted to him, but even with regard to its secondary element, which is reducible to the imitation of Christ.

A final consequence of the relationship between love and law is that when a Christian acts in this way, he is free; for "where the Spirit of the Lord is, there is freedom" (II Cor. 3:17). This is a theme dear to St. Augustine as well as to St. Thomas, who comments: "A man who acts of his own accord, acts freely, but one who is impelled by another is not free. He who avoids evil, not because it is evil, but because a precept of the Lord forbids it, is not free. On the other hand, he who avoids evil because it is evil, is free. Now it is precisely this the Holy Spirit accomplishes, by inwardly equipping the soul with an inner dynamism. The result is that a man refrains from evil out of love, as though the divine law were commanding him; and thus he is free, not because he is not subject to the divine law, but because his inner dynamism enables him to do what the divine law requires." (In II Cor. chap. 3, 1. 3; cf. *S.T.* I-II, q.108, a. 1, ad 2)

2

God Is Faithful

HENRI HOLSTEIN, S.J.

Faith is the experience of a meeting, of a personal discovery: the discovery of the living God. Faith is also a long acquaintance, punctuated with good and bad times and of seeming abandonment by the living God. It is a journey like the one to Emmaus. And, little by little, God reveals himself to be a faithful God. Since he is faithful, he imposes himself on my poor, emotional, egocentric love, a love always threatened with unfaithfulness, to transform it. Faith is the experience of a faithful God.

Consider the experience of Israel on its march toward the promised land: They learned from the start that the name of their liberator was the Faithful One. The experience of the Exodus, the flight from Egypt, the crossing of the "Red Sea," the destruction of the Egyptian army, the manna, the water flowing from the rock struck by Moses—all this was necessary to help them believe in the One Who delivered them from the land of exile:

> And they believed His words, and they
> sang His praises (Ps. 106:12).

But an essential condition of this experience is the fidelity of Israel demanded by the Lord on Sinai. It is when man is faithful that he recognizes God's fidelity and takes heart; when he disobeys and grows restless, man places the Lord's fidelity in question: "Why have you led the people of Yahweh into this desert? To be killed with the animals? Why have we had to go to Egypt? Why have we been led into this evil place?" (Num. 20:4-5). Angry at Moses, Israel became panicky and blamed the Lord Himself. Unfaithful to God, they doubt His fidelity. They no longer know that God is faithful. The light of faith becomes weak as soon as the dialogue between God and man is interrupted.

The fidelity of the believer, a response to the fidelity of God, is a condition of this dialogue. But the dialogue is led by God, Whose grace makes us faithful. God's fidelity is proven by a constant spring of grace. But this grace must be sought constantly through prayer and action: "We must beg the faithful God for His fidelity."[1]

The life of faith is an ever-growing, deepening experience of the fidelity of God. We will first show this by considering the obedience of faith, then by considering events, and finally by studying hope, which leans on belief in the fidelity of God. The life of faith is a journey in the presence of the faithful God; the discovery of God is constantly renewed and grows more profound. It is an uninterrupted source of confidence and joy, until we enter the full light of the Beatific Vision.

"In the Obedience of faith" (Rom. 16:26).

It is remarkable that in Holy Scripture, fidelity and confidence, which seem to be characteristic of the attitude of the believer, are first mentioned about God: *God* is faithful and trustworthy.

God is faithful because "His word lives forever" (Isa. 40:8). He does not contradict Himself. He never takes back His word. He is Truth:

"God is not a man, so He does not lie, nor a son of Adam, so He does not take back His word. Does He say one thing and do another?" (Num. 23:19).

The whole history of Israel shows God's obstinate fidelity to His word. And the New Testament will take up this affirmation to show its full realization in Christ. Christ's work is the Amen of the Divine Fidelity:

"He is faithful, He Who calls you: it is He Who will do that, He will guard and protect you from evil" (I Thess. 5,24; II Thess. 3:3).

This divine fidelity is a fidelity of confidence. In spite of unbelievers and agnostics, God will obstinately remain faithful to man's confidence. His first word is creative: Let us make man to our image and likeness . . ." (Gen. 1:26). And this word is without regret. The choice, taken from the beginning in favor of man, will not diminish. Finally, it manifests itself in the man Jesus, His Word "become flesh" (Phil. 2:7). It is in this way that the Father lets us know the strength and power of His fidelity. The Incarnation is the last word, the one that finalizes all the rest in the "belief" that God grants "His man," as St. Iranaeus says.

Jesus the Man shows God's fidelity by being "the faithful servant par excellence." It is in the perfection of his filial obedience, His very fidelity of God, that He expresses His faithful love even unto death: "There is no greater love than to lay down one's life for a friend" (John 15:13).

Christian faith experiences this fidelity of God. It decodes it, so to speak, in acts that pertain to fidelity, acts that St. Paul calls "the obedience of faith" (Rom. 1:5; 16:26). To obey in faith is, in effect, to recognize, painfully and sorrowfully at first, but also in the joy of the dialogue that follows, the faithful God at work "for the good of those who love Him" (Rom. 8:28).

The first movement, which is decisive and indispensable to faith, is submission to God's will. What God commands must be done. Thus, "Abraham obeys the call to leave for another country . . . and he left not knowing where he was going" (Hebr. 11:8).

At his first call to faithful obedience, the believer feels dominated, even eclipsed by the immediacy of the order. He does not yet know from whence that dominating voice comes, that voice which compels him to leave his familiar universe and enter the unknown. He must go. That is that! The imperative voice forces him to obey without leaving time to consider: "Leave your country, your parents, your father's house to go to the country I show you" (Gen. 12:1). The magnificence of Abraham's faith was shown in his leaving immediately, without asking for explanations or demanding reasons.

At times it will seem as though the believer is being led by a blind, unjustifiable fate. But he soon learns to recognize, in the unseen that is around him, the Will of a God Who is Master of the world. Such is the submission of Job in the face of an evil he does not understand but which he accepts from the hand of the all-powerful God:

> Naked did I leave my mother's womb: naked shall I return. Yahweh had given and Yahweh has taken away. Blessed be the name of Yahweh! (Job 1:21)

But this obscure recognition of a Ruler, without whom we could do nothing, tends to go beyond itself and to reveal partially the mysterious plan of this God Who comes to disrupt our life. The obscurity of faith, loyally accepted, provides a more brilliant light. To accept and do the Will of God leads us to know Him better. In his suffering and dereliction, Job understands that he is seized by God and is forced into a discussion where God reveals Himself. The "hand of God lays heavily upon him" (Job 13:2), not to bend him to the earth, but to return him to the One Who has revealed Himself. In this struggle, from which he cannot escape, Job discovers the living God Whom he did not know before.

"I only knew you by hearsay, but now my eyes have seen you" (Job 42:5). The obedience of faith illuminates, weakly at first, but with an ever-growing strength, the intellect which has consented to yield. The servant learns the master's fidelity. In command or in trial, he recognizes a grace: He is not the victim of an inexplicable misfortune nor of an unfortunate risk, nor of a weakness in the laws of nature. He is a friend whom God, until then unknown, invites to a dialogue with Him in order to reveal His all-powerful wisdom which guides the world and men. If God has treated Job so harshly "a just and honest man who fears God and avoids evil" (Job 1:8), it is that Job may know the faithful God and accept the experience of this terrible dialogue with the living God.

The obedience of faith leads to a meeting with God. Night becomes clear only after it emerges from the depths of darkness. God is there, He waits and He calls. The fatality of accidents and misfortunes becomes meaningful as soon as we recognize their origin. "God speaks to Job from the womb of the storm" (Job 38:1). He is only recognized in the obedience of faith. . . .

"Truly, you are the hidden God, the God of Israel, the Saviour" (Isa. 45:15).

God hides Himself and reveals Himself, while having us search for Him. It is a kind of mystical game in which each player follows the other by obscure clues. Even the fidelity of God wishes to be hidden because His invisibility is the sign of the grandeur of His love. A God Who would impose Himself would be a tyrant or demi-god; God wants to be welcomed, not endured. He withdraws because He wants us to make the effort to look for Him, avoiding the easy solution of a familiarity without mystery. Meanwhile, He is near to us, He is the God Who is nearby, Who marches with His people through the desert, and establishes his tent in the midst of their camp, while waiting for the Temple of stone which would be the center of the religious and political life of His people, while waiting for the *living* Temple, the humanity of Christ: "Destroy this Temple and in three days I will rebuild It" (John 2:19). God, present among us in Christ, will remain the hidden God; He will only reveal Himself to a faith capable of discovering Him. For those who do not believe, the Man, Jesus, will be a sign of contradiction. Their eyes will not recognize Him and their judgment will be so blinded that they will condemn Him as an impostor and evil-doer. But to the one who believes, Jesus reveals Himself: "Do you believe in the Son of Man?" says Jesus to the blind man He cured. "Who is He, Lord, that I may believe in Him?"

"You see Him. It is He Who speaks to you" (John 9:35-37). Personal knowledge is never mathematical, but it is certain. When the resurrected One, at the lake front, invites His disciples, tired after their vain night's work, to taste the dinner He has prepared for them "No one dared ask Him: Who are you, for they knew full well that He was the Lord" (John 21:12).

"I am with you all days . . ." (Matt. 28:20).

Faith begins with a discovery: laboriously, by the slow pondering of the significance of signs, or abruptly, by the realization that an Other is out there, before me, and that I am called by my name with so much authority that I cannot escape. The living God has revealed Himself to me. As long as I remain faithful, as long as my heart is pure and free, the presence of the Lord will always be at hand. The Lord is there. He is faithful.

As faith grows, signs are used less and less. They become more transparent. It was enough for Mary Magdalen to hear her name called by a familiar voice to know that Jesus was there, resurrected. God's fidelity is shown by its constant presence: He is there and the least indication confirms it. "The Master is there and He calls you" (John 11:28).

I find the presence of the faithful God even in the history of my personal faith. I find it in service to others, in sickness, weakness; I even find it in my consciousness of sin and the contrition that follows. Everything tells me that God is there, faithful; and this fidelity is the very strength of my faith.

The believer is a traveler who goes even to the edge of the abyss.

The essence of faith should constantly question itself and find its stability only in its own progress: Peter walking on the water but sinking as soon as he hesitates in his faith in Jesus Who calls him. The constant temptation of faith is to step back. Was I right or wrong? The true test of faith does not come from outward attacks, contradictions or ridicule. Those outside forces hit home only if there is already some internal hesitation. That internal doubt is then nourished from without to make me see things as illusion.

It is our internal attitude that must be purified by our meeting with the faithful God in humble prayer. If I believe, it is by the grace of the Lord that calls me to Him, not by a good action on my part. Even the first movement toward faith comes from grace alone, as noted by the Council of Orange against the "Semi-Pelagians" who attributed to man the initial impetus. The Father Who "has loved us first" (I John 4:19), "Draws us to His Son" (John 6:44). All initiative comes from Him: all we do is to welcome this gift of grace given us through His mercy:

> It is not we who have first loved God, but He
> Who has loved us by sending His Son as a Victim
> of propitiation for our signs (I John 4:10).

From the beginning of our faith, we must see the fidelity of the Father, and we must be assured that this fidelity will not diminish. Being filled with grace during prayer, we must recognize, not only that God has done everything, but also that He works against us at times. But at such troubled times, does not the Lord hold on to us even stronger than before? Why fear that He will leave? Magdalen cried at the tomb on Easter Morning and was upset because they had taken away her Lord. The Lord was there behind her and she did not recognize Him. Often I, too, have not known how to recognize the Lord. I have been tempted to despair when I could not accomplish a goal on which I had decided.

But the Lord is faithful and He has made me feel the force of His fidelity. "It is with stout heart that I extol my weaknesses so that the power of Christ may come over me. For when I am weak, it is then that I am strong!" (II Cor. 12:9-10).

The experience of faith is a knowledge of a faithful God Whose fidelity carries with it assurance and certitude. Each day I understand my faith better as a constant attitude based on this fidelity. To believe in a faithful God is to prove that He is faithful and our faith rests on this fidelity. To pray in order to believe is not so much to implore the gift of faith as to thank God for being, if we can so express it, as faithful as He shows Himself to be. It is from this that the biblical metaphor "God the Rock" takes its meaning:

> "Be my Rock of strength, my Rampart that
> saves me; for my Rock, my protection is
> You!" (Ps. 31:3-4)

The faithful God is unmoved, and it is He Who grasps my trembling faith in a steel grip; His grip never loosens and I test His love by His firmness:

> "The one who does not love has not known God;
> for God is love" (I John 4:8).

And this love, prevenient and full of initiative, of the faithful God, gives me "full assurance" as St. John says (I John 4:17). The peace of faith rests on the fidelity of God!

This fidelity is tested in apostolic activity and charitable works toward our neighbors. It is not enough to say that faith demands our generosity and an effective love of others. All that is true, but the experience of the believer is so much richer. In the famous and beautiful words of Bergson, he feels that he loves men with the very love of God. Through him passes the love of God; through him God loves men and shows them the fidelity of His love. If the saints were sincere when they thought themselves small and poor, it was because they knew God was working in and through them. Jesus Himself recognized that His doctrine and works were "not from Him, but from the Father Who sent Him" (John 7:16; 5:36). Whatever a Christian does, whether he be a Vincent de Paul or a Francis Xavier, cannot be said to be his own work; rather it is the work of the Father acting through His Son and through those who believe in His only-begotten Son. The assurance of the apostles, their confidence and zeal are a witness to the fidelity of God and a unique and never-ending source of devotion.

That is why the separation of faith and charity causes the ruination of both. Faith without works is folly, say the apostolic epistles; but charity without faith—without this contsant reference to the fidelity of God which is the very soul of all apostolic activity worthy of the name—would be like the blind leading the blind and leading them to destruction! But charity which springs from faith possesses, in its very action, the certitude of being the instrument of the love of a faithful God, in Christ Jesus.

It is also in sickness and the weakness of the body and spirit that faith recognizes the presence of the faithful God: a fidelity which is not shown—does not the afflicted one, like Job, seem abandoned and rejected by God?—even to his friends, but which is proven and strengthened in its acceptance. What is asked at first is that we accept the Will of God and submit in silence with a loyal and acquiescent heart. The grace of this acceptance allows the recognition of a God Who is very near and of Whom Holy Scripture says that He prefers the poor and unfortunate. Whereas *men* turn away from those suffering, God goes to them and makes them His friends. Was not the Messiah sent "to the miserable and afflicted" (Isa. 11:4; 61:2)? Does He not always show a predilection for all those who are humbled, exploited, misunderstood? Further, do not the miracles of Jesus announce that the redemption will reach all men even in the cosmic order shaken by sin? God's fidelity brings Him close to all those afflicted, for His choices are without regret. But it is precisely this same fidelity that gives man strength through sickness, sorrow, defeat, or contradiction. It gives meaning to his suffering. What God once accomplished through the suffering of His servant, delivered up to outrage (Isa. 50:6) and weighed down like an innocent lamb, with the "crimes of all" (Isa. 53:6-7), He now accomplishes in our sufferings. A mysterious power of redemption is accorded to Christ's dereliction and death. God owes it to His fidelity to prolong this in His adopted sons. Human suffering is right to turn toward God in faith: God has promised in some way to make the scandal of Calvary meaningful up to the Parousia "For what is God's folly is wiser than man's wisdom, and what is God's weakness is stronger than man's power" (I Cor. 1:25).

Perhaps by looking at our sins, we can come to understand the fidelity of God better and to give it a wholehearted assent. To see ourselves as frequent or constant sinners would lead us to despair, if we did not fix our gaze upon God's fidelity: "Yahweh, Yahweh,

God of concern and pity, slow to anger, rich in grace and fidelity . . ." (Ex. 34:6); God is faithful in pardoning, and does not tire of renewing His paternal pardon each time it is sought. There is only one attitude which can help us accept our congenital state of sin—humble confidence in the fidelity of God Who pardons and greets us, like prodigal sons, with paternal mercy. The grace that pardons is also that which makes us strong against the sin it takes away. God is faithful not only to pardon my present faults but to give me courage and strength against faults to come. If I am uncertain and vulnerable, God is sure and strong. The jealous God gives His love "to produce grace for those who love Him" (Deut. 5:10) and "turning His face from their faults, He made their hearts pure" (Ps. 51:11-12).

God was not content to reiterate statements in the Old Testament to express the fidelity of His mercy when confronted by the infidelity of sin. He wanted also to "give His Own Son" (Rom. 8:32) to redeem our sins: "The One Who had not known sin, took on our sins so that we would be justified before God" (II Cor. 5:21).

While pondering my own sins and the perversity around me, I am tempted to lose heart. But when looking at God's fidelity to His Son Incarnate, I cannot help but be confident in His fidelity also to me and feel Him drawing me closer with His merciful love. In the face of the faithful witness of God's fidelity, anxiety goes and in its place comes a confidence in the justice of God, a stronger faith in Jesus Christ "come into the world to save sinners, of whom I am the greatest" (I Tim. 1:15). God reveals His justice by granting mercy to all, for all have sinned (Rom. 3:23).

An unshakeable faith in a faithful God Whose wish is mercy: "We believe in the One Who rose from the dead, Jesus, our Lord, given us for our faults and resurrected for our justification" (Rom. 5:24). And the peace of one who confides in God's fidelity, finding in every moment the presence of an attentive and forgiving love, assuming our human defeats as well as our apostolic labors and our uncertain resolutions. The fidelity of the Father in Jesus Christ is the only hope and the only certitude on which the Christian can rely. But that is enough. Each day he has the joy of faith. For "God is faithful, Who has called us to the communion of His Son, Jesus Christ our Lord" (I Cor. 1:9).

"Faith is guaranteed as long as we want it . . ." (Heb. 11:1).

The experience of God's fidelity runs the risk of being contradicted and put in question every instant by our fears of the future. Tomorrow, will God be faithful? I well know the absurd character of this question, but I cannot help from asking it as long as I let my mind and heart be overrun with fears about the future.

Will not temptation be too strong? Will not my sin be too great? Today I have resisted with much effort and pain, but tomorrow, can I be assured that I will not give in?

The adolescent, looking to the future, fears and doubts, in his confusion, the realization of his dreams. The adult, through experience, knows the uncertainty of his projects and suspects the difficulties he must face. As the years pass, this fear builds up and invades every area. Every man fears old age. It comes and will not turn back. Old age is the age of fear. Especially in our own day, it is felt more and more; old people become incapable of facing themselves, feel relegated to the side of the road because they have "done their time." Moreover there is the fear of the unknown, of the coming of death, even when the old person knows there are few tomorrows and does all he can to change his surroundings.

Every age of human life needs hope; the more we advance, the more necessary and difficult is hope. The problem is that we try to hang on to *false* hopes that are not stable. Only the hope of faith can support and give courage.

Hope is the projection of my present faith onto my uncertain future. For faith is not only a present experience but also a confident expectation of fidelity in the future. I know that the fidelity of God is unchanging. God does not change, He does not retreat, He knows neither caprice nor omission. And His Christ that He gives us without regret "is the same yesterday, today and forever" (Heb. 13:8).

"I know in Whom I have believed," confided Paul in the evening of his life, "and I am confident that He is capable of keeping my trust up to the present" (II Tim. 1:12). Paul recognized the fidelity of God in Christ; his faith is a constant homage to the Infallible Word (Rom. 9:6), accomplished in Jesus Christ, through Whom "God sends us His mercy" (Rom. 9:16). He knows that he can be confident in Christ until the end, until the "day." His "obedience in faith" is bit by bit transformed into the "hope of faith." This accounts for the serenity of his words.

The object of faith the believer experiences is God Himself: not only an intervention of God, a word or an act, but God Himself Who has revealed Himself to me as "the faithful God." From there, faith goes beyond the immediacy of a fugitive knowledge. God does not only reveal Himself in the light of Sinai, but in the persevering realization of a plan that He works out with patience and steadfastness. Faith becomes habitual confidence in a familiar God. Whatever happens I know that I can rely on Him, tomorrow as well as today, and that till the end of my life when I will see Him face to face, my hope will not be confounded (Rom. 5:5).

Of this dimension of faith, Paul has given a moving account, which is a good example on which to meditate when the future seems somber and uneasy:

"Then what can separate us from the love of Christ? Can affliction or hardship? Can persecution, hunger, nakedness, peril, or the sword? 'We are being done to death for your sake all day long,' as Scripture says; 'We have been treated like sheep for slaughter (Ps. 44, 12). But in spite of all this, victory is ours through Him Who love us.

"For I am convinced that there is nothing in death or life, in the realm of spirits or superhuman powers, in the world as it is or the world as it shall be, in the forces of the universe, in heights or depths, nothing in all creation that can separate us from the love of God in Christ Jesus our Lord" (Rom. 8, 35-39).

And for this optimism, Paul gives the determining reason: "If God is for us, who will be against us?"(Rom. 8:31).

This dimension of hope in faith quiets my concern about the future, appeases my uncertainties, and strengthens my confidence. "God will not fail to give us all He has to give (*cf.* Rom. 8:32), for He loves me in Christ and His love is without regret. Is not hope the source of the "joy in faith"?

Hope pervades the whole Church. In the constant struggle it must wage against the world and its own weaknesses, the Church always wins. Every day its beliefs are attacked. Modern times await the spectacular "retreat of the Church" in a world that seems to nourish the sociological phenomenon of "dechristianization." Like Peter walking on the water and sinking, does not the Church today cry out: "Save us, Lord, we perish"? Made uneasy by so many reliable witnesses, alarmed by statistics and forecasts, can we prevent ourselves from asking that terrible question: "What will the Catholic Church be in the world fifty or one hundred years from now?"—or to pose the disturbing question of Fr. Rahner: "Does the Church have a chance in the modern world?"

To this pointed question, constantly posed by statistics which "in the one hundred years to come" will always be thrown at us[2] one response must be given: God is faithful and Jesus Christ has conquered the world (John 16, 33). The response of faith and hope, of faith working in all our deeds, brings to the uncertain future the quiet of hope. Hope does not give us the answers to the pastoral problems of evangelization posed by the modern world, but it does let us approach them and work on them with a basic attitude of confidence, peace and patience.

Not even Paul knew how the pagan world, to which he had been sent by God, could be reached by the good news of Jesus Christ. He had seen the difficulties multiply. He had made only a few converts and some of those had not given him much satisfaction. And in the midst of his work, he is taken away. He knows that he is through and can see the damage that will be caused by his departure. But, first and above all, he knows Jesus, to Whom he has given his faith. He knows that Jesus is the accomplishment of the Infallible Word, of the indefectible promise of the faithful God. And this certitude is for him a source of peace and confidence: "I know in Whom I have believed."

We have a "faithful and true witness" (Apoc. 3:14) of God's fidelity in Jesus Christ our Lord. In Jesus, the Father gives us an effective proof of His fidelity. For Jesus is the very fidelity of God: He is the true Word of the faithful God, by Whom and in Whom the Father comes to us. To believe in Jesus Christ is to believe in the fidelity of God; to deny Christ is to cut ourselves off from the fidelity of God.

The knowledge of Jesus Christ through faith is a knowledge of the faithful God; this experience of fidelity is the certitude given by God, Who is infinitely true and just, Who wants to reveal His fidelity and save us by this revelation. Jesus Christ appears as the unique mediator, the One Who gives us faith and the One in Whom our belief is placed. He is the *Amen,* the solemn attestation that God gives us of His fidelity and the One through Whom our faith is brought to the Father, expressed in the liturgical *Amen,* the adhesion to the fidelity of God. Jesus is the "Author and Consumator of our faith" (Heb. 12:2). Faith comes from His grace and unites us to Him, since He is the One Who leads us to the Father (John 14:6) and He alone reveals the Father to us: "Whoever sees me, sees the Father" (John 14:9).

In our faith in Christ we know that God is faithful and we become capable of giving a childlike response of fidelity to God. For the fidelity of the Father wanted us to be "His sons through faith in Christ Jesus" (Gal. 3:26).

3

The Meaning of Christian Hope

BERNARD OLIVIER, O.P.

Man cannot live without hope. His daily life is nourished by expectations of the future. When he is beset by trouble, it is hope which gives him patience and the strength to fight.

More fundamentally, in order to live courageously an existence that is constantly subject to change, we need hope that life has a meaning. And not to lose heart amid the immense amount of human suffering and evil, we need a certain hope that humanity itself is progressing toward some end which will justify these incomprehensible ways of getting there. An absurd world where nothing has any meaning can only beget despair.

Hope is a sign of powerlessness; it shows that the realization of our desires does not depend only on ourselves. But it is also an active force. If our hope is well founded, it becomes the staff for our weakness, the assurance we cannot find in ourselves alone.

SUPERNATURAL HOPE

Supernatural hope in a Christian life plays the same indispensable role as natural hope in a human life. The psychological characteristics of one upheld by human hope are to be found, transformed, in the Christian. These characteristics may be briefly mentioned.

The man who hopes is a man of desires, conscious of an insufficiency in his life. The man who hopes is looking to the future. He forms part of the movement in life which is a march forward. But he does not simply sit down and await an inevitable happening over which he has no control. When I hope, I am straining towards the realization of my desire. I have no absolute certitude that I shall reach my aim, and that is why I hope. Hope is mixed with the fear of failure. But if the means I have at hand are efficacious, I am borne up even in the midst of uncertainty by the conviction that I shall triumph. This conviction which overcomes uncertainty is the most typical element of hope; namely, trust.

MAN'S DESTINY

In Christian hope, the stake is nothing less than man's eternal destiny, the realization of the plan of world salvation. This is why Christian hope is born of the faith which alone reveals this destiny. That which we await in hope surpasses anything man left to himself could even conceive: the partaking of the life and happiness of God Himself. Even our hope itself is not of our own creation; only God can give it to us.

God's redemption of the world is historical, temporal in its occurrence and development. Both faith and hope have their history. Just as God did not reveal Himself completely all at once, so He did not reveal a hope complete from the beginning. The great hope which was to traverse the centuries until the end of the world was defined, step by step, only as man became capable of grasping it.

God begins by choosing a man, Abraham, and binds Himself to him by a promise: "I will make a great people of thee" (Gen. 12:2). From that moment the movement of hope begins; for from that nation is to come He who is to realize the true hope, Christ. This handful of men, and little by little this nation, go forward, led by God and sustained by a promise He is constantly renewing and making more definite, towards a future of which they cannot yet suspect the whole brilliance: the installation of the kingdom of God by the Messias.

Finally the imminence of the kingdom of God is proclaimed by the last prophets. But although the object of hope is at last revealed, the messianic kingdom is still generally imagined as an earthly one, an era of material prosperity, and the Messias is imagined as an earthly king. Christ will have to reveal the true meaning of hope and the real nature of His kingdom.

Hope in the Old Testament is characterized by two elements. It is communal in nature—the hope of the nation. The hope of the individual, notably resurrection, remains vague and secondary. Secondly, the hope of Israel is directed towards a definite event in history, the coming of the Messias.

The realization of this hope is awaited from God alone, and thus hope acquires a theological character. God is almighty and He loves Israel. This is the foundation of hope, and God's promise determines the object of hope—the messianic era.

CHRISTIAN HOPE

From the beginning of His ministry, Jesus presents Himself as the Messias foretold by the prophets (Matt. 4:17, 12:28; Mark 1:15; Luke 4:16 ff., 11:20). Will He, therefore, put an end to a hope which finds achievement in possessing its object? No, Israel's expectation has been fulfilled, but a better hope is beginning. Jesus has really come to found the kingdom of God, but it is to be a spiritual kingdom, not an earthly one.

This kingdom is to require two distinct phases. In the first, the earthly, temporal phase, the law is one of growth (Matt. 13:31 ff.). It is also one of imperfection; the separation of the good and bad has not yet been made (*ibid.* 24 ff.). But this spiritual kingdom will find its completion at the "consummation of this world." The kingdom will then pass from the earthly, temporal phase to a heavenly, eternal one; and this passage will be marked by a definite event in time: the return of the Son of Man in glory. It is at that moment that the work of salvation will be completed by the general resurrection and Last Judgment, and Christ will deliver the kingdom into His Father's hands.[1] This is the new hope offered to Christians. The Jews awaited the kingdom; it has come; but it is still only a preparation for the final kingdom, towards which the hopes of Jesus' disciples must turn.

COMMUNAL HOPE

Here again we find the two characteristics which we discovered in the ancient hope. Christian hope is essentially communal. It is not the expectation of an isolated individual; the promises made to the chosen people are inherited by the new people of God, this new kingdom of the spirit which is the Church. It is only by belonging to this new people of God that one can enter into hope. Again, Christian hope is directed towards an event which will put an end to history. By reason of this temporal dimension, hope integrates the whole movement of history until the end of the world into its own movement.

But Christian hope is not simply expectation directed towards a distant event. It already puts us, mysteriously but really, in possession of its object. Even now, in virtue of Christ's first coming, we really possess in germ the eternal life which Christ's second coming will inaugurate fully. "He who hears My word *has* like eternal . . . he *has passed* from death to life" (John 5:24).

Thus the people of God, having already entered upon the new life by Christ's grace, journey through the vicissitudes of time and history towards the final achievement of God's design for mankind. Such, according to the Bible, is the great breadth of hope which fills each one's life, fills also the history of the world, bearing the Church along in its confident march towards the eternal kingdom.

NATURE AND OBJECT

There is only one hope, as there is only one faith, one Lord, one baptism. The Christian is called upon to enter into the unique hope of the people of God. He enters by it into the great stream which bears the Church along and can share in it only in and through the Church.

But evidently hope has no real existence save in the individual hearts of those who form God's people. We must, therefore, determine its nature and object as it exists in the hearts of Christians.

Hope is a theological virtue, by which we reach God directly as the object of our acts. As we have said, the value of human hope depends entirely on the support we have at hand. The same applies to the theological virtue. Here the support is God Himself; our own strength is out of proportion to the object of our expectation. It is only through Him that we can expect what He has Himself promised. We hope in God before we hope for anything, whatever it be.

Because we hope in God before we hope for anything, God is the formal object of our hope. But what is it that we hope for? What is the material object of our hope? We have seen the object of our hope as it is defined in the Bible; but when we open a manual of theology or a catechism, we observe a disconcerting change of perspective. The object of hope is reduced to a purely individual one, "my salvation";

and its eschatological aspect is disregarded. The communal aspect of hope and its orientation towards the return of the Lord must be re-established in an authentic doctrine of hope.

HOPE AND CHARITY

By instinct man seeks his own good, his own happiness. If, entering upon the life of grace, he is content with simply transposing his instinct for happiness, he will quite naturally consider his eternal individual happiness as the object of his hope. But we forget that although grace does not suppress nature, it raises it and transforms it. Entering into the life of the children of God, man becomes part of the Church, sharing its life and hope. Moreover, the fundamental spring of this new life is charity. Faith is perfect only if it translates itself into practical charity. Hope is really itself only if it is nourished on charity.

Now charity unites us to God and to all our brethren and makes us seek God's glory and the good of our fellows as if it were our own. That is why the instinct for happiness, if it is truly transposed into the order of grace, leads us to espouse God's views, the cause of His people, so that we hope no longer for ourselves alone, but for the glory of God and the happiness of His people.

The personal happiness of the child of God thus appears to him as that element—which no doubt touches him most nearly—of the design of God's love for humanity. Hope of personal happiness is certainly not excluded, nor even diminished; it is simply put into its proper place.

We can, then, at the end of this article, determine the object of Christian hope. The son of God, integrated into the people of God, places himself in the hands of the almighty and loving God who has engaged Himself by promise (the formal object). Desiring and fervently awaiting the manifestation of the heavenly kingdom, he hopes at the same time for his own inclusion in that kingdom (the principal material object). But he also hopes for everything that leads to the kingdom: the support of Christ for His Church amidst difficulties—and in his own life, perseverance and the graces he needs. That is the secondary material object.

Hope thus rediscovers its communal value and its "historical" dimension. At the same time hope is not the mere passive expectation that many Christians imagine. It is the strength which gives God's children a conqueror's mentality in their inevitable battles. It is truly that "helmet" of which St. Paul speaks. It is also the "anchor of salvation." Battered about on the surface by the events of his own life and by those of history, the Christian is rooted deeply by his hope in the strength of God Himself. He is with God and God is with him. Who can shake him?

Editor's Note: The author makes reference to the following texts: Matt. 25: 31 ff.; Rom. 8:17 ff.; Col. 3:4; I Cor. 15:24 ff.; II Pet. 3:10 ff.

4

Love of Neighbor

ROBERT W. GLEASON, S.J.

I would like here to elaborate certain themes on growth in charity, by which I have in mind particularly growth in charity toward our neighbor. This of course always runs parallel with growth in charity toward God. It is a subject particularly relevant to the modern world, since today has been called the age of the person. Today we are aware, more than in any other era perhaps, of the reality of what it is to be a person and of interpersonal relationships. As a result this theological virtue of fraternal charity has acquired a totally new intensity and importance, which it did not have for a previous age. Even though the actual theology of the virtue has not changed very much, it is possible that our human preparation necessary to understand the theology has undergone improvement.

We are all aware that Christ has called upon us to love our neighbor with a genuine love. He has even proclaimed this love as a proof of the Divinity of His Church, an extraordinary statement, indeed, and one that requires study. To begin with, this demand of Christ to love our neighbor is something that fits in with our own nature. It is not something simply superimposed from without, but something in accord with our nature as limited human beings. In point of fact, all the commandments of Christ often reveal to us our own inner potentialities, for they all aim at our fulfillment as human and divinized beings. And so fraternal charity, too, aims at man's own self-development for the simple reason that man is most fully himself, most completely in possession of himself, when he is capable of transcending himself and making a gift of himself in love to another. God has made man in such a way that he is related to others. If we are to fulfill our nature as human beings then we are obliged to obey this command of charity, to reach out toward unity, love, and communion with others.

Every created personality is a distant echo of the relational character that we know is in God Himself. In the Holy Trinity, the three Divine Persons are subsistent relations. If we are to grow in resemblance to the Trinity, if in other words, we are to develop as complete human beings, then we must display the same relational character. We must live, not as isolated units within a social body but as members of the true Body of Christ, as branches of the vine. In that way we will live within a higher and more transcendent unity, which is itself living the Mystical Body of Christ.

It is clear then that love for one's neighbor is an absolute precondition for achieving humanity. This fact is itself a revelation, and it is quite possible that if God in the Old Testament and Christ in the New had not commanded fraternal charity, we might never have fully understood our own human nature as well as we do. We could of course have known about this commandment, deducing it from the relationships that exist between man and man. Left to itself, however, human reason, although possessing the bare capacity to arrive at the obligation to love all men, would probably never have arrived at a deep and secure understanding of fraternal charity. It is possible, therefore, that without Christ's revelation humanity would never have had that deep sense of identity that flows from an acknowledged unity with the whole of the human race on its march toward its final destiny. As a result, even on the natural level, man must live relatively in charity, if he is to perfect his personality. For the greatest danger, even to natural self-development, is egotism.

Without Christ's revelation concerning charity, human adulthood might never have been opened up to us as a living possibility. It is the point of wisdom then to make our own the insight that Christ brought to morality. Having been taught since childhood that we should love all men, we sometimes take for granted the idea of fraternal charity. But this is to forget that Christ brought new life into morality. And certainly the Christian notion of what constitutes fraternal charity is *wholly* new. Let us make no mistake about that. It is not a natural thing. The closest approximation to it previously, aside from revelation, is the Stoic notion of unity, the idea that all men have a common destiny. But that notion contains so many distracting philosophical elements that it can hardly even be called a preparation for the Christian revelation. According to the Christian idea, insofar as man is closed, incommunicable, devoid of human relationships of love with others, just so far is he inhuman, unfulfilled, and un-Christian. This remains true no matter what must be said concerning the need for detachment.

Man's existence is diminished precisely in the degree to which he lives in a depersonalized world of objects. Such a state of reality, as we know, is becoming more and more common. Today the trend is toward the mechanization of the human spirit, and men are more and more being looked upon as manipulatable objects, capable of putting in so many hours of work a day, of gaining so much money a day, of being moved about like so many counters. By and large in today's world men are considered fields of force to be worked upon, commodities to be bought or sold. This is why we have the repeated declarations of the Holy See concerning the dignity even of man's labor as such. To treat the personal world as though it were impersonal, as though it responded to the same laws to which matter responds, the laws of force, is inevitably a temptation for those who live in such a culture.

These laws of force are seen at work today not only in the area of the material but in that of the psychological as well. To treat people as though they were objects, exerting upon them psychological pressures from the community, from conformism, and from exploitation by those who know how to shape the urges of men, is to look upon people as though they were objects. Many of the latest trends in advertising, in sociology, and in other areas of our day-to-day world are evidence of this tendency to depersonalize humanity and to treat it as though it were susceptible to the same impulses and laws as brute matter. Such a tendency is even manifest to a certain extent in the Christian world: in the refusal to treat the other person as an inner center of subjectivity to which one must respond. Instead he is treated as something pregiven, something "out there," something which can be manipulated. His intelligence, wisdom, affectivity, individuality become fields of force which can be operated upon with the result that man is reduced to the level of something to be acquired, to be crushed, to be got out of the way, or to be made a means to an end.

In order for me to live as a Christian and as a man, I have to commune with others. This involves the acknowledgment that the other has a destiny open to the infinite, that he has his own God-given individuality which must be respected, and that he has his own personal law of progress written into his being. After observing whatever may be his God-given potentialities for expansion as a person, as a Christian, I must allow these the spiritual space to develop. I must grant them a favorable atmosphere in which the other's inner themes can unfold properly. *The* word which God has spoken in *this* person, and which throughout eternity will never be repeated, *this* word must be given the opportunity to develop.

The commandment of charity tells me that I must establish with each individual, insofar as I am capable of it, a collaboration with him which will grant him a spiritual space to unfold and by which, as a result, the interpersonal distance between us will be diminished. It is a lamentable fact that people can live in close physical contact with one another, day after day, week after week, year after year, without ever crossing the spiritual space between them. We are perhaps familiar with the cynical remark about those in the religious life, "They enter without knowing one another, they live together as strangers, and when they die no one could care less." This is certainly not the Christian ideal. What Christ ordained is rather a Church that is a supremely open communion of all men. But if that open communion is not had, men become a prey to vague anxieties and insecurities at the depth of personality, which work toward the destruction of both the natural and the supernatural.

The Communion of Saints has been established here on earth by God and is a preparation for the Beatific Vision in heaven. But the Beatific Vision does not consist of a multitude of isolated individuals staring fixedly at the same object. In point of fact it is not in any sense an object that is being contemplated but the Tri-personal God. The unity in which this Beatific Vision is beheld is meant to be prereflected here in the open society that is Christianity, that is the Church, and in every smaller open society, such as the family, religious congregation or order, school, or educational group. The individual's own moral personality, therefore, is impoverished the more he is unable to meet others in this genuinely open communion.

What Christ reveals to us in Himself is a revelation of humanity and an example of perfect human nature. We see in Jesus Christ infinite compassion, infinite tenderness, infinite openness, infinite accessibility. He deals with different personalities differently. Revealing to us the Christian commandment of love, He reveals to us what it means to be human, what the ideal exemplar of our human nature is. By the example of His own life Christ shows us the depths of human nature and its unsuspected potentialities.

Once this philosophical or theological insight of charity has become a part of our culture, it is possible for it to retain vitality even when its source has been abandoned. For example, respect for womanhood, to which Christianity greatly contributed, can continue in a culture after the culture has been largely de-Christianized. But to fail to develop this insight of charity to its fullest extent in the supernatural is to frustrate our deepest tendencies, not only as men but as Christians.

It should be realized that as a result of this commandment of charity Jesus Christ has informed all our human affections. I use the word informed here advisedly, in the somewhat hylomorphic sense that Christ imposes a new perfection, a new form upon all loves. But the important thing to realize is that by so doing He does not suppress anything authentic in our humanity or in our affective life. I underscore this because an older generation of religious often seemed to feel that the affective life was something that was to be crushed, or else to be so canalized exclusively toward the Lord that the commandment to love one's neighbor was taken in a highly desubstantialized fashion. The truth of the matter is that Christ does not suppress anything of value in our humanity.

Whatever type of love exists in us, it is only in Jesus Christ that it can find its adequate fulfillment. For it is He who elevates our loves, unifies them, hierarchizes them. Although commanding, for example, that we do not love music more than God, He does not suppress our love for music. If I have love for the music of Bach, I expect to hear it in the next life, perhaps in a higher form. For I am human, I have been promised a human happiness, and I will have a human body with ears to hear.

Christ also gives us a structure by which we may hierarchize our human loves. Many people undergo conflicts in their natural life, whether psychological, ethical, moral, religious, or spiritual. Because of the several loves in their life, which, though perfectly normal, are not necessarily of the same level, they are unable to structure them easily. Christianity provides for man a proper guide to unite these loves, but it does not suppress them.

We must also recall that when Christ newly informs and supernaturalizes our loves, He does something more. He *intensifies* our affective life. We are not supposed to love *less* intensely because we are Christian, but to love *more* intensely. This would seem to be perfectly obvious to anyone familiar with the Gospels; and yet if one reads much derivative ascetical literature, not however written by ascetical theologians, one has the impression of some kind of inner conflict. The truly supernatural Christian, it might seem, has a less intense affective life than the one who is not fully Christian. If we consier the example of certain saints we may see otherwise. We would find, for example, that St. Theresa of Avila, who achieved a degree of holiness that most of us will never attain, seems to have had friendships, even with men. St. Francis de Sales, too, seems to have had friendships in his life and to have been quite human. He was fond of Madame Chantal, and with good reason. And there are other entirely human saints who give the lie to the suggestion that the de-emphasis of one's affective life is a normal result of a higher supernatural life.

At times also, friendship has been so treated in the perspective of Christianity that one is taught to see its dangers more than the values. No doubt there are friendships that are dangerous to morals, to faith, to the community, to Christianity. There are dangers of all kinds and at all times, but this does not alter the fact that friendship is a value and that it is to be cultivated. Friendship in Jesus Christ is more intense on the experimental level than is love without Jesus Christ.

Without disregard for all that the moralists in their wisdom have taught us, we should remember that love is always a value and that *even if it be a guilty love,* it is still a great invitation to grace, so long as it is a *genuine* love. There can be genuine love that is guilty, of course, and one may not condone the guilt. But in order to obtain a practical good in the practical order we may not destroy a theoretical truth, namely the supreme value of charity and love. To destroy theoretical truth is to guarantee that we end by embracing error and nonsense. Christ therefore calls on us to humanize our loves, to hierarchize them, to keep them guiltless, but *also to intensify them.* Thus the charity of Christ informs every genuine human love. Through His charity Christ seizes on our affections as they exist in the concrete historical order and hierarchizes them in His love without change or distortion. Failure to realize this has been the occasion for many peculiar nontheological notions in the matter of fraternal charity.

One conclusion to be drawn from what has been said is that there is nothing contrary to the natural law in simple human kindness. It is, in fact, to be recommended and to be sought for, however difficult for human nature. Nor does it follow that in expressing this familial charity, we must abandon our intelligence and our discretion.

It is not necessary, for example, to deny objective situations. If someone with whom I live is hard to get on with, I am not required by charity to say that he is easy to live with but only to make it more easy for him to live with me. Again, I do not have to abandon my ideas in the name of charity. I should be able to disagree with someone politically or theologically, without hating him because we are in disagreement. All that is required is that I try to come to a knowledge and appreciation of the truth and to see the other side of the question. I do not have to deny that human nature, my own as well as all others, has been touched by original sin, and consequently that there are areas of greediness and selfishness in all of us. In other words, I do not have to close my eyes to reality in order to be charitable and loving. A mother and father will readily admit that their children are not perfect, but this does not mean that they do not love them.

So it is with *us*. We have also to recall very strongly that the genuine Christian idea of charity is not a kind of juridical fiction. In other words, Christ has not asked us to treat other men *as if* we loved them, but really to love them. He has not asked us to treat other men as Christ, unless in some genuine sense they are Christ, so that in dealing with them we are dealing with Christ Himself. When He says, "If you give a drop of cold water in My name, you give it to Me," "I was in prison and you visited Me," He is speaking the truth. Christ does not order us toward sanctity by lies, even though they could produce a good moral effect. Instead it is His method to take our human nature and reality into account.

It is important to stress this idea because at times fraternal charity is explained as though we were supposed to ignore all genuine lovability in people and simply treat them *as if* we loved them, *as if* they were the Christ. But this is not the wish of Christ at all. Rather what we must do is attempt to penetrate to the depths of the individual, where Christ can be encountered because he is *de facto* there. Charity therefore does not demand impersonal kindness, a caseworker approach to difficult children, without involvement or commitment. What it does demand is that we love people because they have within them genuine lovability. They have their God-given natural gifts, which reflect God and reflect His goodness. No matter how difficult it is to love someone, one can always reflect that at least he possesses existence, and existence is identified with goodness, as the metaphysicians tell us. Presumably if we look long enough and patiently enough and lovingly enough we are going to find something genuinely lovable in this person. We are not, then, supposed to deny it and love him only *as if* he were the Christ. Men are the children of God in the natural order and they may be loved for their natural gifts, as well as for their supernatural gifts.

But I do not think that even this is the final theological explanation of what is meant by fraternal charity. The difficulty with the "as if" concept of charity, as I see it, is that one who lives by this concept is doing exactly the opposite of what God has commanded him to do. Instead of loving man, he is attempting to improve his moral stature by acting as if he loved man, which will not at all improve his moral stature. Man has no need to bypass mankind in order to reach God. If we take seriously the datum of our faith, that God became Incarnate, then the "as if" theory of love seems an implicit denial of one of the essential mysteries of our faith. A man who uses such an approach to charity may be morally good, but he misunderstands the intrinsic, theological nature of fraternal charity. One does not need to bypass the individual to love God more securely; in fact we are specifically forbidden to treat men as a means to an end, even if the end be ethical perfection. To use man as a means to an end results in not loving men and not loving God, because one is not fulfilling God's commandment to love men. Fraternal charity implies a genuine response of love to something genuinely lovable in the individual, and not an instrumentalization of the other person to improve *my* moral status.

Since every human being we meet posseses a genuine value in himself, imparted to him by God, it is possible for us to respond to it. I must first, therefore, respond to the dignity and value in the other person and then, as a gift, there will flow back to me an increase in my moral values, because I have obeyed the law of God and responded to the objective situation. Nor are we ever called upon to love exclusively the gifts, natural and supernatural, that God has given to man. The ultimate explanation of fraternal charity is not even that we love in this individual the gift of grace which deifies him, because grace itself is a creature. What we are called upon to do is to love with fraternal charity, not merely as a moral virtue, but as a theological virtue.

The ultimate explanation of how we can find God and love Him in the other is that He possesses the other in the secret part of His personality. Grace itself, which is a created gift, is itself relational, that is to say, it itself reflects something. The whole nature of this created gift of grace, which I may love in the neighbor, is to reflect the One who gives grace, the Giver, God Himself. It not only reflects God the way any other gift would, but it involves God, because grace cannot be given without the presence of the Lord Himself, the Giver. And hence if grace is in this person, finding it in this person I also find the Giver of Grace, the Lord Himself. As a result, we never treat people, it seems to me, as a passive channel or as a function through which *we* arrive at God. We do not instrumentalize them to improve *our* moral status. Since God has joined Himself once and for all to humanity in the Incarnation, humanity itself is exalted. As Emile Mersch says "There is not a single stone in this earth, there is not a single droplet of water that has not been changed by the fact of the Incarnation." Once God Himself took into personal union with Himself matter from *this* world, humanity achieved a totally new status. One does not have to strip humanity of humanity to achieve union with the Godhead, as was thought before Christianity. One does not have to avoid humanity to seek God. God is to be found within the bosom of humanity because that is precisely where He has chosen to put Himself.

As a result of this divine action, fraternal charity is made theologically possible by the fact that what is most deeply individual, most incommunicable about each person is the active personality constantly poured into him by God. Why is it possible for us to state that in fraternal charity what we really love is the uttermost individuality of the other? It is possible to say this because, in philosophical terms, what is most individual to me is my ultimate act of personality, my root of personality? The perfection of personality, which makes me to be myself, which prevents my ever being assumed by anyone else or becoming a part of anyone else, that thing which makes me to be me is constantly poured into me by the action of God Himself. What makes a man unduplicable, is a continued creative act of God in the center of the man's depths. And so if I come to the depth of another person, I encounter there not simply a created person, but the Living God, Who sustains him in existence, pouring into him this ultimate act of existence.

Consequently it is God Himself Who possesses the ultimate secrets of any man's personality. It is He alone who knows the total inner meaning of that pattern, that *eidos* that is unique, in each individual. What we love in fraternal charity is this unique, unrepeatable, concrete individual, with all his personality to its uttermost depths, and in him we love God, because God is *de facto* there, sustaining and communicating the act of existence to him.

If one touches, therefore, the ultimate depths of another, even in the natural order, even if this person is not in grace, one will find the creative God giving Himself. But if one touches someone who is in the state of grace, then one will find this great gift of grace and one will find the Divine Trinity Itself giving Itself to this soul, forming or actuating this soul, and as it were, fusing with it. One will find God dwelling in the soul as a guest.

I conclude, therefore, that Christian charity is genuinely theandric or incarnational, genuinely human and genuinely divine. It is not just a moral virtue, it is a Divine virtue. It is intensely human because it can appreciate, in a way no natural humanist could, all the humanity of the other person to the very depths of individuality, that last act that makes the man unique, the act of existence itself. It is a Divine Virtue because we love within our neighbor the One Who sustains him as an individual. God is present in him, not in the fashion of an inert idol, but as One Who forms the consciousness of the neighbor, renders him open, assists him to be able to enter into a genuine communion of love. It is God who renders the isolated individual courageous enough to break down all barriers and all false security in order to achieve this open communion of charity.

It would be a peculiar, merely juridical approach to fraternal charity to believe that we make God the formal object of our fraternal charity when we love the neighbor because he has *told* us to do so rather than because Christ is present in the neighbor. Through intelligence and faith we are able to find Him there. As a result we have always to be on guard against emptying the message of Christ concerning fraternal charity of all genuine ontological and theological meaning, as though He were telling us some kind of fairy story when He tells us we are to love all men. Christ's message is to be taken seriously here, for He is the revealer of the Divine message and the revealer of what we ourselves are, as human beings, when He tells us that the neighbor is to be loved.

This familial love, this open, honest, genuine love, is a realistic love. It does not deny that some men are difficult, but accepts the fact without attempting to understand why some people are difficult. Realistically, it believes that they are probably difficult for the same reason that we are difficult ourselves. In stressing the realism of charity, therefore, we have to stress its humanism as well.

We can not substitute for God's commandment to love, the words *like* or *tolerate,* or *don't get involved with,* or *leave in peace,* or *don't get in the way of.* We cannot change the meaning of Christ's words or weaken the spirit of what He intended. To desubstantialize charity into some kind of pale and bloodless substitute would be to change its very nature. It is *not* the method of the Incarnate God, Who became human, to suppress our humanity or to divinize us by destroying it. We must love, of course, from a theological and supernatural motive, that is to say we must love God in the neighbor and the neighbor in God as God has commanded, with universality. We must extend this love to all men insofar as we can despite the emotions that may arise in us, such as irritation, distaste, or anger. Without intelligence and will, we accept and continue this love with universality.

But the universality of fraternal charity does not mean either, as some have at times supposed, that we are to love all men in the same way or to love all men equally. That is nonsense, and it is utterly impossible as well. We are expected to love people according to their relationships to us, and obviously we have to love them according to the greater or lesser insight we have into them. If someone constantly opposes me and seems to display all sorts of irrational and hateful behavior toward me, I must love him and collaborate in every way with his own inner theme, do everything that I can to help him to be better, so that he will love me and perhaps treat me better. But I cannot be expected to love him in the same way that I love my mother and father, my brothers and sisters, even my brothers in religion. We do not love people all in the same way, because we cannot explain or understand all to the same degree. To love all equally would seem to demand that I deny my intelligence somehow, since it is obvious that some people are *de facto* more lovable than others. The Virgin Mary is more lovable than any of the saints, and Jesus Christ is more lovable than any human being. The saints are more lovable than most of us, and some of us are more lovable than others. Nevertheless we do have to be willing to show to all a readiness, insofar as is within our capacity, to enter into an open communion of love with them. We must be willing to foster their inner themes—the inner value proper to each—to collaborate with them, to render ourselves approachable to them. We cannot force our friendship on them. We have simply to be accessible, to be open. Friendship is always a gift of freedom.

In conclusion, what we are saying is that Christ has healed everything that He has assumed. Consequently he has healed and divinized our human affections. He did not heal them by eradicating them, so that we are forbidden to love our parents, as some religious seem to think. He loved His parents, He loved His disciples, He loved His friends, and He loved them as they were, each in a different way and in a different relationship to Him.

If we accept this concept of fraternal charity, it becomes clear that charity is by no means that sweet, easy virtue taken for granted to exist in all pious people. It is not at all an easy thing. We can of course substitute various counterfeits for it, which are easy. We can always substitute a kind of casual bonhommie, good companionship, that fragile and imperfect substitution for the genuine community spirit. We can substitute vested interests based on natural sympathies, inclinations or interests. But there is never true charity unless there is genuine victory over self. That is why even a guilty love is an invitation to grace, because it is a victory over egotism.

Charity demands renouncement. If I am to lay myself open to all sorts of people, some of whom like me and some of whom do not like me, I must be humble and I must be mortified. There are times when charity requires heroism. There are martyrs of charity. To live with people who are not naturally attractive or who are different and yet impose themselves upon us by their sheer presence in the Christian community can require heroism.

We know that by embracing the counsel of religious chastity the individual forgoes the most intimate and engaging form of human love, marital love. Religious then ought seriously to reflect that unless this renouncement brings with it deeper and more intense forms of love, then there is something un-Christian about it. There are many dangers involved in a life of celibacy or virginity. By this is not meant the obvious danger of violation of the letter of the vow. The danger that I am speaking about is that, at times, the wellspring of personal love can be dried up within the individual. The grace of marital love is a great invitation to charity, to love of God. The religious, therefore, who does not embrace the married life, has always to see to it that his love and charity be fulfilled in a more perfect way in religion. On this subject we might reflect on the following points, which were raised at an institute where this topic was discussed.

"What ideally should be the character of love among those dedicated in the religious life?" "Is fulfillment of the human personality's desire for love and need to love, simply to be found in a more perfect love of God, or also in a more perfect and more intense love of man?" "What of human love in the religious life?" "Is it simply more universal and less exclusive?" "Does it simply gain in extension what it loses in intensity?"

"To what extent is intimate, engaging, interpersonal love possible or desirable among consecrated religious?" "What light do the life of Jesus Christ and the lives of the saints give us in this matter?" "To what extent should the love of religious be more rational and less emotional than married love?" "Is married love the prime analogue for human love, and the love of the religious a sort of secondary derivative, or is it the other way around?" "To what extent should our love be more effective, that is a love of service, and less affective, that is, a love of commitment?" Sanctity, as we know, is eventually measured by *affective* love.

"To what extent does the training of young religious serve as a help, and to what extent does it serve as a hindrance to fraternal charity?" "To what extent does the training of young religious concerning friendship help them in forming genuine friendships?" "Does our sophistication today cause us to live behind a sort of mask, where our major task is to be disengaged from others, and disinvolved, so that others never know us?" "To what extent should we really try to love others in their individuality? Or rather should we use them as a means to love God?"

"What are the causes and the cures of loneliness in religious life?" "Is there loneliness?" "Is it inevitable that as one grows older in the religious life he is less reluctant to accept the young?" "Is there a necessary cleavage between, let us say the intellectuals and the nonintellectuals, between those more addicted to sports and those less addicted to them?" "As we grow older, should it be more difficult for us to form friendships with the religious and easier for us to form them with lay people, or is there something wrong in that?" "What apostolic value does the vow of celibacy or virginity have for the Church today?" "What witness value does it have?" "Does it have the authentic and full witness value today that it once had?" "If it is not thoroughly penetrated with genuine personal charity, can it function in the Church as an eschatological sign?"

These are important questions, and they demand a thoughtful reflection on our part. Whatever we may say about them, at least we have to conclude that Christ's command to union, to charity, demands of us an open, warm, familial love for all men insofar as we are capable of it, a love which is human-divine, theandric. The closed, opaque personality, incommunicable and unknown to everyone, is not the Christian ideal, or even a natural ideal. It is a deformation, from both the human and the supernatural viewpoints.

5

Poverty

KARL RAHNER, S.J.

THE PROBLEM OF POVERTY*

The history of the religious life for the two millennia of its existence has been, without much exaggeration, a history of various explanations of poverty. True, at times controversies arose about the motives and the reasons for poverty; and if we look more closely, very different motivation has been assigned to it in the various Orders and at various times. But above all, it has been practiced and determined in manifold ways; in its concrete reality it has varied and varies in the past and present from Order to Order. This fact is recognized; in fact, Orders and their "strictness" are gauged by it. Of course, it is possible to rise above all these different practices of poverty and to fashion a formalized concept of *the* religious poverty which fits them all. But then the question arises whether this concept really covers the proper character of poverty in a particular Order, whether the theological motivation which is given as the basis and goal of religious poverty still covers this formalized concept of poverty, and whether this formalized concept of poverty (for example, complete dependence on the will of superiors for the disposition of material goods) still preserves what was meant by "poverty" in Scripture and tradition and in the motivation of the original religious movements.

Today entirely new problems have been added to those that existed previously concerning the true character of poverty. We

* "Die Armut des Ordenslebens in einer veränderten Welt." *Geist und Leben*, v. 33, heft 4 (September, 1960), pp. 262–267. Translated by Rev. Gregory J. Roettger, O.S.B.

live in the midst of an emerging economy which in a forceful manner changes the material content of religious poverty. It would be Utopian to think it possible to carry out exactly what an Anthony, Pachomius, Benedict, Francis or, at the beginning of the modern era, an Ignatius conceived concretely as poverty. Such a concept would surely overlook reality and would bypass the real task, namely, to grasp anew and to realize the essence of what has been traditionally understood by poverty in the changed economic circumstances which are inescapably ours. In the realm of material goods and values more than in any other field, man is a function dependent on the social, collective form of this entire realm, whose formation is almost entirely independent of him: a reality which pre-exists and is withdrawn from his decision.

To wear a shirt or not to possess one, to go barefoot or shod, is at various times and under various economic systems something very different, almost wholly determined in its concrete content by prevailing circumstances. Hence, it happens that the early religious rules regarding poverty—which are intended to describe and determine the material content of poverty in the various Orders —either are no longer in force to a large extent or no longer reflect present reality at all. We shall return to these points later.

In this place we wish merely to call attention to the situation in order to make clear that we cannot expect a satisfying answer, which is strictly theological, regarding the religious meaning and the theological essence of poverty. A concept of poverty in its concrete application is not at all clear and cannot be clear, and we do not sufficiently understand the larger picture of the concrete economy of today, of which the concept of poverty forms only a part. Were we to try to give an exact theological formulation of poverty, this formulation could only be created by withdrawing into the realm of the abstract and the formalistic, where everything would be true, beautiful and marvelous, but where one might wonder whether the subject of the discussion is the poverty with which we have to deal in everyday life.

I shall speak first of all of some traditional problems of the concept of poverty; in later articles I will discuss the theological foundation of poverty in the circumstances which exist, and will sketch certain problems in connection with religious poverty that arise out of the present-day economic and ideological situation.

It may be comforting to stress the point that theoretical uncertainty and theoretical problems do not necessarily affect the practical activity of reasonable and wise persons. In man's concrete life there exist thousands of things which the experience of millennia has proved meaningful and valid, but which lend themselves to a clear theoretical explanation only with the greatest difficulty. The simple experience of life always teaches us more than theoretical discussion, which can never grasp life adequately. We know that religious life is meaningful and good as regards poverty, because it has been lived for centuries according to the venerable wisdom of experience, in the Church animated by the Spirit. And we know, even before we possess certainty, what we are observing and why it is good. This does not mean that reflection loses its meaning and its necessity, but merely suggests the uncertainty and the destructive power which it might have if it remained entirely abstract.

SOME TRADITIONAL PROBLEMS

1. The distinction between the poverty of the individual in an Order and that of the Order as such is well known. Such a distinction has its value. Without doubt the poverty of the individual contains an element of dependence on the community in the disposition of material goods. But dependence in the disposition of material goods cannot be identified with poverty (even if this temptation often assails ascetics and canonists). If the poverty of the community were not presupposed, it would be impossible to speak of the poverty of the individual. The absolutely dependent member of a truly wealthy society could not seriously be considered poor, if words are to retain any meaning. From this it follows that the problem of religious poverty is primarily a problem of the poverty of the community, insafar as its exists in the Order and inasfar as it presupposes that the individual's manner of life is determined by that of the community. This truth should be obvious.

I have the impression, however, that modern religious communities, even if they wished to accommodate the regulations concerning poverty in their rules to present-day conditions, are always tempted to think first of the individual, and to let the question of poverty, as it affects the community as a whole, recede into the background. This can be understood. Nowadays the problem of the poverty of the community is much more difficult to solve than that of the poverty of the individual. But it must be solved. Otherwise legislation concerning the poverty of the individual necessarily becomes formal casuistry, and we try to decide how the *juridical dependence* of the individual on the permission of the superior regarding the disposition of material goods can be maintained, simplified, or made stricter under present circumstances, without regard to the concrete poverty which is involved.

Such things easily turn external formalities which do not necessarily possess supernatural meaning or exert any formative influence on the personality. Dependence and poverty, as we have said, are not identical. This is an old problem, which must be re-thought anew today. To put it in another way: a rich Order cannot have poor members. Its great wealth may be strictly withdrawn from the arbitrary will of the individuals; it may have members who do not own property in a legal sense. But a really wealthy Order cannot have poor members. At most they will be completely dependent members with regard to the common ownership of material goods absolutely vested in the community.

Someone might say that such assertions already presuppose a fundamentally Franciscan concept of poverty, which was not verified, for example, in a rich medieval community (a royal monastery). Over against this objection it may be asserted that this concept of poverty—Franciscan, if you will—is the biblical concept, the early ascetical concept, the "evangelical" concept, which is presupposed also in the mentality of the modern Church and of the laity when the demand is made that religious should be poor. It must likewise be presupposed theologically. Otherwise poverty shrinks together and becomes a mere modality. (No wonder that the old Orders had no vow of poverty in the strict sense of the word!) It forms no proper evangelical counsel nor a real vow nor a strictly theological problem. In a word, poverty of the individual and poverty of the community are, in the last analysis, the same problem. If the community is poor, and insofar as it is so, the individual participates in the poverty of the community, because he is a member of it and therefore shares in its manner of living; and since he is poor, he unites with a community that lives this poverty. What degree and what character the poverty of the communty has or should have remains very much another and an open question.

2. In saying this, the second point to be treated has already been anticipated. Neither dependence in the disposition of material goods nor the juridical concept of lack of private property makes a person "poor" in the sense in which the word "poverty" is used in a theological and ascetical discussion. A person who has no private property cannot, indeed, dispose of material values at his own good pleasure, or even do so validly from a juridical point of view. But if he belongs to a community which is willing to supply him with such economic goods as are possessed by a person who is termed "rich" in relation to the common economic standard, then such a member of such a community cannot be regarded as poor. At the most it may be said that he is economically completely dependent. Such a dependence may indeed be felt as unpleasant. It may make the person in question "powerless" (at least as far as the outside world is concerned), and this dependence and powerlessness in comparison to others may also be acceptable from a Christian and ascetical point of view, within the meaning of religious ideals. But it cannot be called poverty.

If offenses against the vow of poverty were seen only in those cases in which the juridical dependence regarding ownership is violated, this would constitute a legalistic distortion of the genuine concept of poverty. And correspondingly, in circumstances where the superior acts juridically and canonically only as the legitimate administrator of the community property, he may be acting very much contrary to the spirit of religious poverty. If, for example, the superior seeks to increase the wealth of the Order endlessly, in a capitalistic and ruthless manner like a clever businessman, he may offend against the spirit of poverty, even though privately he lives in the same "ascetical" manner as many modern managers of great industrial enterprises. In such a case he has not offended against the principles of dependence, because as superior he legitimately performed these acts of administration; but he has sinned against poverty. If a superioress of a Sisters' Congregation exploits the individual Sisters through overwork in order to make the Congregation rich and powerful through the addition of new houses, she has offended against poverty, even though, because of it, the individual Sisters have to live very "poorly."

3. Religious poverty and *forms* of poverty must not be confused. Certainly poverty may not be theoretically sublimated to

the point where it is incompatible with any kind of use of material goods. Yet poverty demands a certain degree of deprivation of material goods, though we may leave aside the question as to *which* goods fall under the deprivation of poverty (and under what circumstances). Poverty has a very material content. Poverty in religion cannot be simply "poverty in spirit." The relationship to the world of material goods must be made concrete, and separation from it (of which more later) must be concretely realized. Still, a clear distinction must be made between poverty and determined forms of poverty. This has always been recognized. And for this reason, even in those cases which presuppose the common "Franciscan" concept, poverty has differed very much in various times and places.

This is not the place to analyze the various historical forms of poverty, to describe their physiognomies and to differentiate among them. It suffices at this point to call attention to this difference, since it will prove important for later considerations. In earlier days, possibly, the attempt was made to express this distinction too facilely, by use of the categories of "stricter" and "less strict" poverty, and therefore of "more perfect" and "less perfect" poverty. Greater caution will be observed in this regard today. More attention will be given to the difference in form than immediately and directly to "strictness." It will have to be granted that, as in so many other matters, the difference in the "strictness" of the various Orders has tended to level off, and that at present it tends still more toward a rather uniform style in all Orders. This possibly is unavoidable because of the common economic situation and the modern common manner of life.

If this difference between poverty (in its essence) and the form of poverty is admitted as an historical datum, then it is impossible to close one's eyes to the fact that today, both in general and in every individual Order, thought must be given to a form of poverty that is really convincing and liveable at the present time. It simply does not do to assume a rigidly conservative attitude, which tries to preserve the ancient form inherited from the Fathers and thus considers all problems solved. In the face of the modern economic picture such a solution cannot be accepted. If it is still attempted, there results a turbid mixture purely external, concessions to the new age perhaps made in haste and without clarity, together with remnants of the old traditions, which *de facto* are no longer ascetically significant, but only survive as a kind of religious folk-lore.

4. It cannot be denied that both in the tradition of poverty and in the tradition of the theology of poverty various motivations and definitions of poverty have existed. The poverty of the ascetics of Apostolic times and of early Christianity was different from that of the cenobites, both in fact and in motivation. The poverty of pure contemplatives and of the person engaged in the apostolate simply cannot be identical in fact, and consequently cannot be identical in motivation. The poverty of the religious life, leaving intact its essential identity, receives a peculiar character from the varying totalities of the individual Orders and, as a result, has a variously specified motivation. Hence history, which reveals these very different motivations in the many movements and struggles concerning poverty, justifies the conclusion that no absolutely univocal meaning should be attempted in the theological definition and the motivations of poverty. It must be assumed that poverty in the Orders presents a comparatively complex picture, which cannot be reduced to one theological root.

THE MOTIVES OF POVERTY*

Whatever forms religious poverty assumed in the course of history, however different the manner in which it was practiced, it always and everywhere strove to be a fulfillment of Christ's evangelical counsel. Despite the fact that the New Testament teaching on voluntary poverty contains a number of motivations which might well be subjected to analysis separately, every ideal of religious poverty wants to carry out this evangelical counsel, and every form of religious life feels itself justified in its poverty by the fact that Jesus recommended it, even though it may prove impossible to discover clearly the reasons *why* Jesus recommended it.

One aspect of this poverty is precisely its inseparable and immediate relationship to the Lord and his destiny. We may say that the establishment of poverty springs from the theology of the following

* "Die Armut des Ordenslebens in einer veränderten Welt." *Geist und Leben,* v. 33, heft 4 (September, 1960), pp. 267–275. Translated by Rev. Gregory J. Roettger, O.S.B.

of Christ as a sharing in the destiny of Jesus simply because this was the Lord's destiny. The concreteness of the life of the Lord in its absolute reality belongs logically and by presupposition in the life of the person who loves Jesus and seeks to follow him. But beyond that, whatever else the New Testament teaching on poverty contains as a motivation for this poverty will have to be included in religious poverty.

A ROLE IN THE CHURCH

The theology of poverty may not forget that religious poverty has to do with an aspect of the life of a community, which is the historical and economic grasp of essential aspects of the Church herself. Religious Orders are more than private associations of persons who lead an ascetical life on their own account and risk, and are only to some extent under the surveillance of the Church. Further, the Church takes an interest in these societies not only because they render assistance in the tasks of the hierarchical Church, but because religious Orders are a social expression of the charismatic and enthusiastic element in the Church, which must always exist as an essential characteristic in the Church. There can be no eschatological spirit in the Church if the evangelical counsels are not lived as essential characteristics of the Church. The religious Orders are a representational part of the victorious grace of God that has come into the world, which draws man beyond the field of his own possibilities and incorporates him into the life of God himself. This must not be forgotten when we speak of religious poverty. It must be considered in the light of the essence of religious Orders.

Religious poverty has a function to perform for these religious associations as free communities of life. This practical side of poverty, which we experience every day, does not constitute the ultimate essence of religious poverty, but it cannot and need not be overlooked. A certain degree of religious poverty (particularly in a certain dependence and identity of manner of life) is absolutely necessary for the existence of an intimate community of life such as the religious Orders profess to be. From this standpoint the meaning of poverty is determined by the wider purpose of such a community. Inasfar as an Order has an exterior mission, inasfar as the life and activity of the community and of the individual are at the service of such a mission (be it apostolic, educational, missionary, or charitable), religious poverty will also receive its character from this purpose. Its concrete determination in itself and in its manner will derive from the purpose.

A COMPLEX PICTURE

Now it is clear that the various vantage points from which poverty can be viewed are not only legitimate, and make of poverty a complex and varied picture, but also that the significations of poverty produced by these various viewpoints again produce a new problem. For it is not at all obvious *a priori* that these different motivations automatically lead to the same form of poverty. Poverty as an evangelical counsel; poverty as a personal following of the poor and suffering Christ; poverty as a visible part of the eschatological representation of grace, which is the Church; poverty as the organizational principle of a community; poverty as a means of concentrating the forces of a community for the achievement of its task in the external world, need not without further ado lead to the same "poor" style of life. It may even happen that these aspects of poverty mutually threaten and hinder one another. Thus a radically ascetical poverty, for example, may really threaten and destroy the possibility of a community life. The apostolic employment of poverty may seem to call for such wealth on the part of the community that it is no longer possible to speak of the real poverty of the individual member and hence of ascetical poverty.

Therefore, considering the relationship of these various viewpoints, while none need be rejected out of hand, the following may be asserted: poverty as imitation of and participation in *the destiny of Jesus* in a form of mystical identification, and poverty as a New Testament *counsel,* to sell everything and to give the proceeds to the poor, need not and cannot create mutual difficulties. Even if they cannot be directly identified with one another, still there are related totalities, as will be clearly seen immediately. The third aspect of poverty, in which the religious Orders are viewed as aspects of the essential meaning of the Church, cannot be in conflict with the two first-named essential bases of poverty. For the Church (as will be shown later) is to make comprehensible in the world *that* grace which makes up the content of the kingdom of God, for whose sake the disciple of Jesus is exhorted to become poor.

On the other hand, it must be clear from the beginning that poverty as an organizational principle in a community—poverty as a means of concentrating the forces of a community for the achievement of its practical tasks—can claim a right to consideration only in dependence on and submission to the significations already mentioned. Should they impose themselves to such an extent as to injure or destroy the essential foundation, then they would have to be rejected and opposed. If an Order wants to be an Order of the evangelical counsels, then apostolic, missionary, educational, charitable and other goals can never become the decisive element in the manner of life to such an extent as practically to do away with evangelical poverty. If certain goals, entirely legitimate in themselves, would demand a manner of life which truly and honestly could no longer be characterized as poverty, then such goals would have to be worked for and realized outside the religious community. One may not proceed from the axiom that all goals that are significant and necessary for the Church for that reason have to be realized in religious communities. The modern connection of religious life with almost every imaginable effort in the Church has indeed led to the assumption that this axiom exists. But it is and remains spurious and unproved, though it quietly presents itself as self-evident.

THE TEACHING OF JESUS

What, then, is the evangelical meaning of poverty in the teaching of Jesus? We abstract from the fact that in the first place poverty is simply a participation in the life of the Lord who *de facto* was poor, or better, who lived a life of poverty (Lk. 9:57; Mt. 8:20; 2 Cor. 8:9). Likewise, in treating this question, we abstract from the fact that in the New Testament poverty was a recommendation for a manner of life to be led only by individuals as individuals; the idea of a common life of poverty in the evangelical sense, the concept of a poor community, is not yet evident. We shall not take into consideration the "communism" of the primitive community of Jerusalem (Acts 4:32-37) either, because this would lead us too far afield. But we have the right to reflect that patently, in the concept of the Lord, virginity recommended by him "for the sake of the kingdom of heaven" (Mt. 19:12) and poverty recommended just as highly and for the same reason (Mt. 19:21; Lk. 18:22) derive from the identical basic attitude.

On the other hand, it is perhaps unrealistic to regard every moral demand or recommendation of Jesus as not existing prior to him; and therefore we can *reckon* with the possibility that Jesus in his recommendation of poverty adopted a program that was in vogue in late Judaism. Still we may say (though somewhat cautiously) that the poverty which Jesus intends and recommends to his disciples cannot be found either in the Old Testament or in late Judaism, which formed the environment of Jesus. We also presuppose (the proof of it would lead us too far afield) that Jesus in his call to poverty did not want to institute a social program, either as a requisite or as the ideal for the *common* social and economic formation of the world as a whole.

Given these presuppositions, we say: Jesus knows and declares that with him and in him the kingdom of God has arrived, and that this coming of the kingdom places before men an absolute, radical need of a decision of the greatest urgency, setting them in an eschatological situation. Not that man as a moral being perpetually needs to make decisions between "yes" and "no" with regard to God, but that now in Jesus the ulitimate call to salvation from God has come. God in Jesus forces man to make the ultimate decision. In this coming of the kingdom of God, thus understood, the wealth of man, according to Jesus, is so much a danger and an obstacle to the reception of the kingdom of God that it is easier for a camel to go through the eye of a needle than for a rich man to enter this kingdom (cf. Mt. 19:23f.; Mk. 10:25; Mt. 13:22; Lk. 1:53; 6:24; Mt. 6:19-24). Not that possessions in themselves are immoral, or that destitution in itself possesses any moral value. "A fundamental rejection of ownership, as practiced by the Buddhists and the Greek Cynics, is foreign to Jesus" (Schmid, *L Th K,* 1², 880). Jesus does not oppose the rich as a social enemy. But, according to the mind of Jesus, wealth and the heaping up of possessions signifies the direst danger for man. Enmeshed in the cares of this world, he overlooks the coming of the kingdom, hears the decisive call of God only dully, and does not have that radical freedom of heart which is required for the undivided reception of the kingdom. For that reason

Christ encourages those who, in closer imitation of him, want to receive this kingdom, to give their goods to the poor and to become poor themselves (Mt. 19:16-30; Lk. 9:3; 9:57f.; 12:33; 18:22).

Why riches form an obstacle to readiness for the kingdom—from what viewpoints and for what special reason—is not explained very explicity by Jesus. The rich man has cares (Mk. 4:19; Lk. 8:14), wants to have more riches, gives himself over to pleasure, enjoys the power and pleasure and security that go with wealth (Lk. 16:19; 12:15-21); he has his "treasure" on earth instead of in heaven (Lk. 12:33f.).

Jesus' evaluation of the danger of riches closely reflects the observation of ordinary life as it presents itself to the reasonable man who is unbiased with regard to wealth, does not idealize it, and acts soberly. As a result it is abundantly clear that in the list of woes Jesus pronounced concerning the rich and wealthy (cf. Lk. 6:24), his prophetical style of speech must always be kept in mind, if one wishes to avoid a doctrinaire generalization and an attitude admitting of no exceptions, which Jesus did not intend at all, as is clear from his own words (Mt. 19:26).

Furthermore, despite Mt. 8.20, the impression persists that Jesus was not really miserably poor or actually suffered from hunger. He possessed money (cf. Jn. 12:6) and patently had enough opportunity to be supported by rich friends whenever he needed it. Hence one cannot say that the text of the Old Testament (Prov. 30:8f.), according to which the middle way between opulence and misery was ordinarily the best presupposition for the service of God, was simply disavowed by the example of Jesus.

It is evident that with Jesus the motivation of poverty is identical with his motivation of voluntary celibacy for the sake of the kingdom of God. In the evangelical counsel of poverty he exhorts those who want to belong to his closer followers and thus to become "perfect" (Mt. 19:21), to imitate by their own decision in their own lives that situation which is proper to those "poor" whom he styles as blessed in the Sermon on the Mount—that is, the *anawim,* who are socially powerless, threatened and suffering, but who at the same time bear their lot "humbly" and submissively before God. The *anawim* transmute their lot by faith, and so transform it into that which the voluntary poor are to strive for by the intention of Jesus: to externalize their undivided freedom as the internal situation demands, to hear Christ's call to the kingdom of God.

But another dimension has to be added to what has been said. Jesus exhorts those who have voluntarily become poor for the sake of the kingdom of God to give their riches to the *poor*. This is not the easiest manner of becoming poor that might be indicated. For example, were it technically just as feasible, one might just as well destroy one's property by burning in order to become poor. The neighbor who is poor is clearly intended as the goal of this largess of one's wealth. He is to be helped. In the mind of Jesus this certainly does not mean the "disenfranchised" and the "disinherited," who pretend to a socio-political right to wealth. No; the poor man is to be helped because he is a brother in the kingdom of God, because he is loved as such, because by this gesture of belief in the coming of the kingdom of God he is to understand that the kingdom of God has arrived. For it is the function of this kingdom to unite and bring together the men who through the guilt of the world have fallen into disunity and strife. Hence where belief in this coming of the heavenly kingdom is lived concretely through voluntary poverty, belief in the oneness of the love of men united by the grace of God must also be made concrete. Man no longer defends the realm of worldly goods as a bastion of self-defense against his neighbors, but allows them to share in these goods, because he can confidently love them as fellow-citizens of the kingdom.

A kind of community of goods (which naturally may assume the most varied forms and need not necessarily be a replica of the primitive community of Jerusalem) is an important aspect of this poverty as a realistic gesture of the new brotherhood in Christ. (From this vantage-point also might be considered the brotherhood in the Orders, with its accompanying community of goods, through whose service the former private wealth is placed at the service of the universal Church. Naturally this will only come about if private egotism, hankering for possessions, is not replaced by a collective egotism of a larger community in opposition to the Church or other Christians.) This aspect of evangelical poverty must always be taken into consideration when we seek to explain poverty in a more theologically systematic manner as an eschatological gesture of belief in the coming of the kingdom of God from above by grace. It must never be forgotten that this kingdom, the oneness of brotherhood and of love, is to be entered also in a definite manner through the gesture of voluntarily becoming poor.

Jesus considers closer attachment to his person and the consequent voluntary poverty as especially required in the case of those who place themselves at the service of his missionary endeavor (Mt. 10:9).

By way of summary, we may say: With Jesus evangelical, voluntary poverty is not a social program for the reform of economic conditions for their own sake; it is not an aspect of an ever-valid ethic of being (hence, likewise, it is not "ascetical," if that term is to connote demands of abnegation of an essential kind). It is rather a consequence of the eschatological situation of salvation. Poverty has significance only inasfar as it furthers the radical readiness for the kingdom of God, not because there is any value in pure lack of ownership in itself, or in bourgeois simplicity and contentment. It is not regarded as the manner of life of a community, but as the means of making missionary activity possible. It is the abnegation, primarily, of wealth, as wealth showed itself in its ordinary effects in the historical situation of Jesus, so that an application of the counsel of poverty to the ever-changing economic situation is imperative. But poverty is not intended as a mere attitude, as (in this sense) "poverty in spirit" but includes as a material element (despite all inclination toward freedom of soul in the kingdom of God) a concrete act of abnegation with regard to material goods.

If we (while passing over the teaching of Acts, of Paul and of James) seek to penetrate and systematize the intended result somewhat theologically (by which fact it is simultaneously enlarged, since it is brought into contact with more general theological viewpoints), then we may say:

Poverty is simultaneously intentional and actual in the dialectical difference of intention and work. Detachment with regard to material possessions does not yet constitute faith and charity, which alone count; and yet for those who are exhorted to embrace it, this faith and this charity realize themselves in poverty as their manifestation, their "work."

Evangelical poverty (in the form just described) is only meant as a reply to the historical situation of salvation, in which man finds himself in the eschatological presence of the kingdom of God in Jesus. Poverty is, like all abnegation in the New Testament, a concrete expression of faith in the coming of the grace of God, which goes beyond anything man could do of himself. Since this grace is the absolute self-sharing of God as he lives in himself, and since it has only been revealed in Christ, as the glory of God himself which breaks all earthly measures and goes beyond all values of experience, man can only now reply to the coming of God. The act of faith realizes itself and becomes concrete—that is, it embraces the *entire* reality of man, his physical and social sides, his endowments—by jettisoning certain realities and values, the sacrifice of which is either an act of despair (or resignation) regarding the meaning of existence, or a breaking open of the soul to the reality of God, which comes from above as grace.

The meaning of poverty consequently is the act of faith in God's grace as the only ultimate fulfillment of human existence. Thence it follows that, if faith signifies salvation and if it must necessarily concretize itself, such a "giving up" of the world belongs to every faith to a certain extent and in a certain manner. The "poverty of spirit" of all Christians necessarily implies, even though the material limits cannot be determined, a poverty in the sober reality of life. Considered in its essence, the poverty of religious and the rich or poor life of other Christians show only accidental differences; the two cannot be separated into absolutely and essentially different manners of life. And conversely, letting the "world" pass must be regarded as an act of Christian faith, which regards the world in all its aspects as *redeemable;* it is always an act of faith in the capability of the world to be redeemed. Such an act of faith cannot find its absolutely essential fulfillment simply in the possession of nothing (inasfar as this is physically possible). Otherwise it would assert implicitly that freedom from the world in itself constituted possession of God, and this is false. Triumph over the world is a gesture of faith made possible by God's grace—faith in the fact that God gives himself to the world in grace and that this grace can be forced neither by enjoyment of the world nor by flight from the world as such. Furthermore, only he who has a positive relationship to the world can give it up as a positive value in the act of faith. The man who worries, who is disinterested, undeveloped, frugal, regulated by bourgeois standards, is not the kind of man who in any appreciable measure can carry out the meaning of the act of faith in poverty. The "ideal" of religious poverty can therefore never consist in this, that it grows in proportion to the deprivation of material goods; nor can it consist in the narrow pedantry of those who watch over their bourgeois manner of life and the observance of their casuistry for its own sake.

Inasfar as the Church not only has to be the Church of believers, but also must appear as such—must be the sign of faith in the world —the concreteness of the act of faith in the act of self-denial belongs necessarily to her manner of appearance, and it must never be wanting to her. It is an existential witnessing to the faith, which belongs to her as a holy Church just as much as the authoritative preaching of the faith. Hence it can be readily understood that the fostering of this ascetical witness of the faith *of* the Church and *in* the Church is one of the essential tasks of the Church. She must repeatedly form herself and present herself as a Church in which the truth is lived. She must show that she is awaiting the return of the Lord, looking forward in hope to the eternal kingdom of God still to be realized: believing, hoping, loving.

The fostering of such eschatological witnessing to the faith by the "ascetics" of the Church, who always form a "state" in the Church, naturally comes about more easily and more effectively if the Church does not have to turn simply to individual, separated ascetics, but if these, in order to stress their charismatic mission and duty, form a community, and this community and the individual ascetics in it are formed and guided by the Church, enriched with the Church's powers of salvation, and again and again are brought back to the duty to which they—the individuals in the communities and the communities themselves—have been called by God. Poverty as a freely chosen form of life, which proclaims and represents belief in the coming of grace from above, is essentially an ecclesiastical act. Hence it follows that this poverty must be so formed that it reflects the function of witnessing to the faith of the Church both interiorly and exteriorly.

POVERTY IN THE MODERN WORLD*

The most obscure part of our consideration of poverty is reached when we have to deal with the poverty that is to be realized at a particular time, namely, in the modern age. Poverty and wealth are *a priori* relative concepts. They always refer to the amount of material goods at the free disposition of the individual in comparison with the amount of such goods possessed on the average on a given economic or cultural period.

It does not make much sense to call a pygmy of the rain forests of Central Africa "poor" because he does not have a shirt. At the time of Jesus a man was perhaps considered "poor" in Palestine if he owned but one cloak instead of two (cf. Mt. 5:40; 10:10). Today an individual would rightly be called "poor" who has only two shirts to his name. Hence poverty is a term relative to a determined economic system. Still it is not *simply* relative. For within the persistent historical changes of the economic situation a certain constant persists. With regard to man's biological existence a certain absolute minimum is demanded. For example, it can be stated how many calories a man needs lest he die of hunger. Because of this constant it cannot be asserted that the concepts of poverty and wealth are always to be determined solely by the prevailing economic situation; furthermore, it is not permissible to ask whether, for example, our present "poverty" has anything in common materially with "poverty" in the days of Jesus.

But, on the other hand, since man is not purely a biological being, since he has needs which are not determined purely by his life but are subject to historical changes, the concept of poverty contains a variable, historically changeable element, to a great extent withdrawn from determination by the individual. Thence arises the question: What is properly meant by present-day religious poverty? From this question will emerge the fact that simply because of the

* "Die Armut des Ordenslebens in einer veränderten Welt." *Geist und Leben,* v. 33, heft 4 (September, 1960), pp. 275–283. Translated by Very Rev. Gregory J. Roettger, O.S.B.

changes of economic and social conditions rather important changes have also taken place in poverty and the form of poverty. These have not yet been sufficiently recognized in the Church's laws regarding the poverty of religious communities. It further becomes clear that the significance of the poverty of the Orders, for the Church and her witness to the world, has undergone an almost essential shift, and that we are obligated to apply ourselves to evolve a new form of poverty, which will enable the constant function of poverty in the religious life of the individual, of the Orders, and of the Church to stand forth more clearly both internally and externally.

It is very difficult to express what ought to be said about this question in a clear and systematic manner with any degree of completeness. The reader is therefore requested to excuse the fragmentary and disordered character of the following considerations.

1. In the first place, an observation which will perhaps serve to meet the criticism occasionally expressed today by ideal religious: that it is clear and undeniable that modern religious are threatened with the danger of becoming more lax, and that the sole duty of the superiors should be to take a stand against such an aberration.

If poverty signifies economic insecurity and a surrender of the social power connected with wealth, then it may be stated that, by and large, the religious Orders as communities have never been so poor as they are today. If it is correct to say that the individual religious participates in the wealth or the poverty of his community, then this fact also signifies something for the individual members of the Orders. This assertion is well founded.

The aggregate of property in a medieval abbey, in a medieval monastery of mendicants, or in a seventeenth-century college of Jesuits, and the power connected with it, was, by comparison with the goods at the disposal of the entire economy, proportionately far greater than it is today. This holds true even if the comparative figures are adjusted to take into consideration the relationship between the number of religious and the size of the general population at each period. Monasteries have all become poorer than they ever were, if poverty is determined not only by the absolute quantity of goods, but also by their relationship to the amount of goods existing at any particular time. That the increase of poverty is not accompanied by an increase of biological or economic insecurity in the same proportion is simply a consequence of the general economic situation.

Perhaps in former times a religious ran a greater risk of suffering from hunger than now. But this is simply a result of the fact that this danger has become smaller than formerly. Similarly, it can scarcely be doubted that economic insecurity has been relatively increased in the case of religious, more than in many other social groups, in comparison with the security they enjoyed in former times. This fact does not lose its significance even though this increased insecurity in the case of religious does not arise from economic causes (as in former times) but from other causes, such as the threats to religious communities from political powers inimical to religion and to the Church.

On the other hand, we need not hide in shame from our religious ancestors in this matter of poverty, even though we now have a typewriter and a wrist watch and other things they did not have. It is true that the absolute quantity of goods at the disposal of religious today has grown extraordinarily by comparison with past centuries; but this is not the result of a development of the Orders as such, and much less of a loss of the religious ideal of poverty. It is only a consequence of the general economic development. Nevertheless, this fact constitutes the basis of the modern problem of poverty in the Orders.

2. The problem of the security of modern man (and thus also of the religious) is of great significance. In our present-day economy, in contrast to other ages, everyone, including the religious, has at his disposal the absolute minimum necessary for the preservation of life. The possibility of starving to death has been reduced to a minimum in our economic milieu. The poverty of earlier days, however, to a large extent rejected such security. The poor man begged in the strict sense of the word, and not only suffered hunger if he did not receive an alms—which was not guaranteed—but he was also exposed immediately and obviously to common catastrophes (crop failures, pestilence, etc.), which in former ages could come about much more easily and only be avoided with great difficulty. Even though one may assert that, despite this modern economic situation, the fear and insecurity of existence is possibly more characteristic of man than formerly, this does not change the proved fact. For this

modern insecurity of existence is not increased through the poverty of religious. Even a more parsimonious use of the quantity and kind of economic goods would not bring them closer to that limit of the minimum required for existence, which begets this insecurity. They would indeed live more sparingly, and such a manner of life can certainly be defended and praised. But if they were thus standardized on a level of consumption of a very modest kind, then they would really be secure, for this modest quantity of goods is easiest to have.

This arises from another circumstance which changes the situation essentially, and in terms of which religious poverty must be viewed. In an industrial society every person capable of working can share in the production of goods. As a result, begging has become a purely peripheral phenomenon: alms as a means of minimal existence comes into play only in the case of those incapable of working. Money today is a symbol of productive working power.

Even though one may say with a certain justification that today's Orders perhaps have to "beg" more than they did formerly, in order to support and develop their young members who are not yet "productive" (since they are not yet active in the apostolate, and the "income" from this source does not suffice for the support of the unproductive members), still this "begging" is much like that practiced by other cultural institutions to assure their financial stability (through "contributions" of financially able "members," "supporters," etc.). It has in common with begging as formerly understood only the name, and possibly some abstract, metaphysical essence, but nothing more. Religious in our lands, generally speaking, no longer have to beg in the sense in which that word was formerly understood.

Because we live in a productive economy of labor and money, intellectual and spiritual efforts can also be regarded as labor having a commercial value. And so, no matter how we look upon this matter of poverty in theory, religious in fact live largely from the income of their activity, which is considered as labor. Just as the old honorarium of the physician has given way to a direct recompense for his work, so the same holds true of the activities of religious: they receive their wage.

But precisely for this reason, in the judgment of modern man, religious step out of the category of the poor and into that of wage-earners, with all the advantages and disadvantages which that economic situation brings with it. In any case, religious no longer are ranked among the really poor in the opinion of men. At most they belong to those who must be satisfied with a comparatively modest manner of life. Faced with this situation, it does not help to console oneself with the thought that we religious still live rather modestly and simply (even though with a standard of living that inescapably is raised with the common level of living).

It cannot be denied that by this development, however unavoidable, the distinctive character of religious poverty has definitely suffered in significance and power of conviction. Our poverty, from the juridical standpoint, will be regarded as a useful organizational measure for a common life and for an organization whose members have set themselves a common goal (especially since they are celibates, and for that reason almost necessarily are bound to a close community). But this life with its common property will not be looked upon as that poverty which the Gospel calls such, nor will it be regarded as an act of faith because of its hazards of insecurity and powerlessness. Perhaps such an aspect of life will be attributed to one or the other of us, if there is a definite impression that he would have "earned" much more if he had not become a religious. But in general this compliment will not be paid us, and most likely it would not be true anyway.

The fact remains: Since religious poverty at present has little in common with (voluntary) insecurity over and above that of men in general, religious poverty has lost much of its character of witness, which it basically must have as something religious and ecclesiastical. The former insecurity of existence that used to accompany poverty has yielded to a security of monastic existence, from the economic point of view; and this security becomes all the greater if the religious identifies himself with his community and adjusts his personal wants to the economic capabilities of his community. If he does so, then it is scarcely possible to speak of insecurity and of risk regarding earthly existence, from the standpoint of poverty. If and to the extent that such insecurity still exists in religious life, it arises not from poverty but from the threat to the religious and clerical life from powers inimical to God and the Church. In that way God may have supplied a substitute for the believing trust of the poor of Christ. But this new element certainly is not poverty.

3. A further problem has to do with the technical observance of the juridical dependence of the individual on the permission of the superior. Mention has been made several times of the fact that the simple juridical dependence of the religious in the disposition of material goods cannot by itself constitute the essence of religious poverty. To think that such a formal dependence on superiors actually constitutes the essence of poverty would signify the collapse of the whole ideal. But abstracting from this, the modern economic structure produces a serious difficulty with regard to such dependence. All the acts and omissions of a religious can be so construed and understood, in a juridical manner, that every act and omission on his part with regard to material values can be considered as authorized by the religious superiors, and hence there is technically no disposition of private property. But the question is whether that fact guarantees that the religious thereby lives "poor," and whether such poverty produces those results without which it is meaningless. Precisely here we meet with a difficulty.

All of us live in an extraordinarily rich and extremely complicated world of goods, whether we like it or not, whether we live modestly or opulently. It follows that we continually perform (and must perform) a great number of acts regarding the disposition of material goods. Now these acts, it seems to me, because of their multiplicity and variety, can depend only very juridically—by the use of certain juridical procedures—on the permission and approval of superiors, but cannot depend upon that permission in a real sense. In other words, the religious of today whether it be admitted or not, has in fact a considerable quantity of material goods which he treats just as if they were his private property.

Perhaps someone will object that it has always been so necessarily. Even in ancient times a handkerchief in the pocket of a religious was treated in the same way as by a private owner of a handkerchief; and in more recent times it was a ridiculous rather than an edifying fiction for a Sister to speak of her dentures as "our" teeth instead of "my" teeth! That may all be true.

The important point is this: Because of the development of modern economy and the wealth of goods with which everyone nowadays surrounds himself and occupies himself, this circle of factual—even if not juridical—private property and its free disposition has become greatly enlarged. Hence there exists a problem of the practical observance of the concrete economic dependence of the religious on the permission of the superior. It seems to me to be meaningless and to the disadvantage of genuine poverty if these difficulties are hidden under the formal and juridical constructions of permissions which are simple fictions. If these fictions are insisted on, then the modern religious is obliged to observe a multitude of superflous acts of a bureaucratic nature, which the hard-working individual will find it difficult to understand.

We cannot delay at this point to expand these considerations in the way of practical suggestions. We merely ask whether the practical circle of goods, which always existed in reality, ought not perhaps to be enlarged in view of the greatly increased quantity of goods, because the contrary only leads to formal and juridical bureaucracy and contributes nothing to a modest manner of life based on personal decision and personal responsibility.

4. Attention must be called to a further change in the concrete form of poverty brought about by the modern economic situation. The quantity of goods that are *productive* (taking that word in its widest sense) has increased in an extraordinary manner even in the life of the religious. Naturally, such goods always existed—goods which served not merely to preserve life, but which were "means of work," requisite for the attainment of the goals which a religious and an Order embrace. Saint Francis was already forced to concede that even his poor friars needed books, Breviaries and churches. But nowadays the quantity of such goods has increased considerably; one might almost say that they have changed essentially.

If we abstract from land and soil, in former times the classical example of a good was a consumptible good. To understand this, it suffices to advert to the controversy that lasted for centuries regarding the licitness of taking interest. Today the classical example of a good is neither land nor soil nor a consumptible good, but the machine, the tool, the productive good. While in earlier times the concept of the "rich man" immediately conjured up the image of a person who possessed great possibilities for enjoying himself (and who in this sense was also powerful, since he possessed goods which another lacked), the modern classical example of material goods also changed the concept of the rich man. He is no longer so much a man who has great possibilities of pleasure. (On the one hand, they are limited from the biological standpoint in all people; on the other, in our mass-consumption economy, today's "poor" man is not so much behind the rich in this respect as was formerly the case.) The rich man today disposes of a quantity of machines, of productive goods, and in *this* way has power in an entirely different manner than formerly. It must not be forgotten, however, that many goods can serve both productive *and* pleasurable ends (taking both words in their widest sense). A radio set can fulfill two purposes. Furthermore, it should be remembered that the effectiveness of a means for a determined end within a society depends on the general condition of that society. In the time of Jesus a donkey was a useful means of transportation. It is no longer that today.

From this observation a new problem arises for religious poverty and the manner of poverty. If an Order or a religious pursues determined spiritual, apostolic, or educational goals, there is need today for many more means of labor, many more productive goods than before. A suitable library which will at all serve its purpose must have at least ten times as many books as, say, in the Middle Ages; we use watches, dictaphones, cameras, electric razors, typewriters, telephones. No doubt many already (and perhaps quite justifiably) consider a television set and not only a radio as a necessary or useful instrument of work. In the missions the private plane will be regarded as a necessity. Because of lack of manpower and for other reasons, every monastery today has a great number of technical appliances: an elevator, oil heating, cold and hot running water, an electric kitchen, etc., etc. One may continue to insist that all these things do not belong to the individual but to the Order, and that thus poverty is safeguarded. That simply is not true. A truly wealthy Order cannot have poor members. But is not an Order rich, in the modern sense, when its members have at their disposition and actually employ a notable quantity of such appliances?

Naturally it may be objected (and this objection may offer some comfort) that the quantity of such goods, in comparison with the productive goods of other people of the present age, is very, very modest; even today an Order, relative to the rest of society, is still poor. (In fact, from this viewpoint, as was pointed out at the beginning, it has become even poorer.) It may also be asserted that these many labor-saving devices exercise an ascetical effect by increasing the tempo of work (at least in the case of serious persons), and even oblige the individual to an asceticism of work, because he is tied down by this kind of work much more than in the more leisurely days of yore. Perhaps God has thus again supplied a compensation for the loss in poverty. But certainly the penance connected with this fatiguing work has no connection with poverty.

In any case, the great quantity of these aids always represents, in the eyes of outsiders, the possibility of greater enjoyment; and indeed they can serve such a purpose. Consequently, this increase in productive goods in the life of the modern Order, however unavoidable it may be, makes the Orders appear rich rather than poor. The ecclesiastical, representational function that essentially belongs to religious poverty suffers thereby in a practical manner.

Besides, there is also the influence of this situation on the mentality of the religious himself. Today's religious desires to increase the results of his work to an ever greater degree, and therefore wishes to have at his disposal an ever-increasing quantity of goods as means of work. From this standpoint, however, it is not at all easy for him to find an inner relationship to poverty, at least if we mean by it what ordinarily goes under the name of "poverty." He has an appreciation for a highly developed organization for the exploitation of his time, his powers, his work, all of it demanding an extremely high degree of asceticism. He does not want to enjoy comfort. By reason of this will to work and to accomplish, he desires to impose on himself considerable mortification as far as consumptibles are concerned, which is perhaps considerably greater (relative to the respective possibilities) than in earlier days of the Orders, where a great deal of time had to be spent and could be spent in talk, slow trips, care of everyday needs under the most primitive conditions. The modern religious will say: If that is poverty, then I have a great appreciation of poverty, but not if poverty signifies the bourgeois manner of life and work of the eighteenth-century and would make it seem ideal that a religious house should look the same interiorly as it did a century ago, when it certainly was not built by Le Corbusier, like the new house of studies of the Dominicans in France.

So the question returns: Bearing in mind the meaning of religious ideals, is a person still poor if, while observing a strict asceticism with regard to consumptible and luxury goods, he is "rich" in all those things which tend to further the other goals of the Order and of the religious; or must the quantity of means of work be cut back—even though this should bring with it a certain diminution of the effectiveness of work—so that it can be brought under the concept of poverty, since it is not at all clear that an Order may or must pursue a legitimate goal with *all* the means not in themselves unlawful? Is this a justifiable question? Has it already been answered? Can a univocal, theoretical reply be given? In any case, we ought to consider the practical aspects of the problems and the casuistry in the practice of today's religious poverty more precisely and more openly from this point of view.

THE CHALLENGE OF POVERTY*

Does present-day poverty still have the spiritual power that it once had? From some aspects, to which reference has already been made, it is not easy to give an affirmative answer. Modern poverty signifies to an essentially lesser degree exposure to the inescurity of existence, which binds the religious climate of faith to the eternal goods of grace and a trusting submission to God. The considerably enlarged sphere of the individual's disposition of goods, compared to former times, makes the religious of today much more like the layman who possesses private property, particularly since the layman's sphere of action appears to be considerably more restricted than it was formerly. From that standpoint, too, the spiritual power of poverty would seem to be diminished. Less than formerly the religious will be able to imagine himself as one of the *anawim* of the New Testament: the little ones, the humble ones, the powerless ones, with all the religious implications which such an experience could bring with it formerly. We have already seen that by reason of today's prevalent regard of material goods as a means to the attainment of planned goals of a legitimate character, modern man finds it difficult to perceive any meaning in poverty, if it is to be more than an asceticism of consumption, because he will see in such poverty only a refusal to work for legitimate and religiously valuable goals by all available means.

* "Die Armut des Ordenslebens in einer veränderten Welt." *Geist und Leben,* v. 33, heft 4 (September, 1960), pp. 283–290. Translated by Very Rev. Gregory J. Roettger, O.S.B.

There are still other considerations which make the religious effectiveness of poverty seem diminished and therefore questionable. Practically speaking, at the present time poverty in monasteries simply does not signify "deprivation." Of course, even today it may entail the renunciation of luxuries and similar things which the individual might otherwise acquire and use; but in the last analysis these renunciations affect only things whose non-possession does not create deprivation.

If, for example, I do not *want* to make a trip by air around the world, then for me the impossibility of harmonizing it with poverty does not signify "deprivation," pain, or anything that affects me intimately. But those hardships, really worthy of the name, which were usually bound up with poverty in times past, irrespective of the attitude that was freely assumed, practically no longer exist in today's religious poverty: hunger, cold, sickness which could not be treated for lack of money, definite social discrimination with contempt and mistreatment, the need to beg in the strict sense of the word.

In fact, it may be asserted that, under the sway of the modern economic situation, religious poverty has become so sublimated that it is in danger of losing its original meaning. Here occurs in its own way what happens again and again in the social life of mankind: under the old nomenclature and the old juridical forms something really different comes into being.

The question arises whether modern religious poverty signifies anything more than (1) an asceticism with regard to consumptible goods and luxuries, and (2) that community of goods which is necessarily required in an intimate and permanent community of life if such a community is to function. If one had to admit that the real meaning of poverty exhausts itself in these two aspects, then the theological and ascetical basis of poverty, and the concrete manner of poverty, would have to be established clearly and definitely under these two aspects, with the rejection of many outmoded ideologies. Perhaps the prospect ought not to cause undue alarm. For one may say: Even in the asceticism of consumptibles and luxuries, the fundamental essence of evangelical poverty is still preserved. This is a statement, indeed, that still needs much investigation and consideration. One may say that from both aspects of contemporary religious poverty, important and decisive potentialities for religious formation can proceed, which may also cause such a religious poverty to appear as the pillar and support of religious life.

The reply to the question (which cannot be satisfactorily answered here) depends partially on the reply to another question. The basic question is this: Is the manner of living exemplified today by all Orders, with negligible variations, *really* forced upon them unavoidably by the concrete economic situation; or could it, without thereby falling victim to a romantic anachronism, be formed in such a way as to resemble more closely the former style of poverty? There can be no doubt that in very many ways we have simply been obliged to embrace a different manner of poverty than was in vogue formerly; and all attempts to break away from this new manner, however ideal or reactionary the motives may be, would really be disobedience to God and his disposition, which he imposes on man in a given situation by reason of historical development.

If a Capuchin today does not go about barefoot in a large city, that does not imply that he has become unfaithful to his ideal of poverty. For his predecessors did not go barefoot in the city either, and hence, if he would do so today, he would not be imitating his predecessors. Likewise, he cannot feel himself obliged by the ideals of his Order to wander as a poor man through the Umbrian country in the steps of the poor man of Assisi.

And yet the question may be raised whether we religious, in the wake of these necessities, have not embraced without reason and without discretion many things in our manner of living and our poverty which do not belong there, and which *unjustifiably* set us apart from the ancient manner. Led by a reactionary traditionalism on the one hand, and on the other by an indiscreet connivance with the spirit of our age, have we not perhaps delayed in developing our manner of poverty in a creative way? The practice of poverty often gives the appearance of a flaccid and miserable compromise between the modern manner of living of people in the world and the venerable monastic forms of life. That such a situation does exist in a *certain* degree among us religious can only be denied by him who thinks that the common blindness, sinfulness and wordly corruption of men simply cannot be discovered in the mentality of the average religious and the average religious house.

Finally, the problem at hand must be viewed from yet another angle, namely, from that of the ecclesiastico-social function of poverty in the Church, which signified and testified to the man of past centuries, who necessarily was poor, that there exist goods of a higher order than consumptibles; that striving for these consumptibles could not constitute the ultimate of human existence; that even the economically poor man, precisely because of the situation in which he found himself, with its dangers, insecurity, humility, etc., could concretely fashion his belief in God and life eternal; that eternal life could not be merely an opium for the poor, if the rich voluntarily became poor, since these really do not need an analgesic for life's miseries. It is self-evident that this function of example in an economy that was poor in all things was greater and more far-reaching than it can be in a rich and diversified economy. The task of supplying an example to *necessary* poverty is more comprehensive in a society of people poor in the world's goods than in a society where the contrary holds true. If, abstracting from a very thin upper stratum, the *great majority* of people is really poor and in need, then in such a society voluntary poverty has the function of a *general* religious example. If society today is necessarily pluralistic, and consequently those in actual need form but a small group at the most, then it becomes clear that poverty in its function as witness no longer plays the same *comprehensive* role as formerly. The Church needs to proclaim entirely different examples to entirely different groups of society.

Man's continued experience of contingency, which he formerly felt in the insecurity of existence precisely by reason of dire poverty, will show itself today in other areas than in material need. Consequently, this contingency must be interpreted by the Church from a religious standpoint, based on faith, in these other areas. Hence the question very insistenly presents itself: What causes man's contingency and his dependence on God to become present to him in today's mass industrial society, in a world rich in consumer goods, in a planned economy? Modern man cannot experience in the same immediate and intimate manner, as was true formerly, that he must beg his bread from God. Naturally, man as such always lives in the "need" that teaches him to pray. But in the concrete, this existential need has its own history and evolution. As a result, it is impossible for the old manner of poverty to serve as univocally as the comprehensive example of the religious significance of life for all men as was formerly the case. Religious poverty as an expression of this significance no longer serves as the universal religious exemplar for the whole of society.

Does this mean that religious poverty has simply lost its function as a religious example in the Church and for the Church, and so also its ability to witness to the faith over against the world? That is impossible, if poverty is an essential characteristic of the religious life, and this in turn an essential function of the enduring Church. But *wherein* can this exemplary function of religious poverty consist today? Again, as a reply to this question, asceticism with regard to consumptibles and luxuries presents itself. One may say that modern mass consumption threatens the Church, because she has not yet sufficiently succeeded in creating clear exemplars for giving an ethical and humanizing aspect to this consumption. (At best, in this connection, we can console ourselves with the consideration that the trend toward an ever-increasing consumption simultaneously constitutes a much more decisive threat to Communism.) Here religious poverty could find a new and at the same time (as far as essence goes) an old sermon: a definite and convincing presentation of an asceticism of consumption. Not primarily in the sense that we religious to a certain extent represent the finger of the Church raised in threat: "You must not dissolve in an ever higher standard of living; there is something more noble to strive for." But in this, that the Orders, through what we call poverty, demonstrate to modern mankind an asceticism of consumption which would prove itself the only possible, genuine, and workable "hygiene of necessities" there is, an asceticism of consumption in which man simply and self-evidently denies himself a thousand possibilities of consumption because he has a genuine and vital relationship to God, spirit, person, and charity, and because he must refrain from covering up those experiences of contingency which always persist.

Naturally, this kind of poverty must develop in such a way as to become noticeable and convincing. If we are supposed to let men see our works (even though we keep our heart hidden in the intimacy of God), then we ought to see to it that our asceticism of consumption really enters into our lives, that it be rugged and radical in the good sense (without attempting to restore the manner of life of past ages), that it be thus exemplified to men and appear as a joyous carrying out of the duties of the spiritual life. We religious would have to be distinguished by a non-conformity with regard to the typical forms of modern consumption, with its artificial creation of needs, its dictatorship of consumption, its demonstrative consumption, which tends to stress social status and does not serve to satisfy a real need. (Perhaps a Provincial might think that he owes it to his position to drive a Cadillac!)

But in making these considerations, we religious must be convinced that we are still a long way from presenting a concrete example of such an asceticism of consumption as a (partial) form of our religious poverty. Abstract ideas and general principles may be very correct and very important. They substitute as little for a concrete example, which is born of a creative act, as pedagogical principles substitute for the personality of the educator. In this formation of the concrete exemplar of the modern person practicing the asceticism of consumption, we have not yet advanced very far. We are still at the stage, it would appear, of an uncreative compromise between the old manner of poverty and the modern manner of living: the invasion of an unbridled pursuit after consumption even in the religious Orders, and negative efforts on the part of the religious authorities to stem the tide.

In order to increase our courage to work for such a new and concrete form of poverty, the following consideration is offered for what it is worth. We are living in an age of masses: in an age of organizations and tremendous mass movements. The Church and the Orders will also appear in the eyes of modern man to be such and, because they have become very large numerically, will be subject to the sociological laws of such mass organizations. For our purposes this has a twofold significance. The Church and the Orders as a whole will make a very human, very profane, demythologized impression on the man of today. He will tend to put them in the same category as health insurance, unions, and civil institutions; they are unavoidable, heartless, and strictly egotistical associations; they have a very problematic morality; as far as his own life is concerned, they do not offer much power of conviction, because they make great efforts to regulate even the hidden recesses of his life. Hence they are to be viewed with care and suspicion.

The greater such mass organizations become, the more difficult will it be for them to bring to the fore anything new and creative, in the face of the untold complications of institutional existence, the impossibility of fixing responsibility, and the bureaucracy which is inevitable if a great mass is to be governed.

I suspect that all the somewhat older Orders pride themselves on the fact that in the centuries just past they did not need those reform movements and reorganizations which were so common in the Middle Ages and at the beginning of the modern era, particularly in connection with the observance of poverty. It may be asked whether this pride is really justified, or whether this fact, which is viewed with so much satisfaction, is not rather an indication of the dead weight of uncreative traditional elements in all larger societies in an age of mass organization which has brought it about that every attempt at a particular observance in religious life and in poverty had to attain its goal through the foundation of new Congregations.

If there is anything correct about the two observations, then the following would result as far as our question regarding poverty is concerned: In the formation of a form of poverty that produces conviction exteriorly, the individual and small groups are more important and have better prospects than the large Orders as such. This does not mean that individuals and small groups can exist and develop their form of poverty only outside the large Orders. But it does mean that the form of poverty in the large Orders becomes something calcified or softened by bad compromises with the new age, so that the ever creative power of a genuine evangelical concept of poverty necessarily begets new forms outside the traditional Orders, if the Orders do not supply the individual or the small group with the opportunity to work creatively for a new form of poverty without rushing to regulate everything by juridical norms.

Hence the question is this: Could not the Orders, without doing violence to the discipline of the common life, allow more freedom for such efforts at developing a modern form of poverty? If the persuasive force of religious poverty is to become *actual,* should not various forms of poverty perhaps be developed in the same Order? If it is remembered that Ignatius of Loyola even implanted such diversity by rule in his Order (even if not much has remained of it), then such a question cannot be dismissed out of hand. For example, does not the poverty in a rectory of religious, with its few members, have to take on another form and affect outsiders differently than the poverty of a large religious house of studies? Ought we not to have a clearer concept of the way in which a mission preacher, a students' chaplain, a foreign missionary, must exemplify religious poverty in their various ways? If we, for example, consider that the manner of life of modern Orders is pretty well the same in Europe as in Asia, but exercises no convincing impression on the inhabitants of India, even though by European standards life there is very "poor," then perhaps it becomes clear that these questions cannot be summarily dismissed with the assertion that every Order needs uniformity in the manner of life of all its members. It likewise becomes clear that such questions cannot be settled *a priori* by juridical norms. But individuals and small groups within the existing Orders ought to be encouraged to make such attempts.

If we now close, this must not leave the impression we are convinced that we have even alluded to all the essential problems affecting religious poverty today. More attention would have to be given (to mention at least one more point) that the division of labor in the modern economy also has its influence on religious poverty. Religious life necessarily falls under the sway of this economic system, which is based on a highly developed division of labor, extending itself also into the realm of strictly intellectual work.

Even as late as the eighteenth century an intelligent member of an apostolic Order pretty well understood the complete activity of the Order; today that is no longer true. In an active Order no one really understands all the "professions" exercised in such an Order. The preacher, the professor, the procurator, the youth chaplain, etc., etc., have become distinct professions in which each individual understands only his own field.

This has implications not only for the technique of direction and obedience in a religious community, but also for poverty. These professions not only differentiate the education, the manner of life, and the place of the individual in the totality of secular society, but also the kind, the quantity, and the value of the means of work which are the presupposition of the various professions in an Order. This diversity of means of work, which may include special trips for research, acquaintance in various circles of society, expensive instruments, specialized libraries, may again have its effect on the manner of life and of poverty of the individual. From this standpoint, too, it really cannot be denied that within the same Order various forms of life and activity evolve. They have their right to existence, if one regards life in religious communities soberly and with a somewhat sharpened sociological eye. Until now little attention has been paid to them. Attempts still are made to bridge the gaps with juridical norms. The entire question and its difficulties are not studied dispassionately. From this point of view many other matters relating to the question of religious poverty would also merit attention.

6

Love and Celibacy

BERNARD HARING, C.S.S.R.

A deeper undertsanding of marriage as a way to salvation has in our age developed with great emphasis the idea that married love is in God's plan a way to greater love of God and neighbor. Modern psychology, however, especially depth-psychology, has so stressed the importance of married love for maturing and integrating the human personality, that the impression is occasionally given that man is primarily a "sex-being."

This attitude implies that the way to develop man's ability to love is married life. As a result, those who either involuntarily or of their own choice remain unmarried are occasionally advised to seek the full integration of their personalities by friendship with a person of the opposite sex—a friendship not necessarily sexual, but carried along, nevertheless, by sexual desire. Such psychology is all part of an attitude which Pope Pius XII deplored in his encyclical, "Sacred Virginity."

It is important first of all to distinguish clearly the different forms of celibacy. Our Lord indicates them when He says: "Some are incapable of marriage from their birth, and some have been made so by men, and some have made themselves so for the sake of the kingdom of heaven. Let him accept it who can" (Matt. 19:12).

CELIBACY HAS MANY FORMS

First, there are single men and women who have found no love, who perhaps are basically incapable of seeking true married love. They are completely wrapped up in themselves, fearing to expose their impoverished Ego to the danger of genuine self-surrender. Such loveless persons can even be found in the married state. These latter really seek themselves, even when they appear to have established unity. The shell of marriage hides their lonely self-seeking. They cannot make each other happy, because they refuse to give themselves.

There is also the single person who with full consciousness avoids marriage, because he has decided not to bind himself to its irrevocable and sacrifice-filled love.

Again, there are people so entangled in ambition for material success that they never even consider marriage. If such a person enters marriage, he makes no effort towards the fulfillment of its unique purpose.

We cannot approve such loveless ways of life, yet our judgment of these individuals should be mild. Perhaps they are incapable of loving because they have never or rarely received true, selfless love. Perhaps they fit under the category of those "who men have made incapable of marriage."

CELIBACY FOR THE KINGDOM OF GOD

There are still other unmarried persons who with great hope and eagerness were ready for married love, but could not find a companion to suit them. For these the big question is whether they will preserve and develop all their ability to love despite their forced renunciation of marriage. They must realize that their situation is a call to love of a different kind. Perhaps what they need above all is the undertsanding of those around them, particularly of their loved ones. It is even more necessary that they discover that other people have need of goodness and kindness from them. But behind all this is still another question, which is, in fact, the ultimate question: Have they reached, or even begun to strive for, the warm realization that they are loved by God and that He desires and accepts all their love?

Just as married chastity receives its attractiveness from the fervor, the power, and the reverence love brings to it, so to a greater extent does celibate chastity, as deliberate "celibacy for the sake of the kingdom of heaven," grow out of the richness of the love of Christ. Such a celibate has understood that God is love. He is moved and completely taken up with the heavenly love which God has given us in Christ.

Such celibacy can be understood only as a special vocation. This celibacy has nothing to do with a cowardly flight from the sacrifices of marriage. It sees the great value of married love. Renunciation is praiseworthy only when the thing renounced is recognized as being lofty and a source of real happiness.

The special vocation to celibacy for the kingdom of heaven has diverse forms. There is the springtime fragrance of untouched virginity which, from the beginning, thinks only of God and lives faithfully and perfectly for Him. There is also the path of long struggle, disappointment, and the cross. Even an unanswered or disappointing earthly love can be the occasion of the joy-giving recognition that it is indeed good to belong wholly to the Lord.

LOVE FOR CHRIST

In pursuing this celibacy for the sake of the kingdom of heaven, one may renounce a married love desired with every fiber of one's soul. The essence is not the renunciation, but an ardent and overflowing love for Christ. The fire of this love is different from earthly love. It is a gift from above and cannot be understood by the earthly-minded man. Only the life-giving Spirit, the personal Love of Father and Son, the Gift of the Resurrected Christ, can awaken such love and make it triumph. If noble married love is a gift, then also in a much higher sense is celibacy. It is Christ Himself through the grace of the Holy Spirit who allows a person to surmise, to experience, and to see how full of love such undivided friendship is.

Such celibacy finds its most striking symbol in the very special love which married people have for one another. Husband and wife wish to belong to one another perfectly and exclusively. The person who is celibate for the kingdom of heaven realizes that the Lord wishes to have him completely for Himself without the distracting cares of earthly love (cf. 1 Cor. 7:32, 34).

The self-sacrificing and enthusiastic love of the celibate for the sake of the kingdom of heaven is the answer to the unique love of Christ, who nourishes him with His own Flesh and Blood, so that he is in some way "of His Flesh," just as the good husband nourishes and cherishes his wife as his own flesh and blood (Eph. 5:29ff.).

We have already said that voluntary renunciation of marriage is good only when it is joined with a true esteem of conjugal love. Nonetheless, the special love that consecrates celibacy does not depend upon experimental knowledge of conjugal love. Still an earthly love can be a great grace to help us to understand what a strong and warm love Our Lord expects from a celibate person, since even this earthly love grips our hearts so deeply. A spark of love which by its nature would lead to conjugal love can with the grace of God be a profound introduction to the mystery of celibacy. Therefore a heart that is capable of human love seems even more requisite for this vocation than for marriage.

MARRIED LOVE

Who can describe down to the last detail how completely the human power to love has its source and fountain in the example of conjugal love—in the conjugal love of our forefathers, in the love of parents who have given us life and who have cherished us by the strength of their conjugal love? If noble conjugal love were to fail, then the natural requirements for celibate love would also soon fail. Even though we are here speaking of celibate love which is a direct gift of Heaven, in the purest love of a celibate person for God there are energies which come from the sanctified realm of marriage.

But just as conjugal love is the background and inspiration for persons who consecrate themselves entirely to God, so celibate love in turn contributes something to Christian marriage. The ultimate testimony of the celibate is necessary if married people are to hold onto an invincible hope of perfecting their love in God. The illuminating testimony of undivided virginal dedication to God and His kingdom is a help for Christian married couples to overcome the distracting strength of their sexual love and make it their path to God. Through the sacrament, marriage is so enhanced as to become comparable to the virginal love between Christ and the Church.

Genuine conjugal love will naturally intensify parents' love for their children. A love-filled family life is the root from which springs all types of friendship and all forms of human love. Love in marriage and in the family proves its genuineness when it streams out to others. Likewise the touchstone for the celibate's power to love is his love for his neighbor. Whoever opens himself undividedly to love of Christ necessarily finds his heart expanded towards others.

It is also true that wherever tender and warm love rules among men, it is already on the way to the love of God; or rather it is a radiation from what is, perhaps, a still hidden love of God.

But this much applies to all men: (1 John 4:20) "He who does not love his brother whom he sees, how will he love God whom he does not see?" It is especially true of the greatest venture of love on earth, virginal love. This love flourishes only where rich love has been received—in healthy families with parents who are willing to sacrifice. Anyone who denies himself the vital experience of love in marriage for the sake of the all-powerful love of Christ must continually practice the love of his neighbor—a love that is like that between brother and sister, mother and father—if his undivided love for Christ is to remain full of the warmth of life.

Just as the face of a true mother beams forth purity, so the face of so many old and young nuns has many marvelous things to tell us about mature motherhood. A joyful life of celibacy for the sake of the kingdom of heaven is a mightly testimony from God that man is essentially something more than a mere sexual being. In fact, it demonstrates that he is not primarily a sexual being at all. In a way that far surpasses the merely sexual, he is a person; and he develops this personality by being ordered to the person of God and the person of his neighbor whom he serves for God's sake.

7

The Church's Holiness and Religious Life*

GUSTAVE MARTELET, S.J.

INTRODUCTION

Religious life, which plays an important role in the life of the Church, has not been absent from the considerations of Vatican Council II. A place was reserved for it in the *schemas* that were proposed from the time of the first session. When the Council's plan of work was revised from the viewpoint of ecclesiology, a fortunate result followed for religious life (as well as for other matters). Instead of isolating religious life as a kind of "specialty" and in order not to favor the idea that religious hold a sort of "monopoly"[1] on holiness, the Council spoke about religious life at the same time as it spoke of the holiness of the entire People of God. This measure of the Council (one favored by Cardinal Döpfner[2]) was in itself an excellent one. Such an approach no more compromises religious life than one would "dishonor" the Blessed Virgin by failing to devote an "isolated" schema to her. Can one speak of the part except in reference to the whole? Pseudo-Denis treated religious life within the ecclesial framework of the eccelesiastical hierarchy. St. Thomas, followed by all the classical theologians, considered the subject in connection with the virtue of religion. Yet no one has accused St. Thomas of minimizing its value, nor Pseudo-Denis of placing it within a pejorative context. However important religious life may be in itself, it should be studied within the context of the whole. What more appropriate framework could there be than that of the Church and her vocation to holiness?

* This is a translation of a book entitled in the original French edition, *Sainteté de l'Eglise et vie religieuse* (Toulouse: Editions Prière et Vie, 1964). The translation, made by Raymond L. Sullivant, S.J.; 4, Montée de Fourvière; Lyon (V), France, will be published in the REVIEW in installments and, when completed, will be issued by the REVIEW in a clothbound edition.

Why, then, did conciliar discussion on this point betray an uneasiness which the chroniclers of the second session made no effort to dissimulate?[3] One of them even spoke of "subterranean emotional elements" which "conditioned the debate after the manner of the pulsations of the subconscious, the more influential for having failed to express itself explicitly."[4] The remark is rich in imagery! In fact, three questions dominated the debates, whether public or private. The first concerned the meaning of religious life within the Church: theologically, it is the most important. The second problem touched on the place to be given to religious when one analyzes and numbers the states of life that exist within the Church. The thorny problem of exemption constituted the third consideration. Let us consider each of these topics in its turn.

MEANING OF RELIGIOUS LIFE WITHIN THE CHURCH

Since it wished to free the Church from "suffocating juridicism" (to use the expression of Maximos IV), the Council felt impelled to insist anew on the importance of the People of God's vocation to holiness. This vocation is based on the baptismal initiation which introduces every Christian into the very life of Christ and demands of the members of the Body a life that is in conformity with that of the Head. However elementary the concept may appear, it is extremely important to recall this truth. All of this deserves praise on the condition, which is not always necessarily forthcoming, that the rediscovery of Christians' vocation to holiness obscures neither the specificity of the religious life nor its organic connection with the life of the entire Church.

Although the problem was discussed more than once at the Council,[5] the real question is not that of determining whether the bishop or the religious is in the more perfect state. It is rather a matter of clarifying the meaning of religious life in its relation to the vocation to holiness of all Christians. Fortunately, it has become impossible to enhance the former to the spiritual detriment of the latter. In the Church, "laymen" does not mean "profane" in the mundane sense of the term. The word simply refers to a baptized person who is not a cleric. The title of every baptized person is first of all "Christian."[6] Any devaluation of Christian life to the "profit" of the religious life is completely intolerable. Such an action would be an insult to baptism and would represent a failure to recognize that all the members of the Church are called to the holiness envisioned by the gospel. On the other hand, calling attention to the value of baptism should not entail or cause a depreciation of religious life. The unfortunate anomaly of former times which naïvely contradistinguished religious life from Christian life in general must not generate the contrary anomaly: a Christian life radically separated from religious life. In order to avoid such a misunderstanding, it is necessary to meditate ceaselessly on the Gospel doctrine of precepts and counsels;[7] we must also, and perhaps above all, define the genuine place of religious life within the whole of the mystery of the Church.

It is a fact that this question, a central one in the thought of St. Thomas and Suarez, has been too often neglected by professional theologians since the sixteenth century. For all practical purposes, it is absent from the work of Moehler and from that of Scheeben; and it is equally inconspicuous in academic treatises such as Franzelin's *De Ecclesia*. While in our day Journet makes a solid if brief allusion to the subject,[8] one can analyze the new tendencies in ecclesiology without finding a reference to it.[9] The problem appears to remain within the domain of the "spiritually minded" or that of canon lawyers. We should not then be astonished if the manner in which the Council approached such a vast question lacked theological breadth nor if nothing genuinely conclusive was produced by the debates.

Consequently, an effort must be exerted to determine, within the perspective of the councilar *aggiornamento,* the ecclesial value of religious life. In so doing, we must ge to the heart of the matter by starting from the mystery of the Church. A certain misunderstanding of religious life, current in our day, will not cease to exist until theologians dissipate a kind of doctrinal and spiritual inconsistency surrounding religious life itself.

ANALYSIS OF THE STATES OF LIFE

The second question raised by the Council is, even if of less apparent gravity, nevertheless essential. Can the structure of the Church be reduced to the simple distinction of priest and layman? Should we, on the contrary, speak of a tripartite division: cleric, layman, and religious?[10] Those who consider the matter only from the viewpoint of hierarchy are completely opposed to the latter division.[11] The point of view of such persons is certainly a necessary one, but is it a fully complete one? Hence, it seems necessary to restudy the question in depth and not to propose a solution except in the perspective of a problematic that has been thought through in a new way. This we shall attempt to do in the following pages.

EXEMPTION

A more serious question, although one which stood out less clearly in conciliar debate, is that of exemption. This immense historical problem has never been adequately examined, nor does it always possess a spiritual grandeur commensurate with its size. It too is a problem which can be solved only by examining all sides of the matter, since it arises from factors which while essential are too often forgotten. To clip the most obvious misunderstandings in the bud, it will be useful to recall certain historical facts.[12]

The origins of exemptions spring from the very nature of monastic life. The latter, which assembles a community (laymen for the most part in the beginning) around a spiritual master, possesses an *internal* discipline confided to the abbot,[13] while the authority of the bishop concerns the relations of this community with the *exterior*. At least, such a vocabulary is employed to describe and partially resolve the jurisdictional conflicts as they appeared at Chalcedon (for the East) in 451 and at Arles (for the West) in 455. However, the first exemption which historians recognize as such was that accorded by Pope Honorius in 628 to the Monastery of Bobbio in northern Italy: it removed that monastery from the jurisdiction of the local bishop. Though other cases are cited in the seventh century, it is necessary to await the foundation and expansion of Cluny in the tenth century to see this first type of exemption become generalized.

At the time of Cluny exemption was a way of confronting a variety of complex situations. Many bishops were mired in a subjection, at times simoniacal, to the temporal power; they themselves no longer enjoyed, nor did they permit others to do so, the spiritual liberty that was required by their charge and was so necessary to the Church. Cluny inaugurated a vast movement of reform, by the basis of which was monastical and therefore territorial. Having been declared an integral part of the patrimony of St. Peter, the Abbey along with its innumerable dependencies escaped the local authority of bishops and possible confiscation by them. The Abbey thus fell under the pope's jurisdiction and served Rome's centralizing aspirations which were to end with the Gregorian reform of the eleventh century.[14] Being monastical, Cluny's exemption was a complex of components: feudal immunity, spiritual liberty, and Roman centralization. The monastery supplied an answer, by way of opposition, to the unusual state of a "Church" which had fallen "into the power of laymen."[15]

Of a completely different nature was the exemption enjoyed by those orders which made their appearance with St. Dominic and St. Francis in the thirteenth century. Exemptions, that is, withdrawal from obedience to the local bishop in matters concerning the order's affairs, was no longer directed to monasteries, but to communities which were mobile and directly apostolic. Exemption was no longer territorial but personal. The arrangement is a response to the still current situation in which religious orders are scattered throughout several dioceses while depending on a single superior. These groups cannot retain their internal unity unless they are free of the power of local ecclesiastical authorities. This *partial* withdrawal from local obedience implies, as Popes Pius XII[16] and Paul VI[17] recalled, the *direct* attachment of the religious orders to papal jurisdiction. This is particularly true of the Jesuits who are bound to the Holy Father by a special vow of obedience with regard to any mission which he may choose to assign them. Insofar as the hierarchy is concerned, then, exemption does not entail an abolition but rather a transfer of obedience.

Despite the cursory nature of this historical survey, it provides evidence which indicates that the problem of exemption, bound to the Church's very life, should be studied within the context both of her mystery and of her history. Consequently, correct procedure forbids justifying or practicing exemption in the twentieth century as it existed at Cluny. Nor can we pretend that its existence resulted from historical factors alone and that consequently its existence today can no longer be justified. Exemption is bound to the very existence of religious life, although it cannot be simply and absolutely identified with it, since communities of diocesan right do exist which are true to religious even though non-exempt. It is thus imperative to establish the true meaning of exemption, its rights and its limits, and the way it is to be used. A profound understanding of the episcopacy implies the renewal of exemption—not its death—on the condition, however, that religious life regain an awareness of its sources and its meaning.

Our task is an enormous one! Hence it will be necessary to proceed step by step. Since religious life is essentially connected with the holiness of the Church, this holiness must first of all be defined. The Church's holiness being that of a Spouse, we must recall the meaning of the Church's spousehood. Only then will the correlative values in the Church of marriage and virginity be seen. Given virginity's affinity to the religious life, the eschatological import of virginity must be examined. Religious life, which includes virginity while going beyond it, thus appears at the very heart of the mystery of the Church. This mystery is that of the Spirit revealing the depths of Christ. Such is the true source of religious life within the Church and the principle of its true relation to the hierarchical function. Having clarified these points, we shall then determine the place of religious life with regard to the whole of Christ's Body and shall conclude by considering the relationship of religious life with the world. Hence the following four points will constitute the sections of this study:

I. The Church and Holiness
II. The Church's Holiness and Her Spousehood
III. Marriage and Virginity
IV. Virginity and Eschatology

I. THE CHURCH AND HOLINESS

During the Council's discussion allusions were made to the relationship between the holiness of the Church and the existence of religious life.[18] While the relationship is an obvious one, it warrants careful analysis. The first *schema* tied religious life to the Church's *note* of holiness. Being traditional, the doctrine is acceptable on the condition, however, that a narrowly apologetical perspective, admitting as holy only that which is authorized by the miraculous,[19] is not reintroduced in support of this way of speaking. Holiness, no less than oneness, apostolicity, and catholicity, is a *property* of the Church, a trait of her spiritual nature.[20] Religious life being entirely devoted in the Spirit to imitating Christ belongs to the essence of the Church which can and should bring forth men in holiness unto Life.[21] However banal this affirmation may appear, it is nonetheless profound, containing a double aspect of which the second is not always sufficiently stressed. While holiness is a *gift* of Christ to his Church, it is at one end and the same time the Church's *response* to Christ. In both cases this holiness is sacramental in structure.

THE CHURCH'S HOLINESS AS A GIFT OF CHRIST

The end of St. Matthew's Gospel reveals an almost didactic expression of this holiness as it shows the resurrected Christ saying:

> All authority in heaven and on earth has been given to me. Go therefore and make disciples of all nations, baptizing them in the name of the Father and of the Son and of the Holy Spirit, teaching them to observe all that I have commanded you; and lo, I am with you always, to the end of time.

The Lord thus assures us of his indefectible presence—"I am with you always, to the end of time"—and he confers on the Church the triple responsibility of *preaching*—"make disciples of all nations"—of *sanctifying sacramentally*—"baptize them in the name of the Father and of the Son and of the Holy Spirit"—and of *governing—"teaching them to observe* all that I have commanded you." Rather than belabor the question, freely disputed among theologians, of whether Christ thus conferred a double or a triple power,[22] the important thing is to grasp that Christ's indefectible presence in His Church assures her of on inalienable holiness.

Recent crises have revealed that the old Donatist difficulty, so vigorously combated by St. Augustine, which identifies the holiness of the Church with that of her ministers and not first of all with that of Christ, has never been completely laid to rest. There is a constantly reappearing temptation to assess the Church's value by the *manner* in which men of the Church accomplish their mission rather than first of all by the *fact* that this mission, validly exercised, is never abandoned by the Lord. The spiritual fidelity of clerics is infinitely desirable; it is required on ordination day: "Imitate what you do," says the bishop to the ordinands. However necessary and desirable the personal holiness of the members of the hierarchy may be, it remains relative when compared to the objective holiness of the indefectible structures of that sanctification which itself transcends all human fidelity. This structural, objective holiness is not *magic,* as our Protestant brothers sometimes believe. It is rather a matter of *covenant* and should be made to be "credible," to use the expression employed by Hans Küng when speaking of the ecumenicity of the councils.[23] Yet to make this quality credible is not to endow it with existence. The consummate holiness of such men as Irenaeus, Basil, Francis de Sales, or Borromeo is not identical with the objective holiness of the Church's structure. While the former reposes on and manifests the latter, it cannot replace it. There is something existing within the Church, perhaps the most perplexing facet of her holiness, which neither the misery of sinners nor the virtue of saints can damage nor increase. Just as the infidelity of a baptized person cannot destroy Christ's claim on him but can only betray it, so the objective holiness which results from Christ's assistance to His Church is completely different from the spiritual mediocrity or perfect holiness of His ministers. The gospel cannot be truly adulterated by hierarchical teaching; the sacraments cannot be corrupted by the Church's administration. And as for the legitimate exercise of pastoral authority, it cannot lead the faithful away from Christ!

Hence, to believe in the Church's holiness in this first sense is not to assume that the men of the Church are invariably holy but to accept the fact that the Church's holiness is indefectibly communicated by way of her ministers even when they are sinners. In the last analysis (and there only), the most radical holiness of the Church is not to be discovered by investigating whether the Church is faithful to Christ but by believing that Christ is faithful to the Church. If all visible holiness were to become absent from the Church (and this is a pure hypothesis), she would still retain a holiness that is credible, deserving of belief. Relying on the word of Christ alone, in the darkness of faith we would be able to discover in her holiness that no human power can destroy because no human power is the basis for it.

The holiness of institution, resulting from Christ's irrevocable gift of Himself to His Church, is, understandably, the holiness most often studied by theologians.[24] Without this holiness, there would no longer be a divinely assisted structure within the Church but only a community essentially fallible which could one day find itself completely opposed to God. One would then need to circumvent the community to return to Christ. Nevertheless, in spite of the importance of this first type of holiness, it is not the only one within the Church.

THE HOLINESS OF THE CHURCH AS THE CHURCH'S RESPONSE TO CHRIST

Subsisting as a means of salvation through the spiritual power of Christ who endows her with the power to teach, sanctify, and rule, the

Church is thus constituted *by* Christ only in order that she may live completely *for* him. A holiness of return and response thus corresponds to the initiating holiness which is the only orginating source of the Church. To what Christ does institutionally for His Church independently of her will, there does and should correspond what the Church freely does and should do for Him. Instituted as a service assisted by Christ, she does nothing in this capacity *for* Him which she does not do *by* Him. Yet what she accomplishes in accepting to serve Christ's holiness institutionally is not identical with the act whereby her members—clergy and laity—freely partake of the benefit of this institutionally communicated holiness. The fact that the Church receives Christ who *constitutes* her as the indefectible organism of holiness is one thing; but the fact that the Church herself responds to this holiness by which, as it were, she has been involuntarily anticipated, is another thing. And it is only by this response that the Church herself becomes holy with the kind of holiness we are now considering.

In fact, would Christ's gift be a genuine gift if it bore no response by way or reciprocity? What point would there be in infallibly guaranteeing the gospel, the sacraments, the pastoral conduct of God's people, if nothing resulted therefrom on the part of the Church? If no one ever lived the Christ-life, would we know that He had given Himself? A gift attains its end only by arousing the loving response for which it was given. The more we insist as Catholics on the objective holiness of the hierarchical and sacramental structure of the Church, the greater is our obligation to show that this holiness of means, indefectibly guaranteed, produces a holiness of result which is indefectibly obtained. These indefectibilities attract each other, or, to speak more accurately, the holiness of the gift mercifully shapes that of the response.

It is this holiness of result which the Council envisages when speaking of the vocation of God's people to holiness. It is not then speaking of the means but of the goal, and it does not separate Christ's initiative from the response which it should arouse in us. But, as we have seen, the Church's holiness cannot be reduced only to her response to Christ. The Church's most basic holiness is that to which in a sense she contributes nothing. But, having said this, we must add at once: to the holiness in which the Church does nothing but receive is added a holiness by which she, without ceasing to receive everything, responds and gives. In the Church holiness of love given makes response to the holiness of love received; holiness of freedom prolongs holiness of structure! Neither of these aspects can be sacrificed to the other, since the one is for the other and the latter cannot exist without the former. The Church is never objective indefectibility of institution without at the same time being—in greater or less measure according to times and persons—a free and spiritual interiority of conversion. The first form of sanctity does no violence to the second of which it is the condition and the stem; and the second cannot free itself from the first of which it is the flower and the fruit. Both, though of different form, make a unity and truly come from the Spirit. In the one case, the Spirit acts to assure the objective conditions of the sanctifying encounter with Christ; and in the other, the same Spirit acts to obtain from free will the spiritual result which is the institution's reason for being. In other words, the Church's holiness is sacramental.

SACRAMENTAL STRUCTURE OF THE CHURCH'S HOLINESS

The title of this subsection suggests that the sacraments are the means of explicit initiation to the love which God bears for the world in Jesus Christ. But also and especially it indicates that the entire Church—hierarchy and faithful—cannot exhaust the love from which they benefit but rather that they *signify* this love by living in dependence on it.

By the very fact that she exists by and for Christ, the Church also exists for the world which our Lord acquired for Himself and from which He is inseparable. The Church cannot, consequently, appear in the form of a community content to live for its own pleasure. The conscious beneficiary of Christ's life and presence in the world and thereby of the Father's communication in the Spirit of the Son, it is essential for the Church to be a community of dispossession, of emergence from self. True, in Christ she has been loaded with gifts by God as Christ Himself received in abundance from the Father. But the plenitude which she thus receives from God through her Lord is a plenitude that strips and dispossesses her by consecrating her in the Spirit to the Christian bringing forth of the world. As soon as she is explicitly given to mankind and begins her conscious life at Penetcost, she is caught up in an absolutely essential relationship to all men; and she is immediately impelled by the Spirit toward the first fruits of her totality—which, however, she never visibly attains in this world. In her existence among men she is the form and the presence of the mystery of salvation, but she is never its limit. The visible Church is but a sign, a promise of her own totality.

The promise is not misleading; the sign is an authentic one. But since the love by which the Church lives is that which God in Christ directs, gives, and bears to all men, only the universal regrouping of men in a faith in Christ alone constitutes the fullness of her reality. As long as this fullness is not accomplished, the Church hopefully awaits her true self; and the Christian community of which she is now constituted can never be more than a sign of what she is yet to become. Her own mystery thus being only partially visible, the Church knows herself fully only by taking into account her basic unfulfillment.

The Church's holiness is, therefore, never closed upon herself as a purely sociological reality would be. Certainly, the Church is a definite institution in which Christ visibly assumes a body; but she is equally a movement out of herself toward the invisibility of hearts. More profound and no less essential than what is already seen in her is the mysterious face of her hidden identity, made up of all of those who without knowing it give to God something of that love which He Himself gives to them in Jesus Christ. Even if she were as holy a community as her institution demands and enables her to achieve, the Church would still retain a hidden sanctity derived from the totality of the world which unknowingly benefits from the Lord's love.

Are we then to conclude that there is no point in striving for the world's conversion to Christ? On the contrary! From the mountain of the Ascension the Lord gives His Church no knowledge of the invisible aspect of His Body. He rather reveals the visible task which He commits to her and which He expects from her. Hence, irrespective of the extent to which the Church may have extended herself invisibly in the hearts of men, she must regroup them in a visible sign—described by Paul VI as "the unmarked confines of Christ's sheepfold."[25] And this she must do from Jerusalem to the ends of the world and until the end of time. It is only in this apostolic work of preaching and of initiating men into the life of Christ that the Church's holiness is genuine; it is only then that it does not evaporate into a vain gnosis of an already finished salvation of the world—as if, in view of this knowledge, nothing would remain to be done in order that the reality which it contains might be transmitted to men. On the contrary, even as the charity of God in Christ fills every corner of the earth, so the Church has the duty to attempt to touch all hearts that they may know the charity with which they, in spite of everything, are indefectibly loved. Yet the holiness of the Church, which impels her to introduce the world sacramentally into the charity of God in Christ, can never be reduced to the visible results obtained by her efforts. She contains not only the spiritual truth of her own children but also that of all those men who are bound in Christ to the Church by their hidden love of God. Because the Church's holiness at this point surpasses her own visibility in the world, her nature can be called sacramental. Hence it does not suffice to say that the Church *has* sacraments; we must understand that she *is* a sacrament.[26] She is the *finite* sign of an infinite love: that of Christ and of a love returned which should be limitless since it is that of all humanity. By forgetting this truth one renders the Church's sanctity that of a sect—while in reality it is that of the unique and true Bride.

II. THE CHURCH'S HOLINESS AND HER SPOUSEHOOD[27]

St. Paul, in the Epistle to the Ephesians, and the fathers of the Church, following his example, have taught us to refer to the Church as the Spouse of Christ. St. Augustine writes: "There is come into existence the whole Christ, Head and Body, one person out of many. . . . Whether the Head speaks or whether the members speak, it is Christ who speaks: He speaks in the person of the Head, He speaks in the person of the Body. But what is it that has been said? 'They shall be two in one flesh.' 'This is a great sacrament.' 'I say this,' he says, 'in Christ and in the Church' (Gen. 2:24; Eph. 5:31–2). And He Himself says in the Gospel: 'Therefore they are no longer two but one flesh' (Mat. 19:16). For in order that you may know that these are in a way two persons and yet again one person in the marriage bond, He speaks as one person in Isaiah when he says: 'He has bound a mitre upon me as upon a bridegroom, and he has adorned me as a bride' (Isa. 61:10). A bridegroom He has called Himself in the Head, a Bride in the Body."[28] Since the Body is the Church, Christ and His Body are Christ and His Church, the Groom and the Bride, in the union from which is reflected all the holiness of the Church.

OBJECTIVE HOLINESS OF INSTITUTION AND THE MYSTERY OF THE BRIDE

The fact that the Church is holy with an indefectible holiness of institution is inseparable from the fact that Christ loves the Church as a groom his bride; He would not, then, deprive her of the unfailing signs which denote this love. But this love alliance is not merely a human one; it is based on the transcendence of the Groom, Christ Himself. It is in the capacity of the Lord "to whom all power is given in heaven and on earth" (Mat. 28:18) that Christ is Groom. The title, then, is not symbolic or merely human. He is Groom because God, having used His divine power in resurrecting Him from the dead, "*has put all things under his power* and has made him the head over everything for the Church which is his body, the fullness of him who fills the entire universe" (Eph. 1:22–3). It is indeed the Lord of glory who is the Church's Groom. He associates Himself to her by reason of a sovereign love which creates her, not through any affection that would precede Him and on which He would depend. The Bride's beauty is a gift of the Groom. "He gave himself up for her," says St. Paul, "to sanctify her, having cleansed her by the washing of water together with the word so that he might present the Church to himself in splendor, without spot or wrinkle or any such thing and that she might be holy and without blemish" (Eph. 5:25–7). We have already called attention to the last verses of St. Matthew's Gospel which speak of the same love in other terms. There, Christ confides to His Church (condensed to the Eleven), His own Person and His work. He gives Himself to her in the mission which He gives her of announcing His truth to all men, of sanctifying them in His life, and of keeping them in His way. He makes her His indefectible collaborator, His conjural alter ego. The Church will exist until the end of time only because she leans invisibly upon Christ who is always "with her" (Mat. 28:19) as the Groom is always with the Bride. Her ministers, by whom the Church is glorified and who represent her holy institution, are nothing else but the permanent gifts of Christ to His Church and the signs in which the indefectible love of the Lord for His Spouse is clearly visible.

Such gifts are not limited to the Church in the strict sense. To be sure, the world is *for* the Church if one considers the Church as the total Christ. But the Church is no less truly *for* the world if one sees in her the associate of Christ for the world's salvation. Christ gives Himself indefectibly to His Church in order to be able to sanctify men. To do this, He must first overcome in the Church the world and its sin. The fathers of the Church (most notably St. Ambrose[29]) spoke of the Church of this world as the *immaculata ex maculatis*. Our Lord does not prevent the Church from being vulnerable, fragile, and sinful in her members; but sin must not destroy the ministry which He confides to her nor the means supplied that she might exercise it. It is a disposition of love that protects the ministry from the evil of sin without drawing her members from their sinful condition.

The Church in her turn possesses in Christ something that is not of this world and that hence cannot be destroyed or protected by it. Christ's love, which protects His Bride from adultery, is one of the forms that His Lordship over evil takes. The spousal love of the resurrected One for His Church thus becomes the very axis of the world's history of salvation. By His vigilant and indefectible watch over the Church, our Lord wrenches the world from evil. It is by assuring the conditions of constant communion with Him through the Church that He guarantees the world the perennial presence of His grace. At the end of time, Christ's love for the Church and through her for humanity will have traversed the entire span of ages without having been weakened or diminished. From Him alone there will have indefectibly resulted the objective holiness of the Church and hence the sign of the salvation that is always possible for the world.

HOLINESS OF RESPONSE AND THE MYSTERY OF THE BRIDE

The substantial holiness of institution resulting from the Groom's love for the Bride demands a substantial holiness of liberty which is the Bride's response to the Groom. Christ's love could not truly be victorious over the inertias of history and the deadly contradictions of sin, if, when giving such a gift of love to the Church and through her to all humanity, He did not obtain a gift of response in return. Christ is truly the sovereign Groom of the Church only if He is loved in return by her. Not that Christ is ever "received" in the world as He merits. He will never be loved as He deserves, He who should be the supreme love which inspires and structures all others. Christ, like the Apostle, and even more than the latter, is capable of ever giving more even though He be loved less in return (see II Cor. 12:15). But in order to spare humanity the dishonor of being loved to such a degree while returning nothing, He wishes to obtain a minimum of response from men, for without it He would be an unknown and betrayed Love in their eyes. And since it is through the Church that the unfailing love of Christ comes to the world's attention, it must be through her that a little love is returned in exchange for so much love that is given. The mystery of the Church is thus accomplished—by returning to Christ some of what she has received from Him.

This response of love will not consist merely in the objective and ministerial fidelity represented by the divinely assisted, hierarchical function. Since in this function there is manifested the indestructible love of the Bridegroom for the Bride, it is undoubtedly true that the more this function is carried out in a spirit of making a return, the more will Christ be glorified. But the Bride's response to the Groom, without excluding the spiritual fidelity of the members of the hierarchy, nevertheless surpasses it to a considerable degree. As a matter of fact, in the Christian community it is often the unknown faithful who represent and constitute, in every age, this sanctity of response by which the Groom is so deeply loved by the Bride. It is there, in the hidden members of Christ's Body that we must often look for the Church's complete self-giving to her Christ and find the hidden choir where the Bride tirelessly fashions her love song to the Groom[30] and bestows on that part of humanity that loves God silently and without knowing it the explicit language in which the world's unconscious Christian expresses and saves himself. This century-old chant is that of virgins, of martyrs and doctors, of confessors of every kind, of widows and orphans. It rises from cloisters or from the court of kings, from the altar or from the rear of the church, from the swamps of

Nettuno or the roads of Umbria, from a slave's room in Herculaneum or from the noisy shops of a factory! Even as it existed during the somber hours of the Western Schism, it will still survive even if the West decomposes into a universe without the gospel. Having lived in a world which knew no technology beyond the windmill and the sextant, the Church's loving response will continue to exist in future millenia when weightless men will have made a stepping stone of the moon but for all that will not have found another Christ. She will be present until the end of time, never absent, never tired—in the midst of men become the leisured masters of robots while remaining slaves to idols.

But our aim is not to analyze the Church's age-old love in itself, thereby suggesting the sanctity hidden in the world. We have only recalled it in order to situate the religious life more accurately. The latter is not a kind of disconnected absolute. Like all holiness, it is profoundly related to the spousehood of the Church; accordingly it must first be understood in terms of marriage and virginity which are the two faces of a single mystery.

III. MARRIAGE AND VIRGINITY

THE SACRAMENT OF MARRIAGE AND THE CHURCH'S SPOUSEHOOD

SACRAMENTAL VALUE OF MARRIAGE "*For this reason a man shall leave his father and mother and be joined to his wife, and the two shall become one flesh.* This is a great mystery, and I mean in reference to Christ and the church" (Eph. 5:31–2). In this text the sacramentality of marriage finds its most profound expression.

The union of man and woman, restored by Jesus Christ to the original purity of an indissoluble unity (Mat. 19:6), is the sign of the union between Christ and the Church. Hence, marriage, a thoroughly human institution of love, no longer has its ultimate meaning in itself. By uniting Himself to humanity in the flesh, God accomplished a union between man and Himself so profound that in the face of its reality the conjugal union becomes no more than a figure. God wedding Himself to flesh—this is Christ; and the flesh wedded by Christ—this is the Church. God thus unites Himself to humanity through Christ that mankind, having given its flesh to Christ, might receive from Him the divinity which pours out upon man by means of His body. Compared to this communication from the depths of God to the depths of man, the exchanges of conjugal love are no more than figures. Indeed, Scripture tells us that the love of man and wife is an image of the love of Christ and the Church. To the holiness of His own love Christ relates the human love of those whom baptism has incorporated into Him and makes the marriage of the baptized the sacrament of His own union with the Church.[31]

Yet St. Paul does not develop the sacramental relationship of marriage to the mystery of Christ and the Church until after having first recalled that "we are members of his Body" (Eph. 5:30). The Christian couple does not therefore sacramentally represent the bridal mystery of the Church except insofar as they have been introduced into Christ's very *being* by baptism. They symbolize the mystery of which they are themselves a part, and their marriage introduces them sacramentally into a living communion with Christ which passes by way of the forms of their conjugal life and of their reality as man and wife. The indissolute unity in the flesh, the eminent virtues which their common life supposes, the gift of life and their care to foster it, the peaceful acceptance of the harsh realities of existence, all of these circumstances delimit the daily domain which Christ's love assumes and transfigures and which it never dispenses with. Yet the condition which gives the human and Christian power of the image reduces its exactness as well.

SPIRITUAL LIMIT OF MARRIAGE The indissolubility of the bond guarantees an essential aspect of the relationship of the image to the reality. But the purity of this feature cannot be secured and held except at the cost of a life in Christ which at times the flesh paralyzes. Even when it is perfectly realized in its own order, conjugal fidelity implies a love of Christ by means of an intermediate person. The conjugal language of love, to be sure, is in no sense evil. In the eyes of the Church it is even a necessary condition for the definitive indissolubility of sacramental marriage.[32] Was it not through the flesh that God came to meet mankind and that Christ henceforth loves the Church? The Church, accordingly, rises above all Manichaeism which, indeed, she has formally condemned.[33] But however good conjugal love may be in relationship to those who declare it evil, it is not necessarily the most elevated state when related to the absolute of Christ. A man cannot please his wife, a wife cannot please her husband, and both the one and the other cannot face the problems of their home and its multiple demands except by becoming deeply involved in the affairs of the world, the husband for the sake of his strength, the wife for that of her beauty, and both for the defense and development of the life they have brought into the world. In order not to be drawn under by this current, to participate in the world without becoming its slave, to serve without attempting to rule, to speak the language of love by means of the senses without becoming engulfed by them, to love the Lord without seeking self through His image, to be in the flesh the reflection of Christ and His Church whose bond is the Spirit, one must, as St. Paul said, "having a wife, live as though one had none" and "deal with the world as if one had no dealings with it" (see I Cor. 7:29). Even if one observes this admonition, he must continue to watch over his humility. "It is to the extent," it has been written with a courage unusual in our day when treating the subject, "it is to the extent . . . that a Christian marriage is the most visibly successful that it is confronted by a temptation to install itself in this world—an idolatry of the creature, of self-satisfaction with one's present state which has not been regenerated in depth by death and resurrection with Christ."[34]

Are we saying that the sacrament is only a decoy? Certainly not! But the human love which the sacrament sanctifies is the *image* of the reality and not the *reality* itself. It is to be admitted without scandal or resentment that marriage, even though a sacrament, is no more than a sacrament; it designates the love of Christ and the Church and is nourished by His grace; but marriage does this under carnal conditions which Christ will abolish in His final reality and which He sanctifies only to teach us how to surpass them. Even though it represents the undivided love of Christ and the Church by its quality of indissolubility and even though it sanctifies the spouses, conjugal love involves, in fact, a domination by the desire which closes in upon themselves those whom, from another point of view, it causes to go out from themselves. If it is true, then, that there is dispossession even in possession itself, this dispossession is never free from this desire;

and conjugal love is not yet that charity which sustains the Church. This is what medieval thinkers meant when they said that marriage "signified" the union of Christ and the Church but did not "contain it."[35] In other words, the latter union *escapes* conjugal union and, without being foreign to it, is nevertheless not fully identical with it.

Yet it is possible to conceive of a love which, by foregoing the human language of desire, thereby also avoids its divisions. But not implying the conjugal love of the other union, it would not be a symbol of the union of Christ and the Church and consequently it would not be sacramental. But by having renounced the human image of the Church's status as spouse, it would aim at the reality this image represents and would concern itself with loving Christ for Himself and in Himself without going by way of the detour required by an intermediary. Not that Christ can ever dispense Himself from loving Himself in others. But consecration of self to the Lord and to others while foregoing the demands of the flesh is one thing; acknowledging Him (real enough though it is) in a love determined by desire is another. That is why virginity will always surpass marriage in the Church.

VIRGINITY AND THE CHURCH'S SPOUSEHOOD

"Virginity has accomplished what marriage only signifies," says the Preface of the consecration of virgins.[36] Far from condemning marriage, Christian virginity appreciates its sacramental depth and desires to fulfill, in a fashion exclusively spiritual, the meaning signified by the sacrament. Characterized by a holy impatience with the weakness of figures, virginity unreservedly vows a love of Christ alone; and while sacrificing the image of conjugal love without disdaining it, it gives itself to the reality without passing by way of the symbol. Thus virginity really enters into the spousal mystery of the Church even though it does not signify that mystery in a sacramental way.

St. Augustine was the first to say: "Even those who consecrate their virginity to God, while possessing a more elevated degree of honor and holiness within the Church, are not deprived of nuptials. Their nuptials are those of the entire Church in which the Groom is Christ Himself."[37] Since it is love alone which makes a spouse of the Church, the Christian virgin, who loves Christ with the love of the Church, becomes a bride after her image. And even as the sacramental character of Christian marriage is not a reality of the moral or psychological order, neither is that of virginity. Virginity is inseparable from the baptismal *incorporation* which is brought to full flower in the former; virginity, then, possesses all the spiritual and human realism of which Christ is the source and end. Just as the Christian couple lives by reason of the union of Christ and his Church in the daily reality of the conjugal life, so the Christian virgin lives in terms of Christ's preferential love in a most complete way, thereby representing the Church's mystery in a special way. She does not live it *hierarchically* as do the bishop and the priest associated with him, nor *sacramentally* as the baptized bound by the conjugal tie; she lives it spiritually by vowing an *exclusive* love of response to Christ, thereby expressing before the entire world the most profound secret of the Church.

"Given the fact," writes St. Augustine, "that the universal Church is a virgin united to a single spouse, Christ Himself, as the Apostle says (II Cor. 11:2), of what great honor are not those members worthy who observe in their very flesh what the entire Church observes in faith?"[38] True, all love of response in the Church is a part of the reality of her love as Bride. Clerics as well as married Christians, being devoted to Christ, are the Church answering her Lord in love. But the characteristic quality of Christian virginity is that without any hierarchical function and in the absence of conjugal love it represents the Church's undivided love for Christ. Virginity manifests the bridal being of the Church for whom Christ suffices and who views all things only in Him. And in this way virginity enters the domain of the virgin par excellence, the Virgin Mary.

St. Augustine in an extremely dense text evokes in a single declaration the relationship between Mary and the Church and the incomparable dignity of virginity in terms of the Church herself: "Mary brought the Head of this Body into the world," he writes, "the Church gives spiritual birth to the members of this Head. In neither case does virginity hinder fertility; and in neither the one nor the other does fecundity destroy virginity. Consequently, if the universal Church is holy in body and spirit without being in every case virginal in body but only in spirit, how much holier is she in those of her members in which she is virgin both in body and spirit."[39] Once again virginity appears as inseparable from the mystery of the Church of which the Virgin Mary is, according to the traditional language of the fathers, the figure.[40] She is this figure not in virtue of a conjugal bond of any kind but entirely because, like the Church herself, she belongs entirely to Christ and to Him alone. And the same is true of all virginity which draws from this attachment its true eschatological meaning, thus announcing what, as far as it is concerned, true religious life will be.

IV. VIRGINITY AND ESCHATOLOGY

The eschatological character of Christian virginity is an evident element in tradition. We shall briefly recall this doctrine, and afterwards we shall show that it is consecration to Christ which endows virginity with this eschatological value and which explains the relationship between viriginity and the mystery of the Church.

THE TRADITIONAL AFFIRMATION

Virginity's relationship to eschatology is based on our Lord's affirmation concerning the world of the resurrection. When the Sadducees pretended to be disquieted by the final fate of a woman with seven husbands and asked: "Whose wife shall she be?" Jesus answered that in the world of the resurrection "there will be neither marrying nor being given in marriage—men live like the angels in heaven" (Mat. 22:30). This world is *angelic* by its irrevocable surpassing of generation; and yet this world of incorruptibility must be populated by beings that are truly human. "It is for this reason that he did not become an angel but became a man, a descendant of Abraham," as Scripture says (Heb. 2:16): It is possible to question whether the traditional comparisons of virginity with the *vita angelica,* arising from the words of our Lord in St. Matthew, respect a wholesome human realism.[41] But one thing, at least, is certain: virginity, by freely sacrificing carnal generation, anticipates the world of the resurrection. "What we shall be," writes St. Cyprian, in a frequently cited text from *De habitu virginum,* "you have already begun to be. You already possess the glory of the resurrection in this life; you pass through this world without succumbing to its contagion."[42] In his turn, St. Ambrose says to virgins: "You have already received what has been promised to us; what is hope with us is already at your disposal. You are from this world, but you are no longer of it. The world had the good fortune of containing you, but it was unable to hold you."[43] Yet nothing more correctly justifies the thought of the Fathers concerning the eschatological value of virginity and therefore that of the religious life[44] than the way in which virginity is related to Christ Himself.

ESCHATOLOGICAL MEANING OF VIRGINITY AND THE MYSTERY OF CHRIST

As Father Congar has written: "Religious life is one element of the eschatological right which the Church affirms and translates into the world."[45] But religious life in general and virginity in particular are not purely objective, and, as it were, sociological, figures of eschatology; they are *spiritual* figures. They exist only within the context of a relationship with Christ that is as personal and as profound as possible.

One of the fears, perhaps a well-grounded one, of religious orders during the second session of the Council was that religious life might be reduced to a matter of "form," to a kind of "style," to use a current expression, a mode of life admittedly respectable but emptied of all spiritual content proper to it. "One kind of life is as good as another!" it is said, expressing an opinion uncomplicated by careful analysis. The choice of virginity and more generally, of religious life, is not spiritually different from the choice of the marriage state provided that the latter be Christian. Is not marriage a sacrament? All true perfection flows from God who can give, and in fact does give, as much grace to those in one condition as to those in another. Consequently, there are no special vocations in the Church. As for the religious state, it can give an objective and social form to convergent individual choices; but it cannot pretend to a greater love of Christ nor aim at a more profound union to His mystery than any other state. Whence, and we are returning to our point of departure, the simply *figurative* content of virginity and of religious life. Eschatology is *represented* in the Church by these states, but Christ is present in them to no greater degree than elsewhere.

Hence, any consideration of virginity must avoid in this matter of eschatology the errors made by the ancient Jews with regard to messianism. The eclipse of the person of the Messiah by reason of the good things his coming would bring was one of the striking features of the messianism that Jesus rejected.[46] The kingdom that we await and that virginity for its part anticipates cannot be a kingdom without a King; or, more precisely, it is only a true kingdom because of its King; or, as Origen said, the kingdom is the King Himself. The age to come is empty for us if Christ is not its only content. He will introduce us personally in the fire of the Spirit to the glorious life of the Father (I Cor. 15:27–8). Hence, in order to discern the true eschatological value of virginity, one must restore to the Person of the Lord the place which continually risks being surreptitiously taken from Him. This can be done by turning to the comparison, constantly made by the fathers, between virginity and martyrdom.[47]

VIRGINITY AND MARTYRDOM St. Cyprian, when commenting on Matthew 7:14 concerning "the narrow way which leads to life," had already said: "Rough and hard is the path which leads to glory. This path is traveled by martyrs to the very end, virgins walk thereupon, and the just set forth on it."[48] This gradation, martyrs, virgins, just, is a well-known one. In terms of the parable of the sower (a common subject of meditation for the fathers), the scale assumes a quantitative form. St. Augustine's commentary on the parable represents a highly developed state of the tradition.[49] He proposes several possible classifications of the terrains.[50] But whether he attributes the prize of highest spiritual returns to martyrdom, or whether he consigns it to virginity, or to the two in association, one point stands out: he spontaneously considers one and the other, martyrdom and virginity, as the two forms par excellence of fidelity to the Lord. The greatness of the combats sustained by both is sometimes used to justify the comparison. Thus, Methodius of Olympus, imitating Plato's *Symposium* in his *Banquet of Ten Virgins,* wrote at the beginning of the fourth century: "Virgins have been considered martyrs not for having briefly undergone corporal torture but because they have not feared to patiently endure the truly olympian combat of chastity during their entire life."[51] Yet Methodius' interpretation is not the most usual point of view in tradition and for us is certainly not the richest.

Following the best tradition of Ignatius of Antioch,[52] of the martyrs of Lyons,[53] and of Origen's *Exhortation to Martyrdom,*[54] Nicolas Cabasilas, a Byzantine author of the fourteenth century, gave an interpretation of martyrdom which can be remarkably helpful in understanding its counterpart, virginity. "Whether they were previously in the ranks of the faithful," writes our author speaking of martyrs, "or whether they received the life of Christ in the course of persecution, they all alike proclaimed their faith in Christ in the face of the executioners, confessed His name, and asked for death. In a single voice, women, girls, men, children, of every state of life, of every condition, called out to the persecutors as if to obtain a good which was already in view. . . . There is no need to show that the strength which inspired these martyrs to such courageous daring, fervent endurance, and ardent perseverance transcends human nature. . . . It is because they were pierced through by the love of Christ that they offered this spectacle, one without precedent."[55] Having scarcely become "new men, they lighted Christ's flame in themselves and in others."[56] "This love," he continues, "has all the appearance of a true transport, for those beloved of Christ were effectively carried beyond the laws of nature." The point is admirably illustrated by a pagan actor who (like St. Genesius before him) was converted to Christ at the very time he was parodying the holy mysteries: the object of his mockery instantaneously became the well-loved reason for his death. "From having said that he loved Christ," explains Cabasilas, "he came to love Him in reality; like fire, the love went from his lips to his heart."[57] In this way he entered the number of those who, freshly baptized, "lit Christ's flames in themselves and in others."[58] Our author attributes martyrdom to the effects of baptism. And though he does not compare martyrdom with virginity, still by giving martyrdom an interpretation directly linked to the baptismal discovery of Christ, he effectively enlightens us as to the manner in which we are to understand virginity, a state never separated from martyrdom by the fathers.

MARTYRDOM, VIRGINITY, AND LOVE OF THE LORD What does martyrdom find and what does Christian virginity seek by thus exceeding, each in its own way, the natural possibilities of man? A vain anticipation of the world to come, an esthetic mimesis of the future life? By no means. What virginity seeks and what it finds is what the martyrs sought and what they found: Christ in person who calls and attracts them. They are not only His "imitators," but lovers who are transformed. "My love is crucified," said St. Ignatius of Antioch in order to justify his thirst for martyrdom. "If he had this astonishing desire for death, if he has no more use for corruptible nourishment, it is because he loves Jesus Christ and Jesus Christ alone."[59] It is in this attitude that virginity is extraordinarily like martyrdom. Resulting from baptism as does the latter, virginity and the joy it gives have Christ as their origin, their milieu, and their end.[60]

Now if eschatology concerns the term of all things, and if this term is truly the Lord on whom was "bestowed the name which is above every name, that at the name of Jesus every knee should bow in heaven and on earth and under the earth, and that *every tongue confess* that Jesus Christ is Lord to the glory of God the Father" (Phil. 2:9–11), then virginity, which entails a total and exclusive consecration to Christ, receives from this dedication its true eschatological meaning. Borne along by the entire force of its love for Him beyond whom there is nothing except the Father to whom Christ brings us in the Spirit, virginity in its decision as martyrdom in its act is an absolute choice of the Ultimate and a passage into the exclusive domain of the Principle and Goal of all things (Col. 1:16–9). The eschatological meaning of virginity, as that of martyrdom, rises in the baptized from the love which consecrates the virgin and the martyr in an undivided way to Him beyond whom there is nothing.

If it is true that virginity announces the future state of the world in its own distinctive fashion, it does not do so by losing that essential part of glory which St. Paul defines as "always being with the Lord" (I Th. 4:17). All other aspects of eschatology: transformation of the universe, incorruptibility of man in his body, glorious surpassing of history, and even the triumphant integration of humanity in the trinitarian life, all of these things which are of great importance and without which humanity would not find in Christ the end destined for it—all of these exist for man only in Jesus Christ, with Him, and by Him. Even at the present moment indissoluble union with Christ is eschatology in its source; to resort to an apparently naive but actually a profoundly Christian formula, it is paradise begun! Virginity understands this and lives it. In the eyes of virginity the love of Jesus is the whole of its consecration. And He is also the spiritual "whole" of the world which will never fulfill its purpose except through communion with the Lord. Can one say too often that the eschatological excellence of virginity is not limited to foregoing generation? To desire this latter for its own sake could be a means of refusing the body, life, or of seeking passage into a chimera. Virginity's value lies in its search for an undivided love of Christ; it is constituted by the completely Christian desire of "belonging totally to Christ" (I Cor. 7:29).

Virginity's value does not lie in its refusal of the human love that is born of desire, but in its preference for Christ's call to love Him without division. It sacrifices those things of the flesh which remove it from exclusively belonging to Christ. Virginity freely accepts what death imposes on all men and anticipates through love the spiritual plenitude of the resurrection which will be free of carnal forces. Without being dispensed from death—the virgin consecrated to Christ dies as do all human beings—virginity consecrated in one stroke (and this is the excellence it seeks) frees a person from having a heart and a life divided with respect to Christ. But since it is united to Him without division, it finally rejoins Him, and this with joy. This is why tradition, especially the liturgy,[61] depicts the virgin as being able to follow in the steps of the Bridegroom at whatever hour of the night He may come. This total openness of love with regard to the coming of Christ in a death not by martyrdom but by nature is a perfect summary of the unexcelled eschatological value of virginity. It also explains why virginity is directly connected with the mystery of the Church which forms and constitutes us.

CHRISTIAN VIRGINITY AND THE MYSTERY OF THE CHURCH

The excellence of Christian virginity is, then, the choice of love which puts it in an exclusive dependence on Christ. The excellence of the Church is of the same nature. Depending on Christ by the prevenient institution which makes her the unfailing sign of Him who is the Fullness of time, the Church responds to this love by living not only *in dependence on* Christ her Source but also *for* him as her Goal, doing this in a free consecration of herself. While waiting for Him (and she awaits the coming of Christ with impatience [Ap. 22:16]), the Church does not see in eschatology a life that is purely in the future. For the Church eschatology is her present life with Christ in the structure of a divinely assisted ministry and in the liberty of a divinely inspired response. The Eucharist which she makes and which makes her[62] gives her each day the assurance that He whom she awaits is also the One who comes, who knocks, enters, is seated, and makes His own life the nourishment of His Bride (see Ap. 3:20).

It is true that the Church awaits a radical renewal both of the world and of men in "a new heaven and a new earth" (Ap. 21:1). She knows that "until that day all creation groans in travail" in the desire and "hope of being freed from the servitude of decay and thereby of obtaining the glorious freedom of the children of God" (Rom. 8:21–2). But the Church's expectation for the world of creation cannot be separated from a spiritual groaning which has Christ Himself for object: "Come, Lord Jesus" (Ap. 22:20). Eschatology is resolved for the Church by the return of her King—and until that day in a daily existence under Christ's direction. The last words of the Apocalypse: "May the Lord's grace be with everyone! Amen" (Ap. 22:21) are like an actual response to the eschatological supplication of the Bride. And St. Paul in his turn says: "The grace of the Lord Jesus Christ, the love of God, and the fellowship of the Holy Spirit be with you all" (II Cor. 13:13). This disposition (and it is a true response of Christ to the prayer of waiting uttered by His Church) contains the certainty that the Christ who is to come is already mysteriously present and that He makes possible a real communion with the still hidden fullness of God. For the Church as for the virginity inspired by her, eschatology is, then, the absolute love of the Lord opening upon the world which He has created for His Glory which He anticipates by His grace (II Cor. 13:13).

Those in the Church who love Christ with this love of absolute preference of which virginity is the sign are, then, dependent on the love which characterizes the Church as the Bride of Christ. Their love of Christ is enrooted in her love: it is she who in the Spirit leads them to love Him, for it is first of all to her that the indefectibility of love which He gives her has promised a corresponding indefectibility in the love returned to Him. Not that Christians' love is not their own or that they are dispossessed of their own heart or that the Spirit no longer has a role to play; but, being called to form in Christ a single Body whose mystery encompasses individuals without destroying them, we fulfill ourselves only by entering this totality of love which day after day flows from the desire of God formed in Christ to make all humanity a community of sons (Eph. 1:4). That is why when men and women give themselves to Christ either in an initial way or in the supreme way we have described it is the very love of the Church as Bride which they manifest. The Church is there to introduce them to Christ through the gospel, through baptism and the sacraments, through her authority, and through her entire life.[63] In thus forming them according to the depths of the love they receive and of that they should give, she assimilates them to what is infallible in her own love and strips them of what is infirm in theirs. As we fulfill ourselves through her, she fulfills herself in us as well!

Although being the first to be loved in order that she might be the first to love, still the Church never exists except in those who constitute her. As we have said, our love of Christ is hers; but we must also add at once that her love is ours. We can love Christ only if we are within the Church and only if we have been engendered by her unto this love; on the other hand the Church in her turn loves Christ only in and through the love of her children. Her love of Christ is deprived of substance if it is deprived of ours. That is why she begs with such insistence that we love Christ as she knows that He deserves to be loved; she does this so that she may love Him through us as she desires to do. That is also why the priority of the love of Christ which virginity represents and which assumes canonical form in religious life has awakened and will continue to awaken such profound echoes within the Church.

8

The Psychological Possibility of Intellectual Obedience

THOMAS DUBAY, S.M.

If anything is anathema to our western world it is thought control in whatever guise it may appear. Understandably enough, our democratic horror at the least restriction on freedom of thought and expression strikes a sympathetic note in the heart of the western religious, for even he cannot escape the moods of a pluralistic society. So true is this sympathy for freedom, that not a few religious find the commonly taught doctrine on obedience of the intellect an incomprehensible, if not impossible bit of spirituality. One can encounter good religious whose very constitutions carry a stipulation on obedience of the judgment and yet who are almost scandalized by that stipulation, who may even think it a mistaken insertion because they view it either as impossible of fulfillment or as an unjust attempt to curtail reasonable freedom.

In this article we propose to investigate psychologically the theory and the practice of intellectual obedience, that is, the conforming of one's judgment to the judgment of the superior. We will preface our analysis, however, with a review of the commonly received doctrine on obedience of the intellect, a doctrine classically enunciated by St. Ignatius of Loyola in his well-known letter on obedience and recently sealed by the strong words of Pope Pius XII in his 1957 address to the General Congregation of the Society of Jesus.

WHAT IS INTELLECTUAL OBEDIENCE?

Before answering our question positively, we might with profit dwell for a moment on what intellectual obedience is not. Conforming one's judgment to the superior's judgment does not mean merely that upon receiving an apparently unwise command, the subject judges that in these concrete circumstances he (the subject) intellectually agrees that the superior is to be obeyed. A religious does not make the superior's judgment his own simply by accepting the intellectual proposition that this command must be executed, for that is accepting a solid truth of ascetical theology, not a superior's judgment. Obedience of the understanding is more than an intellectual acceptance of the theory behind religious obedience.

Secondly, obedience of judgment does not mean that a religious violates his intellectual honesty by "agreeing" with the superior no matter how patently wrong the latter may be—and sometimes is. Nor does it mean that a subject must think as his superior thinks on any subject whatsoever. The superior has no infallible authority from God and no universal commission to teach, and so he has no right to expect his subjects to be of one mind with him on free questions unrelated to religious obedience.

If intellectual obedience is none of these, what, then, is it? Although a religious can avoid an offense against the virtue or the vow of obedience by a mere execution of the matter commanded, yet perfection adds to execution a full surrender of both the will and the intellect. There are, consequently, three elements necessarily included in an act of perfect obedience: *execution* of the superior's directive, *wanting* to execute it *because of the superior's authority,* and *thinking* in its regard *as the superior thinks* insofar as such is possible. As regards this third element, we can hardly improve on St. Ignatius' explanation, an explanation ratified by the explicit authority of the Sovereign Pontiff: "He who aims at making an entire and perfect oblation of himself, besides his will, must offer his understanding, which is a distinct degree and the highest degree of obedience. He should not only wish the same as the Superior, but think the same, submitting his own judgment to the Superior's, so far as a devout will can incline the understanding. For although this faculty has not the freedom which the will has, and naturally assents to what is presented to it as true, there are, however, many instances where the evidence of the known truth is not coercive, in which it can with the help of the will favor one side or the other. When this happens, every obedient man should bring his thought into conformity with the thought of the Superior" (*Letter on Obedience,* translated by William J. Young, S.J. [New York: American Press, 1953], p. 10).

It is not our purpose here to develop the idea of intellectual obedience, but rather to analyze its possibility from the psychological point of view. Our aim, then, can be satisfied by two or three illustrations of the Ignatian teaching. Father X, a religious priest, is attached to a parish, and during Lent is charged by his superior to preach a series of sermons on the capital sins. Father X rightly believes he knows the parish and its needs well, and he further thinks that those who come to Lenten devotions need a series of sermons on fraternal charity far more than one on the capital sins. Surely the difference of opinion between Father X and his superior is not black and white either way. As is the case with most commands in religious life, the evidence is not coercive; the matter is at least debatable. If Father X has a "devout will" in the Ignatian sense, he will try insofar as he can to see and accept his superior's judgment about the advisability of a series on the capital sins. Rather than adduce mental or vocal reasons against the superior's view (and that is his natural inclination), he summons up reasons that support the superior's position, and he tries to solve his own objections. In other words, he makes a serious attempt to judge the matter as his superior judges it.

Sister Y is denied permission to invite to the parlor someone she thinks she could aid spiritually by a word of encouragement or advice. Sister conforms her judgment to her superior's, not merely by agreeing to the proposition that she ought not to invite this person because she has been denied permission, but by trying to agree to the proposition that, all things considered, seeing this individual now is not wise *in itself.*

Brother Z is refused permission to buy tools that he obviously needs to do his job competently. Brother knows clearly that the monastery is not hard-pressed financially; and he knows, too, that his present set of tools is simply not adequate. What must Brother's "devout will" do in this situation? Rest in peace. He need not even try to conform his judgment to his superior's, because the case is clear (in our supposition, at least). Since it is patent that the superior is wrong, even the perfection of obedience does not require Brother to believe that he is right.

NATURE OF INTELLECTUAL ASSENT

The difficulties involved in seeing the advisability and even the possibility of a submission of the judgment are prominent in the cases of Father X and Sister Y. Brother Z's situation offers no great problem. If the intellect is a necessary, determined, non-free faculty, how can it be moved to accept one view rather than another? If Father X's intellect is determined by the evidence at hand and if he can see his motives for assent but not his superior's, how can he honestly conform his judgment to his superior's? And the same is true of Sister Y.

The intellect, the faculty that knows in an immaterial manner, the faculty whose proper object is the universal idea, is admittedly a non-free cognitive power. It can know only what is given it, for the knowing intellect is what the scholastics call the possible intellect, and the possible intellect is determined by the impressed species. Though this terminology may be obscure to the non-philosopher, the fundamental idea is quite simple. Just as the eye is passive and determined in the sense that it can see only what is given to it, so also on the more immaterial plane is the intellect passive and determined because it can "see" only what is given to it to understand.

While we readily grant the non-free character of the intellect's grasp of the idea (the simple apprehension of the philosopher, the knowing of what a thing is), we do not grant that all of his judgments are determined or non-free. By a judgment we mean, of course, the attribution of one idea to another or the denial of one idea to another. I attribute white to house in the judgment, "the house is white," or I deny right of James in the judgment, "James is not right." Some of our judgments are necessary: "seven times four is twenty-eight," or "any being has a sufficient reason for its existence." These propositions are overpowering in their evidence; the intellect must accept them. It cannot do otherwise, for there is no theoretical or practical difficulty in the propositions that could distract the intellect's attention and so render the assent unnecessary.

But—and this is important for religious obedience—most of our judgments are not necessary. Even more, many of our *certain* judgments are free even though perfectly certain and established by irreproachable evidence. Although the judgment, "God exists," is certain, and metaphysically certain at that, it is a free judgment, for it is not coercively obvious. A man can choose to be unreasonable, to look rather at difficulties practical and speculative, and thus choose to reject a truth that is amply demonstrated beyond any reasonable doubt. Because the intellect is not necessitated by the evidence in these many free certitudes, the will must enter into the picture and decide whether a judgment is to be made, and, if so, what kind. The fact that the certitude of faith (another example of a free assent) is free is one reason that it is meritorious of eternal reward.

And so the will has a decidedly large part to play in our intellectual life—far more than most of us would like to admit. If I am a Democrat (or a Republican), I am such not because of clear, cold reason alone. The positions taken by the two parties are by no means obviously right or wrong, at least when considered as two systems. If I am a Democrat, there are intellectual reasons, of course. But there are also a host of factors that have influenced my will quite aside from my desire for efficient government: parental persuasions, educational exposures, attitude of friends, personality traits of political figures, my home city and state, income bracket (if I had one!), social position, religion. If you wonder whether rural life is superior to urban, whether married women ought to work outside the home, whether your religious superior is right or wrong in a given case, you may be quite sure that your will is going to have an important role in your final yes or no to each question.

The will exercises this role in two ways, indirectly and directly. The will indirectly influences our intellect in its act of judgment by determining whether and for how long the intellect is to consider the various pieces of evidence pro and con. If a man refuses to study the evidence for the divine origin of the Catholic Church, his final judgment, "She is not Christ's Church," has been very much determined by his will, even though he might flatter himself that he has been quite intellectual in building up his case against her. If a religious refuses to examine carefully the favorable motives for his superior's decision, his judgment that the superior has erred is shot through with the volitional element.

The will plays a direct role in the formation of a judgment, not because it elicits the very act of judgment (this is a cognitive act and therefore an operation of the intellect), but because it imperates or commands the intellect to pass judgment, to link one idea with another. This direct role is found in both certain and opinionative assents. Although we have thus far considered chiefly the certain assent, what we have said bears even more pointedly on the opinionative. If certitudes can be free, it is obvious that opinionative assertions must also be free. If certain motives often do not determine the intellect, surely probable ones do not. And so because the opinionative judgment is not one forced by the evidence, the will must enter into the matter directly and command the intellect either to assent, not to assent, or to suspend assent altogether.

APPLICATION TO RELIGIOUS OBEDIENCE

From all that we have said it appears, then, that a definitive disagreement with one's religious superior is not usually a purely intellectual affair. The reader will note that we specify a *definitive* disagreement, that is, not a mere difficulty in seeing the superior's position, but rather a mental assent, certain or opinionative, that the superior has erred. If we may return to a previous example, our point may be clarified. If Father X makes a judgment that his superior is wrong in directing a Lenten series on the capital sins, Father X's will has probably entered into his decision both indirectly and directly. On the first score, Father X's judgment has been influenced indirectly by his will, if he declined to look for and consider reasons supporting his superior's view. If, in addition, he chose only to adduce mental evidence to prove his own view, he chose so to act by his will, not his intellect. On the second score, Father's judgment has been directly influenced by his will, since the evidence is not compelling for either opinion, and in order for him to make an opinionative or a certain assent either way the will must intervene.

It now becomes apparent that obedience of the judgment involves both the intellect and the will though in different ways. It is the intellect that is here conformed to the superior's, but it is the will that sees to the conforming operation. However much he might like to think so, the religious is not subject merely to objective evidence in his intellectual reaction to his superior's commands. His final assent or dissent is very much determined by his *desire* to assent or dissent, and that desire will be shown probably by both an indirect and a direct influence on the part of his will.

We may next inquire into the reasons why the will enters so pronouncedly into a realm that seems no great affair of its own. Why does the will step into the intellect's own proper sphere and influence its own proper act, the judgment? The underlying answer to this question may be deduced from what we have already said about the indetermination of the intellect in any of its judgments that lack compelling evidence. In these cases it is the will that must decide finally whether an intellectual assent is going to be made and, if so, what kind: affirmative or negative, certain or opinionative. Without this volitional push the intellect would operate only when the evidence for its assent is overwhelming and bereft of any difficulty, practical or speculative. While the intellect's frequent indetermination is the underlying reason for the will's entry into the act of judgment, we may still ask why the will chooses an affirmative assent rather than a negative one (or vice versa) or a certain rather than an opinionative one (or vice versa). Why, in other words, do we choose to hold what we do hold? Does our will always follow the objective state of evidence?

To answer this question is to answer also the problem of why we err when we do err. St. Thomas does not hesitate to place the root cause of error in the will, and he therefore finds at least a material sin (one without guilt) if not a formal sin (one with guilt) in our errors of judgment. "Error obviously has the character of sin," points out the Angelic Doctor. "For it is not without presumption that a person would pass judgment on things of which he is ignorant. Especially is this true in matters in which there is a danger of erring" (*De malo,* 3, 7). Why the sin? Because there is a deordination in the will's extending an assent beyond evidence, in judging without adequate information. We do not err because our senses and/or our intellects deceive us.* Being passive faculties they cannot register except what is given them, any more than a catcher's baseball glove can catch a golf ball if a baseball is thrown at it. If as I ride down the highway I see a peach tree and declare it to be a plum tree, I have erred not because my eyes deceived me (for they indicated precisely what is there), but because through an over-eager will my intellect

* The senses can err, of course, when either they or the medium are defective. Of themselves, they are inerrant.

was pushed to extend its assent, "Look at the plum tree," beyond the given data. An ordered judgment, one supported by available evidence, would have been, "Look, I *think* that is a plum tree." In this judgment there is no error for it does appear to be a plum tree.

In pinning down exactly why the will imperates unjustified assents epistemologists offer a wide variety of causes and occasions. These may be seen in any complete text on the validity of human knowledge. We will apply these same reasons and add some of our own to the subject's judging of a superior's command when the rightness or wrongness of it is not obvious. We may note that in the subject's disagreement with his superior there will often be an inordination of one kind or another. We qualify our statement by the word *often* because it can also happen with some frequency, and even in matters debatable, that a subject judges his superior wrong for objectively valid reasons. But even in this latter case perfect obedience will prompt the religious to seek to conform his thought to the superior's insofar as he can, and that by trying to see the superior's *reasons rather than his own.* What, then, are the inordinate causes for a subject's willed intellectual disagreement with his superior?

(*1*) *Precipitate judgment due to levity or lack of maturity.* Many people, not excepting religious, have a tendency to pass judgment on ideas or persons or events on the spur of the moment and without allowing themselves the leisure for mature consideration. This undue haste could be willed insofar as an individual realizes his tendency to ill-considered conclusions and yet does not take adequate means to overcome it. A religious who is wont to have and express an immediate opinion regarding decisions of authority is probably beset with this defect.

(*2*) *Innate tendency to disagree.* Closely allied with our first cause for a religious' intellectual disagreement with his superior is the odd perversity by which some men almost automatically choose the contradictory position to an expressed proposition. This type of person, when a religious, will find himself spontaneously thinking that the community should buy a Ford once the superior has decided upon a Chevrolet.

(*3*) *Desire to appear informed and/or as having a mind of one's own.* To suspend judgment upon hearing a statement or to agree with it can in the first case appear to be due to ignorance of the situation or, in the second, to a lack of intellectual initiative and originality. Sister X may disagree with a superior's directive regarding classroom procedure primarily because she wants her community to realize that she, too, knows something about matters educational. Brother Y may be at odds with his superior about some extracurricular activity just to let it be known that he still has the use of a good set of reasoning apparatus.

(4) *An attachment to an idea or to a thing with which the superior's directive is incompatible.* Father X in our above example could have been willing his intellectual disagreement with his superior because of an unreasonable clinging to his own idea of what the people need most to hear about in a Lenten series. Although this clinging to an idea may be solidly motivated, it may also spring from an intellectual pride or from a self-centered attachment. If we refuse to examine honestly the evidence supporting the superior's view, we have cause for suspecting a self-centered attachment.

(5) *A preformed set of pseudo-principles.* Not unrelated to simple prejudice is the phenomenon by which a religious builds his own cozy living of the religious life upon a set of principles hardly deducible from gospel asceticism. When his superior's directives clash with these "common sense" principles, the former are judged to be defective, not the latter. Fit forms of recreation, the amount of money available for a vacation, types and amount of work assigned are all illustrations of the kind of material in which intellectual judgment is likely to be mixed with an abundance of will.

(6) *Dislike for the consequences of the superior's judgment.* Even when no principle is immediately apparent, a religious can disagree with his superior's judgment because he can see that it is going to conflict with his own plans and purposes. A teaching sister who wishes secretly to run a particular extracurricular activity can easily be tempted to find intellectual fault with a command whose execution will disqualify her for the job she seeks. If she succumbs to the temptation, her judgment is probably rife with will.

(7) *Dislike for the person of the superior.* If my memory does not fail me, Ovid once observed that love is a credulous sort of thing. And we might add that hatred is incredulous. The same man will strain to put a favorable interpretation on a wild remark of a true friend, while he will unabashedly reject a moderate statement of an enemy.

A religious who feels a natural antipathy towards his superior is by that very fact predisposed to disagree with his judgments on non-intellectual grounds. Because women admittedly tend to judge with their hearts to a greater extent than men do, sisters who note this inclination in themselves should observe carefully its bearing on intellectual obedience.

These, then, are some of the volitional factors that can be present in the religious' failure to conform his judgment to that of his superior. Lest we be misunderstood, we repeat that a lack of conformity of judgment can also be due to solid intellectual reasons held by the subordinate; and in this case he is not at fault, provided he has honestly tried to see the superior's point of view. But we do insist that many of our disagreements can be influenced, perhaps strongly, by any one or several of the factors we have outlined. When such be true, our disagreement may not be flattered by the pure name of intellectual.

SOME DIFFICULTIES

Does not intellectual obedience smack of the unreal, the dishonest? Is not a mature man or woman being asked too much in being urged to surrender not only the will but the very intellect itself? Is the religious to enjoy no personal independence at all? These questions almost answer themselves in the asking. Intellectual obedience is honest and realistic for the simple reason that it requires only that a subject look frankly at evidence favoring the superior's viewpoint. Since he already knows his own opinion, the subordinate violates no honesty in trying to see and accept that of God's representative insofar as such is possible. Nor does this ask too much, for every faculty of man belongs to God, his intellect included, and they all, therefore, should be surrendered to Him. As regards independence, we must note that no man is independent of God. A religious obeys with his understanding, not because the superior is more intelligent than he, but because he commands with God's authority. There is an immense difference between the two motives.

Would not the faithful practice of intellectual obedience cripple a religious' later ability to rule? Hardly. This difficulty is based on the tacit premise that the subordinate's viewpoint on a debatable command is the more correct because it is the subordinate's, that he will learn how to rule by attending to his reasonings rather than those of the superior. The contrary seems more likely. A subject already knows how he would judge in a given situation and why he is inclined to disagree with his superior. It stands to reason, then, that he will be broadened, not narrowed, if he honestly tries to see this same situation from another man's vantage point. I would expect obedience of judgment to improve a subject's later ability to govern wisely rather than hinder it. After all, who of us is so brilliant that he has nothing to learn from another?

And finally, does not the conforming of one's judgment to that of another tend to smother magnanimity and zeal, bigness of mind and accomplishment? I think I might be pressed if I had to give a convincing theoretical answer to this objection, but I find that an adequate concrete answer could scarcely be easier. We need only look at the lives of the saints and then ask whether their perfect obedience of intellect and will smothered their zeal and accomplishment. We need only recall, for example, that towering figure of magnanimity, St. Francis Xavier, corresponding with his superior on his knees. The objection melts away.

Intellectual obedience, then, is not only psychologically possible; it it logical, helpful, desirable. Without it obedience of execution and will can hardly be perfect. The subject who is at intellectual odds with his superior's directives is likely to murmur, to cut corners, to be lacking in promptness and cheerfulness. With intellectual obedience he is completely subordinated to God. He enjoys peace because his holocaust is entire.

9

Some Reflections on Obedience*

KARL RAHNER, S.J.

In contributing to a periodical which is commemorating the fourth centenary of the death of St. Ignatius, the founder of the Jesuit Order, what theme should a writer choose? If he prefers not to speak directly of the Saint himself and still wants a fitting topic, he could choose nothing better than the concept of obedience. Jesuit obedience—some like to call it *cadaver* obedience—is a well-known and even notorious tag. It is also something which is poorly understood. Ignatius stressed the importance of this virtue for members of his Society, since it is a matter of great moment for an order engaged in the active care of souls. But in reality Jesuit obedience does not differ from the obedience found in the other religious orders of the Catholic Church.

In choosing obedience for his topic this writer does not flatter himself that he is rediscovering a long neglected subject. In the last ten years, in Middle Europe alone, at least fifty books and articles have been devoted to this theme. In attempting to say something on the subject of obedience the writer is troubled by a suspicion that possibly he merely wants to be numbered among those who have had something to say on the point. Besides, in a short article like this, one can scarcely hope to say anything that is at all comprehensive or conclusive. Hence these few lines do not pretend to be more than marginal notes, and the writer is resigned to face the possible accusation that he was incapable of conceiving a livelier topic for discussion.

* The German original of this article: "Eine ignatianische Grundhaltunf," appeared in *Stimmen der Zeit,* 158 (1955–6), 253–267. The present translation was made collectively under the direction of Joseph P. Vetz, S.J., and the supervision of Gustave Weigel, S.J.

VARIOUS MISCONCEPTIONS

Considered in its essence, obedience in religious life has nothing to do with the obedience which children owe to their parents and to others who are in authority, supposedly equipped to care for their upbringing. The reason is that this latter type of obedience has as its very aim its own eventual transcendence. By means of this training in obedience, the obedience of childhood later becomes superfluous, since the adult, having achieved liberation from the domination of blind instinctive drives, is able to command himself. On the other hand, in the case of obedience in religious life, we assume that the subject is already an adult. But we do not assume that the person who commands is necessarily more intelligent, more gifted with foresight or morally more mature than the person who obeys. If such an assumption were in order, the relationship of superior to subject would be an educational relationship. The one obeying would be a child or a man of infantile character, who is not yet responsible for his own behavior. Human nature being what it is, there are such persons even in religion. Still their percentage should not be greater than that found in other walks of life. And I suppose that, generally speaking, it is not. After all, childish persons can find too many havens to which to flee from their unfitness for life without having to seek out religion as their only refuge. One conclusion that can be drawn from these rather obvious considerations is this: Superiors should not act as if by nature or by reason of their office they are more intelligent, more clever persons, more morally steadfast, more provident and wise in the ways of the world. This may be true in individual cases, for the world is not so constructed that only the more stupid become superiors. But it should be soberly stated (for subjects, lest they demand too much of superiors, something which would be unjust and show a lack of charity; for superiors, lest they delude themselves): the higher the office, the smaller the possibility, humanly speaking, of fulfilling it as well as in the case of a man faced with a lesser post. For we may reasonably presume that the degrees of variation in mental and moral gifts among men and less than in the degrees of difficulty found in the management of various social enterprises. From this it follows that, as a rule, more important duties will unavoidably be more poorly performed than lesser ones. No judgment is passed here on any particular case. As a matter of fact, sometimes people do grow in stature in performing more difficult tasks. But for the most part, the opposite takes place. Along with the assumption of a more important responsibility comes the painful realization, felt both by the superior and those about him, that the man is far from being equipped for his task. The defective fulfillment of higher obligations cruelly lays bare the shortcomings of a man's capacities which previously escaped our attention.

Let us repeat once more: obedience in religious life is not the obedience of children. Therefore, the religious superior should not play the role of an Oympian papa. In the life of the cloister (even in orders of women) there are still to be found age-old rituals governing the etiquette of superiors, involving demands of respect from subjects, secretiveness, manifestations of superiority, appeals of superiors to a higher wisdom, displays of condescension, etc. All this should gradually be permitted to wither away. Superiors should cast a long and quiet glance at the world around them: those who are truly powerful and influential, who receive a great deal of unquestioning obedience, place no value on ceremonial of this sort. They find no need of concealing their weakness, anxiety, and insecurity behind a pompous front. Superiors should quietly admit that in certain circumstances their subjects know more than they do about the matter at hand. Given the specialization of modern life with its need for countless types of ability to cover its many areas, present-day superiors can no longer act as if they can understand any and every matter that falls under their authority. In the good old days a superior could do everything that he commanded his subject to do. He had previously done the very thing himself. He had distinguished himself (and otherwise he normally would not have been made superior) and so had given proof that he understood at least as much as his subject. At least this was the rule in the past, though naturally there were exceptions to it even then. Today it is quite inevitable that what formerly was the exception should become the rule. Every religious superior has many subjects who necessarily possess a knowledge of science, of pastoral functioning, of current affairs, which the superior (who can be a specialist himself only in a single limited field) cannot possess. He finds himself or ought to find himself, in the same position with regard to the knowledge of others as Eisenhower does with respect to the mysteries about which his atomic experts advise him. The superior, therefore, is dependent upon the information of counselors to an extent not required in the past. The advisors, usually provided for superiors by the constitutions of an order, today in many ways possess an utterly new and more urgent function than in former times when they were in practice only a democratic check on an excessively authoritarian and uncontrolled government of one individual. It would be well, therefore, if superiors would always seek the information they need in a spirit of objectivity and concreteness, for they must give commands for objective and concrete situations, no matter what be the value of obedience to an objectively erroneous command. This is not always done. A secret-cabinet policy may often be a well-intentioned means of acquiring such objective counsel, but it is not always effective. In religious life, on final analysis, there can be no real democratization of obedience, as will later be shown. But there can be objective and clearly determined methods of procedure for achieving the counsel and information needed for decision. Unfortunately this is not always the case. Once again I insist, mostly for the benefit of the secular opponent and hostile critic of religious obedience: the people in religious life realize that religious obedience is not the obedience of children. It does not presuppose children, but mature adults. And only in the measure that it can legitimately presuppose this can it be at all true to its own proper nature.

Again, religious obedience is no mere "regulation of traffic." Certainly where men live together in a community there must be order. That there be order, the power to command must be present. Not everyone can do as he pleases, and moreover, not everyone can discover for himself just what is required by the total whole. Command, however, implies obedience. When obedience is conceived merely as a rational or rationally prescribed function of order for the life of a community and for the coordination of its organs and activities toward a common goal, then perhaps the pattern has been discovered which can intelligently explain civic and national obedience. But in this concept the peculiar nature of religious obedience has not been grasped, even though it cannot be denied that in religious life this aspect of obedience is also present, and necessarily so. Religious obedience is not rational and inevitable regulation of traffic, by which every sensible person submits himself to the traffic policeman, and in which a coordinating agency takes care that everything moves without friction toward the common good. At times attempts have been made to explain religious obedience in his merely rational fashion. But this explanation is too easy and cannot reach the real roots and depths of religious obedience. And yet the obedience entailed in the rational regulation of traffic and of the sensible coordination of work in a common effort is part of religious obedience, though it is not the most characteristic nor the most profound element of the evangelical counsel. For the daily functioning of obedience in religious life it ought to be noted that this element of obedience is present; yes, that it is almost identical with the superficial tasks of quotidian obedience. For day-to-day life, therefore, a certain de-mystification of obedience should quietly take place, perhaps to a greater extent than is now permitted in some parts. In the many small details of daily life, obedience is in reality nothing else than a rational method by which rational beings live together. Therefore, the superior should not try to give the impression that he stands under the immediate inspiration of the Holy Ghost, but should be courageous enough to seek approval for his commands by giving reasons for them. It is incomprehensible how such an approach to mature and much-loved brothers or sisters in the Lord should be a threat to the authority of the superior, who, according to the command of Christ, should see in the authority of his office only the greater obligation to serve. This does not mean that there should be long debates and discussions over every small decree of a superior. That was the folly of the Parliaments in the past. This would be irrational and childish (although unfortunately it does occur). The problem can be met and overcome by an appeal to higher ascetical motives. Without irritating himself or others, the subject should calmly and maturely consider the many unavoidable regulations of daily life in a religious community for what they really are: inevitable burdens of earthly life which weigh upon people in the world just as much as they do on people in religious life. Much irritation among religious persons caused by details of common life flows solely from immaturity which does not comprehend that a person does not prove his independence and personal integrity by rebelling against communal rules and regulations. And yet it still remains true: religious obedience, according to its own proper nature, is more than a merely rational regulation of traffic.

There is a third consideration which will preserve religious obedience from misconception and excess. It is not true, even in religious communities, that all initiative should takes its rise from superiors. Nor should we be too quick to consider this statement a mere platitude. To comprehend it really, we must make use of metaphysics, a metaphysics which consists in pondering with wonder on the commonplace and the obvious and then drawing some conclusions. Human authority (even when exercised in God's name) must not be conceived as adequately and exclusively competent to monopolize all initiative, all effort and all personal decision. Nor does it imply that subjects are called to initiative and decision only when authority gives the signal.

One frequently gets the impression, both in religious orders and in the Church in general, that initiative, action, militancy, and the like, are indeed considered necessary and desirable in subjects, but only on condition that the go-signal be given "from above," and only in the direction which has already been unequivocally and authoritatively determined by superiors. Unconsciously and spontaneously a tendency is vigorously at work to make the subject feel that he is so built into his order or the Church that only the total structure through its hierarchy is capable of initiative; that opinion or enterprise find their legitimacy only in the express, or at least tacit, approval from authority.

Unless we wish to absolutize the community, the principle of subsidiary has application not only between smaller and larger societies, but also between individuals and their communities as well. Yet there can be no subordination of the individual to a community and to the authority representing it, if it tries to make the individual an exclusively dependent function of the community and its authority. We need only put the question in all simplicity: may one propose a wish to a superior, or, with due modesty, propose an alternative policy? Everyone will answer: "Obviously, yes." Hence it is unnecessary first to ask the superior whether he wants the request to be presented or the alternative proposed. Yet this request, this alternative suggestion is also initiative, in which one must take the responsibility of deciding whether it is to be presented or not. For even when with all obedience and modesty the decision is left to the superior, the suggestion alters the situation of the superior in making his decision. It broadens or narrows the field of choice. Indeed even when the subject shows the greatest discretion, the superior is "influenced," whether he likes it or not, whether or not he would have followed the suggestion on his own. In the whole world there is no autarchic human authority which is pure activity and in no way passivity. To command absolutely is proper only to the Creator who is not faced with opposing structures and unavoidable initiatives, because He Himself in the strict sense makes everything out of nothing. All other authority, even in the Church and in religious orders, is not the only determining initiative but is one force in an immense network of forces, active and passive, receiving and giving. Authority has and should have the function of directing, coordinating, overseeing, and planning the whole interplay of human initiatives. It is not, to speak strictly, even in the ideal order, so representative of God that it alone is the autarchic planner and designer of all human activity. This would be the hybris of a totalitarian system which cannot exist, and, more significantly, should not exist.

Hence, authority, even in religious orders, in practice needs, calls for, and puts to use the initiative of subjects. Even in the abstract, there can be no *absolute* ruler and director of it. Independently of authority there exist initial sparkings of forces which cannot be controlled by authority. Because this is so and cannot be otherwise, it also *should* be so. That is to say, in no community or society, not even the Church or religious orders, *may* authority act as if all good initiatives originated from it, so that every execution of plan, command, and wish originated in authority alone. Even the most laudable initiatives of the Holy See often are only the reaction to an action which originated elsewhere, and this is important. The same is true in the case of authorities of religious orders. Subjects are not mere receivers of commands, because that is simply impossible. The aim of obedience is not to make merely passive subjects. This is not even an "asymptotic" ideal, but a chimera and the usurpation of the creative power reserved to God alone, which He can delegate to no one. Only God has "all the threads in His hand," and He has empowered no one to act in His fashion.

Consequently the superior cannot be a god in the fulfillment of his office. Not to prevent his subjects from assuming initiative is not enough for a superior. He must positively count on it, invite it; he must not be irked by it. He must, to a certain degree, recognize himself also as only *one* of the wheels in a heavenly mechanism whose ultimate and comprehensive significance is directed by one only, by God and no one else. The superior always remains something moved. In an ultimate sense, he does not know exactly to what end evolution is moving. In spite of all the authority given him, and in spite of all the supervision he is charged with, he acts in trust and ventures into the unknown. He too never knows exactly what he is doing or starting when he commands or refrains from doing so. He must remember that authority is not the only source for heavenly impulse, direction, and stimulation. He must realize that God never took on the obligation first to advise the authorities selected and authorized by Himself about God's own activity in the Church for the salvation of souls and the progress of history. The superior has no exclusive vision of the divine will with the mission to pass it on to his subjects. There is no God-given warrant for such a process of communication. Rather the superior must also be an obedient man, a hearer. The formal correctness and juridical validity of his commands does not guarantee that they are likewise ontologically guaranteed. If the subject must obey in order not to be disobedient before God, this fact is no proof that the command given was the command which, according to God's antecedent will, should have been given. It can be the product of a permitted fault in the superior. It can proceed from dead traditionalism, from human limitations, from routine, from a shortsighted system of uniformism, from a lack of imagination, and from many other factors.

There is in the world a plurality of forces which can in no way be hierarchically subject to authority—though such forces cannot contradict authority as far as the latter succeeds in bringing them within the field of direction and command. This latter task, as has been said, can and should be only partially achieved. Hence the subject in religious life has no right simply to take refuge behind obedience, as if he could thus be free from a responsibility which he himself must bear, the responsible direction of his own personal initiative. We often hear apologies of obedience which praise this supposed advantage. It does not exist. At least not in the sense that the religious can thereby escape from the burden of personal responsibility. He himself chooses obedience; otherwise he would not be in religious life. He must then answer for the consequences of his choice.

The received command is a synthesis of elements. One is the superior's personal and original activity, the other is the external condition for that activity. This condition is constitued by the subject himself: his mode of being and action, his capacities and incapacities (perhaps culpable), his approach and attitude to the superior. This conditioning is prior to the command and makes the subject co-responsible for the command itself. Certainly the religious can often say to his own consolation that the superior has to answer for this or that decision and not the subject. But the extent of this consolation is not great. Taken as a whole, the religious cannot escape the responsibility for his own life, down to its last details. He simply hears in the command the echo of his own character and activity. There does not exist in this world a control-center of action from whose uninfluenced motion all else in existence originates. A human being cannot relinquish his personality to a representative, not even in religious life. That is in no way the purpose of obedience.

TRUE OBEDIENCE

To provide a positive definition of religious obedience is by no means a simple matter. We could immediately and without further examination maintain that religious obedience is an abidingly vibrant obedience to God and the fulfillment of the Divine Will. But if we were to do that, we would have to determine how it is possible to know in what sense it can be said that that which is commanded is the will of God. For the fact remains that there can be commands which the subject must obey, provided that the things commanded be not sinful, but which in the objective order, are wrong, and which, in given circumstances, have been commanded with real culpability on the part of the superior. In cases of this kind it is no simple task to say why and in what sense the fulfillment of such a command could be the will of God. Nor should we over-simplify the matter by praising without qualification the "holocaust" and "renunciation" which obedience entails. For it is obvious that pure subjection to the will of another who is not God has no value as such in the realm of morality. In itself, pure dependence of self on the will of another is amoral, not to say even immoral, unless some further element be added to it.

We might add that if religious obedience is subordination of one's own will and decisions to those of another who holds the place of God and is the interpreter of the Divine Will, we must at least determine how we are to know how this other person received the divine commission to be the expositor of the will of God. This question is a difficult one; even more so than that of poverty and of the evangelical counsel to renounce the blessings of conjugal love. For these two evangelical counsels are recommended directly in the words of Holy Scripture and by Our Lord Himself. As far as these two counsels are concerned, it is always possible to fall back on this recommendation, even when we do not succeed in achieving a crystal-clear understanding of their inner meaning. In this matter it can be said that the religious is walking in the way of the Gospel. And to him who has set out on this path in unquestioning surrender, the meaning of these counsels will be more and more fully revealed. He can always say that he is imitating Christ. And hence he needs no further argument over and above the fact that the disciple does not wish to be above his master, and that love understands what it recognizes as a fundamental characteristic in the beloved Lord.

Concerning obedience, however, the problem is not as simple as all that. As a matter of fact, we see that in the days of the early Church, in which a continuous procession of ascetics and virgins was already a fact, there was as yet no mention of religious obedience. Nor can any direct affirmation of this concept be found in the pages of the Gospels. The early ascetics lived the life of solitaries, and so there was no stimulus to the evocation of a notion of obedience. And even for a long time afterwards, obedience was not raised as a third vow. The religious accepted a celibate or monastic life in any form, and obliged himself to remain in a definite community which lived such a mode of life. It is clear that we will have to proceed carefully if we are to specify the content and arguments for religious obedience.

Before we proceed in the question of the meaning of obedience precisely as it exists in a religious community, we must be clearly warned against another simplification which superficially gives a quick and easy solution to these questions. We cannot simply refer to the example of Christ. Beyond a doubt He was obedient. Obedience to His Father, according to His explanation, was the form, the driving power and the content of His life. We must by all means imitate Christ. But this is precisely the question: how do we know that in subordination of self to human authority we exercise the deepest obedience to God? Christ did not do it. Certainly the Apostle knows that there are human authorities which in some fashion take the place of God as far as we are concerned, and whose decrees ought to appear to us as the will of God. But Paul is speaking of the authorities which are not freely chosen nor created by us, but exist prior to us and prior to our will, namely parents, masters, and the civil governors. Can we extend and complete this Divine Will imposed on us by subordinating ourselves to new régimes of our own making? If we answer that religious superiors have ecclesiastical authority because they are appointed by the Church, this reply alone does not lead us to any clear-cut doctrine. Subordination to the authority of religious superiors is not imposed on men by the Church without their own free and deliberate consent as implied by the vows. Hence the question remains: why is it meritorious to submit to the authority of another, when it has not been imposed on us by God Himself? Should we not safeguard the freedom that God has entrusted to us as much as our function of personal responsibility, since, as we have already said, an absolute surrender of innate responsible freedom is in no way possible or reasonable?

Hence the argument from the Gospel in favor of religious obedience is not so simple, nor can it be proved immediately or without further examination. Our problem could be expressed succinctly in the following question: is religious obedience a concrete prolongation of obedience to the will of God, either in general, as it finds expression in the commandments of God, or in particular as it is manifested in God's direction, inspiration and providential disposition of the lives of men?

Religious obedience should by no means be considered primarily as obedience to individual commands, nor is it even the abstract notion of a general readiness to fulfill such commands. Primarily it is the permanent binding of oneself to a definite mode of life—to life with God within the framework of the Church. It involves the exclusive dedication of one's energies to those things which are the concern of the Lord and to what is pleasing to Him. We accept as a form of life the expectation of God's coming Kingdom of grace from on high. Obedience is concerned with the sacrifice and renunciation of the world's most precious goods; the renunciation of the right to erect a little world of our own as a field of freedom through the acquisition of wealth; the renunciation of the right to one's own hearth and the felt security to be found in the intimate love of another person through the conjugal bond. It is concerned with prayer, and with the testimony to God's grace which is to be found in what is commonly known as the care of souls and the apostolate. Beyond this we need no further description nor argument for the life of the evangelical counsels. Obedience is a permanent life-form giving man a God-ward orientation. It does so ecclesiologically because by it the religious manifests the peculiar essence of the Church. It is the manifestation of God's other-worldly grace beyond the reach of earthly merit, to be accepted by faith alone in spite of all human impotence. In this manifestation the Church achieves her existential visibility and becomes historically tangible through doctrine and sacrament. This is the life to which the religious immediately and primarily pledges himself. His obedience, with reference to the individual commands which a superior may enjoin, is specified by this life-form giving it its definite religious significance. Otherwise there would be no sense to vowed obedience. It would not be a religious matter at all. It would rather be perversity to praise this kind of obedience in any other field of life; for instance, if one were to vow obedience for the better functioning of a center of chemical research in which one is employed as a research collaborator. If we suppose that a permanent vowed obligation to a religious life is of positive value in the moral order (and this is presupposed here), and if we further assume that it is proper and reasonable, though not necessary, to lead such a life in a community, then it follows that obedience to the directors of this community is justified and meaningful in the concrete pursuit of this permanent way of life.

Hence we are not trying to canonize an abstract notion of obedience as the execution of another's will as such. Such abstract obedience is due to God alone permitting no transfer to another. Beyond this case we cannot obey purely for the sake of obeying or of not doing our own will and determination. Something like this, considered abstractly in itself, would have no positive significance in the realm of morality. It would be downright absurd and perverse. The fact that this sort of thing would be "difficult" and "a perfect holocaust," hard and troublesome for him who is obedient at all times and in all things, can scarcely be itself an argument for the meaningfulness of obedience. The implied presupposition of this argument, namely that the more difficult and repugnant thing is always better and more pleasing to God, just because it is a renunciation difficult for man, cannot be the legitimate starting point of discussion.

Our concept of obedience also explains why religious obedience has its place exclusively in a religious society approved and sanctioned by the Church. The content of obedience must be guaranteed, if such obedience is to possess moral value. It is not enough that commands be morally indifferent. They must be morally good in their total context. The totality must represent for the Church and to the world the content of the evangelical counsels. One can vow only that which is better. Thus one cannot vow directly and as an end in itself to do something which under certain circumstances (even if not sinful) is less prudent, less good, less significant. Whence it immediately follows that the proper and essential object of religious obedience is an abiding way of life according to the evangelical counsels. For in accord with the teaching of the Church this is certainly the better thing, but in what this superiority consists will not be further explained here. Obedience is not at all to be conceived as the "heroic" (or almost foolhardy) concession of a *carte blanche* to a superior, so that the religious simply does not do his own will, either because this is always pleasing and hence its renunciation especially difficult, or because it is fraught with danger and hence to be avoided. Thus it is that obedience is always specified with reference to the constitutions of the given Order, and the superior can only command within the framework determined by the constitutions. In seeking the real essence of obedience, the most important point is missed if only the particular command of the superior is primarily and abstractly considered according to the formula: I declare myself ready to execute the command of another, if this command be not evidently immoral. This is not the case. Obedience is the acceptance of a common mode of religious life in imitation of Christ according to a constitution, which the Church has acknowledged to be a true and practical expression of a divinely oriented existence. By virtue of this acceptance and obligation the vow explicitly or implicitly includes the carrying out of the just commands of the authority necessary in any society, when they are directed to the concrete realization of the life-form of religious commitments "according to the constitutions." Such realizations cannot be determined *a priori* once and for all. Whoever, therefore, is critical of the notion of religious obedience, is really attacking the wisdom of the life of the counsels in the Church. He is attacking, moreover, the wisdom of a life that is not primarily concerned with the tangible realizations of worldly objectives, but which through faith makes the expectation of hidden grace the ground of existence, and translates this faith into act. Without such an act, faith itself would be meaningless. This act is representative of the Church and bears the Church's witness to the world. If this mode of existence is to have meaning, then it must inspire a willingness to carry out in any given instance the concrete actions, undertakings and renunciations, which in the judgment of competent authority are deemed necessary for the concrete realization of this way of life.

This is why obedience is connected with the teaching and example of Christ who was obedient even to the death of the cross. Whoever enters into a religious community, whoever perpetually and irrevocably makes this way of life his own, chooses for himself an unforeseeable destiny. For the consequences of such an election and dedication to the community and its rationale of action cannot be foreseen in detail. And these consequences can be difficult and painful. But this gamble (considered in its formal structure) is involved in every human obligation, whereby another person with his own proper will becomes an inseparable part of one's own life. We find it in marriage, acceptance of the duties of citizenship, the responsibility of office, and so forth. Hence if the religious community and its basic ideals are justified and meaningful (which in our case we legitimately assume to be true), so too is the obligation toward all its consequences which cannot be seen in advance. A human mode of life which consists in the free subordination to something higher than itself cannot exist without this element of risk. And without such a surrender the individual will remain in his own egotism behind the defenses of his own existential anxiety, which is the surest way to destruction. But the man who gives himself to what is higher and nobler, who takes the gamble, knows that he is only doing what Christ Himself did in His obedience.

Under this aspect, that which in a given instance is irrational and indefensible but actually unavoidable really becomes the will of the Father. In this way the cross of Christ, a crime of the Jews and the pagans, "had" to be; it was the will of the Father who had planned it, even though it came about only as the result of the shortsightedness and guilt of men. The permanent dedication to the ideal of the counsels in imitation of Christ, who was poor and self-denying, the crucified legate of God, consecrated to prayer and atonement, is lived all but exclusively in a community professing the same ideal. Hence the obedience which it entails must be regarded as the will of God, even if a particular command appears to be senseless (just as death, failure and the other tragic circumstances of human existence appear), provided of course that what is commanded is not immoral in itself. Religious obedience is thus a real participation in the cross of Christ. Nor should one protest that the irrationality of a mistaken command frees the subject from his contract, and cannot be considered as a share in Christ's mission. We must realize that religious obedience is more than a rationally accepted agreement governing "traffic-arrangements" in a common enterprise. This, of course, is included, for life in any community demands obedience, though in our case community life is directed to God. Obedience in any other society, in the event of an unwise command, would be justified only by the rational insight that such unavoidable eventualities must also be reckoned with in the original bargain. Otherwise, obedience, which is always to some degree necessary, would end, for it would be left to the direction of the subject to obey. But in religion the imitation of Christ is practiced. There the cross of Christ is considered not merely as something inevitable, or as the misfortune of life, by and large to be evaded, but rather as the embodiment of grace and its acceptance through faith, as something which "must" be, "so that the scripture might be fulfilled," since only "thus" can one enter into one's glory. There the command, judged unwise according to its immediate historical context, will be seen as something which in the framework of religious life is worth-while, even desirable. This of course does not justify the superior in issuing such a command. Yet such an order can be understood in the same way as the saints in their imitation of Christ understood failure, shame, the shattering of cherished plans, martyrdom, and thousands of other unjustifiable contingencies. They secretly longed for them as the embodiment of their faith in God's grace now reaching its perfection.

It might here be in place to recognize that morality and spontaneous moral judgment have a greater function than is ordinarily supposed. The command of a superior may be objectively sinful, and if recognized as such by the inferior it should not be put into execution. Everyone will agree that a superior, even with the best intentions, can issue an order which is objectively wrong. If one does not consider as sins only those things which are expressly labeled as such in confessional manuals, then it will be hard to deny that that which is materially false can also very often be objectively immoral. What is more, it is not easy to explain why this is not generally so. Let us offer a fictitious example. A higher superior instructs the principal of a boarding school that he must under all circumstances make the boys go to confession once a week. Let us suppose that the subordinate, in this case the principal of the boarding school, clearly realizes what the superior in his idealistic remoteness cannot comprehend, namely that such a demand will eventually prove very harmful to the spiritual life of his charges. Question: have we here merely an inept pedagogical practice, which must be "carried out" because commanded, or have we in fact an innocent but unjustified demand which, since it is actually a serious threat to the genuine spiritual development of these youths, should not be carried out by the subordinate? The very ineptness of the practice offends against moral principals. Must the subject now declare that he cannot square it with his conscience, and ask to be relieved of his office? Reading the older moralists one gets the impression that they were more concerned with such cases than we are today. Have we today become more moral, or has the principle "an order is an order" gained foothold even in such holy quarters as religious communities? Do we avoid talking about such possibilities out of fear of evils produced by the conscientious objector, and so act as if something of this kind practically never occurs? But is not the consequent evil caused to conscience greater than the utility of a frictionless functioning of external government requiring of subjects a literal obedience to commands? Even the subject has the duty in conscience of examining the moral admissibility of what has been commanded. The just "presumption" that the command of a superior is not only subjectively but also objectively morally unobjectionable does not constitute a simple dispensation from the essential obligation of every man to attain to moral certitude respecting the moral liceity of a free action before it is undertaken. This action is no less his own and no less one for which he will be responsible, simply because it is commanded.

As a religious grows older he asks himself with a deep and secret anxiety whether he has done anything in his life which can stand judgment in God's sight. Nothing of course can so stand, except what He has given out of pure mercy. What is worthy of God comes from God's grace alone. For this very reason what one does is not indifferent. There is an absolute difference between man's potentialities when God's grace is accepted and when it is rejected. God has told us, and He is greater than the human heart, that there are deeds of selfless devotion, obedience to God's holy will and self-forgetting dedication. Yet we always discover in ourselves, if we are not stupid, naive or conceited, things which always make us afraid that there is nothing in us but open or disguised egotism. Are we sure that God's grace was ever operative in us? Such an event should have been life-transforming. Yet was there ever a moment when we did not seek ourselves, when success was not the fruit of egotism, when our love of God was not anxiety, when patient prudence was not really faint-heartedness? The divine achievement of miraculous sanation takes different ways, giving us the right to hope that not everything in our life was open or covert self-seeking. Nor need painful anxiety about it be another manifestation of self-seeking or secret self-justification before God. Whoever is so concerned has made his life essentially simple and easy. We act on our own but the last and most important deed will be effected in us by God Himself operating through the bitterness of life itself. The individual can always do one thing at least. He can give himself over to something greater than himself. He can also see to it that this greater Reality be more than an ideal or a theory, which on final analysis is under his own control, and can be constructed according to his fancy, so that it can no longer be distinguished from the mere idols of the heart. The individual can strive to make this nobler Reality actual. This Reality must make demands on us, when we do not desire to be constrained; must act even when we do not wish it; must cause us suffering when we ourselves would rather avoid it. This happens when the greater Reality to which we dedicate ourselves becomes a tangible force of incomprehensible greatness, whose word of command is directed towards us—and we obey. This means to obey silently, and in the true sense, unquestioningly; to serve, and to submit to a demand we have not ourselves invented. When this happens we have too little time and too little interest to defend or develop our personal integrity. The self has lost its importance. We might even be so fortunate as to become a true person, who exists in so far as he forgets and sacrifices self, in so far as he obeys. But we must remember that life's good fortune is God's grace. In order to become obedient, and in transcendence lose ourselves—the only way of ever really finding ourselves—we must perhaps see nothing at all extraordinary in obedience, hardly ever think of it reflexly. We should rather think of the Reality which we serve as a matter of course. That Being is worthy of all love and service, because ultimately it is no mere cause, but *the Person*: God. Perhaps the truly obedient man is simply the lover, for whom the sacrifice of self-surrender is sweet and a blessed delight. Perhaps we should not speak so much of obedience, for it is already threatened when we praise or defend it. Either tactic is only meaningful as an encouragement for the young in order to strengthen their wills to embrace in silence a matter-of-course service of God in the Church through a life of prayer and witness. They must learn that this is meaningful even though the heart shudders and the wisdom of this world panics at the thought of losing self in the loss of freedom. The ultimate obedience, that which demands and silently takes everything, will be exacted by God alone. It is the command to die the death which overshadows every minute of our life, and more and more detaches us from ourselves. This command, to move on and to leave all, to allow ourselves in faith to be absorbed in the great silence of God, no longer to resist the all-embracing nameless destiny which rules over to us this command comes to all men. The question, whether man obediently accepts it, is decisive for time and eternity. The whole of religious life grounded in obedience is nothing more than a rehearsal, a practical anticipation of this situation, which more and more envelops human existence. For the religious it is the participation in the death of Christ and the life concealed in Him.

10

Authority and Power in the New Testament*

JOHN McKENZIE, S. J.

Biblical scholarship lies very near the center of the campaign for the *aggiornamento* of the Church and the ecumenical movement. Depending on the point of view of the observer, biblical scholarship is thought to be either the Moses of a new exodus or the Pied Piper of a new Hamelin. We really do not deserve either the credit or the blame which we have received; but we have a modest role in contemporary theological events, and we ought to be aware of our responsibility. Our role is, I think, less modest than one would judge by the number of biblical scholars included among the *periti* of the Second Vatican Council. This illustrates rather well a common conviction that biblical scholarship is a fringe activity tolerated to prevent a greater evil. Biblical scholars are not thought to speak for the Church, nor even in the Church. Most of us, I am sure, can accept our uncertain status graciously and continue to do what we can. And what we can achieve is considerable. The absence of biblical scholars in numbers among the advisers of the Council does not represent the influence of biblical scholarship in the Church; and those who think that biblical scholars do not belong with the *periti* know this.

Our place in the ecumenical movement is large and evident. Most of us have found ourselves more and more frequently engaged in panels and discussion groups with Protestant clergymen and scholars. The reasons for this deserve to be recalled. We deal professionally

* Presidential Address, given at the twenty-seventh general meeting of The Catholic Biblical Association of America, at the Vatican Pavilion, New York's World Fair, on September 1, 1964.

with that theological source which Protestants accept as primary. They believe they can talk with us; they have or think they have a genuine problem of communication with our colleagues in dogmatic theology. More important is the widespread impression that biblical scholarship has become the very model of ecumenical discussion. The consensus of principles and methods of interpretation which exists and the exchange of opinion which flourishes, the free use of literature written by members of different confessions—these have no parallel in other areas of study. Theological ecumenism, if it is to advance at all, must follow the lines laid down by biblical scholarship; so at least many theologians, both Catholic and Protestant, are convinced. In biblical studies we have reached a degree of mutual respect based on candor and communication in a common body of learning which is not yet found elsewhere.

Just as most of us have engaged in ecumenical discussion, so I am sure many of us have found that it is at times embarrassing to have the respect and friendship of Protestants. A witty colleague of St. Vladimir's was kind enough to say in an article published two years ago that he hoped his approval of the theories of some Catholic scholars would not get them in trouble with their own superiors. The remark is partly serious; and I am sure that some of us continue to circulate freely only because Protestant exegetical journals are not widely read in certain ecclesiastical offices. Where ecumenism is thought of as capitulation rather than discussion, it is often believed that a Catholic scholar can win the approval of his Protestant colleagues only by compromising the faith, or at least by compromising *doctrina certa et communis;* and the line between these two doctrinal areas has grown incredibly thin here and there.

As a consequence of exegetical collaboration we are faced with a paradoxical situation; I do not wish to exaggerate its import, but I do not think that it should be entirely ignored. Catholic exegetes, while they move toward a greater consensus with Protestant exegetes, are drifting away from the theological positions held in some Catholic circles. Perhaps the word "position" is too flattering here; we are often puzzled by the problem of how to deal with irrational prejudice and tribal attitudes. I observe that we have had more genuine theological dialogue with Protestants than we have with some segments of Catholic theological opinion. The phenomenon will probably become more disturbing before it ceases to attract attention. The rift does not seem to be growing—if anything, it is narrowing; but it is still there, and every now and then one is astonished to notice how wide and deep it is.

A number of theologians and exegetes have voiced their concern over the relations between theology and exegesis and their desire for a closer integration of the two disciplines, or at least for friendly relations. The existence of this division could easily create a false impression; and this impression, in turn, could hamper exegesis in its work. It is no secret, although no one to my knowledge has published it, that the encyclical *Divino afflante Spiritu* has never been entirely received within the Church. This phenomenon ought to be considered whenever such topics as obedience and devotion to the Holy See are discussed. We know that we cannot afford to dismiss the problems of the relations between theology and exegesis; and I trust we know also that the problems will not be solved by granting control to one theological method.

The Bible, which was once a point of division between Catholics and Protestants, is now becoming a point of union. But the same Bible is still a point of division between Catholic theologians and Catholic exegetes. This is the paradox of the present situation; and we exegetes cannot expect others to resolve the situation for us. The resolution could take the form of a power play which will interdict the most important factor in contemporary biblical interpretation, the free study of biblical questions and the unimpeded discussion of the problems of learning by scholars. Should such an unfortunate development occur, we shall see no more either of the ecumenical movement or of the biblical movement in our generation.

The relations of Catholic exegesis with Protestant exegesis on the one hand and with Catholic theology on the other seem to come to a focus at a single point; and it is to this point that I direct your attention, because it is a point which exegesis has not yet explored. Ecumenical discussions rarely fail to uncover the vital point of division between Catholics and Protestants; it is the problem of authority in the Church. Similarly, the position of Catholic exegesis in the Church is obscure not so much because of anything in exegesis itself or in theology itself as because of some very common and some extremely distorted conceptions of authority in the Church, the same misconceptions which make Protestants hesitate. The discussion may take the form of a study of the structure of the Church, and even of the nature of the Church; or it may deal with the idea of power, or with the relations of obedience and freedom. But in the last analysis it is a single problem with numerous aspects; and this problem deserves the attention of exegetes as much as it deserves the attention of anyone else—assuming, of course, that the nature of power and authority can be legitimately discussed by others than the bearers of authority.

That this problem lies within the area of exegesis should need no explanation; but the number of studies carried on by Catholic exegetes is small enough to permit one to mention the reasons why exegesis should be concerned. The original grant of power and authority to the Church is conferred in the New Testament, and the books of the New Testament show the exercise of power in the apostolic Church. We cannot deny the evolution of power and authority in the Church; this belongs to legitimate doctrinal development as do other theological ideas, and no biblical study of any theological problem can be conducted with the presupposition that legitimate development ends with the apostolic age. But the genuine nature of the power of the Church cannot be seen unless the original state of that power is examined; and the legitimacy of the evolution of power is most clearly perceived in the unity and continuity of power throughout the history of the Church.

It is necessary to insist firmly on the distinction between the nature of authority and the exercise of authority. The nature of authority in any human society is more or less obscured by the practical use of authority; purely theoretical discussions become unreal, and the question of what authority can do is usually and quickly answered by seeing what authority has done. Sacral authority is more liable to be obscured by practice than secular authority because of the sacred character of its personnel. The theoretical implications of the use of sacral authority are closely scrutinized by theologians, who then make these implications a part of the teaching of the Church. They are, of course, no such thing. To base theory upon the actions of men who in their actions are subject to error and to malice is to make it impossible to distinguish between the nature of power and the abuse of power. Power which justifies itself by what it does is absolute and unrestrained. Unless one admits that power can be and has been abused in the Church, no reasonable discussion of the nature of authority is possible. Without this admission, whatever is done is then right because it is done; the agents are by hypothesis incapable of doing anything which is not right.

I spoke of misconceptions of power and of the theological development of the idea of power. Surely one basic misconception touches the development of the idea. For there has really been very little development of the idea of ecclesiastical power for several hundred years. I see no theological development corresponding to the evolution of man in civil society. And I trust no one will say that theological development has never been affected by the evolution of civil society. At the height of the Renaissance, at the moment when the power of the Church was challenged by the Reformers, ecclesiastical power had become a counterpart to secular power and had followed rather than led in the evolution of the idea of power. Both temporal and spiritual power stood as absolutes in their own realms. The subject of a Renaissance prince saw no difference between the power of his prince and the power of his bishop. Both powers were from God, and the subject owed absolute obedience to both. There was no appeal from either absolute except to the other. The theory of civil power was evolved later, principally by revolution; the theory of ecclesiastical power has more or less adhered to the medieval and Renaissance idea of absolute power. It is somewhat strange that only in this area of theology is theoretical evolution inhibited.

But man in civil society is no longer the subject of an absolute Renaissance prince. It would be foolish to suggest that most men in the modern world have achieved stable democratic institutions; it would be historically unsound to assume that democracy itself is a terminal political state. But modern man is wedded to democratic processes for better or for worse, and he has learned to think of himself as a citizen and not as a subject. The members of the Church also have evolved, and this itself is enough to suggest that they may have difficulty in understanding how they are to act when they are confronted with a society which they think is absolute.

In touching upon the abortion of development in the idea of ecclesiastical authority, I risk committing that fault for which we exegetes will surely be rebuked: the fault of talking about things outside the field of interpretation. We have enough trouble vindicating our office of talking about biblical interpretation. Therefore I do no more than suggest this as an interesting area for our colleagues in theology and ecclesiastical history to explore. We exegetes can examine the idea of power and authority in the Bible. A full-scale exploration of this idea would be a book-size job. All that can be done here is to point out a few leads for such a study; this address, if it succeeds, will be the type which is dignified by the term programmatic. A study of authority in the Bible need not be and should not be militantly critical of existing institutions and practices. I observed that we must explore the idea, not the practice; and we are in danger, if we discuss the practice, of speaking about something which we do not know. If what we find is relevant to existing practice, it will be recognized as relevant.

I suggest first that we locate authority and power in the Church within the controlling theme of the New Testament idea of community. It should not be necessary in an assembly of biblical scholars to prove that this controlling theme is love, and that the Church in the New Testament is a community of love before it is anything else. If the Church should arrive at a point where its nature as a community of love is no longer perceptible, then it would lose continuity with the Church of the New Testament. The continuity of the Church need not be more perfect than we can expect in a society of men; the notion has to be flexible. Continuity can be obscured in various periods and in various areas of the Church. Quite clearly the Church has had members and does have members, some of them in official positions, to whom the idea of a community of love comes as a surprise, and perhaps an unpleasant surprise; the existence of such members does not destroy continuity. The Church maintains her identity in spite of her failures to achieve the perfection of love; but we must be concerned with maintaining the primacy of love.

Love is the quality by which the genuine Christian is tested and judged, and no other quality is relevant unless it is a function of love. When I read a letter in a clerical journal in which the writer reaffirms as traditional his conviction that obedience is THE WAY (*sic*), I can only reflect that Father has not been reading the New Testament lately. I know the sources of his conviction, I think, and I know that he, like many others, has mistaken the part for the whole. Unless authority commands in love and the subject obeys in love, we are not dealing with a Christian obedience. And at this point one must risk being banal by recalling that love is directed toward persons, not ideas or objects. Christian obedience is intelligible only as a work of love, not as a substitute for love.

Authority reposes on power; and the power base of authority in the New Testament must be clearly recognized. The number of texts which deal with authority and power is not great, and I think I may be dispensed from treating them here; if any texts have received their due attention in theology, they are the texts on which authority is based. I would like to see the treatment expanded by some other texts not usually found in theses which deal with *potestas ecclesiastica*. These would include the lines which say that the greatest among the disciples should be a child (Mark 9:33-37; Matt. 18:1-5; Luke 9:46-48) and that the disciples should not lord it over one another like the great men and kings of the nations, but that the first among them should be the lackey and the slave of others (Mark 10:42-45; Matt. 20:25-28; Luke 22:24-30). Children and lackeys are not the bearers of power in secular society. What Jesus meant was at least that power and authority in the Church should have no resemblance to secular power and authority. Ecclesiastical power has a different end, and it disposes of different means.

The power base of authority in the New Testament is love, not the power to command or the power to coerce. Had Jesus wished to express dominative and coercive power, the words child and lackey are singularly inept for the purpose. For a practical demonstration of the power of love in action one can usefully study the letters of Paul. The efforts he makes to explain his position to his churches offer an interesting contrast to many communications from modern church offices. He meets the members of his churches person to person, and not through official channels. That they criticized him is evident, and that he took fire at the criticisms is also evident. But he responded to the criticism; it did not occur to him to deny that the members of his churches had a right to criticize. He was much more sensible of his responsibility than he was of his dignity. The only power which he saw in himself was the power which entered the world in Jesus and endures in the Church; it is the power of love which saves. The apostle is expendable; he exists not to be served but to serve, and to give his life as a ransom for the many.

Love has its own way of commanding and its own way of coercing. And it is sadly true that those who do not know it cannot be taught it. The weight of love is far greater than the weight of mere authority, and the response of love is far in excess of the response of obedience. These things seem so obvious that I am almost ashamed to utter them; but why are we so often reminded of our duty of obedience, submission and respect, and so rarely challenged by love? Do we fear the reality of Christian love, or are we deeply aware that we lack it, or are we too self-conscious to admit that it is meaningful to us? And when I speak of the challenge of love, I do not mean exhortations to our duty to love—as if love could be conceived as duty; I mean active love which overpowers the reluctant by the depth of its devotion. The New Testament shows us leadership in love, and it shows us no other type of leadership. Love empowers some members of the Church to occupy hierarchical positions, and it vindicates their management of their office.

A second aspect of power which deserves study is power as the operation of the Spirit. In the New Testament the Spirit by its coming evokes the Church into existence. Every work of the Church is a work of the Spirit, just as every Christian work of the individual members of the Church flows from the dynamism of the Spirit. If authority in the Church is not an operation of the spirit, then it ceases to be authority in the Church; it would no longer be truly Christian leadership. Authority in the Church must be charismatic; its power is not from any human factors of intelligence, experience, or organization, but from the indwelling Spirit which enables the bearers of authority to achieve that which is impossible by merely human means. Charismatic leadership does not make these human qualities unnecessary; but it means that the leaders and the other members of the Church should not depend on the Spirit for that which human qualities can achieve, nor should they depend on human qualities for what is achieved by the Spirit.

St. Paul presents the charismatic Spirit as a unifying principle. There are different gifts, but the same Spirit; and the one Spirit is the one life of the body, whose members fulfill diverse functions in harmony. No member can say of the other members that it does not need them (I Cor. 12:4-31). Not all receive the same gifts, nor should one envy the gifts of another; the gift which all share is the highest of gifts, the gift of love. The gift of authority is completely safeguarded in the Pauline conception; but other gifts are just as carefully safeguarded.

Authority has its proper position as one of the charismatic offices which the Church needs; and without other charismatic offices in the Church authority cannot fulfill its task. The principal of unity is the principal of the Spirit of love, not authority itself. The Spirit belongs to the whole Church and is possessed by each of its members; it is not the privilege of authority alone. Nor is the Spirit, the dynamic principle of life and action in the Church, subject to the authority of the Church. The Spirit can and does act outside the channels of authority.

This introduces us to the relation of authority to the prophetic office in the Church. It is an easy assumption that prophecy as a distinct function has ceased in the Church, or that the prophetic function has been subsumed into the official teaching office. The gift of prophecy is not as clearly described in the New Testament as some other charismata. But it is obvious that the Church needs prophets and has had prophets. It is clear also that the relations of prophets and official leaders have been hostile more frequently than they have been anything else. If there is no prophecy in the Church, then the indwelling Spirit dwells only in the officers of the Church, and the Spirit is under the control of the officers of the Church. Prophecy is the voice of the Spirit which speaks to the officers and to the members of the Church when either officers or other members are unfaithful to their own charisma. No conception of ecclesiastical authority is complete unless it leaves room for the prophetic utterance. Surely the prophetic office deserves serious study; and biblical scholars are better equipped than others to state clearly the place of the prophet in the Church. Perhaps we shall never accept the function of the prophet any more gracefully than it was accepted by the kings and priests of Israel and Judah; but even if the prophet must always be an outsider, the legitimacy of his role in the Church must be affirmed.

For the prophet is the means by which the Spirit protects the Church against corruption; and it takes a prophet to point out that there are other forms of corruption besides concubinage, nepotism and simony. The Church posseses within herself the principle of regeneration; but the authority in the Church does not possess this principle detached from the whole Church. Life is renewed by an exchange between the members. The officer of the Church can indeed receive the prophetic charisma, but he does not receive it in virtue of his office. It must be understood that prophecy is not normal and regular, like other offices in the Church; it is rare and exceptional, and belongs to times of crisis. But prophecy has its place, and it must be recognized as such when it appears. That there are false prophets does not take away the office; popes, bishops and priests have been false to their trust, but this does not take away the clerical offices. The spirit often speaks to the officers of the Church through those whom the officers govern; if the officers do not hear the voice of the Spirit from this source, they will not hear it at all.

Our study of the authority of the Church in the New Testament ought to make it clear beyond dispute that Jesus established something entirely new in the authority which he conferred upon the Church. Authority as a function of love and as an operation of the Spirit has no precedent in societies which existed in Old Testament times or in the Hellenistic world, nor does it appear in social ethics of ancient or modern times. The relations of the officers and of the governed are totally dissimilar to the relations of officers and governed elsewhere. The Church has its own unique end and it has its own unique means of achieving that end. The use of means other than those with which Jesus endowed the Church not only do not advance its end, they may positively retard it. This danger, present in all the activities of the Church, may be peculiarly acute in the area of ecclesiastical authority.

Jesus commissioned his Church to create an entirely new social structure; and this means an entirely new conception of authority and leadership. The Church has indeed created such a structure; and it exists, even if not all the members of the Church nor all her officers are aware of it. The Church is a community of love in which the Spirit dwells. But our realization of the Church is still imperfect. We face the danger that the structure of the Church will take on the forms of secular society and that the Church will employ means proper to secular society. When the Church becomes a power structure, unless that power be the power of love, it takes on a secular character. When coercion replaces inspiration and love, the Church takes on a secular character; it can even take on the unpleasant aspects of the police state. When the officers of the Church dominate the faithful rather than become examples for the flock (I Pet. 5:3), the Church takes on a secular character. I suppose the one thing that is clear from the New Testament description of ecclesiastical leadership is that one person does not impose his will on another. If the members of the Church are not united in that love which makes all seek to serve each other, then coercion and control are no substitute for what is missing.

I said that we must distinguish between the idea of authority and the practice of authority, and I mean to maintain this distinction with no reference to any concrete situation. But one must point out that the new and revolutionary idea of authority which the New Testament discloses is constantly threatened by assimilation to that society which most resembles the Church externally, the political society. I have already alluded to certain assimiliations which have occurred and which can scarcely be denied. The political society is an existing structure for the management of large numbers of people which appears, with certain adaptations, to be well suited to the management of the Church.

In modern times we have in addition the theories of corporation management; and I wonder if it is a tribute to the Church when it is said to meet the standards of good management practice. No doubt the Church must grow with history and live in it; but to yield to creeping secularism in its authority is not to grow with history. To adopt the workings of the political society converts the Church into a power structure. It introduces politics in the vulgar sense of the term, by which I mean the manipulation of people and things in such a way that one gains and keeps office. It means that office is conceived primarily as power over others and as control, not as service, and certainly not as a function of love. The enumeration of the effects of the introduction of political structure could go on and on and could become much more concrete and particular, but this I wish to avoid. All of us are aware of certain realities, unless we have deliberately refused to recognize them. We may not be as well aware of our duty in these realities, and of our resources. Exegetes have little to say; but they can study the power and authority of the Church in the New Testament, and they can present their conclusions as studies of theological sources which never lose their value. They are as relevant now as at any time in the life of the Church.

11

Reverence for the Individual as an Expression of the Divine Mind and Will

JOHN NAVONE, S.J.

"No one who does not act uprightly or does not love his brother is a child of God. For the message you have heard from the beginning is this: 'We must love one another.' "[1] This is one of many instances in which the sacred writers insist on the love of others as a prerequisite for salvation. Jesus insisted that we must love our enemies, do good to those who hate us and seek reconciliation with others before offering sacrifice.

Jesus' insistence that we love every man was not an arbitrary discipline for his followers, but has its roots deep in metaphysical reality. The hatred and utter rejection of any man implies the hatred and rejection of God Himself; whereas our acceptance and love of others unites us, in some way, with God.

The mystery of the "I" in its uniqueness and myterious depths has never been appreciated so keenly as in our own day. And, if it has, this appreciation has had scarcely sufficient repercussions in theology and asceticism. It would be undeniably beneficial that a reaction should set in to force us to recognize the importance of this dimension of reality. For a great source of boredom with the spiritual life, and life in general, is the loss of the sense of wonder and awe which proceeds from the partial loss of the true image of man. Wonder at his own marvellous origin and nature, and the worship which this wonder impels, are what nourish the psyche of man. Boredom is subjective. Life is not boring, *we* have become bored.

God possesses within Himself a plan for all that He causes; otherwise, He would not know what He was doing. God is Intelligence itself and is in no way ignorant of what He is causing. Consequently, there exists within the divine mind an intelligible plan for every man that exists, and this is called a divine idea.[2]

God, therefore, has an idea of me. God *is* thinking of me and *is* willing that I exist. I am not existing here and now by chance, and no one is forcing God to think of me and will my existence; but He freely and intelligently expresses Himself by my existence, so to speak. The deepest relationship between myself and God is not one of resemblance or of difference, but this "existential" relationship which is one that is strictly speaking impossible to define. My existence is that act by which I am both made present and present myself before God. And thus I am at once distinguished from God and turn towards God, adhering to Him as to the Source on which I depend. This relationship, once grasped, can follow out two divergent paths within me, that of love or of hate, that of confident adoration or of rebellious pride.

If someone should, therefore, hate me, he is implicitly turning away from God. He is hating what God thinks and loves. How, then, can such a man say he loves God? If he wills that I did not exist, and turns in aversion from me, his will is diametrically opposed to God's will and providence.

This depth of personal subjectivity includes all that is unique, irreplaceable, and incommunicable in my consciousness and the exercise of my liberty. The existential values of subjective distinctiveness must be appreciated by every Christian. My consciousness of myself —not as the knowledge of a particular object which happens to be me, but as the absolutely incommunicable presence of the "I"—is not nothing. In one sense, it is everything, since the universe of objects exists for me only through it. The "I" which thinks existence, the act whereby I think it, the liberty which takes sides with respect to it, all that is most interior and most singular in my personal attitude—is existence. And the idea of existence is a "mystery" which cannot be made perfectly clear. It is a mystery which Gabriel Marcel described as "a question which encroaches on its own data."

I originate in mystery and my existence is mysterious. Despite the depths of my self-knowledge, I cannot hope to know myself perfectly because I am not causing my own existence in its fullness. The truth of my existence implies, firstly, that as a creature I correspond with the archetypal creative thought of God, in a correspondence which formally constitutes the truth of my existence. Secondly, I can speak of the truth which other men know about me. Their knowledge is true insofar as it corresponds to the objective reality which is myself. No man, including myself, can properly grasp the correspondence between the original pattern of myself in God and the created copy. The relationship between myself and the creative mind of God, in which the truth of my being primarily and properly consists, and which in its turn first renders human knowledge of myself possible, is the root cause of my mysterious inscrutability as well as my knowability.

The relationship on which the truth of my being is fundamentally based, the relation between my existence and the archetypal creative thought of God, cannot be known formally by any man. Someone may know me, but he cannot formally know my *truth,* of which his knowledge is a certain effect. The common root of my paradoxical knowability and unknowability is in my createdness: the truth that the design, the archetypal pattern of myself dwells within the Divine Logos. It is my origin in the Logos which makes me knowable, partaking wholly of the nature of the Logos with a lucidity and limpidity that extends to the very depths of my intelligibility. But because of this origin in the Logos, my existence mirrors an infinite light and can therefore not be wholly comprehended. It is not darkness or chaos which makes my existence unfathomable, but rather an abyss of *light,* which overwhelms the limited capacities of the human intellect. My unknowability does not denote something in itself dark and impenetrable, but only something that has so much light that a particular finite faculty of knowledge cannot absorb it at all. It is too rich to be assimilated completely; it eludes the effort to comprehend it, because the knowability of Being, which we are attempting to transform into knowledge, consists in its being creatively thought by the Creator. Hence the reality of the individual is unfathomable and mysterious and should urge us not so much to communication as to awe and wonder. But it would not be a wonder of resignation or despair. It would be the awe of reverence.

As we have seen, if God communicates Himself by calling me forth into existence in His presence, then I must pre-exist within God in some manner. But it would not be adequate to conceive this in terms of the mere pre-existence of my image in a model. For the model contains my image only insofar as the later resembles it, whereas God causes me in my totality. Hence He must contain me according to all that I am, according to my very subjectivity, the very aspect which opposes me irreducibly to Himself. What else can this mean than that I am present to God in the only manner in which it is possible for me, as other, to be present, namely according to the mode of thought and love? It is by a love which is God Himself. Nothing has been added thereby to His existence. My Creator, precisely because he precontains within Himself all other acts of existence, every man according to his subjective depth, cannot be conceived save as an absolute Love. "God is love." And thus the metaphysics of existence squares in its own way with the intuition of the apostle of love.

Everything is present to God in the single grasp He has of Himself. God can never be an object to Himself. God does not know me as an object, but rather I am present to God in my lucid subjectivity in the simple act whereby God is present to Himself, present, needless to say, as subject. Though I am present as other, as distinct from God, this does not make me an object, because my "otherness" is transparent to God, who project me as other, to be other. Thus I am closer and more transparent to God than to myself, whether as a creature or an adopted son. And, secondly, since my personal presence to God, which, willed, gives me existence, there is no opposition in God between presence and actuation. When God is causing, it is a person who is causing.

Fr. David Burrell, in his article,[3] "Indwelling: Presence and Dialogue," asserts that this personal grasp which God has of us is nothing less than our salvation, unless we sin in that terrible refusal to be human. Our salvation is accomplished and revealed by Christ—not in such a way was to preclude our co-operation, as though eternity were some static, impoverished state before history. Eternity comprehends time in an ever-present now, so that the will and achievement of our salvation is contained in the eternal act whereby the Trinity redeems us. This is why, Fr. Burrell continues, that the essence of the indwelling of the Trinity in the souls of the just is their presence to God from all eternity. This fact does not deny the reality of their created response. The dialogue is constituted by an eternal act which in no way compromises the fact of a dialogue. The created response of the individual is real even though it adds nothing to eternal love. The explanation of this dialogue begins with the truth of God's personal love for the individual which God Himself has revealed. The very truth of this revelation demands an external term in the individual loved. It is a created, contingent term, because God's eternal love terminates in history. The beginning of God's dialogue with a person at a given point in history does not indicate something new in God, but rather in the person. It is through this created term that the person loved may personally verify God's love for him and respond to it.[4] What constitutes the indwelling and dialogue of God with the person is not the created term—the temporal expression of eternal love, the created effect of uncreated presence—but the eternal mission of the Holy Spirit. It is not the fact of arriving that marks the mission as personal to the Holy Spirit, but the fact of being sent. Our presence to God from eternity constitutes our union with Him. But if this presence is to be personal, we must be known and loved by each Person according as He is God and distinct: to the Father as initiator, to the Son as the means of our salvation, the perfect witness of this loving initiative, and to the Spirit as sanctifier. The divine missions are coeternal with the processions and imitate them. Just as the personal, enduring acceptance of the other that *is* love does not dispense with but rather calls forth concrete expression, so the union willed and worked by God elicits in man a created term, an instrumental power whereby he may recognize the reality of union, express this recognition, and through this expression grow in intimacy with God Himself, who has eternally and personally loved and accepted him.

Despite the awesome significance of the individual, He exists not only for Himself, but also for others. They see Him, hear Him and even with regard to what escapes them he can communicate to them by language a knowledge which already extends quite far. Furthermore, he does not gain full self-confidence and assurance except through the opinion which others have of him. Aristotle noted this point well. In order to *be* truly in our own eyes, we need to know that we are accepted and supported by our equals. Our reason would be in grave danger if everything around us proclaimed our non-existence. And yet the knowledge of others reaches us only from without. There is always the inner fortress of our own inviolable intimacy, but this would vanish into illusion were it no authenticated by the divine Thought and in some way an object of this Thought.

Gabriel Marcel, in his *Philosophy of Existence*, graphically describes the role of others in keeping us in contact with reality. Marcel holds that each one of us becomes the center of a sort of mental space arranged in concentric zones of decreasing interest and participation. It is as though each one of us secreted a kind of shell which gradually hardened and imprisoned him; and this sclerosis is bound up with the hardening of the categories in accordance with which we conceive and evaluate the world. Fortunately, he continues, it can happen to anyone to make an encounter which breaks down the framework of this egocentric topography; "I know from my own experience how, from a stranger met by chance, there may come an irresistible appeal which overturns the habitual perspectives just as a gust of wind might tumble down the panels of a stage set." What had seemed near becomes infinitely remote and what had seemed distant seems to be close. It is an experience which leaves Marcel with a bitter taste, an impression of sadness and almost of anguish; yet he believes it is beneficial, for it shows us all that is contingent and artificial in the crystallized pattern of our personal system. For Marcel it is, above all, the sanctity realized in certain men which reveals to us that what we call the normal order is, from a higher point of view, from the standpoint of a soul rooted in ontological mystery, merely the subversion of an order which is its opposite. In this connection, the study of sanctity with all its concrete attributes seem to Marcel to offer an immense speculative value and the true introduction to ontology.

In so far as every man is the effect of God's thought and will, he embodies a special facet of reality and a mysterious truth which we can never completely comprehend. He is the correlative of a divine idea and love. My encounter with him enables me to establish, however obliquely, a contact with the mind and will of God. In knowing and loving him, I am knowing and loving this particular expression of God's love and knowledge; and thus God and I are united in both loving and knowing the same object. And thus I reverence every man for that sacred quality which enables me to commune with my Creator. Through each man God is revealing Himself in an inimitable way, for He never creates the same man twice.

In proportion to their existence, God loves all creatures. He hates no man, for without His love and thought even the damned would cease to exist. The real tragedy of sin and damnation lies in the fact that God is loving a man who has turned away from Him, knows of God's love, but has become incapable of returning this love.

Every man is called into existence at a particular time and to a particular milieu. Consequently, a man not only evokes our reverence for what he is in himself, but also for the special and mysterious purpose for which divine Wisdom has created him. The Creator is always thinking of the good of the universe with the creation of each man, intending that the universe will be a better place because of this man's particular role in it.[5] All creation benefits by this particular act of creation whereby I am initiated on my special mission. The universe derives a particular good from this mysterious mission on which I alone have been sent.

A fully distinct idea of this individual mission would involve nothing less than the exhaustive knowledge of all existents in their unity as well as in their distinctions and interactivity, a knowledge in which the most minute details, and the most individual particularities, and the most intimate secrets would be exposed in full light and grasped in a single look.[6] A knowledge which would see the effect of my every action, my very presence, on all creation; which would see how I was related to every other existent in the universe and would influence them as a pebble generating concentric ripples in the center of a vast surface of water. Now such an adequate and concrete idea of existents does exist in the Word of God. And all the progress of human thought tends but to the one goal of imitating in the least imperfect way possible this inaccessible ideal. Only in the Word of God is my mission understood in its totality.

Paul Claudel seems to have grasped the special Providence governing each individual and its relation to himself, when he wrote:

> The second of the great Commandments enjoins us to love our neighbor as ourself. This is called solidarity. That means there is not a single one of those people whom chance puts in our way and proposes to us, with whom we do not have everything in common, and with whom we do not inherit, as children of God, a certain indivisibility. Providence made them holders of a part of our own destiny, depositaries of a certain amount of possibilities. *They bring us something from Providence, a pass word.* It is worthwhile to look at this fellow, to study him, to understand him, and more-

over, to try him. With him he brings something we needed and also something for which our help is needed, an action from both of us for which the time has come. But I am aware of the business he came to consult us on, without realizing it, and for which he submits his files in bulk, and the matter at hand is none else than his eternal salvation and mine along with it. Yes, the leathery faced peasant, the alcoholic, the timid and cantankerous bourgeois who looks like the fat dog of the concierge, the business woman with the awful gaze putting lipstick on her widened lips, are our brothers and sisters. Jesus Christ died for them. There is a star deeply hidden within that flesh, more deeply driven in than the legal coin in the carp of Gennesaret. It is a long distance between heaven and earth, and the adventure that leads all those obscure figures to me would take a long time to tell. But there is no gainsaying it.[7]

Only in the Word of God is my existential significance fully known and appreciated. In God I am known and loved more than I could ever know and love myself. In His knowledge and love, my existence assumes an infinite significance. Who could say that what God has known and loved from all eternity is insignificant and meaningless? This was the clown's beautiful message in *La Strada* when he assures a distraught, feeble-minded girl that her life has a very special providence and purpose. To deny this fact would be to deny the existence of God himself. It would be asserting that Intelligence had acted irrationally in creating a particular existent without a particular purpose.

The same reverence for the individual that Federico Fellini had expressed so poignantly in *La Strada* has been stated in its theological and philosophical dimensions by St. Thomas: *"Every creature is nothing other than an objective expression and representation of what is contained in the concept of the divine Word."*[8] Again, St. Thomas asserts that "Knowledge and will mean that the thing known is in the knower and the thing loved is in the lover. Thus according to knowledge and will, things are more in God than God is in things";[9] "We know that everything done by God dwells in Him as known, so it follows that all created things are in Him as in the divine life."[10]

This wisdom of St. Thomas was deeply rooted in the revelation of Christ which had added a new meaning to human life. The world of Aquinas was a deeply personalist world characterized by the interpenetration of the sacred and the profane, the secularization of the sacred and the sacralization of the profane. This deeply religious age keenly appreciated symbols, for all knowledge of God is analogous and mediated. There is an opposition between what is mediated—"a spade is a spade"—and what is beyond it. This is obscure, and we do not know it properly.

The medieval man reverenced the individual within the framework of order and mystery. The old wisdom of the middle ages discovered order everywhere. Order represented the clear and intelligible building up of reality, as well as the teaching which reflected that reality; it represented the satisfaction enjoyed by the mind in surveying and penetrating the pattern of life, as well as the ways of life which can be trodden and followed by its thought. The individual was embraced by this order established by God and leading to God. It was the wise man who could see the basic order of the universe: "The wise man knows that things have been made and ordered by God, and that, as a consequence, things are hierarchized by their relations to their Ultimate End Who is God."[11] The Wisdom of a loving God has ordered all things, and every man to Himself.

But the wisdom of the middle ages also recognized mystery. Anyone who did not see this world, apparently explained with the utmost clarity of reason in the *Summa,* surrounded on all sides by mystery did not do justice to Aquinas. Not only did mystery limit the penetrability of reality, but order itself was interwoven and crossed by mystery. And it was not only mystery in the theological sense, likewise flowing through every part of the world, which eluded us. No, the boundary between order and mystery passed through the world itself and the lives of every individual.

Two mentalities have clashed throughout history. They may be described as that of the "old wisdom" and the "new knowledge." The confrontation, dramatically recorded in the clash between Plato and the Sophists, is basically between religious and moral men on the one hand and antireligious, immoral rationalizers, on the other; between the philosophy of truth and the rhetoric of slogans and "isms"; between the man who integrates new events with religion and morality and the man who seizes upon these events to destroy or discredit religion and morality; between men for whom the ultimate is God and those for whom it is themselves. In this essay, the clash is, more specifically, that between the religious and moral viewpoint of the historical Judeo-Christian tradition and the positivist mentality which rejects it on the basis of new scientific knowledge.

Today, the many who have exchanged the old wisdom for a new enlightened existence, or perhaps have never even heard of the old wisdom, find reality staggeringly impersonal. Economy becomes a philosophy of life, statistics are ethics and knowledge is power. For the human heart there is no peace on earth. At least, the old wisdom had offered a good way to live and a good way to die, a way in which a man's being and doing was rooted in a personal God who fortified and enriched him with that wisdom which existed before the beginning of time.

We live today in a scientific culture through which the elements of modern science have filtered, unevenly, incompletely, with results good and bad, but so marked that they characterize the whole unmistakably. It is a culture in which art and science—the two remaining idols of the tribe—stand unchallenged as institutions that a man can give his life to and feel pride in. The state is considered a fraud; religion, a private hobby; the reality of love is doubted; life itself is frequently repudiated.

Modern science is that body of rules, instruments, theorems, observations and conceptions with which modern man manipulates nature in order to grasp its workings. These ideas, symbols and apparatus form the subject matter of the so-called pure sciences. But the word scientific is often applied loosely to things non-scientific such as an advertiser's latest product. Our scientific culture owes its character as much to the derivations of science as to the rigorous core. Just as there were few Aquinases in the religious culture of the middle ages, there are few Einsteins in the scientific culture of modern times. While the spreading of theological truth was the highest aim of that age, the spreading of scientific truth is the highest aim of our age.

The common man has acquired an unquestioning respect for science, although it is largely unintelligible, even to the educated. For the positivistic mind, science is an absolute. In this respect, science is in the saddle and rides modern man. This unsynthetic mentality views the knowledge of the positive sciences as the only true knowledge; everything else is a matter of mere opinion, until it is authenticated by the method of the positive sciences. The positive sciences represent the "new" knowledge, which ushers in a new way of human life in which the "old wisdom" has become obsolete and meaningless. Marxists, Scandinavian Socialists and many leftist liberals subscribe to this thesis; they are antitraditional on nearly every level. Traditional wisdom is dismissed as "bourgeois," in the case of morality, and as "superstitution," in the case of religion. Even where the scientific cast of mind has not led to atheism or Marxism, it tends to suppress the personal and individualistic by its insistence on method. Method supplies assurance, persuasion, and perpetual self-correction.

On the other hand, the scientific civilization supported in authority by technology, leaves the individual puzzled, if not paralyzed in the exercise of his judgment. The lack of practice in judgment, the fear of doing something outside one's specialty, the belief that judgments can or will be handed down ready-made by some infallible agency, leads to a statistical living—or counting before you think—that postpones judgment. The individual ventures to express his views after discovering that they square with the findings of the pools. The faculty of judgment is impaired by the ritual of accuracy demanded at every turn. Factual error becomes a mortal sin with the concentration on minutiae established as the universal law emanating from the laboratory.[12]

With its stress on minutiae, science frequently engenders a cast of mind found in the counting-house, in the keeping of precise books and balanced accounts. Balancing accounts of energy and mass becomes the book-keeping of science. With counting-house virtues, science can turn out tremendous results with lesser minds working as an organized group. It is a mind which desires to see and count everything, which regards the numerical as objective and the personal as useless. Numerical support transforms the useless, untruthworthy, subjective views of a man into valuable, reliable, objective fact. Without the old wisdom how does modern man maintain his ability to distinguish between big and little things?

The multiplication of social sciences follows from the multiplication of sciences. Man's behavior, it is assumed, is governed by physical laws. Therefore, we have behavioral science based on the visible, measurable facts of human action. In the study of man the inner is separated from the outer self, excluding the subjective element from the material studied. Society is dependent on common action and must measure human desires, actions and responses. Personal impressions are useless. What counts are numerical facts. What is material can be known scientifically: it can be measured and is governed by physical laws and is, therefore, subject to prediction and control. By ruling out the subjective as unmanageable, science rules out a man's personality. Scientific systems neglect man's will with the assumption that a man must follow scientific postulates like the interaction of particles in a lab. Without the balancing effects of wisdom, reality becomes unbearably impersonal, and the subject of man becomes a playground for mathematics.

Science has also established the cult of research. Teachers race for distinction in the field of research. Seeking for truth is the only honorable life. The search for new truths is over-rated to the detriment of the transmission of truth, which is more important. The newest becomes the truest, and the past is slighted and disregarded.

The obsession with minutiae, the new, the objective and impersonal, the numerical, creates an atmosphere in which the individual is no longer seen as the framework of order and mystery, is no longer reverenced as the expression of the divine mind and will, and no longer feels in harmony with a world that was made for him.[13]

The new knowledge has helped man to overcome his fear of God. With his new freedom and independence, man won anxiety. He dreads being alone and grows old with the horrible sensation of having passed the peak and of looking down at the shadowy exit. With his own wit he has created his own world, and on the seventh day, he finds it good-for-nothing—but bungling. He has created chaos, and has said "let there be darkness"; now his anguished spirit hovers over the void.

God is not hiding, yet this man cannot find Him. He cannot hear God because he is too noisy. He cannot see God, because he is too enlightened. He never really discovers what he is looking for, yet he despises the old wisdom which refreshes the human spirit and give a freedom of soul less boisterous, less forced.

This is the man for whom reality is primarily a question of things: status, money, amusements, cars and clothes. Life is identified with things; death is followed *nothing*. To die means to be without *things*. Persons, too, become things when friends are reduced to "contacts." Reality is only a concatenation of events, a vast complexus of things, occasionally relieved or heightened by "kicks." And even that God who had once left the ancient Hebrews breathless, now becomes reduced in the popular imagination to a kind of immobile diamond out there in the blue.

It is not so paradoxical, then, that with three billion people contributing to a so-called population explosion, one major complaint of our times is loneliness, isolation and the inability to communicate. A southern friend put the problem concretely: "New York is a city of feet: New Yorkers walk about looking at their feet and never at one another."

Thornton Wilder's *Our Town* gave the problem of depersonalization dramatic universality when Emily returns from the dead to relive her twelfth birthday with her family, a day which she had thought her happiest:

> Oh, Mama, just look at me one minute as though you really saw me. Mama, fourteen years have gone by. I'm dead. But just for a moment now we're all together. Mama, just for a moment we're happy. *Let's look at one another.*

Broken-hearted, Emily returns to the dead. All had gone by so quickly, and they never had the time to look at one another. They had never realized all that had been going on.

In a depersonalized universe, the man confronting mystery seeks for an explanation in science, a philosophical system, or even a mystique. Turning away from the old wisdom of Augustine and Aquinas, the Renaissance looked to art, the Enlightenment to reason, and the Twentieth Century to science for the ultimate answers.

According to the old wisdom, however, reality is personal. The only adequate explanation of all reality is found in a Person, not in a philosophical system, science or a mystique. For the men of the old wisdom, reality originates and terminates in a Person, the personal God of Job, the three Persons of the Trinity revealed by the Son of God. The significance of every existent is personal in a world where everything exists for man and man exists for God.

No philosophical system completely explains a universe that is, in one sense, only half created. The totality of reality is never present to our consciousness, but only to that of the three divine Persons. All that the Father knows and loves, He expresses in His Word, God the Son. Thus, the full significance, expression and understanding of all reality is found only in a Person. In comprehending His own personal, triune reality as externally imitable and in willing that His personal perfections be actually imitated, God brings into existence the totality of created reality. Whatever exists is, therefore, personal in its intelligibility, goodness, beauty, and significance; and has a special role to play in a personal universe filled with the mystery of an incomprehensible Person who reveals Himself through His creatures.

Confronted with mystery, the Christian accepts a person as the answer to the riddle of the universe. He accepts Jesus Christ as the personal, concrete expression of an essentially transcendent, personal mystery. He is the person, together with the Father and Holy Spirit, who is the ultimate reality behind every reality, through whom, with whom and in whom all that is exists. He is the Alpha and the Omega from whence all reality originates and for whom it exists. Reality is personal. It is *for* a person. It is His Kingdom, the Kingdom of Reality, as opposed to the Kingdom of illusion, make-believe, deception, lies and what is not.

The old wisdom teaches us that we encounter *the* Person in other persons. St. Augustine had said that we err in looking for God in the sky rather than in our neighbor. If God were in the sky, the birds would be closer to Him than ourselves. In the presence of another, we stand before the fingertips of God. We stand before someone of whom God *is* thinking, *is* loving, *is* willing to exist. *This* person is someone for whom there is a special mission in the universal plans of a mysterious Providence, known only to God. He has not come into the world by accident! To reject or ignore this person is to reject what God thinks and loves. It is to reject an occasion for learning more about *the* Person, more about God's thoughts and loves and the special way He communicates Himself to us in a concrete, personal act of divine friendship. This is the old wisdom of which St. John writes: "How can be who does not love his brother, whom he sees, love God, whom he does not see?" Can we say we love God, if we do not love His reflection?

Had not St. Paul and St. Thomas taught that the purpose of all law is the establishment of friendship, either between man and man, or between man and God. St. Paul[14] and St. Thomas[15] agreed that the whole Law was summed up in the one commandment, "You must love your neighbor as yourself." Salvation came through friendship with God and man.

The old wisdom taught that the sight of God constituted our eternal happiness, and that it does not start after death, but now . . . even though in a mirror darkly. We are on the way to happiness, to *the* Person, *the* Friend, when we begin to see and love Him in other persons. The surest index of our knowledge and love of God is our loving response to His personal images, those finite reflections of His infinite personality, which mirror in a unique, incommunicable way a facet of the Divine Person. It is as if God had created this person to tell us something special about Himself which only this person and no other shall ever express.

The old wisdom taught us respect for things, even a glass of cold water. But this respect was personal: the glass of water was to be given to a person by a person in the name of a Person. It was very clear that things were for persons. Consequently, it was wrong for persons to become preoccupied or obsessed with things in themselves: large surpluses of grain, pieces of silver and costly perfumes.

The old wisdom taught us to make a loving response to the goodness and truth we found in every person, even our enemies.[16] And we did this because of *the* Person whose reality, goodness and truth was expressed in this person. Neither was there any personal loss or degradation in the service of other persons, because *the* Person had been, and still is as we believe, in our midst as one who served. Aquinas had taught that God loved even those in Hell. Their Hell, however, was in not being able to love God, in that unintelligible refusal to be human, to receive *the* Person who alone communicates the power to become a son of God.

If to be made in the image and likeness of God meant that human activity works in the likeness of the divine, then the life of the three divine Persons furnished the motive and pattern for friendship. To become perfect as our heavenly Father, meant that we, too, must live a life of self-communication, self-giving and friendship with God and man. It was a life of openness to others, freely giving what we had freely received. The Trinity was the key to understanding friendship: three distinct Persons living the same life, communicating in the same thought and love in an eternal act of perfect self-communication and identity of being in an eternal presence, dialogue and loving responsiveness to the eternal truth of the other.

The old wisdom ruled out isolation and alienation. It was not good for a person to be alone. To "pray always" was an invitation to communicate always. We were to open our minds and hearts for a dialogue with God whom we recognized in His myriad images. To these images, often the hungry, the thirsty and the naked, we were to manifest the loving face of God. If the shadow of any momentary sparrow could be a message from the Sun, perhaps the smile of any person could tell another that Love exists and loves us.

The old wisdom would not have been very consoling if it had not taught that the world was created, sustained and redeemed by a Person who is also a Friend. The human heart only rejoices when *the* Person reveals in His Word[17] that He is love and loves us, and brings it to the realization that the loving self-communication of God—of *the* Person—creates, sustains and redeems the world.

Unfortunately, in this whole matter of persons and friendship with their perfection in self-communication through the sharing of thoughts, hope and loves, the new, enlightening knowledge deceived us. It taught us to live as if persons were merely side-issues or incidents to the main problems of life. Yet the truth of the old wisdom was that we lived our lives for persons. They are the goals not the means. Through the friendship of persons, the Divine Person intends that all men become His sons. Comradeship and serious joy with persons are not interludes in our travels, but rather our travels are interludes in comradeship and joy which through God shall endure forever.[18]

The new knowledge is the spirit of eternal dissatisfaction which forever cries out for new experience, but seeks only. It is the forceful restless surge for sensations, pleasure and status which produces a fun culture both egocentric and dehumanizing. But that wisdom which is older than Job taught us how to hold on to things with open hands. A Personal Friend had given and He had taken away, bless be the Person, my Friend.

The new knowledge teaches us to say, "No, with thunder!" The old wisdom taught, "Thy will be done," "Be it done unto me according to Thy Word" (a Word which was both a person and a Friend, to whom we lovingly acquiesced). A destructive New Order based on dangerous new knowledge proclaimed the expediency of exterminating six million persons; but the Old Order, eternally creative with the eternal generation of the Son, created man and the world, a personal world. The new knowledge engendered disgust for a world that seemed one dark kingdom of absurdity; the old wisdom evoked complacency with the realization that the universe is ultimately intelligible. The new knowledge affirmed the enormous emptiness and anguish of the human spirit in the absence of God as the ineluctable status quo. The old wisdom led the person to an abiding faith in the Second Person, the Incarnate Word who alone explained the totality of reality which, like an iceberg, is nine-tenths hidden from us in mystery. The new knowledge taught men to fret and to reject; the old wisdom helped them to achieve a delightful tranquillity in the knowledge of the good that is, and gave them power to joy in its being.

The old wisdom is really the Eternal Wisdom, not just an idea but a Person . . . whom we know and lovingly accept as Jesus. The Eternal Wisdom is not a cold abstract concept, but a Person revealed to us in both Old and New Testaments. Reality is personal because it has been fashioned according to that Eternal Wisdom which has existed even before the world began. In Christ Jesus, Eternal Wisdom has become flesh and no longer calls us servants but friends. In Him, Eternal Wisdom reveals to us that it is a person, and that this person is the Way, the Truth and the Life. The Way, the Truth and the Life are a person, they are Jesus. Goodness, beauty and love are not mere abstractions; they are ultimately a Person—"God is love." God can, therefore, be found in all things and all things are personal, for all the goodness, truth, beauty and reality of the universe are an actual, created participation in the perfection of a beneficent, self-communicating Person who delights to dwell among the children of men.

Christ is "the wisdom of God,"[19] "in whom are all the treasures of wisdom and knowledge hidden."[20] Many of the Greek Fathers, following the tradition of St. Paul, used "Wisdom" as a synonym for the Incarnate Word or Logos. Wisdom is the gift of the Holy Spirit. God is Wisdom and has manifested His wisdom in the person of Jesus Christ. In giving us Christ, God has given us His Wisdom.

The wisdom of the believer consist in recognizing the Wisdom of God manifsted in the history of salvation, and to confess the mystery of God, "of Christ, in whom are all the treasures of wisdom and knowledge hidden." This was the old wisdom which enlightened the soul in search of *the* Person to speak with, to love and be loved by. This ancient wisdom is not what once was, but what has always been and will always be. And many are aware of its beauty who have never been to school. The new men of the Renaissance—to paraphrase Hermann Gressieker's *Royal Gambit*—turned their backs on the old wisdom and learned to cross the oceans in daring curiosity, and where they searched for India, they conquered a new world. The new knowledge, whether of the Renaissance, Enlightenment or Modern Times, is to keep crossing the oceans again and again, and to keep forever searching for the new beyond the ocean. But the old wisdom—is the ocean!

12

Evangelical Prayer

LOUIS LOCHET

Every moment of our existence is intimately connected with our own personal background, and in a sense, with the history of the whole world. This can be seen on a very human level: Our passions, desires, reactions, temperaments, etc., are all rooted in that past, near and remote, the humus of which is formed by the entire range of historical events. We are not free to snap off these links with the past. Rather we must delve into history, take on the role of the past, and consciously strive to redirect its outcome. Even if we regret the past, this should not lead us to break with it, but rather to abandon ourselves totally to its betterment in the future.

We can see how this applies even more on a supernatural level for our life of prayer. The Gospels tell us: "Pray constantly. Never cease . . ." (Luke 18:1; cf I Tim. 2:8; Luke 21:36) and we say to ourselves: "Pray all the time? That is impossible. I simply do not have the time." This answer, given by everyone, is rather simple and seems quite reasonable and decisive. Perhaps however we should examine it a bit more closely. Have we not somehow misunderstood this apparent incompatibility of the evangelical call and our concrete way of living? Is this call really incompatible with a man's work or a woman's housework? It would not be the first time that a too literal interpretation of the Lord's words has led to a stumbling block. When Jesus spoke to Nicodemus about being reborn, Nicodemus asked how it was possible for an old man to re-enter his mother's womb. The danger for us is much more serious than it was for that wise old sage of Israel who waited for a reply from the Lord. We are like those invited to the feast in the Gospel. We have found good and rational excuses. One cannot deny that there are other things to do in life besides pray. But perhaps this simple call to prayer has a meaning which has escaped us all, one that we do not want to hear. However, we were made for just that purpose. There was life, there was joy—and the Master sees us leave to become preoccupied with our own ambitions. And with a heavy heart He follows those who have not followed Him.

Perhaps we should ask ourselves if, when we do pray, our *prayers* are worthy enough to offer Him. Are they what He actually expects? Not that they are evil or offered in bad faith; but do they express the authentic idea of the evangelical call to prayer? Perhaps they are anachronistic; perhaps they are prayers from another age—half-pagan prayers that have not yet become fully *evangelized.* We Christians must realize that for a long time after baptism we remain semipagan, especially in our customs. The grace of Christ must penetrate slowly, like the chrism on the forehead of a new Christian, to transform lives that have become encrusted by our human actions and reactions. This is also true of prayer. Prayer is simply another expression of our total life before God.

We must, then, look seriously into the demands and dimensions of evangelical prayer to discover its true meaning. It is at this level that we should set our prayers, and it is toward this maturity that we should grow. Not that we can change our method of praying in an instant, but we can begin to direct it to its proper perspective and allow the Spirit of Jesus to help us. For, once having cut the path, we can easily see our whole life in its proper place. Anyone can squeeze a few prayers into a life that remains outside the meaning of the Scriptures, but one cannot live a life of prayer, as the Gospels invite us to, if our human, this-world life is the center of our existence. With the grace of Christ we can really direct our life toward a total abandonment to the meaning of the Gospels, through a life of faith and love.

In a very real sense, there is no more beautiful prayer than that of a child. At five, one can pray one's best. Why? Because our prayers are total. They are totally us. A child's prayer is so pure, so simple-so beautiful that even the most indifferent person is shaken at the child's expectation to see God. A child's prayer is not scheming, nor tainted by sin. It is not complicated by deep reflection. It goes straight from the child to the God he loves, and it is to Him that the child you will not enter the Kingdom of Heaven" (Matt. 18:3).

But, the Gospels emphasize, one cannot remain a child and live an incomplete adult life, for then the forces of evil and the world would never be faced, and the person would not be formed by making individual choices. To continue to dwell in complete naivété and the carefree joys of childhood right through adulthood would result in infantilism.

There is one constant element throughout life. Beyond any of life's experiences, beyond all interests and desires, beyond the difficult submission to God's Will, beyond tormenting pain, the boredom of work, the suffering of defeats, beyond the experience of pain, sin, suffering, hate, beyond all this—we are still in search of a new simplicity. This peace of mind is above and beyond a full adult life. It is a peace that has given everything to the Father. It is also the filial trust of a child. But this total abandon, this gift of ourselves is also weighted down with the deeds of an entire lifetime. This unity, which rules the soul and which is expressed in prayer before God, is no longer the childlike simplicity of a child who has not yet experienced struggle and who does not realize the full meaning of these words: *I love you above all else.* This regained unity is above and within man's actions and passions, reuniting them in a single effort that will draw everything together in the thrust of his return to the Father.

Between the infantile prayers of the very young, who give everything they touch a remarkable simplicity, because they do not know what they are giving, and the unified prayers of adults giving their all, not only once a day in words, but moment by moment in all their actions, because love has unified their whole life—between these two points, we must strive toward the latter.

It is, in effect, like cutting the apron strings, like growing up to become involved in the world. We must form a strong relationship with all the good around us, with people, with the world. All our interests, pleasures, work, distractions, should bring us closer to God, not push us further away. If it does the latter, our prayers become lost, unprotected, smothered in a world that has thrown away the invitation to God.

WHAT SEPARATES US FROM GOD

We must shut ourselves off from the world in order to fly freely into the sky and sing with the psalmist: Blessed be Yahweh Who has not made us fall victim to their teeth. Our soul, like the bird, has escaped the trapper's snare (Ps. 124:6). Yes, without a doubt, retreats, silence, the mountains, evening are all good places to find God. We have fled the world to find God. But that is not enough. We must bring God to the world. We must bring the effect of our prayers to the world. But the world is not the only thing that keeps us from God. Sometimes it is we, ourselves. What keeps us remote from God is not only the sin of the world, the distraction of work or play, but our own sin, the overbearing influence of our own ego and vanity. The world is not all black. Does it really prevent us from finding God? Or is it our own view that is clouded? Perhaps our hearts are not pure enough to find Him, even though He is waiting. The Scriptures say: Blessed are the pure of heart, for they shall see God (Matt. 5:8).

It is indeed a captivity and a severe one that keeps us from God, from freedom, from the continual intimacy of the Father's house, because we are made for this joy. However, this captivity is not primarily that of the material world. Rather it is sin. It is from this captivity that we must be delivered, to find in the world, even among all its creatures, our encounter with God. The stages of our prayer are the stages of our deliverance to find, even in the midst of life, that childlike joy that is always nourished by the father in a family atmosphere. This deliverance, which permits us time for praise, is not accomplished by our own merits but by the Spirit of God in us. That is why along with the psalmist we so often appeal to Him in these words: Deliver me, oh Lord. Set me free from prison, let my soul sing the praises of your Name (Ps. 142:8).

PARADISE LOST

This experience of a forgotten, childlike simplicity, this painful search for peace of heart and an encounter with God, is not only found in individual men but is common to all mankind.

This revelation from above gives our personal experience a deeper meaning by plunging it into a living history, as God would have it. Everything becomes a part of our own personal existence, and each step we take is only one step in the great march of all men to reach God, if that were possible (Acts 17:27). This is so true that we can only measure the value of our actions, deeds, and prayers by referring them to the people of God. We really do not know whence we come or where we are going: We do not know where we are or who we are unless we relate ourselves to that gigantic human exodus, under the leadership of God. That is exactly what the liturgy constantly reminds us to do, by putting each year, each day, each prayer into the perspective of a total salvation history. It is only in this light that one can put events in their place in God's time and live them according to their full potential, in His plan of salvation.

We have lost the secret of praying easily, that *joie de vivre* in a childlike world under the eye of God. We have lost Paradise. We were made for that. We are still made for it. We carry in our hearts a nostalgia for a Paradise Lost. Everything then was good, everything was beautiful, everything was pure. All creation was created to be the meeting place between God and Man. In some marvelously simple pictures, Genesis lets us see what would have been if we had not sinned: God planted a garden in Eden, in the East, and in it He placed man, whom He had made . . . (Gen. 2:8) and they heard the footsteps of Yahweh God Who was walking in the garden at dawn (Gen. 3:8). What can we learn from this picture? What marvel is revealed to us? All creation was given to man for pleasure, and God, above and beyond this, was always present for a personal encounter with man. A wonderful and peaceful encounter. But this is what should have been and not what is now.

GOD, HIMSELF, IS AHEAD OF US

Everything was jeopardized by sin. From the beginning, man turned away from God. He looked for his happiness not in submission to the divine plan but in his own plans. From then on, there has been trouble. Having turned away from the Supreme Good, man's vision has become blurred. He has become his own trap, his own idol. He seduces himself and draws his body to destruction. He hides from God, fears Him and his own sin, which God's brilliance brings to light. He flees. Creation, which should have been the meeting place with God, has become a screen that hides Him from man. Finally, all beautiful and good things, which were paths through which God came to man and up through which man climbed toward God, became obstacles, where man could lose his way. All creation is still good, but it no longer leads man directly to where he should go. The world now deceives him as he once sought to deceive God. Paradise is lost forever. Creation is no longer a bush behind which man can hide from God and push himself further and further away from Him. And the man and woman hid themselves before Yahweh God among the trees of the garden. He banished man and placed before the garden of Eden, cherubim with flaming swords to guard the road to the tree of life (Gen. 3:24).

Is this the exile that puts us far from the glory of Paradise and makes it very difficult to pray?

It is not. Such a state of sin, without salvation, and of banishment, without hope, is what could have been, if Christ had not come. But it is precisely for this reason that He has come—so that this would not be. We have lost our ease in encountering God in this world. No one will deny that. But God comes before us in this *sinful* world—this is even truer. This is the definitive truth of the history of man: We exist in a world that was lost, but one that was also redeemed. We now enter into a history of redemption. Paradise Lost is behind us, but a Paradise regained is before us in Jesus Christ—a paradise far better than the first. Our prayers were also lost by sin and saved through Christ, and His life is the history of their salvation.

OUR PRAYER IS SAVED IN CHRIST

Revelation shows us what could have been, without sin, through its description of Paradise. We should not think of Paradise with regret, however, but rather strive toward the new path that has been opened for us. For what we have lost is nothing, compared to what we shall receive, through the grace of Christ. For a long time man wandered through the world as through an empty house, as if he lived in a secularized temple. How great was the number of people who lived in this almost total blackout, guarding in their hearts a nostalgia for a love they no longer knew, groping for the divine (Acts 17:27) and falling helplessly, unable to surpass their senses, before idols they had built, adoring and serving created things in preference to the Creator of all things (Rom. 1:25).

TO BE CLOSE TO GOD IS TERRIFYING

Even when God showed Himself from a distance to His chosen people, above and beyond natural phenomena, He engendered fear and trembling. God's approach always remains a terrifying experience to sinful man; His light is menacing and His Face terrifying. On Sinai, where God Himself came to set up the terms of His alliance, all the people tremble with fear and keep at a distance. And they say to Moses: You speak to us and we will be able to hear, but don't let God talk to us because that would mean certain death! The people, then, kept their distance and Moses approached the obscure cloud where God was (Ex. 20:19-20).

It was forbidden to speak or even write His Name, even by the people He had chosen. If His law imposes prayer, if His Spirit suggests the format, the heart was too often absent from the praise coming from men's lips.

In a secular world, in a nature where mountain and wood have become dens of idols for hearts weighed down by sin, minds clouded by ignorance, God is absent. In Palestine He kept His people, in Jerusalem His house, but even for His elected people He was a Lord who must be sought from afar. Even when the high priest entered the Holy of Holies, the heart of God's house, once a year, he found two cherubim—another sign that they *wait* to see God.

BUT HERE IS CHRIST

Now we have the Christ. In Him the prayers of mankind are restored, the ties of intimacy with God are found again. Here is the new Adam, the new Paradise. Here a new world comes into being. Man starts over again with Christ. Prayer once again discovers its purity and original facility. Christ is above all prophets, above all visionaries, recluses, mystics, saints. He is God's Son and He sees God. He lives with the Father and the Father with Him.

What is striking is the ease, the simplicity, and the universality of Jesus' prayers. He prays as He lives, as He is. He receives each moment from the Hand of the Father with a spirit of submission and grace, which makes every moment a perfect time to pray. He sets aside the night to pray and sanctifies the day. He celebrates the sabbath and the feasts and makes each day a day of the Lord. Each event resounds in Him like a prayer: The lives of men, the faith of the poor, the joy of children, the song of the world, all of these He consecrates and offers in thanks to the Father. The place does not matter, it is good for prayer. The entire world has become a temple where the Son meets the Father in the Spirit. Woman, know that the hour is coming when you will worship the Father neither on the mountain, nor in Jerusalem. The time is coming, and it is now, that the true believers will adore the Father in spirit and truth (John 4:21). He prays in the temple, in the synagogues, on the mountain, in private homes, on the banks of the river, in the midst of the flowers in the fields, in the country, on the streets, at the tomb of his friend, and even on the cross, outside the holy city. He has made the whole world His prayer. He has given the world a sacred character. He has made it the place where man once again encounters the Living God and where the Son meets the Father.

His prayer is not superficial, for it is rooted in the depths of His heart. There is its source. It is from here that everything springs by which the world is transformed and made new. His prayer is nothing more than His life, His very Being: it is the intimacy of the Son with the Father. It fills His life because it completes His being. It is given in everything, His words, His deeds, and His prayers. He captures everything in His giving, for it is the Son of God, the creator of the Universe, who comes to get the world to join Him in His praise, His eucharist, His offerings to the Father. Every prayer is fulfilled in Christ.

His prayer is a mystery. It is the prayer of the Word Incarnate in which the whole world is assumed, in order that we may return to the Father and share in the life of the Trinity.

ONE DAY HE WAS PRAYING SOMEWHERE

The apostles stopped and marveled in silence: Look how He prays! Lord, teach us to pray (Luke 11:1). Did He reply: You cannot pray as I do. You were not meant to. No, He called them to a life of celibacy, a perfect life, He showed them the way to perfect prayer: When you pray, say: Our Father (Luke 11:2).

It is not the abundance of words that matters, not the external attitude, not the place for the formulae that count, it is the filial heart, it is entering into the prayer of the Son. A new era of prayer has begun—evangelical prayer. It is a new world, Paradise rediscovered. It is better than that, it is a Christian world, a filial world.

13

Work in the Christian Life

NIVARD KINSELLA, O.C.S.O.

COMPLICATED PROBLEM

At first sight it appears easy to arrive at a theology of work. Yet one of the recurring motifs in the present spate of writing on the subject is the heading "Towards a theology of work." Evidently we have not yet arrived at a complete and satisfactory synthesis. The reasons for this are several. It is not immediately clear that there can be a real "theology" of work. Has work for the Christian something to do with salvation, so that it is itself theological in some sense? Or is it simply a matter of work being good or bad according as our motive in it is good or bad? In that case our enquiry would better be directed to a theology of motive.

The problem is a modern one and has been exacerbated by two present-day phenomena. One is the de-Christianisation of the masses. This means that in some countries at least the Church appears to have lost the working class and much Catholic activity in this century is directed to remedying this. The other phenomenon is in fact precisely part of this activity. The worker-priest movement of the post-war years in France was one attempt to bring the workers back to Christ. It raised some problems including that of whether the priest should work for his own support and it appears to have confirmed the biblical practice in this matter by proving the other course as practically impossible.

The question is further complicated by the extraordinary variety of occupations that come under the term "work" today. We talk of agricultural workers, factory workers, white-collar workers, skilled and unskilled workers (by this latter meaning heavy manual workers generally) and so on. We rarely reflect that the surgeon is a manual worker just as much as the gardener is, even though he does not have clay under his finger nails. We may also decry the artificiality of much in modern city culture and lament that modern man is so far from the soil and the elemental things of creation. This is true enough, but a little unreal. If modern man is an office-worker and if the soil has been replaced for him by the asphalt of the city street, then we must take him as we find him. He still needs redemption and a theology of work. It will always be only the very small minority who can get away from this artificiality and asphalt. So many men are born, grow up and die in city streets that we must regard their work as truly work and so capable of a "theology" (or not) just as manual work is. When we talk of work, then, we mean whatever one does for one's livelihood, provided only that occupation be honest and upright. So a man works if he digs the ground, sows and reaps, makes pots or tables or washing machines, builds houses or designs them, sweeps the streets, operates an adding machine or typewriter. Whatever we say applies to him if he works for his living, however he does so.

THE SCRIPTURES

Let us see first what Scripture says. The most important piece of teaching in the Old Testament is that God gives Adam work before the Fall (Gen. 2:15). It is the difficulty of work that is a punishment for sin, not work itself. Even without sin, man would still have to work. Apart from this, work is praised throughout the Old Testament, especially in the Wisdom Books. The industry of the workman is said to be rewarded, while the sluggard is upbraided and told to imitate the diligence of the ant (cf. e.g. Prov. 10:4; 6:6-11; Eccl. 5:11; 11:6; Ecclus. 7:16; 10:30; 20:30; etc. But note that Job 5:7 "Man is born to labour" implies more than work. Labour here includes suffering and toil—better translate "travail"). Anna, the wife of Tobias, is praised for "working daily and bringing home what she could gain by the labour of her hands" (Tob. 2:19) and the valiant woman in Proverbs 31 is the diligent hard-working housewife "who did not eat her bread in idleness."

It appears then that work is part of God's plan for man and that its toilsomeness alone is the effect of sin. Work is the accepted rule of life. Industry, diligence, hard work and a care to provide for one's needs are all praiseworthy and virtuous. The lazy man is left in want and the toil of the worker is blessed materially by God. All this appears from even a cursory perusal of the Old Testament. We can however go further than this. The creation story shows us God making man (Adam) his co-operator in dressing and keeping the garden. Therefore work is a co-operation with God. It is a matter of tending God's creation and drawing out of it what man needs for sustenance. The work that is paised throughout the Wisdom Books is generally the simple work of agriculture of various crafts, and the corresponding feminine skills of weaving, spinning and housework. These could all be considered the continuation of the work of Adam, as given him by God before the fall, with the added element of difficulty resulting from sin.

In the New Testament we find the same essential outlook. Christ himself is a workman, member of a working-class family and lives by the labour of his hands. He drew a great many of his illustrations and parables in preaching from the world of work and referred to all sorts of avocations—farmers, fishermen, housewife, sower, merchant, publican, vine dresser, etc. He nowhere suggests that any honest occupation is an obstacle to following him. He notes that the workman is worthy of his wages (Luke 10:7) and in this repeats the Old Testament verbatim (Deut. 14:14 and Lev. 19:13. Note also that his statement here about the labourer living by the gospel repeats the Old Testament system of priestly support). He calls his disciples away from their nets, but only in order to give them the higher vocation of fishers of men. He stresses only that a man must subordinate all things to the salvation of his soul—for what does it profit a man if he gain the whole world and lose his own soul? (Matt. 16:26). He says too that our toil for material things must not leave Providence out of account (Matt. 6:25-34).

St. Paul repeats this teaching of Our Lord and generally considers work under the aspect of support for oneself. He insists that he always supports himself by his work, that if a man does not work neither should he eat (eat here means receive food and shelter from others) and exhorts the Christians to earn each one his own living (2 Thess. 3:8, 10, 12). Throughout this chapter Paul attacks idleness and recommends work as a means of avoiding mischief (cf. vv. 11 and 12 esp.). Further motives for work are e.g. not to be a burden to others, not to be an object of scorn to unbelievers (1 Thess. 4:11) and to be able to give something to the needy (Eph. 4:28). Finally, the apostle tells servants that in their work they should regard God rather than their masters and do all things for the Lord (Col. 3:23). The saint's views on the right of the missionaries to their support by the gospel are set out at length in 1 Cor. 9. He insists on his own right and that of every preacher to support by the Church. The fact that he personally renounced this right does not alter the situation—the right exists.

We have then in the New Testament a repetition of the essentials of the Old Testament teaching on work. Our Lord and the apostle repeat the obligation and value of work for self-support, but say also that the priests of the New Law like those of the Old have the right to support by the altar. Our Lord stresses that work should take account of Providence and be subordinate to man's salvation, while St. Paul insists that it be done for God and relates it to charity and edification.

In this question of work, then, as in all else, we do not find a finished theology presented to us in the scriptures. Can we deduce some principles from what we have said above and indicate the lines along which such a theology might be worked out? It seems we can and they can be summed up under three heads: (1) work is incumbent on man by the Natural Law; (2) as a result of sin work is penitential; (3) work has a social value—that you may be able to give to others. A consideration of each of these points will show the place of work in the life of the Christian.

WORK AND THE NATURAL LAW

Work comes from the Natural Law. It is important to be convinced of this. Otherwise we look on work itself as a penance for sin and from this certain undesirable consequences follow. Since Christ was not a sinner he did not have to work, but freely undertook to do so. It is better to say that the Son of God worked because work is part of man's nature and therefore as perfect man he worked. Otherwise his work has little real meaning. Again if work is merely a penance, it appears to follow that if we can replace it with another penance then we may do so, and this other will be equally valuable. On the other hand, if we see work as coming from the nature of man, as part of the divine plan from the beginning, then the dignity of work is enormously increased. Further, work thus becomes a necessity of nature, so that idleness is seen to be, in a sense, unnatural. God so made man that he finds fulfilment in work. In it alone is he truly and fully man. Without it he is deprived of something integral in his make-up, shorn of an essentially and divinely intended perfecting influence. In this light the apostle's dictum that only the worker should eat takes on a further clarity. The idle man, the sluggard, is a parasite not only because he depends on others for food and support, but also and more so because he refuses to fulfil the needs of his own nature. God has made man to a particular pattern and to be fully and perfectly a man he must respond to this design and live according to it. Refusal to work implies refusal to do this. Work maketh a full man.

But work has a precise meaning. Generally speaking all work is an attempt either to impose order on things or to maintain that order. Now disorder and sin are synonymous. Therefore the work of the Christian (since sin) is not the imposing of order, but the restoring of it. All work, of its nature, for the Christian is precisely this—the re-making of the world in the image of the original plan. If Adam had not sinned, his work should have consisted in maintaining the order placed by God in creation (the garden) and so finding fulfilment. The Christian still finds fulfilment, but for him work is a restoration and a pushing back of the limits of the reign of Satan.

WORK AND PENANCE

Work is Penance. It is not precisely work itself, but the toil and labour that inevitably now accompany it that constitute the penance. This toilsomeness of work is the great penance laid on man for sin. No matter how he perfect machinery and how he advance in technology man is always subject to toil and weariness. He cannot get away from these since they are part of God's plan for expiating sin. But again the Cross gives a new dimension. Expiation is now atonement with Christ. And the two meanings of this latter word (at-onement) show the riches of work done and toil accepted in penance for sin. Our penance united with the sufferings of the Crucified make us one with him. And so our work, our sweat and toil, the monotony of the daily task, the irksomeness and sameness of repetition, all become part of our cross, enabling us fill up those things yet wanting to his passion. This is so from God's ordination back at the beginning, and not merely because we "offer it up." The toil of work is the universal penance laid on all in *Genesis*. Our recognition and conscious acceptance of this provides a means of close union with Christ on Calvary. It also lends a new significance to Our Lady's request for penance, which was explained at Fatima as the fulfilment of the duties of our state in life.

SOCIAL VALUE OF WORK

Work has social value. St. Paul considers work from the viewpoint of edifying others, of not being a burden and of enabling us give alms to the needy. In other words he stresses the social impact of work. This also appears to be basic in any consideration of work. We never work in isolation, but always as members of society. Others depend on us and we on them. No man can work alone and the more closely-knit society becomes, the more our work redounds to its total good or harm. By our work we make a contribution, of whatever kind and whether we will it or not, to the life and welfare of society as a whole. We further the cause of the human family and in some sense better it. But once again Christianity gives a new dimension. This society becomes the Mystical Body and the good of the neighbour attained through work becomes the exercise of charity.

These three elements appear to be basic to a proper understanding of the place of work in Christian life. We have only outlined them and can but allude to the other values contained in work. There are the various virtues brought into play by it; its effectiveness in inducing a realisation of our dependence on God; its utility in revealing the beauty and bound of God in creation, and so leading us to gratitude and adoration; and so much else. But these points are to some extent accidental and vary with the kind of work. The essentials are that work fulfils man's nature, expiates sin and performs a social duty. In the light of these three we see how it readily links up with the Mass. The sacrifice sums up man's life—and so his work—and offers it to God. The Mass thus reminds man of his creaturehood and obligation to work, while making of that work the stuff of adoration. The Mass is Calvary in mystery and Calvary is expiation for our sins. So the toil of our small cross of work is united with the blood of Christ on his Cross—and that uniting takes place at Mass. Finally, through the Eucharist is effected the unity of the Mystical Body that makes of work not merely a social service, but the building up of the Body of Christ.

14

Contemplative in Action

EMERICH CORETH, S.J.

The formula of Jerome Nadal, *Contemplative in Action,* is the classical expression of the Ignatian ideal of perfection. This form of life, however, is not confined to the Society of Jesus. It is valid for every Christian life that seeks its perfection amid the difficulties of external work rather than in the quiet of contemplation. I would like, therefore, to justify the historical and theological bases of the meaning of this formula. Its immediate meaning, of course, must not be overestimated. The context of the single place in which Nadal uses these words clearly shows that he did not intend to give a final and sharply delineated formulation after the manner of an essential definition; rather he uses, in the course of a spiritual instruction, an incidental expression the ideas of which are rooted in tradition.

Herein lies the value and limitation of the formula. It is of value because it places the spiritual doctrine of St. Ignatius in the historical tradition in which the concepts *action* and *contemplation* were alive, and because it sharply delineates Ignatian spirituality, which rises above all tradition by reason of its fundamentally new relationship between *action* and *contemplation.* But herein also lies the limits of the formula, since its meaning can be completely uncovered only in the broad historical background that burdens it with a host of problems and runs the risk of many errors. Therefore we must first investigate the historical meanings and changes of meanings of the notions of *action* and *contemplation,* so that we may then determine the philosophical and theological meaning of the words *contemplative in action.*

ACTION AND CONTEMPLATION

AMONG THE GREEKS

Both the indicative opposition between action (*praxis*) and contemplation (*theoria*) as well as the superiority of contemplation over action stems from Greek philosophy. The great permanent contribution of Greek thought is its discovery of the spirit, of a spiritual sphere of being, existing beyond the material world and accessible only to the human spirit. In view of this insight it is no wonder that the spiritual world seemed to the greatest Greek thinkers, especially Plato, the only true reality; the rest merely appearances. No wonder they placed the essence and dignity of man in the spirit alone and assigned no true value to the body. No wonder, therefore, that they settled upon a spiritualism and an intellectualism that regards the body as the enemy of the spirit. And so they logically placed the perfection of man in the perfection of the spirit, in the greatest possible dematerialization and spiritualization of life, and so in *theoria:* the turning of the spirit to the eternal truths and values, not in *praxis:* activity amid the things of the world. Here we stand at the historical source of these concepts: *praxis* signifies external activity, whether it be manual work or the business of politics; *theoria* means "studium," intellectual cognition of a scientific and especially a philosophical type: knowledge of the eternal truths.

The metaphysical foundations for the evaluation of *action* and *contemplation* were created by Plato in the sharp dualism between the mundane and the supra-mundane, between nonbeing, the realm of unreal appearances of sensible things, and the world of true being, the realm of truly existing, universal and necessary essences. As human activity is directed toward nonexisting things, the vision of the ideas is directed to the purely spiritual world and finally to the highest idea, the Good itself. Union with the idea of the Good, therefore, is the highest human perfection. It is achieved amid the passivity of spiritual vision, free of all activity. Of course *theoria* here must not be taken in the cold, theoretical sense in which we take it today. It is rather the goal of a gradual dematerialization and spiritualization of the *eros,* which is the highest form of love, but a love developed and perfected in intellectual cognition. So the dualism of *action* and *con-*

templation conforms to the harsh dualism of the Platonic world, and an evaluation of the former is conditioned by the latter. Throughout the centuries this evaluation has become deeply woven into Christian thought, and the metaphysical roots of platonic dualism have forced upon it a heavy burden.

These philosophical foundations were partly corrected by Aristotle. He at least mitigated the Platonic dualism by locating the essences of things within the things themselves as intrinsic forms, and he sought by his theory of abstraction to do justice to the activity inherent in intellectual cognition as opposed to the simple representation theory of Plato. Nevertheless he remained basically dependent upon Platonism with its fundamental dualism between matter and spirit and its consequent evaluation of action and intellection. For if the universal forms are limited by the eternal uncreated principle of prime matter, then the material universe stands in opposition to the being of God, for although it is not radically evil, nevertheless it is a reality intrinsically estranged from God. Hence, for Aristotle human perfection cannot be concerned with mundane affairs, but only with intellectual knowledge of universal and necessary truths, of divine things, which are the highest object of the intellect. And so it is that the relationship between *action* and *contemplation* remains essentially the same as it was with Plato.

Because of his deep influence upon later Patristic thought Plotinus is the third representative of Greek thought, which reaches in him its final synthesis. He proposed to overcome the Platonic-Aristotelian dualism: the divine One is the primary source of all being, matter included, although its necessary emanation is not yet a free creation. But there is a strange contradiction in this new sharp break which is to characterize all subsequent Platonism: the transcendence of the divine One is so emphasized that it is unattainable to the thinking spirit, and although matter depends upon the divine emanation like all being, it is the principle of all defectiveness and imperfection and evil. And so here again the spiritual and moral ascent of man consists in a gradual dematerialization and spiritualization; perfection consists in a likeness to God and a union with Him, in an intellectual knowledge, which however, is not accomplished through the personal thought activity of man, for it is a "knowledge which no longer knows anything," a "vision which sees nothing," a benumbing and blinding of the human faculties, a purposeless and even unconscious dissolving into the divine One in a mystical ecstasy. And so here again, only in a slightly different perspective, perfection is placed in intellectual contemplation to which all action is subordinated.

PATRISTICS

Very early the Greek intellectual contribution streamed into Christian thought and especially into the theoretical principles of Christian asceticism. In the evaluation of *action* and *contemplation* the Fathers followed the Greek pattern, but they did not pass it on unchanged. An interpretation is perfected here which is found already in Clement of Alexandria and actually remains in all the Fathers: action (*praxis*) no longer means external activity but moral and ascetical striving, the battle against sin and passion, and the struggle for virtue and perfection. This is the necessary prerequisite for contemplation (*theoria*), which is the union of the soul with God. This is the true essence of Christian perfection. Surely this contemplation means something entirely different from that of the Greek philosophers: not intellectual cognition alone and not only theological studium, but prayerful and reflective union with God. Surely this is something different and new, even if the difference and novelty is not clearly seen until much later in the history of Christian thought. And so it is that even this "religious contemplation"—as we will call it to distinguish it from speculative contemplation—takes on a predominately intellectual aspect. The contemplative search for God is achieved in an intellectual ascent according to the Platonic and Neoplatonic pattern by which the spirit ascends from the knowledge of the world to its divine principle and attains its summit in a mystical union with God in this life and an immediate vision of God in the life to come.

It is clear throughout that very different facts are assumed in the one idea of contemplation. It is partly a pure intellectual comprehension of a philosophical or theological type, partly a personal relationship with God in a faithful and loving surrender to prayer—both ordinary prayer and mystical prayer, and even the beatific vision of God in the world to come. All of this is so mixed up that it is often difficult, even impossible, to determine whether it is the Christian theologian or the Neoplatonic philosopher who is speaking of immediate contact and possession of God and vision of God.

The assimilation of Greek thought had already begun with Clement of Alexandria, for whom perfection consists "in the knowledge of the Good and union with God." He distinguishes an intellectual and a moral element. The intellectual and theoretical element is Gnostic in origin as that Gnosticism that raises itself above the darkness of faith to a continual vision of God. The moral and practical element is stoically expressed in the idea of *apatheia,* which constitutes the goal of the moral-ascetical struggle. And so again we encounter the old dualism, albeit in imitation of Gnostic and Stoic thought.

Although with Clement both elements belong together and complement one another, as early as Origen contemplation possesses a definite superiority, and this is fixed for the future. Only contemplatives "live in the interior of the house of God," while those who lead the active life "remain in the courtyard." In his development of this idea, Martha becomes the symbol of the active life, Mary the symbol of the contemplative life, and this notion is to live on in ascetical literature. In his division of the contemplative life Origen marks out three steps of the spiritual ascent. The first is the practical life, the moral battle in which the goal is the *apatheia.* The second is the consideration of the created universe through which we ascend to the third step, loving union with God in contemplation. Here already we have the trilogy which through Dionysius Pseudo-Areopagite enters into ascetical-mystical theology: the purgative way, the illuminative way, the unitive way. The effect of this is clearly seen in the Capadocians: for Gregory of Nyssa, progress in virtue is essentially bound up with progress in knowledge; and Gregory of Naziansus explicitly takes over the order of precedence given by Origen: "contemplation is the work of perfection; activity is for the masses."

With Augustine Neoplatonic thought re-enters into Christianity. For him perfection consists in the contemplation of God, true Wisdom —*sapientia* as opposed to *scientia* or the knowledge of created reality. All ascetical practices he subordinates to this end. And so in a Neoplatonic guise he represents the gradual ascent of the soul which terminates in the vision of God, in an immediate contact and apprehension of Him.

The same is the case with Gregory the Great. The practical exercise of virtue is a necessary prerequisite for contemplation, in which essentially consists the highest perfection. Nevertheless one idea comes to light here, which heretofore had received surprisingly little attention: the worth and dignity of the apostolate. An apostolic life, in which action and contemplation are united—we would say a *vita mixta* —Gregory seems to prize above a purely contemplative life. Action and contemplation constitute a certain higher reciprocal activity in which they perfect one another—after the example of Christ, who spent the night in prayer and consecrated the day to apostolic work.

Then, of course, the contemplative life received a definite reaccentuation within the Monasteries when Benedict explicitly made the *Opus Dei* the heart of the monastic life and cast the mold of the monastic form of life in the Occident. Heretofore the focal point of the contemplative life lay in an individualistic striving for the vision of God. Now the indiivdual as such recedes and is replaced by the praying community. This does not mean that the aim of the contemplative life is changed. It is the way that is changed, for the way now leads through the community. Surely Benedict desires that the chanting of the Psalms be animated from within, that "our souls be in harmony with our voices," and he desires a realization of God not only by prayer but by constant recollection. Nevertheless he scarcely regarded the formal prayer of the individual.

More important still for our present investigation into the nature of action and contemplation is that the idea of the apostolate gets no recognition. The flight of the monks from the world is a renunciation of apostolic work. To be sure the monasteries even before Benedict were engaged in apostolic activity, and in the West they bore the brunt of the great missionary movements, but this was done independently of the theoretical foundations of monasticism. The attempt to fit positive apostolic activity into the theology of Christian perfection has not yet succeeded and cannot succeed as long as the Platonic-Neoplatonic ideal even theoretically holds sway. The split between purely contemplative theory and active apostolic practice must first be healed. This appeared more and more in the new structures of the apostolic orders of the Middle Ages, and it is for them, under the guidance of Thomas Aquinas, to penetrate more deeply into the speculative problems of *action* and *contemplation*.

SCHOLASTICISM

Since the restless Platonic tendency is still unconquered, the Greek and Patristic traditions live on in the scholastic theology of the Middle Ages. This is manifest even in St. Thomas Aquinas, who in the II-II of the *Summa Theologica* attempted to master the old problem, and whose doctrine alone we will here single out and briefly sketch for our discussion.

Thomas begins by asserting that human life may conveniently and sufficiently (*convenienter* and *sufficienter*) diivded into an active and a contemplative life. As proof he offers the duality of intellectual activity: if its aim is the understanding of truth, you have the contemplative intellect (*intellectus contemplativus*); if its aim is external activity, you have practical intellect (*intellectus practicus sive activus*). What then does Thomas mean by active and contemplative life?

Life in its totality is active life if it is ordered not exclusively, but principally to external activity. The practice of the moral virtues belongs here, especially prudence, which although of the intellectual order, has as *recta ratio agibilium* moral activity as its end. In his notion of *action,* therefore, Thomas has united the ancient Greek and Patristic ideals: Action is not only external activity in general, but moral activity as well. This has its deeper roots in the fact that for Thomas every free act in the concrete has some moral significance.

Contemplative life, however, is principally ordered to the understanding of truth, and of course principally to the undertsanding of divine truth, secondarily to the consideration of the works of God through which we must ascend to the contemplation of God Himself.

At first glance these definitions seem quite clear. That they are not, becomes obvious when Thomas poses the main question. His main theme runs thus: contemplative life, considered in itself, is better than the active life. Upon this principle he hopes to achieve a Christian theological evaluation of the actual relation of action and contemplation with Christian perfection. If this thesis is understood in virtue of the notions defined above, it is absolutely unacceptable. For the definition understands contemplation as the understanding of truth and is therefore a purely intellectual contemplation according to the Greek ideal. Since intellectual understanding as such, however, even considering its moral and supernatural value, is not superior to every kind of external action, surely it is not to be evaluated above moral activity. On the contrary: knowledge as such is ethically unrelated to perfection. If moral worth is constituted by a free, personal act of internal assent to which there corresponds an external materialization of that assent, then moral worth resides essentially in the will. And so Christian perfection does not mean perfection of the undertsanding, but perfection of love. Greater knowledge can and surely should imply a deeper, more mature personal attitude to the apprehended moral value, and so should contribute to the increase of moral perfection. In other words, knowledge can and should lead to the love of God, in which consists Christian perfection. But it is only the preparation for perfection and does not lead to it of its own intrinsic necessity. It is even possible for one to devote himself to the highest object of knowledge, the deposit of revelation, without any personal self-surrender to that knowledge and so without any moral and supernatural merit. Without love, even without faith, but from a purely theoretical inquisitiveness and interest in Holy Scripture, an unbeliever could read or study Catholic dogma merely to learn what is taught therein. If, accordingly, there is any true meaning in the words the contemplative life, considered in itself, is better than the active, it must be upon the supposition that the contemplative life is understood not in the intellectual sense alone, but a religious contemplation concerned with personal acts of faith and love.

Now this is obviously what St. Thomas intended. He knew that a religious order was different from a scholarly society organized for the purposes of philosophical and theological study, that it was concerned essentially with religious values. Actually he did not make this distinction, but arrived at the evaluation of contemplation from its intellectual element alone. This is obvious from the eight reasons he borrows from Aristotle as proofs of his statement, which he corroborates theologically with examples from Holy Scripture. The fundamental proof from which all the others more or less stem is the fact that the intellect is the most noble and essentially characteristic faculty of man. But the intellect is concerned with spiritual cognition (*intelligere*). So intellectual cognition is the act and perfection of man according to his highest tendency, and hence the highest possible human activity. A life, therefore, which is totally ordered to intellectual cognition is the highest possible type or human life.

That this is Greek, not Christian, thought cannot be denied. It stems directly from the ancient spiritualism and intellectualism. The peculiarly Christian notion that perfection consists in love has not yet come to full maturity. Surely Thomas was aware of this and sought to fit it into his thought.* Thus love is the beginning and end of the contemplative life, inasmuch as it both incited us to the knowledge and contemplation of God and is in turn the goal and fruit of contemplative union. Nevertheless the essence of contemplation consists in the intellectual aspect alone and this alone is the basis of its superiority over action.

On the other hand—and by comparison mark the weakness of the ancient Greek evaluation—the supernatural value of the contemplative and the active life derives from love: the contemplative life is "directly and immediately" ordered to the love of God, and the active life is ordered to the love of the neighbor. And because the love of God is higher than the love of the neighbor, it is also more meritorious. Now prescinding from this systematic ordering of contemplation to the love of God and action to the love of the neighbor, which oversimplifies the interrelations of the two and so brings everything into a false light—apart from this, two essentially diverse trains of thought overlap one another in the evaluation of contemplation: on the one hand its superiority over action based upon its purely intrinsic, intellectual nature; and on the other hand its value proportioned to the degree of love. But since love is extrinsic to the essence of intellectual contemplation, although it can be the source and end of contemplation (and yet must not be) then it follows that intellectual contemplation as such (without love) remains without moral and supernatural value for perfection—and thereby the first order of values is abolished. It also follows that this contemplation, which should become the activating form-principle of a life of striving for perfection, is something entirely different, namely religious contemplation, which considers love not only as the source and end, but is intrinsically constituted through personal acts of surrender to God in faith and love. In as much as this distinction is not perfectly clear, the notion of contemplation remains indefinite, and no one has succeeded as yet in breaking up the narrow intellectualism stemming from Plato.

The fact that Thomas—taking the Dominican view—held that form of life we call the *vita mixta* as the highest form of life, preferring it to a purely contemplative, and all the more to a purely active life, does not change at all the basic superiority of the con-

* St. Thomas treats this matter in the *Summa,* II–II, qq. 179–188.

templative over the active life. An apostolic life which is devoted to teaching and preaching and so to any task that derives from the fullness of contemplation, belongs in the realm of the contemplative life, but rises above pure contemplation in as much as others are given to share in the overflowing fullness of one's own light: for as it is better to illuminate others than merely to shine, so it is better to give the fruits of overcontemplation to others, rather than merely to contemplate. And so the value of an active-apostolic life is appraised from its contemplative element and not—at least primarily and directly—from the intrinsic worth of the apostolic work itself.

IGNATIUS

The Ignatian spirituality is essentially different from this, and we must not understand the words of Nadal, contemplative in action (*in actione contemplativus*), apart from Ignatian idea. In the type of life Ignatius gave to the Society of Jesus, the contemplative element—if this can still be called so—is subordinated and ordered to the active-apostolic life; but perfection is to be realized in the perfection of action guided and impregnated with love. Let us sketch it—again only in its broad outlines—from the writings of St. Ignatius himself.

In the "Formula of the Institute," the structure of the new order along with its revolutionary point of view is discernible. Here you have the service of the King under the banner of the cross (*sub vexillo crucis*), the service of the Church, the defense and spread of the Faith, apostolic work for the salvation of souls, instruction, education, preaching, distribution of the Sacraments, poverty, and obedience as the type of life of the apostolic worker who must stand prepared to be sent to all parts of the world by one who holds the place of Christ upon earth—to work in the Lord's vineyard. All the forms of priestly apostolic work are mentioned, and a form of life is outlined which will guarantee the greatest possible freedom of activity for such work. But there is no mention of "contemplation," and the heretofore recognized goal of one striving after a life of perfection. There is only mention of "action" for the glory of God.

When in the "General Examen" a twofold end of the Society is given: the salvation and perfection of one's own soul, and the salvation and perfection of the neighbor, this could at first glance seem to be related to the dualism of contemplation and action. But the idea is no longer that perfection be achieved in the quiet of contemplation and then others share in the overflow of light and grace—in the Thomist passing on to others the fruit of contemplation—but rather both should penetrate one another to perfect unity so that apostolic work for the salvation and sanctification of our fellow men is the form-principle of the life of the Order, and hence the form-principle of its striving after perfection.

Neither in the "Constitutions" do we find the historic twin notions action and contemplation. And you will scarcely find other concepts that really correspond to them. The twin ideas prayer-action and interior-exterior come closest to the idea behind action-contemplation. Prayer-action appears in the ninth part of the "Constitutions," when Ignatius speaks of the General of the Society and outlines the ideal of the Jesuit. He especially demands: He should most closely be united to and familiar with God, our Lord, both in prayer and in all his actions.

Thus the dualism of prayer and action is subordinated to a higher unity, and its apparent opposition is united into a third element: union and familiarity with God, or more briefly as Ignatius says in another place: union with God. Now if you understand by *oratio* actual prayer—religious contemplation as we have indicated above—so this third, union with God, stands out as something entirely different from it, which is not limited to formal prayer, but designates both action and contemplation in the same way.

Thus it is that the other dualism, interior-exterior, is to be understood not simply in the sense of contemplation (prayer) and action, but in the sense of union with God and action. Ignatius speaks of this in the tenth part of the "Constitutions": those means which join the human instrument to God and dispose him to the governed rightly by the divine hand are more efficacious than those which adjust men to other men. . . . For the former are interior qualities, from which efficacy can flow to assist us to our proposed end. Among these interior things are the virtues, especially love, a "right intention," familiarity with God, which must be acquired and cultivated in spiritual exercises of devotion, but which, as an interior disposition, should animate and sanctify all action. A life of explicit prayer is necessary, but it is no longer the highest end of a contemplative life;

it is rather *exercitium,* that is "exercise" of that attitude and disposition which is not limited to the time of prayer, but fills up the whole active life. And because it is not an end in itself but "exercise," and so—in a properly understood sense—a "means" to an end, it is limited by this end: action performed with a pure intention for the love of God.

This is especially clear where Ignatius considers the spiritual exercises of the Scholastics: let them not put no such emphasis on long prayers and meditations. Sometimes a devotion to literary work, pursued with a sincere desire to serve God, and which moreover helps to form a full personality, will be even more pleasing to God our Lord. The train of thought here is noteworthy. Immediately before this Ignatius had warned that zeal for studies must not harm the zeal for the religious life. If experience shows that this danger exists, it must be encountered by the protection of the practice of definite prayers and devotions. On the other hand, this is a minimum requirement since it suffices to keep alive the sincere intention of serving God, for the fulfillment of the duty of one's vocation, accomplished with a pure intention, is the highest service of God, even greater than prayer and contemplation.

Although Ignatius left no directions for the personal prayer of the Jesuits, and set no limits to it—only that which discrete charity dictates—still he set down the universal principle that prayer, bodily austerities, and the like must be governed and limited according to the demands of apostolic work.

From this it is clear that perfection is determined not by the extent of "exercises," as important as they are, and as much as they are repeatedly emphasized by Ignatius, but by the love-inspired execution of all our actions in God. Thus the "right intention" holds a central place in his spiritual teaching. It demands that we love God with the greatest possible purity in all creatures and all creatures in Him. This is to find God in all things—as the contemplation to obtain divine love of the "Exercises" teaches.

Ignatius, therefore, places perfection no longer in a contemplative element, not even in religious contemplation, if by this is meant formal prayer, contemplation and other "exercises," but essentially in the perfection of action undertaken purely for the sake of God, directed to Him and fulfilled in Him. Ignatian asceticism is an asceticism of action. And all contemplation has a necessary service to perform: continually to supply the active life with new religious energy so that from this "interior" the "exterior" of action may be filled up with the pure love of God and elevated to a continual union with God.

SUAREZ

While Ignatius himself did not take over the traditional notions of *actio* and *contemplatio,* and accordingly neither sought to order the life of the Society in terms of action or contemplation nor attempted to give a speculative-theological justification of the active life. Nevertheless, Suarez, in his work "De Religione," explicitly proposed the question: whether the Society of Jesus embraces the contemplative or the active life.

Suarez follows St. Thomas in the distinction of the three basic types of Orders. All strive after the perfection of love, the one by way of contemplation exclusively—which of itself perfects man's love of God—the other through actions of love and mercy towards the neighbor, for since these two are done for God, love of God is perfected by them; and the third in a mixed life—partly contemplative, partly active. It is clear from this that Suarez has overcome the intellectual evaluation of contemplation and appraises perfection only according to love. If he borrowed from St. Thomas the ordination of the contemplative life to the love of God and the active life to the love of the neighbor, that one-sidedness is nevertheless moderated by this, that for him external activity is done for God, for the love of God, because Christian-supernatural love is especially concretized in action.

But neither extreme is ever exclusively realized. No contemplative life can renounce all action, neither can an active life surrender all contemplation without abandoning the religious life itself. In this sense every order of life is a mixed life. But the peculiar structure of an order is manifest when the principal, dominating end of its entire form of life is considered. To this extent the dualism is justified. For, as Suarez says, the one order of itself tends to contemplation and devotes only as much energy to action as is necessary for the leading of a contemplative life; the active element, therefore, is ultimately ordered to the contemplative. The other order directly intends action and devotes only as much energy to contemplation as is necessary to act perfectly . . . or to render to God a due religious cult. Here the contemplative element is ultimately ordered to the active element, to the perfection of action, as far as prayer and especially the love of God can be ordered to an end and do not themselves constitute an ultimate end in themselves. A *religio mixta,* finally, is an order of life which unites both ends: both are directly intended in a proper and special fashion; both stand together as of equal value, neither element ultimately leading to the other or being ordered to it.

In this sense, according to Suarez, the Society of Jesus is a *religio mixta; Dico ergo Societatem ex vi sui instituti utrumque vitae genus per se ac principaliter intendere.* While he was aware that this was obviously true regarding the active character of the society and needed no proof, he realized how questionable it appeared with reference to its contemplative character, and therefore attempted to verify it through a line of reasoning. As proof he proposed the twofold end of the society, self-sanctification and the sanctification of the neighbor, and attached to both elements the dualism of contemplation and action. But this can be doubted, for surely according to Ignatius perfection is to be attained in apostolic action and not in the quiet of contemplation, for action itself is extolled as the form-principle of self-sanctification, just as necessary as formal prayer, contemplation, and the "exercises." All of these are necessary as exercises whose function is to inspire action: *ad actionem ipsam perfecte agendam.* After citing the great amount of time devoted daily to prayer and contemplation, Suarez also uses as a proof the apostolic activity of the order, which necessarily presupposes a contemplative life, not directly and principally intended as an end in itself alongside apostolic work, but again: that action itself might be perfect.

These proofs are not convincing. Suarez proposes the characteristic features of the Society of Jesus after the pattern of the old orders, especially as they are found in Thomas, and accordingly interprets the Ignatian contemplation in action according to the Thomist *contemplata aliis tradere, i.e.,* bring to others the fruit of over-contemplation. The new specifically Ignatian idea is not proposed in its purity: Through a complete renunciation of a contemplative life (in the monastic sense), God can be found and loved in activity itself; amid the active encounter with men and the things of the world an order of life of complete surrender to God can be lived. Striving for perfection, therefore, must not be accomplished independently of and apart from this external activity—as it were in another room apart—until one may dare to share with others the overflow of his own light and grace; rather it is to be accomplished in the midst of action itself, which is performed for the honor of God and the salvation of the neighbor, and so for the love of God and the love of the neighbor. Here lies a truer way of Christian perfection.

Now if we want to answer the question proposed by Suarez according to the peculiar characteristics of the Society of Jesus, we can look for an answer first of all in the actual amount of action and contemplation in the concrete life. Then the society is doubtlessly a *religio mixta:* apostolic action to which every other form of work is ordered, combined with contemplation, both in the intellectual sense of philosophical-theological study which occupies a relatively large space, and also in the religious sense of interior prayer to which even more space is devoted. But in this sense every type of life, indeed every religious life, is ultimately a *vita mixta.*

But the characteristic structure of an order of life is first known from its dominant end. In the Society of Jesus is the contemplative life alongside the active directly and principally intended in the same way? It is not a question of the ultimate end, since both forms of life, as definite ways of perfection, seek a common ultimate end. The question, rather, is whether between action and contemplation there exists any subordination of means to end, whether perfection is to be striven for *per se* in apostolic activity, and contemplation exercised only in so far as it is necessary—as Suarez says—to act perfectly and render God due religious cult. The fact that explicit prayer is necessary for the religious fulfillment, animation, and sanctification of external activity—to act perfectly—needs no justification. Nor is any proof needed for the fact that duty to prayer and the service of God is part of an active life—to render cult to God. This formula in which Suarez defines the characteristics of a purely active life seems to us a very appropriate way of expressing Ignatian spirituality: the contemplative element, both the study of theology and the sciences (intellectual contemplation) as well as the interior life of prayer (religious contemplation) are ultimately ordered to the perfection of action. Study has no longer, as for St. Thomas, the function of an intellection, but the natural capacity to accomplish the work in the kingdom of God. And the life of prayer is not a contemplative quiet with God, but ever more and more fills up our entire activity with God so that it becomes perfect action—not a mere natural accomplishment, but a supernatural perfection.

If this is the relationship between action and contemplation—and it seems to correspond to the Ignatian spirituality—it follows that the Society of Jesus is not a mixed life but wholly an active life. The actual amount of prayer and spiritual exercises is no consideration. They are necessary, but necessary precisely for the inspiration and perfection of action to which they remain ordered.

CONTEMPLATIO IN ACTIONE

THE STATE OF THE QUESTION

The question of fact poses a question of right order. Is it not a complete inversion of objective values, that contemplation is degraded to function as a servant to action? Religious contemplation, and so interior prayer, which as the formal glory of God represents the absolute zenith of human life, must not be relative, ordered as a mere means to an end of inferior standing. The traditional evaluation of contemplation and action can give no response to this, for tradition regards Christian perfection as essentially a thing of contemplation, and accordingly every action is more or less sharply evaluated as a defection from this essence. Although it is a defection that appears relatively justified because of the practical necessities of life, the common social activity within the Church, the necessity of caring for souls, and so on, still the essential thing is the purest possible contemplation.

Any attempt to answer this question must first of all consider the intrinsic nature and value of the end to which the contemplative element is ultimately referred in an active life. We must achieve a philosophical-theological evaluation of human activity in general and of apostolic activity in particular. Thus it is necessary that we lay bare and cut out the roots of the historical errors, which have worked deeply into Patristic and Scholastic theology and definitely prejudiced our evaluation of action and contemplation. We will call them intellectualism, spiritualism, and individualism. To understand each we must understand their three inherent polar tensions which greatly affect human life: intellection and volition, interior and exterior, individual and society.

INTELLECTION AND VOLITION

The intellectualism of which we speak considers the intellect the highest faculty of man and the intellectual comprehension of truth, especially eternal truth, the highest human act. From this it follows that a life devoted exclusively to the understanding of truth is the highest type of life. It demands the surrender of all worldly obligations and affairs which detract from a contemplative's absorption in the truth and fill the spirit with the concern of other affairs, even though it be a task undertaken for the highest love of God. Pure contemplation is still higher.

From a point of view like this it is easy to overlook the fact that intellection, of its very nature, is not isolated nor can it be, and so it must neither be considered nor evaluated in isolation. Rather it is a part, however essential and fundamental a part, of the complete picture of human endeavor. And in this complete picture intellection as such is never an ultimate for it demands as its complementary counterpart action in which the unity and totality of interior activity is perfected. If the knowledge of the understanding conforms to the decision of free will, then it is an idle question to ask which of these powers is the "higher." They are both of complementary greatness, both equally and essentially arise out of spiritual-personal being.

But if there is question not only of the ontological grade of the perfection of being but of the moral value of respective acts (in the natural and supernatural sense), taking moral activity to mean the essential perfection of man according to the spiritual-personal totality of his nature, then a moral act takes place when man in a free self-determining choice of means in their relation to the totality of his personal existence, takes his stand on authentic or non-authentic possibilities of his own self-perfection. A moral act takes place in active conduct grounded in the free self-determination of the will. Previous intellection is the necessary condition of free will, but intellection as such, even the highest intellection of divine truth, realizes no moral value. Moral value resides in the free answer of the will to which it turns and accepts moral worth; it follows upon intellection, but not necessarily. And so neither the dignity of intellectual knowledge is disparaged nor is the absolute character of intellection *qua* intellection made relative, but surely, as far as the total development of human life is concerned, intellection remains a torso if it does not find its fulfillment in free surrender to the known value. For the Christian this means that even the highest knowledge of God remains empty and incomplete and worthless, if it is not succeeded by a free surrender to God in acts especially of faith and love.

Now actually in the evaluation of action and contemplation—in the Greek position of Plato and Plotinus, and all the more in the Patristic and Scholastic theology—intellectualism was tempered by the fact that striving for contemplative union with God was accompanied and penetrated with love of God. And so too for Thomas love is the beginning and end of contemplation. But it remains a love that is essentially and primarily realized in contemplation. It is not a love ordered to an inspiring penetration of all action.

INTERIOR AND EXTERIOR

Having attempted briefly to clarify the relation between intellection and volition, let us consider the relation of interior and exterior. The classical evaluation of action and contemplation, with its historical roots in the philosophical dualism between spirit and matter, permeated Greek thought and drew Christian thought into spiritualism. The human soul, according to spiritualism, is more or less pure spirit extrinsically riveted to matter and seeking to free itself as much as possible so that its spiritual powers may be developed and arrive at the perfection suitable to spirit. The human body and all its external activity is scorned. Human existence is properly spiritual, and it is realized primarily in the intellectually knowing spirit.

It is true that the roots of this notion are cut away by the Christian teaching on creation, in which matter finds its origin, and by the Thomist teaching that the soul, as the form of the body, forms a substantial union with the body. Nevertheless, the ultimate consequences of this doctrine have not been drawn, and they are important for our discussion. While we do not intend to pause upon the ontological relationship between soul and body, we would like to consider their psychological relationship, grounded as it is in the ontological. The poles of each are called "interior" and "exterior."

If the spiritual soul is actually related to the body and has it as a medium of its own existence and activity, so much so that only through the body is it conscious of itself, and achieves a spiritual self-possession, it follows that there is no such thing as a pure interior—the ideal of every spiritualism. Rather the spiritual-personal life of man is essentially constructed upon the tension of interactivity between interior and exterior. Thus in understanding we are orientated "outside," and "from without" must conquer the area of the spirit. Thus, too, we must go out from ourselves and walk abroad into foreign regions in order to bring these regions into the interior of our own spiritual house. Here we find ourselves. It follows, therefore, that we—to use the terms of Hegel—stand in a dialectical self-estrangement, and only in its resolution and accomplishment do we find our own peculiar identity and attain to a new actuation, enrichment, depth, and fulfillment of our own spiritual existence.

But since intellection demands the personal self-determination of free will as its complementary function, this tension between interior and exterior means not only that we bring the exterior world into the interior of the spirit by knowledge, but also that we are drawn "outside" of ourselves by actively willing, and seize upon the external world by actively forming and determining it. Thus in free activity we form our thoughts and plans, we reproduce our spiritual interior and objectify it in the work we perform in the world. Thus the world is stamped with man's impression, nature is formed and elevated to a cultural level—taking culture here in its widest sense as the exterior life of the world formed by man and for man: from the primitive forms of life, customs and mores which determine actual life, all the way up to scientific knowledge of the world, artistic moulding of it, technical ruling of it, philosophical and religious conception of it, and the vast reaches of social life with its many forms of societies and associations. Nevertheless all of this is not an alienation, self-estrangement and self-surrender of an interior spiritual life. It is founded in the very essence of man and has its ultimate meaning in this, that the totality which forms every culture and every social life reacts upon the spiritual-moral being of the individual who lives amid this totality and is formed by it, and the individual, in turn, is so constituted that his interior strives to represent and express itself exteriorly. An inner conviction, if it is genuine, necessarily demands self-expression in exterior activity. It seeks to strengthen and perfect itself—yes, even to perfect itself—because the interior act first achieves its proper fulfillment in the external act. Surely the exterior flows from the interior: its accomplishment is determined by free will, and its moral value is specified by the interior disposition. But the exterior also reacts upon the interior, so that the interior act itself achieves its ultimate intensity by being externalized. Hence in the interaction of interior and exterior, of interior will and exterior action, true human conduct attains its perfect maturity and completion.

If this is true of moral conduct, it is also true of the love of God, which, as Ignatius says in the book of the Exercises, "must be shown more in deeds than in words." A love that consists merely in the words and feelings of prayer, and remains merely an interior conviction that is not strengthened and perfected in action, is not yet a genuine and true love. Even the monk, who leads a most purely contemplative life, cultivates his love of God not only in contemplation as an inner conviction, but in exterior action as well. He performs deeds of the love of God: physical work, penitential work, and especially the liturgy, which above all is an external act, for it is determined in its moral-religious value by the interior disposition with which it is performed, and in turn it reacts upon the genuine intensity of the inner disposition, bestowing upon it, its final perfection. Thus pure interior is neither possible nor, in so far as it is possible, is it an ideal of human life. And hence it is that ideals have been envisioned of purely spiritual forms of existence, but they are never realized, and all the while the perfection of will and action, which is altogether in harmony with a human nature composed of body and spirit, is sadly neglected.

This specifically human structure of being and activity is exposed to the specifically human danger of alienation: the interior becomes lost in external action so that activity is no longer action perfected by personality, but degenerates into a thoughtless and purposeless course of empty external flurry. In modern times it is scarcely necessary to enumerate the more terrifying dangers. But that these dangers exist is no argument against the purpose and value of true action. It merely stresses more clearly the tension between the two poles, neither of which must be reduced to the other. As there is no pure interiorness but only an interior that stands in continual reciprocal interactivity with the exterior, so all the more there can be no pure exteriorness without forfeiting the true moral worth of human activity, since this worth has its foundation in the free self-determination of the human person. To that extent the unity of this tension has its primacy in the interior, for conduct is essentially evaluated from within by the interior disposition of the free will (*essential perfection*). But conduct substantially achieves its perfected unity in the external act, which springs from the free personality and reacts upon it (*integral perfection*). Therefore, that conduct has the highest value in which interior and exterior act are united in perfect unity, when genuineness of interior disposition is adequately expressed in exterior action, which is perfectly determined and animated from within, and at the same time reacts upon the interior act to give it its ultimate intensity and integrity.

INDIVIDUAL AND SOCIETY

Aside from the value of action in general, let us consider more particularly the significance and value of apostolic action. A true perspective demands that we eliminate a vast source of error which we have termed individualism. It stands in close union with intellectualism and spiritualism. As long as human perfection is estimated either as the perfection (in the rigid intellectual sense) of contemplative understanding as opposed to active volition, or as the perfection (in a broader spiritualistic sense) of pure interiorness of the spirit as opposed to the exteriorness of action, then perfection remains a thing of the individual alone, demanding the surrender of all human associations and relations in order that the soul in its communication with God alone might attain to its perfection. Perfection, then, would be acquired in the contemplative love of God alone, and demands a withdrawal from any active part in the love of the neighbor. This ordination presupposes first of all that the love of God is essentially a thing of contemplation and not also a thing of action—a notion we have already disproved—and secondly, that perfection consists in the love of God alone and not just as essentially in the love of the neighbor. If Christ explicitly compared the command of the love of the neighbor to the first and highest commandment of the love of God (Matt. 22:38), and if John says: "How can one love God whom he does not see, if he does not love his brother whom he sees? . . . Who loves God, must also love his brother," (I John 4:20), surely this means that the love of God must be strengthened in the love of the neighbor. Indeed the love we have both for God and for our neighbor must be the very same love. Love, then, of the neighbor is just as essential and just as basic as the love of God. Of course this is never denied, but in the teachings on perfection it frequently does not receive sufficient attention.

Every individualism basically contradicts the spirit of Christianity. Philosophically it is unsound. The wealth of value in the personal relations of man with man are natural unsurmountable bounds which bind the individual to society. Just as the individual man depends for his physical life upon society (marriage and the family), so his growth and maturity, the self-development of his spiritual-personal, and moral life is guided by human companionship, communication, spiritual contact, mutual help and enrichment, association and co-operation. Absolute eremiticism is impossible. And to that extent to which it is possible, it must always be preceded by social experience, for man as a complete personality is incapable of living without society. Hence, individualism contradicts the basic structure of man's essence and the laws of human life.

It is all the more erroneous theologically. For the individual is not redeemed and sanctified as an individual but as a member of the supernatural society of the Church. As the Mystical Body of Christ, this society is redeemed and sanctified as such, before the individual is incorporated into it and made to participate in salvation. But because this supernatural order of salvation is necessarily concretized in an empirical society, its members live together and depend upon one another, they are responsible for one another, and they are a source of natural and supernatural help to one another in attaining their common sanctification. The Christian life is lived amid the totality of these relations. Since, moreover, Christian perfection is not devoid of the laws of life of a mankind redeemed in Christ, but brings these to pure and rich development, perfection remains essentially related to the society of the Church and has to serve it, whether that be by actively working for the salvation and sanctification of men or by a contemplative life of prayer and penance for the growth of the kingdom of God in the world.

But if exterior activity is action produced by the complete personality, not a self-estrangement of the spiritual interior but its normal self-realization and perfection, so that in the interplay between interior and exterior human conduct actuates its highest possibilities, then that rich fullness of life is produced that, from the pure love of God and of the neighbor, places at God's disposal all its exterior activity and works with all its strength for the salvation of souls. In apostolic work of this sort interior and exterior, intention and activity are not only perfectly united, but in this unity the whole commandment of love given by the Master, love of God and love of the neighbor, is fulfilled. In this fulfillment of the whole law of love and not in an isolated love of God alone—and in such an isolation love would no longer be genuine—consists the self-sanctification of one's self, just as work for the sanctification of others is not only the highest fulfillment of the love of the neighbor—because it concerns itself with the highest good obtainable for another—but is also the highest fulfillment of the love of God, insofar as all the toil and anxiety of work, yes even the renunciation of the peace of contemplative quiet with God alone, is undertaken for the love of God as a surrender of one's self entirely to the plans and wishes of God in order to work with Him in His redemptive mission in the world.

All of this is certainly true—*mutatis mutandis*—also of the contemplative life of the monastic orders. In its austerity it is undertaken for the love of God and realizes likewise the love of the neighbor, for it is lived in society, and by prayer and penance it remains related to the whole Church and is called to serve the salvation of men. Cherished rays of apostolic light stream out from the cloister, even if the individual monk is not directly engaged in apostolic activity. Because there is a multiplicity of different works and tasks, vocations and missions, within the one Church, and so a multiplicity of concrete forms of Christian perfection, any objective appraisal of the different forms of life is very questionable and one-sided. Nevertheless it seems that *in itself* an apostolic life is the highest type of life. In this opinion we agree with St. Thomas, but we disagree with him in assigning the reason: it is not the highest because contemplation (primarily meaning intellectual contemplation) in the sense of giving to others the fruit of one's contemplation is more perfect than pure contemplation, but because it embraces in a unity both interior and exterior, the love of God and the love of the neighbor, and brings them to their highest development in an external act, which is animated by the interior conviction of Christian love in its two inseparable dimensions. In its concrete fulfillment this surely presupposes that the unselfish conviction of love is both interiorly and exteriorly a life-giving power actually penetrating every act with the greatest possible purity. And this is the end that interior prayer and the contemplative impulse serve: contemplation in action.

MEANS AND END

We are prepared now to answer the question whether and to what extent "contemplation is to be placed at the service of action" without foolishly inverting the right order of things. We are not concerned with purely intellectual contemplation, but with religious contemplation, with an interior act of personal surrender to God, with that prayer that, as the formal glory of God, is of the highest value and must no longer be subordinated to an inferior end without surrendering its own worth.

First, let us recall that an action for the sake of God is a form of glorifying God, yes, it is the most perfect and the highest form of glorifying God. The glory of God (formal glory) surely does not consist in intellectual cognition alone, but primarily and essentially in a free personal recognition of the creature-Creator relationship with a corresponding attitude of will, which finds its most perfect expression in the love of God. This attitude attains its perfect form, as far as is humanly possible, not in a pure "interiorness," but in the unity and totality of "interiorness" and "exteriorness": inner conviction and exterior action animated by this conviction. Affective love is true and mature when it has stood the test and becomes perfected in effective love. Hence it is that the formal glory of God accomplished in prayer loses nothing of its value if it is ordered to an end that is the perfection of activity: to act perfectly. This would be an inversion of the true order of things only if the surrender of the supreme good was made to a finite good. But if this ordination elevates action so that it become perfect action, and this not for the sake of perfecting man but for the glory of God, then the ordination is one of affective honor of God to effective honor of God, an ordered unity which has its roots in the very material-spiritual nature of man himself. And in the accomplishment of this ordination the honor of God results in the total and true fulfillment and maturity of man.

Secondly, it should be clear that the life of prayer is not completely subjected to this end. At least this is the meaning of the formula of Suarez, in which he defines the relation between action and contemplation in an active life. For in such a life contemplation has not only the function to assist one to act perfectly, but also to render due religious cult to God. This means that the explicit honor of God, which is of obligation in prayer and worship, remains relatively independent of the ordination to the perfection of action. We said "relatively independent" because contemplation can never be absolutely independent of perfect action. Prayer does not consist in speaking with God in order to impart self-revelation, which is always antiquated by God's omniscience. The meaning of prayer rather lies in ever striving after an expressly new actuation of an interior attitude toward God which is suitable for us, an attitude that must not be restricted to the time of prayer alone but should penetrate and transform our whole life. Since this is a personal attitude toward a personal God, it can be properly actuated only by a deliberate personal acceptance of the divine intimacy in prayer: to this extent prayer is absolutely necessary in every Christian life. But in so far as it is an attitude which, because of its basic significance, should determine and transform the whole course of life, prayer also remains—in spite of the lofty values it possesses unimpaired—essentially ordered to a sanctifying permeation of all our activity, so that it become perfect action. The more this prayerful attitude permeates our whole life, the less is a definite time of prayer necessary in itself. St. Ignatius thought it an imperfection that long periods of prayer should be needed in order to find God and unite oneself with Him. The ideal—which, to be sure, can scarcely be realized in all its purity, for it is the highest sanctity—is that one's entire life be so ordered to God, saturated and filled with Him, that nothing of this union with God be lost even amid the activity with men and association with the things of the world, but that it become a unique prayer in which all action participates.

THE FORMULA OF NADAL

This is the meaning of the formula in which Nadal compresses Ignatian spirituality: contemplative in action. It is valuable not only for Jesuits but for everyone who is striving for perfection in apostolic activity, for diocesan priests especially, and for every Christian endeavoring to sanctify his particular vocation. Let us explain this formula against the background of the teaching of St. Ignatius.

The word *action* scarcely needs further elucidation. It is concerned primarily with apostolic work, be it direct or indirect, since all work undertaken in an active-apostolic life serves this end. Secondly the formula refers to every other active life capable of moral value and Christian sanctification. Action, therefore, here means simply work, intellectual or physical, of any type whatsoever, as long as it can be concretized in moral and Christian value by being performed for the glory of God. It does not mean action in the sense used by the Fathers as moral-ascetical activity, as a mere prerequisite condition for a perfection that consists in contemplation (of an intellectual and religious sort), for in the Ignatian sense action itself becomes the field in which perfection must be attained and realized in the interpenetration of action and contemplation.

Nor must *contemplation* be taken in the ancient sense of intellectual contemplation, since as such it does not depend upon intellection as long as this does not lead to personal, religious value. Nor does it mean, at least it does not merely mean, what we have designated religious contemplation, formal interior prayer. In the "Constitutions" Ignatius speaks of union and familiarity with God and demands that it exist not only in prayer but in all one's actions. Now if this is expressed by the twin classical concepts as contemplation in action, then the word contemplation corresponds not to prayer, but to union and familiarity with God, in a word to union with God, which must be present as well in prayer as in action. Contemplation, then, is a union with God, which clearly stands out against explicit, formal prayer, which surely is actuated and realized in prayer but is not restricted to it. Hence, Ignatius presupposes that action also can be elevated to continual union and intimacy with God.

The next obvious question concerns the degree of knowledge required, for it is clear that in action, in pressing work, God cannot be continually discerned with the same clarity of consciousness as He is in prayer, in explicit prayer. Now in itself clarity of reflexly conscious motivation is no yardstick for the moral value (natural and supernatural) of conduct. That degree of consciousness suffices that makes possible a free, personal self-determination and action springing from it. For this a continual reflexly conscious intention (actual intention) is not necessary; an implicit but effective continuation of the intention suffices (virtual intention). This universal teaching of moral theology is clearly applicable here. Even if it is impossible, during a multiplicity of activities, continually to think explicitly of God (with an actual intention), still the love of God should become an effectively guiding principle, which (as a virtual intention) directs all activity to God. Now the virtual intention is nothing else than the determined continuation of the actual intention already made. The effective strength of the virtual intention, therefore, is measured, not by the clarity and distinctness of the recollection, but by the genuine animation of the actual intention, that is, by the personal surrender to God, freely and consciously made. And when one realizes how easily base and selfish intentions insert themselves into activity and tarnish the purity of the love of God which should govern action, then the necessity of a continually renewed control of the intention and the actual direction of it demands that the union with God become more and more actuality.

Ignatius points out two stages in the growth of this union with God. The first is the "right intention." Since the union with God amid an active life is concretized precisely here, it is a critical point, which Ignatius continually stresses. In the "Constitutions" he writes: all should try to have a right intention, not only concerning their state of life but also concerning each particular action. And in the same place he continues: that in all things, putting off self, they may seek God, as far as possible, in all creatures they love, that they may give their whole love to the Creator, loving Him in all things and all things in Him. These words surely go beyond the mere "right intention" to point out a second and higher step of the union with God, which we wish to designate as contemplation in action in its full meaning.

In the instruction in which Nadal fashioned this formula, we have its clearest illustration. After having treated of the graces of prayer of St. Ignatius, he clearly distinguishes from these ". . . but he knew still another prayer," which was no longer regarded as "a privileged grace of an altogether peculiar type," as merely a personal grace bestowed upon the Saint, but as a "privileged grace which has been granted to the whole Society." With a certain definiteness Nadal maintains that this grace is "a part of our vocation." Because the perfection of the active life consists in this, everyone who is called by God to perfection in an active life is likewise called to this grace. Its particulars Nadal describes when speaking of Ignatius:

> It allowed him to see God present in all things and in every action, and it was accompanied with a lively feeling for supernatural reality: contemplative in the midst of work, or to use his favorite expression: to find God in all things. This grace, which illumined his soul, became clear to us by a kind of light that beamed out from his face and by the radiant trust with which he worked in Christ. It filled us with a great wonder, our hearts were greatly comforted by the sight of him, as we were aware that something of the overflow of this grace flowed out upon ourselves.

We will certainly not do justice to these words if we see in them only the "right intention." Obviously this is something greater, and Ignatius himself teaches us what it is in the Contemplation to obtain divine love of the "Exercises": to know and love God present in all things, living in them, working through them, and in them giving Himself to us. Thus will the vision of things in God grow and the consciousness that we, for all the activity we carry on in the world, are nothing else than "streams from the Sun" of God and "water from the spring" of God—as the "Contemplation on Love" says in the book of the "Exercises"—ourselves not only created and blessed by Him, but also chosen by Him, and sent into the world as instruments of His grace, instruments whose effectiveness is measured by how perfectly we fit into the hand of the Divine Master-worker.

15

Transformation of the World: Flight from the World

KARL TRUHLAR, S.J.

In an earlier article, "De viribus naturae humanae in vita spirituali,"[1] I studied man's relationship to his specifically human powers. I might equally well have entitled it, "The Development and the Crucifixion of Man's Powers." The title of the present article, another in the discussion of Christian Humanism, has to do with man's relationship to "the world."

The term "world" is used here in the sense given it in the current discussion of Christian Humanism,[2] where it regularly means the irrational universe containing man, who has been implanted therein; who by the power of his spirit, of hands and tools, molds for his own human ends both himself immediately and the universe under various aspects, physical, biological, psychic, social.[3] Thus understood, "the world" embraces human beings and the rest of creation with all that has arisen in the course of history and that arises from human beings: the products of education, of organization, of science, art, technology, of economics, of politics.[4] And "the world" is considered independently of its goodness or badness.

Among Catholics there are two positions with regard to man's relationship to "the world": One may be designated "the formation, or molding, of the world," and comprehends the use of the world; the other, "flight from the world." Or they may be called respectively "incarnationalism" and "eschatologism." The former tendency inculcates the idea that Christians have a duty to use the world aright and transform it in keeping with the ideas and the will of God; that as servants of Him, who by his Incarnation consecrated the world, they have the duty of "making Christ further incarnate" in every civilization and culture. The second tendency, contrariwise, betrays a mistrust of the values of civilization and culture, and until the day of the *Parousia* keeps looking forward to the victory of Him who by His Cross crucifies the world.[5] A special aspect of the opposition between these two tendencies shows up in the treatment of the theology of history.[6]

I

The creatures the world contains were created good. Holy Scripture in Genesis represents the Creator as creating with great care and solicitude (1:31). Elsewhere it shows Him explicitly as creating with wisdom and prudence (Ps. 103 (104): 24; Jer. 10:12; Prov. 3:19-20; 8:22-30). Since He created thus, with wisdom and prudence, He had *ideae* of all the things that He made: such is the clear teaching of the Fathers. And from this teaching theological speculation later went on to make further deductions: that since the divine *ideae* are not really distinct from God, He Himself is the world's first exemplary cause, and this according to His essence—not as His essence, but to the extent to which He understands his essence as variously imitable outside Himself. In their *ideae* creatures share the divine life:

> God's act of living is his act of understanding [they are the same]; now in God intellect and the object of intellection and the act of understanding are the same. And hence whatever is in God as an object of intellection is His very act of living or His life. And hence, seeing that everything made by God is in Him as an object of His intellection, it follows that everything in Him is divine life itself.[7]

The Word of God proceeding from the Father through the divine act of intellection expresses the Father Himself as well as all that the Father knows by his act of Self-knowledge; expresses, therefore, both the Father and the whole universe. As the Father's Image, the Word represents to the Father the divine essence and everything that has its foundation therein; represents the images, that is to say, of all things. But these images, proceeding as they do by the same act of cognition as the Word proceeds by, are not created or made, but begotten.[8]

From this, however, it does not follow that the world is the absolutely best world. True, the most perfect cause ought to operate most perfectly. But from this principle the deduction may be made that God operates in the most perfect manner, but not that the effect produced outside of God must be most perfect. Rather, the notion of a world that is absolutely the best in repugnant; for a creature, however perfect by supposition, must remain only finite; and so another more perfect may always be imagined. The world is, however, relatively the best world, insofar as God has freely determined the degree of glory that he wills to have from creatures and insofar as he has chosen the best means of getting it.

A further attribute of God mentioned in Holy Scripture in connection with the creation is His goodness. Psalms 135 (136); 1-9, celebrates creation as the work of God's mercy and goodness. The conservation, too, of creaturedom is the effect of His goodness (Wisdom 11:26).[9] This teaching comes down through tradition and is taken up by the first Vatican Council: God created "by His goodness . . . in order to show His perfection through the good things that He bestows upon creatures."[10]

This holds true of all, even of material, creation. The Scripture texts that speak of God's goodness and wisdom in His act of creation are in no way restricted to the purely spiritual creation. "And God saw *all the things* that He had made: and they were very good" (Gen. 1:31). "In wisdom hast Thou made *all things* (Ps. 103 [104]:24). The first Vatican Council explicitly states:

This God, the only true God, by His goodness and by His "almighty power" . . . in order to show His perfection through the good things that He bestows upon creatures, did by His free purpose "at once from the beginning of time create out of nothing both [kinds of] creature, the spiritual and the corporal, namely the angelic and the earth [*mundanam*]; and thereafter, the human, made as of both spirit and body together."[11]

But although the goodness of all, even of material, things was clearly expressed in Holy Scripture, St. Paul was obliged in his time to utter a warning.

Now the Spirit explicitly says that in later times some will leave the faith, minding deceptive spirits and doctrines of devils, speaking lies hypocritically, with their consciences branded by the searing-iron, forbidding marriage, [bidding] abstinence from meats that God created to be eaten thankfully by the faithful and by those who know the truth; because everything created by God is good, and nothing is to be rejected that is taken thankfully; for it is hallowed by the word of God and by prayer (I Tim. 4:1-9).

The Holy Ghost speaks clearly through persons gifted with the charisma of prophecy—perhaps through St. Paul himself—to say that in the following or in some later period (ἐνὑστέροις καιροῖς)[12] some will abandon the faith that brings salvation, for they will give ear to false teachers with devil-inspired doctrines—doctrines of those who utter lies and who are hypocrites: They give themselves out as inspired by God; in reality they are inspired by demons,[13] whether because they simulate an austere life while inwardly their conscience is "marked with a branding-iron" *(cauteriatam);* that is, a mark of shame has been branded upon it as if with a heated iron.[14]

Their conscience is burnt with a heated iron; *i.e.*, in the moral sense, it is seared with a brand of shame. There is a pejorative reference to criminals or runaway slaves, and a contrast with the στίγματα τοῦ'Ιησοῦ (Gal. 6:17). These apostates bear in their utmost depths the indelible marks of their master, Satan (Spicq).

St. Paul mentions two errors soon to arise, against which Timothy is to fortify the faithful in advance, and which he now points out: marriage will be forbidden as something intrinsically evil. The basic error is that of a dualism that considers matter evil in itself and which looks for a solution to its difficulty in the most intense possible renunciation of matter.[15] The first error, inspired perhaps by a false conception of the resurrection (Matt. 22:30; II Tim. 2:18) and refuted in First Corinthians, 7, is not explicitly refuted in the present passage. (It had been implicitly refuted by the statement [I Tim. 2:15]: she "will be saved by childbearing.")[16] The other error St. Paul—although he had previously had to justify the use of food in other passages too (cf. Rom. 14:1 ff.; Col. 2:20-23)—refutes expressly here:[17] God created foods for men to eat, and for believers and those instructed in revealed truth to eat with thanksgiving: "It is hallowed by the word of God and by prayer": according to Genesis 3:17, the earth is cursed because of man's sin; and according to Romans, 8:19 ff., all creation groans and awaits its deliverance. Therefore, the pronouncing of a blessing over the foods appointed for man's nourishment—the biblical foundation of church blessings—may easily be understood. St. Paul mentions the "word of God," whcih is pronounced over foods and the "prayer" of blessing, which is added. Probably they mean the words of the inspired Old Testament, just as today the blessing at table is still aptly composed of words of Holy Scripture (*v.g.*, Ps. 145:15 ff.; *Pater Noster*). The text clearly presupposes the custom of a blessing at table, which even apart from this can be evinced from primitive Christianity (cf. I Cor. 10:30; Matt 14:19; 26:26-27) Meinertz).

The error foretold by St. Paul soon developed. It appears for rebuke in the Letter of the Church of Lyons occasioned by the martyr Alcibiades, whose rigor of life is blamed in a revelation received by Attalus.[18] Such excessive propensity to asceticism is blamed also by Denis, bishop of the Corinthians (*ca.* 165-175), writing to Pinytus, bishop of the Gnosii.[19] The same error is later on condemned in the heresy lists, published by bishops and councils, especially those by Irenaeus (end of second century),[20] the Councils of Ancyra (A.D. 314) and Nicaea (325), Epiphanius, bishop of Salamina in Cyprus (374-377), Filastrius, bishop of Brescia (*ca.* 389-391); the lists in the Canons of the Apostles (*ca.* 400);[21] in writings against the Manichaeans;[22] in the Council of Gangra, against the false asceticism of the Eustathians (*ca.* 340-343);[23] in the *acta* against the Priscillianists (Council of Saragossa of the Twelve Bishops, A.D. 380, and other councils);[24] in the decrees against the Albigensians, the Waldensians, etc.[25]

In these documents the Church was defending the goodness of the corporeal, material world. The Council of Nicaea declared: "We believe in one God, the Father Almighty, Maker of all things visible and invisible."[26] As the Council was aiming at the Gnostic dualists, who considered the corporeal world as proceeding from an evil principle, and who denied it goodness, the Council's proposition should read: "We believe in one God, *the one and the same* Maker not only of heaven but also of earth, not only of things invisible but also visible." "The Church's first great doctrinal struggle was not against those who denied God but against those who denied the world; and her first victory—almost forgotten today in our theological *summas*—consisted in 'saving the earth'!"[27] And so every act of contempt for earth involves contempt for God its maker.

Since everything comes from God, the only Creator, and since all things have a divine significance, worship of God and striving toward Him on the one hand, and on the other, respect for the world and the remaining faithful to it are not two divergent attitudes or tendencies between which a choice must be made. They are two solidary, complementary aspects, which are both logically and naturally bound together, of one and the same duty and of one and the same love. It is because God is the universal Creator that to blaspheme the earth or the body or things is an act of impiety, just as to scorn a discourse is to insult its author. Christianity, then, is not to be presented as a choice between two incompatible realities, but as a universal synthesis.[28]

Original sin has among its consequences an effect upon matter too. For man is intimately connected with matter, both with that of his own body, which was formed from the slime of the earth (Gen. 2:7), and with the rest of corporeal creation. Implanted in the universe, man is not shut up within himself nor isolated, but at least mediately has an influence upon the whole universe and is subjected to its influences.

Because of this connection, man's works have repercussions even upon the irrational world: his good works a positive, his evil works a negative repercussion.

According to Romans 5:12: "Through one man sin entered into the world [εἰς τὸν κόσμον], and through sin, death." "The world" here is taken by some to mean the human race. Cornely, however, says that "along with Origen a considerable number take it as 'either the place in which men dwell—the globe—or earthy and bodily life in which death has its place'; this means the *complexus* of earthly and human things."[29]

The fellowship between man and irrational creation, so far as sin is concerned, is further expressed in Romans 8:19-22.

For the eager expectation of creation is looking for the revelation of the sons of God. For creation has been made subject to vanity not of its own will, but because of him who made it subject in hope that creation too will itself be set at liberty from its enslavement to corruption unto the freedom of the glory of the sons of God. For we know that all creation is groaning and is in labor until this time.

In this passage too πᾶσα ἡ κτίσις can only mean human creation, as in Mark 16:15: "Preach the Gospel to very creature [πάσῃ τῇ κτίσει]."

Romans 8:19-22 is so understood by St. Augustine[30] also in his attack upon the Manichaean interpretation, and after him by some interpreters, especially in the Middle Ages.[31] Yet it is to be noted that according to St. Augustine man is *"omnis creatura"*—not *tota creatura* —only insofar as like a microcosm he contains all the rest of creation: "But let us without any calumny consider all creation in man himself"; "All creation is in man."[32] Thus, according to St. Augustine, *creatura* in a way designates irrational creation as well as man, and at the same time *all*—not *the whole*—of it.

A fuller repercussion of human sin upon irrational creation emerges in an opinion which today is practically general. This opinion holds that the word "creation" signifies not only *all* but also *the whole of* creation. The further exegetical question, whether the whole of irrational creation is to be understood here in an exclusive sense—that is, without man—or with man,[33] is of scarcely any importance for our subject; for even were it to be taken in an exclusive sense, the slavery of corruption in creation arises from man's sin.

The creation of which we are speaking here is subjected to "vanity" (ἡ ματαιότης) and "corruption" (ἡ φθορά). According to St. Augustine and some others[34] likewise, "being subjected to vanity" is the same as "having surrendered to the things of time that pass away like a shadow."[35] Cornely, following Tertullian, Toletus, Cornelius à Lapide, and others, understands "vanity" as

> those vain and empty things and those perverted and base pursuits of fallen man which since Adam's fail creatures are compelled to serve. For creatures have been deprived—orphaned and disinherited—of the end for which God made them, to the extent that fallen man, who now walks in the futility of his mind with his understanding darkened (cf. Eph. 4:17), no longer minds the end God set for them, but sets up strange and perverted goals for them according to his own will [*arbitrium*].
>
> Man does not make use of creatures to progress in the knowledge, the praise, and the service of the true God by means of them—the purpose for which they were given man—but abuses them, either in such a way as to look upon them as gods, giving them the worship due to God alone, and so to exchange God's truth for a lie; or in such a way as to obey his concupiscences and to seek through creatures either empty and shameless pleasure and delight, or vain and impious praise and glory, etc.
>
> So far, then, is man at present from using creatures to glorify God that through them he is continuously offending God.

In this passage, therefore, as in Ephesians 4:17, "vanity" connotes perversion, though it does not mean that alone. . . . Hence we find no objection to understanding "vanity" here to mean the ownership which the devil, the prince of this world, the ruler of this darkness, is allowed to exercise over creatures, and which he employs to seduce men and to turn them away from the service of God.

Père Viard, after investigating the meaning of the related words μάταιος and ματαιοῦσθαι concludes: "The abstract noun ματαιότης may be admitted to designate in fact the concrete power to which creation, escaping from the submission it owes to God, has been subjected."[36]

Η φθορά, according to Cornely, means, as in II Peter 1:4 and 2:12, all the moral and physical debasement which sin brought into the world. Lagrange opposes Cornely and insists upon the use of the word in *St. Paul,* and excludes from it the sense of *moral* corruption. But he adds: "Because of δουλεία [servitude], however, and because of the parallelism with the positive deliverance, φθορά is to be taken as a kind of personification of a state. Paul . . . speaks of enslavement to a power of death to which creation in general submitted."[37]

To this "vanity" "creation has been made subject, not of its own will, but because of him who made it subject in hope." So far as our subject is concerned, it does not matter whether he "who made it subject" is taken to be God, who willed the subjection of the irrational world when He appointed man head of visible creation (Gen. 1:28) and cursed the world because of man's sin (Gen. 3:17), or to be Adam, or to be man in general[38]; for the *vanity* to which creation is subjected is conceived in any case as having been caused by man's sin.

But just as Adam's sin and man's personal sin affect not only man but the rest of the universe at the same time, so too does Christ's redemption affect them: everything has been signed with Christ's Cross. As for Holy Scripture, this is clear from St. Paul's Epistles to the Colossians and the Ephesians. In Colossians 1:19-20 there is the statement: "It has pleased [God] . . . to reconcile all *things* [τὰ πάντα, not τοὺς πάντας] through Him to Himself, making peace through the blood of His cross, whether things on earth or in heaven." Similarly in Ephesians 1:10: "He determined . . . in the dispensation of the fulness of times to restore all things [again τὰ πάντα] in Christ, both those which are in heaven and those which are on earth in Him." Christ is "the Firstborn of every creature. For in Him were created all things in heaven and on earth, visible and invisible. . . . All things have been created through Him and unto Him [εἰς αὐτόν], and He is before all creatures and all things endure in Him" (Col. 1:15-17). This conception of St. Paul's is further evolved by the Fathers[39] and the theologians.

Scheeben writes: That the supernatural order is brought to its perfection through Christ even in material creation, of which the natural head is man, insofar as it is in and with man that creation receives its own supreme glorification, and is called to the highest glorification of God. The recapitulation [restoration] of all things in Christ means that all creation gathered together again in Christ as its head, united and brought to its perfection, is in a perfect manner brought back, as to its ultimate end, to that principle from which it came through the act of creation, and from which it has been in part separated by sin.[40] In the work of recapitulating irrational creation the connection of the bodies of the sons of God with the corporeal world holds a peculiar importance—these bodies which are to be configured to Christ's glorified body (Phil. 3:20-21) and are already so configured inchoatively through grace. The important connection is this: as the body is the soul's dwelling-place, so material nature is the dwelling-place of the whole man; indeed, the human body has been taken from it, and after being united to the spirit, ceases not to be connected with it. Therefore, the glorification of the human body ought to some extent to be communicated to material nature, which surrounds and is united to the body, in order to become a worthy dwelling-place of man in glory.[41]

This doctrine also underlies the liturgy. In the hymn, *"Pange, lingua, gloriosi,"* the Church sings of the river of Christ's blood wherein not only man but earth, sea, sky, and universe (*"terra, pontus, astra, mundus"*) are laved. To be adduced also is the prayer that, before the reform of the Holy Week liturgy, used to be said on Holy Saturday after the second prophecy:

O God, unchanging Power and Light eternal: look favorably upon the marvellous sacrament of Your whole Church. Bring to pass peaceably the work of man's salvation by the operation of Your unfailing economy. May all the world experience and see that what had fallen is raised erect; what had grown old is made new; that all things return again to integrity through Him from whom they took their origin: Our Lord Jesus Christ,

Your Son, who lives and reigns with You in the unity of the Holy Spirit, God, forever and ever. Amen.

But in the case of man the effects of redemption are not yet definitive; they will be such only in the glory to come, which shall be revealed after the resurrection of the dead, and which we wait for with groaning (Rom. 8). Similarly, in material creation, too, the repercussions of grace have not yet overcome those of sin except in principle, and consequently are continuously at war with sin. Therefore "the eager expectation of creation is looking for the revelation of the sons of God. . . . Creation too will itself be set at liberty from its enslavement to corruption unto the freedom of the glory of the sons of God. For we know that all creation is groaning and is in labor until this time" (vv. 19-22). The words, "the eager expectation of creation," used by St. Paul have in Greek [ἡ ἀποκαραδοκία τῆς κτίσεως] the force of showing creatures with heads thrust forward and eyes alert watching for the glory of the blessed as it comes from afar and waiting anxiously for its arrival. It is to be remarked, moreover, that St. Paul employs in this passage a two fold *prosopopoeia,* or personification: irrational creatures are spoken of as persons waiting for something; and the eager expectation itself is personified: not only is "creation" said "to be looking for," but "the expectation of creation is looking for."[42] That the coming of the new world is to be like a painful childbirth is attested also in these passages: Jeremiah 30:6-8; Michah 4:9-10; likewise Isaiah 26:16-18 (cf. besides Matt. 24:8; Mark 13:8; Gal. 4:19).[43]

The freedom of irrational creation grows or lessens according to the growth or lessening of man's liberty with its repercussions upon the irrational world. Man will enjoy full liberty only in his future glorified state. Irrational creation too will pass to complete liberty only on the day of the general judgment, when it will associate itself with the glorified children of God as "the new earth wherein dwells justice" (cf. II Pet. 3:13).

Material creation, then, has also been consecrated by the Redemption. No wonder, then, that matter too enters fully into the supernatural economy.

In the case of the sacraments, corporeal matter belongs to the visible sign which signifies and confers invisible grace. St. Thomas explicitly notes that on this account the sacraments testify to the value of bodily things.

This kind of remedies required to be transmitted with visible signs. . . . For it was by undue adherence to visible things that man had fallen into sin. Therefore, lest it be believed that visible things are of their very nature evil and that this was why those who clung to them had sinned, it was fitting for the remedies of salvation to be applied to men through things themselves visible: that so it might be evident that visible things are themselves good by their nature, as having been created by God. . . . Hereby is excluded the error of those heretics who would have all such visible things removed from the Church's sacraments. No marvel: for they are of opinion that all things visible are by nature evil and are the works of an evil creator.[44]

Bread and wine are changed into Christ's Body and Blood; and in this change the manifestation of the goodness of matter reaches its peak.[45]

The liturgical year takes its rhythm from feasts deep-rooted in matter and corporality, or which clearly express man's fellowship with matter: the Angel's Annunciation to the Virgin, with the virginal but real conception; Our Lord's Birth, in which a Virgin, yet true Mother, "brought forth her first-born son and wrapped him in swaddling clothes and laid him in a manger" (Luke 2:7); Our Lord's Epiphany, with the star that went before the Magi "until it came and stood above where the Child was" (Matt. 2:9); the whole liturgical Passiontide, in which, among other things, is recalled the memory of the blood shed, of the sun darkened, of the Temple veil, which was rent in the middle (cf. Luke 23:45); Our Lord's Resurrection, whereon "let the globe of earth also rejoice in the rays of such shining lights, and aglow with the brightness of the eternal King, let all the earth be ware that its mists have been dispelled"; Christ the Light is represented by the candle, which is the "work of bees"; its light, "though divided into parts, yet knows no loss from the borrowing of its light, fed as it is by the melting wax that the mother bee produced for the substance of this precious lamp"; and for this product of irrational creation the Church has a prayer:

Therefore, O Lord, we pray You: that this candle, consecrated to the honor of your Name to dispel the murk of this night, may last without failing and be accepted as an odor of sweetness and mingled with the luminaries on high; may the morning-star find its flame still burning—that Morning-Star, I mean, that knows no setting; that Morning-Star that has returned from the dead and shone serene upon mankind." (*Exultet*);

Pentecost, when the Holy Spirit fills the world and renews the face of the earth (Mass of Whitsunday); Corpus Christi, as the feast of a *body* and of the glorification of matter.

By its sacramentals and by its other rites the Church enters fully even into the bodily world. She blesses homes, wells, fields, meadows, vineyards, fodder, smelting-furnaces, printing presses, machinery, seismographs, ships, railroads, gear for mountain-climbing, aeroplanes (*Rituale Romanumm*). All these blessings and rites, whose effect is derived from the work of the Church acting (*ex opere operantis Ecclesiae*), insofar as she is holy and most closely joined with her Head,[46] weaken the influence of sin upon matter or eliminate that influence from matter, and the way is paved for the influence of grace.

With Christ and the Church individual Christians should redeem irrational creation.

This they do first and foremost by right use. The Christian has got to use irrational creation; for in his personal life, bodily and spiritual, individual and social, natural and supernatural, man depends upon irrational creation. But his use of creatures must be right, must be for the purposes of grace, not those of sin. Earth's treasures, for example, are not intended for the egotistic opulence of some, but for the just and natural prosperity of all; for all are children of one Father, who is the owner of these treasures; but natural prosperity must serve supernatural prosperity—the increase of divine life in men. By such use irrational creation is directed not to sin but to the liberty and glory of the children of God. And this orientation is something entirely real.

The *Fontes theologici* (sources of theology) that show the goodness of the right use of things are the same texts that were adduced above for the goodness of things themselves; for those texts prove, in addition to the goodness of things, the goodness of the right use of things. Even Origen himself—who again and again exhorts "to leave things bodily and visible and hasten on to those which are incorporeal," and to "think not at all of earth but wholly of heavenly things,"[47]—does by no means reject the use of material creation:

"We must not refuse to use the things that were created for us, giving thanks to the Creator,"[48] and more at length:

It is not then from the demons that we receive whatever is useful for this life—we especially who have learnt to use them as they ought to be used. Nor is it with demons that they feast who enjoy earth's produce, wine, fruit, the air and water; but rather with the angels, to whose care these things have been entrusted, and who are as it were invited to the table of the godly who obey the saying which teaches: "Whether you eat or drink or do aught else, do all things for God's glory" (I Cor. 10:3). Therefore, when we eat or drink or breathe for God's glory, and are in everything obedient to reason, we banquet not with any demon, but with the angels of God. "For every creature of God is good, and nothing is to be rejected that is accepted with thanksgiving. For it is sanctified by the word of God and prayer" (I Tim. 4:4, 5). But it would neither be good nor able to be sanctified if, as Celsus imagines, the charge of these things had been entrusted to demons.[49]

The things man uses are partly in a primary or unimproved state, partly have been improved upon or given some shape or form. The shaping of irrational creation directs it toward the freedom of the sons of God, and in this sense redeems it, if the shaping gives expression to truth, goodness, and beauty. Such an expression is to be found, for example, in a land formerly an unhealthy and barren marsh, and now after being drained, dry, healthy, productive, affording men labor and food, providing a site for beautifully constructed homes, bestowing on men houses and fields for just ownership: it forms the basis of due material prosperity, and this serves the growth of Christian personality.

The further shaping or formation of irrational creation is necessary for the reason that in His creative act God did not unfold definitively, or bring forth from creation, or express all the possibilities of which earth has the seeds within her. Along with earth God created man, who as God's fellow worker is to develop earth further according to the possibilities and finalities placed in each thing. The first word God spoke to Adam and Eve is: "Increase and multiply and fill the earth, and subdue it, and master the fishes of the sea and the birds of the air and all the living things that move upon the earth" (Gen. 1:28). "God therefore took man and placed him in the paradise of pleasure to till [it]" (Gen. 2:15; cf. 9:1-7). In this shaping or molding, farmer, delver, merchant, householder, statesman, organizer, scientist, parent, educator, artist—each has his role.

With regard to this formation God has His ideas and purposes. They are made known by supernatural revelation and in the natural powers of man's spirit, which can both deduce much from revelation and decide and construct many things even in those areas about which revelation says nothing. Men who mold the universe frequently fail, in all truth, to regard God's ideas and purposes; but when they do not do so, but bring them to realization, in many ways they express the truth, goodness, and beauty that are ultimately an image of the Most Holy Trinity. Thus such molding of the world makes it like God.

And at the same time it leads to God. Man's supernatural life is bound to his psychophysical[50] structure; and this is subjected to influences from the direction of the "world," as is shown by scientific data in biology, psychology, pedagogy, sociology.[51] And for this reason the Church's supernatural life also is bound up with the "world": this holds true for the insertion, conservation, and spread of grace in the "world." Grace, though an entirely gratuitous gift of God, yet presupposes—in keeping with the supernatural ordinance of Divine Providence—by the ordinary law certain natural conditions (which God Himself, the Author of Grace, established by His law). Consequently, unless those conditions are present, either grace is not given; or, if given, is ineffective.

> All commentaries (*commentarii;* properly, "notes") on the Missions agree on this particularly: that conversions, whether of individuals or of nations ordinarily presuppose certain natural conditions—a certain mental culture, habituation to work, stability of life, order. Everyone knows the value that works of charity, care for the sick, and what is in our times . . . daily more evident, social action and social institutes (*instituta*) have for winning souls to the Christian religion.[52]

Here, too, Cardinal Billot's warning has its force:

> To be avoided by all means is that divorce between nature and grace which some posit, apparently from fear of the error of Pelagius, where really there is no need to fear.[53]

God bestows grace in the manner indicated just above, "according to the supernatural ordination of His Divine Providence." The natural conditions of the "world" with respect to grace are not conditions of themselves (*ex se*), or of their nature (*ex sua natura*), because grace does not need them. But they are conditions because God Himself, the Author of Grace, by His ordinary law supposes them in view of His activity. Nor are the conditions here in question a positive reason for the bestowal of grace. Rather, it is a matter of the bond that is, in Suarez' phrase, "simple consecution" (*simplex consecutio*). "The reader will never find in Molina's book [the statement] that grace is vouchsafed as a result of natural works . . . but only that when such and such a work is posited, such and such a gift is given."[54]

The law of grace is a law of harmony. This means that there is between nature and the activity of grace some outward connection. On this point, compare St. Thomas (*S. T.*, I, *q*. 62, *art*. 6), where he takes up the question whether the angels acquired grace and glory according to the amount of their natural endowment.

> My answer is that, reasonably, the angels were given gifts of graces and the perfection of bliss according to the degree of their natural endowment. The reason for this can be gotten at from two considerations. One: God by an ordinance of His wisdom established in the angelic nature differing degrees. Now, as the angelic nature was made by Him in order to reach grace and glory, so the degrees also of that nature appear to be ordered to different degrees of grace and glory. If a builder, for example, polishes stones for a house that he is building, and if he matches some of them with greater artistry and beauty, it is evident that he intends them for the part of the house that is more important. It is evident, then, that if God made some angels of a higher nature, He ordered them toward greater gifts of grace and ampler bliss.

The first of the objections against this is couched thus: "It appears that angels did not acquire grace and glory according to the amount of their natural endowment; for grace being given in accordance with God's mere will, the amount of grace also depends upon God's will and not upon the amount of the natural endowment." In solving this objection, St. Thomas insists upon the assertion made in the body of the article, that God Himself, the Author of grace, can according to His will order degrees of nature to degrees of grace: "Just as grace is from God's mere will, so too is the angelic nature; and as God's will ordered nature to grace, so too He ordered the degrees of nature to the degrees of grace."

This article of the *Summa,* deals with the relation of natural endowment to grace in the case of the angels. The same relationship in the case of human beings is treated in St. Thomas' commentary on the Sentences (*I Sent., dist.* 41, q. 1, a.4), in an article entitled: "Is Predestination Furthered by Any Work of Man?" Among the objections in the introductory portion of the article, the third is especially pertinent to our present subject. "The effect of predestination is grace and glory. Both of these are from God alone. Nothing else, then, helps toward the effect of predestination." Among other observations in the *sed contra* is this:

If predestination is not furthered by our works, it is unnecessary to do any good work; and so, vain is the divine law that leads us on to do good; vain, too, will be natural potencies and gratuitous habits of grace, since we need not work for the achievement of the end—But all these conclusions are unsuitable.

St. Thomas' solution is as follows:

The relation between help or furtherance and the effect of predestination is the same as that between the effect of predestination and its cause. And hence, according to this, every cause by the intervention of whose working the effect of predestination is completed, is said to aid predestination: [1] whether as a meritorious cause; [2] or *ex condigno* (suitably), in the way that the act of one who has grace merits life eternal; [3] or even by persuading toward good; hence, it is said (I Cor. 3:9): "For we are God's helpers"; [4] or as disposing, as when someone prepares himself to have grace; [5] or even *by natural operation,* just as . . . all natural causes help predestination inasmuch as by their office or service the generation and sustenance of the elect is perfected.

In *Ad priman* St. Thomas adds:

This assistance is not given because of any inadequacy in predestination itself, but for the saving of the orderly relationship established by Divine Wisdom; the relationship, namely, that effect shall proceed from the First Cause by the mediation of second causes.

In this Article the word "cause" is not restricted to a positive reason (*ratio*) but designates everything "which by its working intervenes to complete the effect of predestination." This is evident from the solution. If the term "cause" is thus understood, the phrase "cause of predestination" will also include the conditions treated above; and these conditions being given, grace will be given by simple consecution (*per simplicem consecutionem*), without the one being a positive *ratio* for the other.

Padre Suarez in his work quoted above—*Tractatus de vera intelligentia auxilii efficacis,* c. XI [Treatise upon the Genuine Meaning of Efficacious Grace, Ch. XI]—explains the bond between natural endowments and grace in a way that bears more directly upon our subject. The natural conditions for faith in a heathen are comprised in the term "external call," which is explained as consisting in purely natural endowment and as being subject to God's supernatural providence. To be noted is the distinction between

a merely external call—one to which as yet inward enlightenment and inspiration have not been added—and an inward call—whether a merely, purely inward call or one joined to the external call.

The external call may be understood as beginning in relationship, or in order, to faith, when, for example, a heathen hears a preacher explaining matters of faith; or even earlier, when he is invited by the preacher to come and listen; or even still further back, when from rumor and news he receives intelligence that there are preachers who claim to teach the true way of salvation. All these outward facts may be comprised by the name "grace" insofar as they belong to a gratuitous providence and not to the providence due to nature. Nevertheless they do not belong to assisting grace (*gratia adiuvans*) proper; and they can all, when heard, be apprehended by the intellect alone, by the powers of nature, without any special help from assisting grace.

After the apprehension by the intellect, the will can be stirred up to a desire to hear the teaching about the true way of salvation, and can proceed from there to deliberate about whether the teaching is to be listened to or not, and to the inquiry whether it is worthy of credence or not.

From our analysis of this process we may gather that the first grace that inwardly *arouses the heathen to faith* is preceded by a number of acts performed by the power of the will alone; and these acts appear to be necessary according to the ordinary law before that first grace and to be, moreover, its cause and reason (*causam vel rationem eius*);—acts like the purpose of going to hear the teacher of the faith, and of considering attentively and of grasping (*expediendi*) what he says.

And after this purpose it evidently follows that while the heathen listens outwardly, God is inwardly assisting, directing, and enlightening his intellect to form suitable concepts of what is explained and right judgments about its credibility.

In this interior teaching it is evident that the first inward exciting grace begins in the intellect, gradually drawing in the will toward faith itself. . . .

Moreover, although that will and purpose whereby by the heathen applies himself to listen is not necessarily supernatural *in se*, it nevertheless proceeds from a supernatural and gratuitous providence, by reason of which whatever arouses him to entertain that first purpose from a morally good motive, can be reckoned among the *gratiae excitantes*. And the concursus, too, by which God concurs toward such a purpose, though natural in substance, yet is given in accordance with the providence of grace and in order to a supernatural end, and may for that reason be called rightly *gratia adiuvans*.

Finally, this whole kind of grace belongs evidently to external teaching, and therefore, following upon it there is need of an inward grace of illuminations and inspirations of the Holy Spirit—the sources from which the spiritual and supernatural edifice takes its beginning, and this edifice the Holy Spirit begins within us in a purely gratuitous manner.[55]

The bond between natural conditions and grace is said to be "of ordinary law." God in His freedom and omnipotence can infuse the life of grace into a society that is without truth, goodness, beauty. But ordinarily He does not do this. Ordinarily for the implanting, sustaining, and spreading of supernatural life He demands certain conditions on the part of the "world."

Further it is said: "For the implanting, sustaining, and spreading of supernatural life": A heathen can receive baptism even in a "world" in whose structure none of the conditions just noted exist. But the question is: Can supernatural life thus implanted be also sustained and spread in such a "world" by the ordinary law?

Finally, there is mention of "*some* mental culture, *some* being accustomed to work, order, stability of life." There is in no way a question of any rather lofty degree of what is called "civilization" or "culture."[56]

The Incarnation took place in a concrete milieu in the concrete "World."

Now it came to pass in those days: a decree went forth from Caesar Augustus that the whole world should be registered. This first registration was made by Cyrinus, governor of Syria. And all were going to register, each to his own city.

Now there went up also Joseph from Galilee from the city of Nazareth into Judaea to the city of David, which is called Bethlehem: because he was of the house and family of David: to register with Mary his espoused wife, who was with child. . . . And she gave birth to her firstborn son . . . (Luke 2:1-7).

This Son then "suffered under Pontius Pilate" (Apostles' Creed). The concrete milieu was being prepared by the preceding periods of time and events, by history both sacred and profane. For the part played by sacred history see the Holy Scripture, which puts the Old Testament into relation with Christ. The Law, which preserved the Chosen People from becoming mingled and confused with the heathen world that surrounded them, and which by its precepts and by a multiplicity of observances stirred the People to moral effort, and which kept alive the desire for Redemption, etc., was a "tutor unto Christ" (Gal. 3:24). The Old Testament rituals were types and obscure significations of the New Testament reality; *i.e.,* significations of Christ the antitype of the types. "Let no one criticise you with regard to eating or drinking, or in the matter of a festival or a new moon or of Sabbaths: these things are a shadow or what is to be: but the body is Christ's" (Col. 2:16-17). The milieu of the Incarnation was being prepared by profane history. Sacred history is inserted into profane history; the facts and structures pertaining to sacred history presuppose those that pertain to profane history. Therefore, to say that the Incarnation was quite independent of concrete becoming, independent of the concrete state of the "world," is to teach a sort of Docetism, denying Christ's humanity, which was inserted into a concrete time and a concrete space.

Christ, too, afterwards in His earthy life makes Himself dependent upon the "world" in its concrete reality, and takes into account the cultural milieu in which He lives. Thus, His words, though containing the deepest religious ideas, are perfectly suited to the Palestinian Jew of the time of Tiberius.[57]

And so the Church's supernatural life, which emanates from Christ, is not quite independent of the "world." This holds for the propagation of the faith outside of Christendom, as has been shown above.

But even within Christendom, for the maintenance and spread of the supernatural life, certain goods are required which pertain to the "world"—like a family wage, public assistance, social security. The Pastoral Charge is no longer effective if bereft of any of the modern means that pertain to the "world." The practice of some duties of the

Christian life is improved by the assistance of modern institutions; *v.g.*, the elimination of dangers connected with pauperism.

Were the supernatural life altogether independent of the "world," all the Church's striving throughout the ages—helping the poor, alleviating the unfortunate of every class, improving men's temporal lot—would be quite without hope of bringing men by that striving to the goal for which she was directly established.

From the gratuitousness of the supernatural order it is clear that the "world" before Christ did not positively produce the Incarnation. Similarly, the "world" of today does not positively produce the supernatural life. The Incarnation and the supernatural life do not represent a kind of homogeneous continuation of civilization and culture of the "world." But this fact by no means allows us to deny that the values of civilization and culture have some importance for the insertion, preservation, and spread of the Kingdom of God.

The molding of the "world" according to the ideas and designs of God is, finally, "for the praise of God." Thus transformed, the "world" is a cosmic liturgy. The forms of the world transformed are in P. Claudel's phrase, "man's voice lent to the world for praising God." Without human striving that liturgy would remain an undeveloped seed.

The explanation so far given of the Christian's molding of the "world" makes it clear that such transformation is his duty, especially as a claim of that charity—toward God, the neighbor, and self—in whose control over the whole of life Christian perfection consists. It is not a question of charity only towards God, to whom the world is assimilated by the transformation, and towards whom the transformation leads, and whom it praises; but it is a question also of the duty of charity to the neighbor, with whom the Christian has been united in the one Mystical Body of Christ, and whom, too, he is bound to assist by transforming the world. This help he must also bestow upon himself: hence it is a duty also of charity to self.

Sanctifying grace invisibly affects even the body, the temple of the Holy Ghost, with a certain glory; and this kind of glorification is a beginning of the glory to come, which the glorious body will enjoy. In this way also the redemption of the world is in this life the beginning of the "new earth" to come. But as the body's glorification in the life to come is not a kind of unbroken and homogeneous continuation of the "sort of" glorification by which the body is affected in this life—for death and bodily corruption come in between, while the glory with which the body is clothed at the Resurrection surpasses that of the body here on earth as much as the Beatific Vision surpasses grace—so neither is the "new earth" a sort of uninterrupted and homogeneous continuation of the world's transformation here on earth: for "the earth, and the works that are in it, will be burned up" (II Pet. 3:10), "the heavens that now are, and the earth . . . [are] reserved for fire" (*ibid.,* v. 7), "but we look for *new* heavens and a *new* earth according to his promises, in which justice dwells" (v. 13). Nevertheless, the *same* body shall rise from the dead, according to dogmatic teaching on the identity of the body at the resurrection from the dead. Likewise, the universe to come, spoken of in Holy Scripture, will be *new* indeed, but it will be *earth* and *heaven:* The fire will not annihilate, but will renew irrational creation.

The Old Testament texts about the restoration of the world (especially Isa. 51:6, 16, 65:17; 66:22) sometimes contain images that express, rather, a complete newness in the new heavens and the new earth, while elsewhere they insinuate simple transformation of the present world.[58] Corresponding to this in the Rabbinical and pseudepigraphic literature are two conceptions of the world's future renewal: either of a whole new creation, or of a world to come which is only transformed or glorified.[59] The New Testament dispensation, however, although describing the renewal of the world in Old Testament terms, is a genuine inception of the world to come. According to St. Paul, the coming age has already begun with Christ's Resurrection. Christians have already been "delivered from this present world" (cf. Gal. 1:4), have already "tasted . . . the powers (δυνάμεις) of the world to come" (Heb. 6:5); he who believes "has passed from death to life" already (John 5:24).[60] In this beginning, irrational creation is associated with man; it too, then, is fittingly to be renewed rather than annihilated.

This deliverance, these birthpangs (Rom. 8:19-23) do by no means call for the suppression of the present world, but for its renewal. The Christian dispensation is already a new creation (II Cor. 5:17; Gal. 6:15), the arrival of the new man who ceases not to grow (Eph. 2:15; 4:24). The age to come, holy and incorruptible, will be the issue and development of an indefinite series of renewals. We believe that this view agrees with numerous eschatological speculations which place the new order on our earth, which shall have been marvellously transfigured. Would we not find similar conceptions in the Apocalypse of John in his picture of Mount Sion situated between heaven and earth (14:1-5) and of the Heavenly Jerusalem coming down upon our earth? (21:2; 22:5).[61]

A renewal, as opposed to a complete annihilation, of irrational creation is drawn in a special way from the connection that the corporeity of irrational creation has at the present time with the bodies of the children of God that shall be configured to Christ's glorious Body.

We do not know in what state the artistic works, the products of craft, and the other forms of the transformed world of this time are to be in the world to come. One thing is sure: All that these forms have contributed in the manner explained to the supernatural life of the free children of God will remain forever just as that very life will remain forever.

The transfiguration of the world is a task. And its value is to be estimated also in the context of the present antinomy.

The idea of the transfiguration of the world is not at all new in the Church's life. Tertulian in *Apologeticus,* a work completed in A.D. 197, and hence from his orthodox period, writes:

But we are charged with yet another piece of wrong-doing. We are said to be useless for business. How is this possible, when we live with you as we do, using the same kind of food and clothing as you, having the same mode of life, subject to the same necessities of existence as you. For we are neither Brahmins nor gymnosophists from India, dwelling in the woods, apart from society. We recall that we owe God, our Lord and Creator, gratitude. We reject none of the fruits of His works. Only we control ourselves to keep from using them excessively or wrongly. This is the reason why we dwell with you in this world, frequenting your forum, your market, yours baths, your shops and stores, your hostelries and your fairs, and the other places where business is conducted. With you we go to sea; with you we serve as soldiers and work the earth, and do business, exchange the handiwork of our skill and labor.[62]

And shortly afterwards, *ca.* 220, the unknown author of the *Letter to Diognetus* writes:

Christians are indistinguishable from other human beings in country, speech, and customs; nor have they private cities for themselves alone to live in; nor employ an unusual language; nor practise a remarkable style of life. Their creed is not a thing discovered by the reflexion or the devising of men curious for knowledge; nor is the teaching they uphold, like that of some, a merely human thing. Christians are found living in both Hellenic and non-Hellenic cities, according to each one's lot, and following regional customs in dress and food and mode of life. But they give evidence that their real citizenship and real life is an object for marvel and admittedly wonderful. They dwell in their native countries like aliens; they take their share in everything like citizens; they endure everything like refugees and foreigners. Every foreign land is native to them; each one's own country is strange to him.

They are "in the flesh," but do "not" live "according to the flesh" (II Cor. 10:3). They live on earth, but their real civic activity is in heaven. They obey the established laws; and their private lives excel what the laws demand. They love all and are persecuted by all. . . . They are put to death and are quickened. They are in beggary and enrich many (II Cor. 6:10). They are in want of everything and in everything they abound.

Simply put: What the soul is in the body, Christians are in the world. The soul is spread all through the body's limbs: Christians are scattered throughout the cities of the world. The soul dwells in the body without originating there: Christians dwell in the world without having their origin there. The soul is invisible and is kept in the body, which is a visible thing: Christians can be seen living in the world, but their piety toward God remains invisible. The hate and hostility of the flesh pursue the soul, though the flesh is not unfairly treated, for being forbidden to enjoy pleasures: the world, though nothing wronged, hates Christians because they are opposed to its pleasures. The soul loves the flesh and limbs that hate it: Christians love those who hate them. The soul has been confined within the body, yet maintains the body: Christians are detained in the world as in a prison, but it is they who hold the world together. The soul is immortal and dwells in a mortal tabernacle: Christians sojourn among corruptible things while looking forward to heavenly incorruptibility. The soul improves when treated ill in the matter of food and drink: Christians when punished daily grow in numbers. Such is the high post God has assigned them to; and sin it were for them to beg off from it.[63]

Similarly in the centuries following,[64] down to recent documents of the Church's magisterium.[65]

II

1. Irrational creation is certainly good in itself. But man, using and transforming it, was wounded by original sin. Use and transformation,

then, are easily affected by disorder; namely, when determined not by grace but by sin. The products of modern technology—like radio, film, television—can serve mankind's prosperity, but also its hurt. The police can further good morals in public life, but they can also further a dictator's or a government's malice. Business, which unites mankind, can be a natural substratum of unity in the Mystical Body of Christ, but it can be a means for organized struggle against Christ. Legislatures can pass just laws, but likewise unjust. Education can develop a "humanitarian" sense; it can equally crush it.[66]

2. So too man's corruption affects the world so that the world itself becomes partially corrupted. Think of the dailies, radio, films, the forms of private and public life. A world thus corrupted can by its forms, which have originated from sin, undermine the foundations of Christian existence, weaken them morally, block up the well-springs of Christian vigor, and exert in this way a countereffect upon man by the malice it has received from him.[67]

3. Corruption, issuing ultimately from originating original sin, grows through the activity of "the prince of this world" and of "his army." This activity is described as a knd of "atmosphere" which envelops Christians. So Ephesians 6:12: "Our wrestling is not against flesh and blood": that is, it is not a struggle[68] aaginst weak men like ourselves. We have as enemies "the principalities and the powers" (τὰςἀρχάς, τὰς ἐξουσίας). Earlier (Eph. 1:21), St. Paul uses the same names for the good angels; but in the present passage, for the malign spirits, whose hierarchical names he retains. These wicked angels he represents as κοσμοκράτορες—rulers of the world, which is sunk in the darkness of religious ignorance and sin. As such, they are opposed to God, who is often called παντοκράτωρ (II Cor. 6:19), and nine times in the Apoc.:[69] The Almighty. They are "*spiritualia*" (τὰ πνευματικά) "the spiritual things." The use of the neuter "seems to place the spirituality of our foes in a stronger light" (Vosté). They are the spiritual things "of wickedness," whose will is fixed and stable in evil and wholly applied to mankind's destruction. They are "on high"—that is, scattered in the air; which means that they surround us and lie in wait for us on every side.[70]

To the Biblical data much more is added by the Fathers, especially Tertullian and Origen, and they exerted a decisive influence upon subsequent theology.[71]

According to Tertullian the whole public life of a pagan city is penetrated by demons: "Streets, market-place, bath, dwellings, our very houses, are not altogether without idols. Satan and his angels have filled the whole world (*saeculum*)."[72] Angels of vices are identified with pagan gods. Apollo and the Muses, to whom the arts are dedicated, are merely names of dead persons. "But we are fully aware that underneath those names and beneath those statues that have been erected wicked spirits, demons, are at work and rejoice and feign divinity.[73] Moreover, spectacles are diabolical, not merely because they are idolatrous, but also because they arouse passions which proceed from the demon. Spectacles, festivals, the public offices of the pagan world on account of the idolatry that underlies them are the "pompa diaboli,"[74] which is to be renounced at baptism.[75]

According to Origen, the spiritual struggle of individuals is merely the individual expression of a cosmic reality, namely, of a struggle between the world of the good angels and the world of demons. Both classes exert an influence, first, upon the inorganic material world; *v.g.*, on water, on air. . . . Famine, plague, diseases, are from the operation of demons. Both, further, have influence over animals, the several kinds of demons having an affinity with the several kinds of animals. Furthermore, each human being has his good and his bad angel. The demons hide their activity under the guise of different sciences, such as astrology, divination, and magic. Each nation, too, has its good and its bad angel. Before Christ's coming the good angels are powerless; the nations are dominated by the demons. At His coming the demons in great part[76] oppose Him, are vanquished in substance, but nonetheless continue their activity until the *Parousia*[77] by tempting Christians.

Patristic testimonies representing the whole Christian life as a struggle with demons are numerous. This theme then passes into subsequent tradition. The marks of it are to be found in St. Jerome, St. Augustine, Prudentius, and down to St. Bernard, St. Thomas, St. Ignatius of Loyola, Scupoli. The fundamental idea of the theme is this: Because of original sin man remains in some way under the *power of the demon*. Thence the doctrine of the "corpus diaboli" with its "ministers and members,"[78] and St. Augustine's idea of the "city" of the demon opposed to the "City of God."[79] This theme renders intelligible the expressions in the Roman Ritual where the exorcisms and blessings ordinarily suppose that the devil is actively present in creation, which has been reduced by original sin to a worse condition.

We may instance the rite of baptism with its exorcisms and the renunciation of Satan and his works; and the prayers of those in their last agony, especially "Libera, Domine, animam servi tui" and "Commendo te Omnipotenti Deo."[80]

In his activity the devil looks for human allies; man seduced by the devil does the "works of the devil" (John 8:41, 44; I John 3:8; perhaps Matt. 13:38, 39).[81]

In his temptations the devil makes use of the corruption already existing in the world.[82]

4. It is especially such a corrupt world that the Christian has the duty of avoiding—especially, not solely, such a corrupt world; for, as will be shown below, the world in a certain sense must be avoided even apart from its corruption.

The corruption of the world and avoidance of it are to an extent expressed in the Old Testament.

> For having well pleased God he was beloved; and he was brought out of the midst of sinners among whom he lived, was snatched off before malice should alter his mind, or guile cheat his soul. For the witchery of trifles tarnishes what is good; and desire is inconstant and undermines an innocent mind. . . . For his soul was pleasing to God; for this cause God soon led him forth from the midst of evil.
>
> . . . .
>
> We have wandered from the way of truth; and the light of justice has not shone on us; and the sun of understanding has not risen for us. We are forspent on the way of wickedness and ruin; we have trodden hard ways. What use was our pride to us? What gain did our vaunting of riches bring us? Those things are passed away like a shadow. . . . (Wisdom 4:10-12,14; 5:6-9)

The New Testament speaks of the corrupt world and of avoiding it when it uses the word *"mundus"* or *"saeculum"* in a pejorative sense.[83] So the world which Our Lord blames because of it scandals (Matt. 18:7); the world whose spirit is not the spirit of God, whose wisdom is declared vain because it refused to receive the wisdom of God (I Cor. 2:12; 1:20-21); the world the saints will judge (I Cor. 6:2; cf. 11:32); the world spoken of in the text: "Religion pure and undefiled before God the Father is this: to give aid to orphans and widows in their tribulation, and to keep oneself unspotted from this world" (James 1:27); the world that hates Christ and His disciples (John

7:7, 15:18; 17:14); the world whose prince is the devil (John 12:31; 14:30; 16:11); the world that will rejoice when Christ's disciples weep and lament, that will persecute them, but that Christ will conquer (John 16:20, 33); the world of which Christ says: "And I am not of the world" (John 17:16), "The world has not known Thee [the Father]" (John 17:25).[84]

Similarly, Christian tradition, when exhorting to flight from the world, has before its eyes the world corrupted. Thus, *v.g.*, Tertullian addressing the Christians in prison (A.D. 197):

Nor let yourselves be frightened by your being kept apart from the world. If we recall that the world itself rather is a prison, we shall clearly see that you have left prison rather than gone into prison. The world is in thicker darkness that blinds men's hearts. The world puts on [its prisoners] heavier chains that shackle men's very souls. The world breathes out worse uncleannesses—men's lusts. The world, finally, contains more criminals, namely, the entire human race. And again, it is not the judgment of a proconsul, but the judgment of God that lies in store for it. You may consider yourselves transferred, Blessed Martyrs, from this prison of the world to a place of safekeeping—a darksome place, yes; but you are light. (Eph. 5:8) It has its bonds, but you are loosed from bonds unto God. (Gal. 5:1) Its atmosphere is foul, but you are an odor of sweetness. (II Cor. 2:15) There you are waiting for your judge; but you are to pass sentence on judges. (I Cor. 6:2) Let him be sad in that prison who sighs for the profits of the world (*saeculum*). Even outside of prison the Christians has renounced the things of the world (*saeculum*). Inside of prison he renounces even his prison. Where you are in the world (*saeculum*) matters not for you who are outside of the world (*saeculum*). And whatever you have lost of life's joys—it is good business to lose something to make larger gains. So far I speak not of the prize that God invites His martyrs to. Meanwhile, let us compare your very life in prison with your life in the world, and see whether in prison your spirit does not gain more than the flesh loses. Rather, the Church, the charity of the Brethren, sees to it that your body loses nothing that is just. And besides that, the spirit gains what is ever serviceable for the faith. You have not to look at strange gods. You are not running into their likenesses. You do not take part in heathen holidays. You are not struck by the noisome steam, the din of their displays and shows, the cruelty or the madness or the immodesty of those who throng to those shows. Your eyes do not crash upn the sites (*Locos*) of public lusts. You are remote from scandals, temptations, evil memories, and now from persecutions. Prison is a better place for Christians than the desert for prophets. Many a time Our Lord Himself went into seclusion to pray with greater freedom and to leave the world (*saeculum*). It was in a lonely place that He showed His disciples His glory. Let us drop the name "prison" and call it a retreat. Your body indeed is under lock and key and your flesh in durance. But to your spirit everything is open wide. Wander abroad in your spirit; travel far and wide in your spirit—not with shady walks and extensive colonnades in mind, but that highway that leads to God. As often as you walk that way you shall not be in prison.[85]

In Christian tradition, when "world" and "supernatural life" are placed in opposition, it is the corrupt world that is especially meant. Thus St. Clement of Rome:

Moreover, this world and the world to come are two enemies. The one boasts of adultery, corruption, avarice, deceit. The other renounces these things. We cannot, then, be friends of both. We must renounce the one and take advantage of the other. We think it better to renounce the things here in this world, because they are unimportant and short-lived and subject to corruption, and to love what is yonder in the world to come, as being goods incorruptible.[86]

The "pomp of the devil," which every Christian must renounce at baptism, is the corrupt world, as has been shown above.[87]

The same is to be said of the world that must be renounced by a person who is peculiarly dedicated to Christ, as a virgin. Compare the text of St. Cyprian:

What room is there at a wedding for a virgin whose mind is not to wed? There what pleasure or joy is possible for her, where interests and vows are so different from hers? What lesson does she learn there? What does she see? How far a virgin fails of her purpose who had been modest when she arrived and is immodest when she leaves? And even should she remain body and soul a virgin, her eyes, ears, and tongue diminish what was hers. But what of those who go to promiscuous baths and expose their bodies, dedicated to modesty and chastity, before lustfully curious eyes? . . . But as things are, while they wish to dress more elegantly and to go about with greater freedom, virgins cease to be virgins; are spoilt by secret disgrace; are widows before marriage, adulteresses unfaithful not to a husband but to Christ. For loss of their maidenhead they are destined to experience punishments as great as the rewards they were destined for had they remained virgins.[88]

Likewise in subsequent tradition the world the Christian must avoid is the corrupt world especially. Book I *De Imitatione Christi* is entitled: The Invitation of Christ, and the Contempt of all the World's Vanities. St. Ignatius of Loyola in the *Constitutions of the Society of Jesus* requires that all who are examined for admission to the society should carefully observe "how much it helps and contributes to progress in the spiritual life to abhor wholly and not in part whatever the world loves and embraces, and to seek and desire with their whole strength whatever Christ our Lord loved and embraced."[89]

5. There is no question of merely avoiding gross forms of corruption in the world—on the part of Christians who are seriously striving for perfection; but rather of avoiding a subtler form of corruption, one which is therefore far more dangerous to the soul.

Because of this ease in insinuating itself even into fervent souls, and because of the secret complicity that it finds in them, the spirit of the world is a particularly dangerous thing for Christians who are striving for perfection—much more dangerous, in a sense, than open temptations, such as to anger or to impurity. Indeed, more than anything else, this natural —human and earthly—spirit contributes to keep these souls in their mediocrity, to crush and paralyse their *élan* toward the fulness of the love of God by weakening the spirit of faith, the truly supernatural spirit; by impelling to trust in human means and earthly supports, while entertaining those subtle forms of self-love that arrest the growth of charity; by preventing true interior liberty, true detachment from every created thing. And this explains Our Saviour's severity towards the world in His discourses with His Apostles: He knew that it was the great obstacle to their spiritual formation; that there was the source of all those completely human ideas about the Kingdom of God, which they would be entirely shed of only on the day of Pentecost.[90]

6. But harm can come to the soul even from the world that is incorrupt. Things in themselves true, beautiful, and good can render the approach to God much harder, man being in himself corrupt and so able to attach himself inordinately to truth, goodness, beauty. More, it is precisely the fuller and richer forms of civilization and culture that the more expose man to such peril.[91]

7. Christian use and transformation of the world, therefore, presuppose Christian control or a crucifixion of human powers.[92] The more profoundly the crucifixion has purified the soul, the less will it inordinately tie itself to the truth, goodness, and beauty of things; the more easily will it shut itself off from the influence of the corrupt

world; the more freely will it stand in the midst of the use and transformation of the world. Only then can be realized the relationship St. Paul speaks of in First Corinthians 7:29-31. "The time is short; it remains that . . . they who buy [should be] as though they did not possess, and they who use this world, as though they did not use it (καὶ οἱ χρώμενοι τὸν κόσμον ὡς μὴ καταχρώμενοι), for the outward shape (τὸσχῆμα) of this world is transitory." Καταχρώμενοι means "use to the full, use much *or* at will, abuse."[93] Use and transformation of the world ought not to fill the soul with mere earthly reality to the extent that man no longer has any internal freedom left in the midst of the world. Only the supernatural ordination of use and transformation of the world toward God prepares the new earth that is to come, which will never be destroyed; all else that we see (τὸσχῆμα) will pass away in that visibility.[94]

8. In this sense, "we have not here a lasting city (πόλιν) but look for one that is to come" (Heb. 13:14). And in relation to the future city "the sufferings if this present are not worthy to be compared with the future glory that shall be revealed in us" (Rom. 8:18). "And [the just] are revived with temporal help in the way that a traveller uses a bed in an inn: he pauses for rest and is in a hurry to be gone; his body rests, but his soul is striving toward another goal."[95]

9. Because of concupiscence, which inclines man to an inordinate bond with the world, inward freedom in use and transformation of the world will not be realized—according to the doctrine of acquiring "indifference"—unless a contrary tendency is carefully preserved of separating oneself interiorly from the world. The just

> sometimes seek to suffer adversity, and avoid prospering in the things that pass away, lest the delight of the journey delay their arrival in their true country, or hold the footsteps of their hearts fast in the way of their pilgrimage, so that they reach sight of their heavenly homeland without reward. They rejoice in being despised, and feel no pain in being afflicted with want.[96]

10. *Interior* separation from the world will not be realized or will not be maintained without a certain *exterior* or effective separation—that separation especially that is not self-chosen (in active asceticism) but is imposed upon us by God, and which we accept (in passive asceticism).[97]

11. But even in the case where use and transformation of the world involve no inordinateness, the world remains a created value, wholly subordinate to the Increate Value, God. This conviction is betrayed again and again in passages dealing with avoidance of the world.[98] The goods of this world are subject to corruption: God is incorrupt.[99] The world passes away; God is eternal.[100] Only with God is the "fountain of life."[101] Only with God is there tranquillity, solid and firm security, unshakable fixity.[102] Man, being "greater than the age" (*saeculo;* perhaps, time),[103] "greater than the world" (*mundo*),[104] ought to be borne not toward the world, but toward God. This conception of God—Increate Value, and therefore to be placed before this world—is carried through all subsequent tradition. For the most recent period, compare the statement of Pope Pius XII on technical progress.

> As in creation—"in the beginning was the Word"—and not things, not their laws, not their power and abundance; so in the execution of the mysterious enterprise entrusted by the Creator to humanity, the same Word, His truth, and His grace must be placed at the beginning; and science and technology only after It.[105]

To the extent that contact with the world—with certain works of art, for example—brings loss to the soul, the world must be avoided, according to the Wisdom of God: "For what does it profit a man, if he gain the whole world, but suffer the loss of his own soul?" (Matt. 17:25). Now, if avoidance of the world is strongly inculcated in Christian tradition, this is largely so because of the primacy of spiritual values.

12. God, the Sovereign Value, revealed Himself in Christ Jesus as the Author of Grace. This revelation invites and draws man to transcend that existence of the world that is determined by the law of nature alone; to open himself to the influence of grace, to the free demands of God revealed as Trinity, which have to do with, and which are binding upon, human life; to enter into the vital sphere of participation in the life of the Trinity—a life that lies beyond human efforts, since man has only natural powers as his endowment; a life which, in this sense, is "outside of" the world that is determined by the sole law of nature. In this sense, God's revelation in Christ draws man out of the "world," and essentially demands flight from the "world."[106]

13. For intercourse with God as Trinity, for the establishment of its exigency, there is need of recollection of soul. Recollection, to be fully harmonized with simultaneous activity in the world, supposes intense spiritual maturity. When this is missing, recollection in the midst of activity is not fully, and is hardly, preserved. Then is valid the observation of St. Gregory the Great:

> When intent upon the cares of the world, we grow inwardly more insensible in proportion as we appear interested in what is exterior. The soul hardens against the desire of heaven as it grows used to the cares of earth. And while by very custom it hardens through worldly activity, it cannot be softened toward what pertains to the charity of God.[107]

And yet the "desire of heaven" is altogether necessary for overcoming the inordinate love of the things of time. "For the love of things temporal would not be defeated save by the sweetness of things eternal. . . ."[108]

Thus, too, from the difficulty of harmonizing recollection with activity in the world, there is partially explained the strong tendency of tradition of "having time only for God" (*vacandi soli Deo*) as expressed in "the praises of the desert."[109]

14. There is the additional consideration that in the work of salvation man ought to proceed with security: and therefore flight from the world is to be preferred.[110]

15. Finally to be considered is the influence of Greek philosophy proceeding from Neo-Platonism and Stoicism, insofar as within those systems the soul avoids the world in order to emerge from bonds of sense and be absorbed in contemplation of the Intelligible, which it seeks as its proper bliss. That tendency is not, of course, the Christian "ideal," which is essentially *agapé.*

It would be an exaggeration to derive the *entire* thematic of Christian contemplation and contemplative life from the contemplation of Greek philosophy. For Christianity, too, by its own structure tends toward contemplation. The Gospel is, of course, the announcement of redemption and salvation, but at the same time it is the revelation of the mystery of Christ. That revelation is indeed opened to *faith,* which is dark, and is fully penetrated by charity, but which is *knowledge* tending toward, and unfolding toward, the Beatific *Vision.* "To reduce the whole of Christianity to brotherly love (*agapé*) and to shut out of it every element of intellect, every desire for knowledge and "contemplation" would be to impoverish it in a singular manner and to deprive it of all relationship to the Johannine writings."[111]

But if in tradition this Christian tendency is often expressed in *terms* out of Greek philosophy, still it does not by that very fact always express Greek contemplation as well. Though expressed in Greek philosophical terms, Christian contemplation can remain contemplation of "Jesus Christ, God." Its beginning and its crown can remain charity. Christian *apátheia* is not necessarily the *apátheia* of the Stoics, but can be the "interior freedom" of the Christian; the active life and the contemplative life can be two forms of one and the same charity.[112] In his eminent trilogy, *Das Vollkommenheitsideal des Origenes* (Beiträge zur historischen Theologie: 7. Tübingen, 1931),[113] *Fortschrift und Vollendung bei Philo von Alexandrien* (Texte und Untersuchungen zur Geschichte der altchristlichen Literatur: 49:1. Leipzig, 1939),[114] *Der wahre Gnostiker nach Clemens Alexandrinus* (T. u. U.: 57. Berlin-Leipzig, 1952),[115] and his most recent book, *Gregor von Nyssa alsa Mystiker* (Wiesbaden, 1955), W. Nölker has plainly proved that neither in Clement[116] nor in Origen[117] nor in Gregory of Nyssa[118] did Greek philosophy make a decisive inroad at any point upon the Christian manner of thought.

But from this it does not follow that it exerted, and exerts, no influence upon the esteem for contemplation and the contemplative life within Christian spirituality.[119] Compare *v.g.,* how one-sidedly and exaggeratedly the cognoscitive element of mystical experience is insisted upon in mystical theology, and how there is excluded within that element the activity of the senses, imagination, and mental discourse, how the suspension or weakening of this activity—which [suspension and weakness] ordinarily are only transitory and caused by the weakness of the human being's psychological substratum—are proposed as the Christian's "ideal" without any thought being given to the fact that a state is proposed as an "ideal" in which the Christian is without the possibility of serving his neighbor in effective *agapé, agapé* becoming impossible when activity of senses, of imagination, and of mental discourse is excluded.[120]

16. A further explanation of the insistence upon flight from the world within Christian tradition is to be found in pedagogical wisdom, which demands that a relationship (*habitudo*) toward which one is

less prone in his condition is more insisted upon than a relationship toward which some vital tendency already exists in man. But now, this second is the case in the use of the world, toward which concupiscence inclines man.

17. Then, in texts regarding flight from the world the purely contemplative vocation must sometimes be considered. This is what the texts on the subject have an eye to, and as such are not valid for any and every Christian vocation.

18. Finally, the right *avoidance of the world* is at the same time the right use and the right transformation of it. For one who avoids the world has that attitude (*habitudo*) toward it which is according to God's idea and will. Such an attitude necessarily completes and transforms it, since it brings into the world something of the likeness of God.

19. Despite the multitude of reasons in favor of avoidance of the world, there are undoubtedly texts in individual authors of the Christian ages that inculcate such avoidance so much and in such a way that they can scarcely be harmonized with the certain duty of the Christian to transform the world. As if the God whom the soul should seek after by fleeing from the world were not at work in the world to spread His Kingdom against that of the devil; as if in that work He did not associate human beings with Himself as coworkers![121] As if the free will of God in Trinity, who is above the limits of nature, and in this sense "extra mundum"—beyond the world—to which Will the Christian soul must take its flight, were not at the same time requiring service for this world.[122] Certainly the Church as a visible society ought to represent visible also the contemplative element of her life: and hence the purely contemplative religious orders. But they too must transform the world—namely, indirectly, insofar as by their prayer and self-denial they must support those who directly transform it.[123] As if God were not giving the grace necessary to fulfill His will regarding service for the world—even direct service! As if that grace were not more powerful than sin![124] Besides, in such texts the possibility of a synthesis between contemplation and action is hardly considered.[125] Otherwise it is sometimes plainly manifest that such and such a text does not betray the constant attitude of the respective author, or at least not the attitude of all his contemporaries. Thus, *v.g.*, St. Jerome writes:

Why, you will say, are you off to the desert? Why, to avoid listening to you, seeing you, being upset by your anger, putting up with your wars. . . . You will reply: "This is not fighting but running away. Stand in the battle-line! Use your armor to withstand your opponent, so that when you win you may be crowned." I admit my weakness. I do not want to fight in hopes of winning, lest I lose the victory at some time. If I run away I have avoided the sword. If I stand and fight, I must either win or be killed. But must a sure thing be let go, and what is uncertain be pursued? We must avoid death either with our shield or with our feet. You that fight can both be defeated and win. When I run away, I do not win by so doing; but I run away to avoid being defeated.[126]

St. Jerome's contemporary, St. Augustine, writes quite differently.

Terrified by my sins and by the mass of my wretchedness, I had mulled in my heart and meditated flight into the desert. But you forbade and strengthened me saying: "Christ died for all men, so that they who live may now not live to self but to him who died for them." Behold, Lord, I cast my care upon you that I may live and ponder the marvels of thy law. Thou knowest my unskillfulness and my weakness. Teach me and heal me.[127]

The Christian's duty, then, is to use and to transform the world, but at the same time to flee from it. Both are required. Only a synthesis of both attitudes is truly Christian. One who would transform the world without avoiding it would be drinking a poison, little by little, which would destroy the moral power of his soul—the power that man needs to transform the world aright. One who would merely avoid the world would be neglecting one of the essential functions of Christian existence, and consequently, would necessarily little by little mutilate himself; he would also mutilate, instead of effectively fleeing from, the world.

16

The Loss That Is Gain

BARNABAS AHERN, C.P.

The Gospels speak little of our Lady. But that little tells a great deal to those who know the charted ways of holiness. For Mary, too, had to follow their course. It is true, she was lovely with a holiness beyond our fairest dreams, from the moment of her immaculate conception. But all through life this first beauty matured with mellow richness. Mary was always growing in virtue the way her children grow, God's way; there is no other.

This means, then, that her faith went through periods of change. Of course, it was always the same faith, a great, strong spirit of loving surrender to whatever God said and to whatever He asked. But this faith had its marked moments of development, when she saw with fresh awareness "how incomprehensible are his judgments and how unsearchable his ways" (Rom. 11:33). These moments of insight impressed her with new certainty that God and His plans are beyond the reach of human thought. Yet, by divine paradox, this thickening of the veil of mystery flooded her soul with joy. For it all meant that God is too great and too glad to be contained within human limit or angelic measure. "Eye has not seen nor ear heard, nor has it entered into the heart of man" (1 Cor. 2:9)—this motif sounded the surging rhythm of our Lady's growth in faith.

But each advance had to follow the law of loss and gain that marks all spiritual growth. As with us, so with her: the nearer she came to God, the more she had to lose the bright human comfort of previous thoughts about Him to enter the darkness of richer certainty; for His greatness is so transcendent it "has made darkness the cloak about him" (Ps. 17:12).

This fact helps us to undertsand the third great sorrow of her life, the loss of the Child Jesus in the temple. Twelve years is a long time, long enough, to become familiar even with God, especially if God lives close at hand as the best little boy in the world. In a certain sense, our Lady grew accustomed to Him, the way we grow accustomed to Him, the way we grow accustomed to Him in the Blessed Sacrament. Faith and love and adoration fitted familiarly into the pattern of her daily life, forming a habit of devotedness that vitalized every thought and action. Certainly she understood, as no one else could, that there was something about Him beyond all human thought, something divinely good that she could never love enough. That is why her whole being breathed adoration and surrender. But at the same time, there was much she did understand; after all, she was His mother. Each time she took Him into her arms and felt Him clinging to her, she glowed with the warm comfort that every mother feels in the love of a babe who looks to her for everything. Thus the twelve years at Nazareth mingled deep spiritual living with radiant human joy. At any moment the young mother could look upon the divine Child at her side and could whisper the words, "My Boy, Jesus," words that overflowed with lowly adoration and tender human love.

But now the hour struck for signal growth in the spiritual life of Mary. The change involved one of the great sorrows of her life. It is always God's way that the cross should bear the best fruit of holiness: "The purest suffering bears and carries in its train the purest understanding" (St. John of the Cross, "Points of Love," 48; Allison Peers, III, p. 231).

The Holy Family was in Jerusalem to celebrate the feast of the Passover. Mary saw and felt the crowd milling about her; but she was happy and tranquil, for the presence of Jesus always creates a vast solitude and a heavenly peace in the hearts of those who love Him. Long before the author of the *Imitation* wrote the words, Mary tasted their truth: "To be with Jesus is a sweet paradise." Like an oasis amid waves of shifting sand the Holy Family poured life and love and blessing upon every person they met. Our Blessed Mother never feared people or held aloof from them; she knew too well how dear they are to the Sacred Heart of her Son. Keeping close to Him, she moved among "His own," putting into practice one of the most beautiful sentences St. John of the Cross has written: "Where there is no love, put love, and you will find love." To every person she met she could whisper the words, "God is my witness how I long for you all in the heart of Christ Jesus" (Phil. 1:8).

Thus the days of celebration passed, bright and halcyon from first to last. But on the journey home, a storm broke. Joseph and Mary were probably apart when they left the city, in the separate caravans of men and women. Each took it for granted that Jesus was with the other, or with some of their relatives. Not until the end of the first day did they realize He was missing. Search among their acquaintances was fruitless; no one had seen Him. Mary sickened with a sense of void. The loss was Simeon's sword of sorrow piercing deeply in a way of which she had never dreamed. To lose anyone who is dear dashes the heart and drains it of all joy. A mother is empty-souled when she sobs the final word, "He is gone!" In a single moment, then, Mary's heart became a void; for that heart knew no other love, no other joy, but only Jesus.

Even more, He was her God-given charge. She was the Virgin all faithful whom God had chosen to mother His Son precisely because she would never fail. For her, motherhood and a life for God were one and the same task. Mother love was the Virgin's devoted fidelity to the God who chose her above all others. Yet now she had failed Him. Night closed in upon Mary's soul; and emptiness: Jesus was gone.

Back in Jerusalem once more, she and Joseph wandered the streets of the city, seeking everywhere for the lost Child. What Mary was thinking we do not know. How she ever spoke His name we cannot understand. Even an ordinary person who loves God can hardly reason when he feels the loss of God; he simply suffers. And should he hear the name of Jesus—or, worse still, have to pronounce it—he feels a choking lump in his throat. St. Joseph, then, must have made the inquiries. Our Lady was bound with silence in a sea of suffering.

At last, someone suggested the temple. There they found Him, "sitting in the midst of the teachers, both listening to them and asking them questions" (Luke 2:46). At the sight of Him, His mother poured out her whole being in the cry, "Son, why hast thou done so to us? Behold, thy father and I have been seeking thee sorrowing" (Luke 2:48). There was no petulance in her words, but only the pure love that has lost and found. There was no lack of restraint; she simply gave utterance to a devotedness that knows no measure. Everything was just as God wanted it at that moment—a woman loving Him with all the power of her soul and, therefore, full ready for new growth.

It was His word that accomplished it, His word that opened a new, dark depth of faith for her advance: "And he said to them, 'How is it that you sought me? Did you not know that I must be in my Father's house?' " (Luke 2:49.)

Through that word Mary "lost" Him again. It poured thick darkness around Him, closing Him off more securely than ever before from touch of her feelings and the grasp of her understanding. For it made her feel with new awareness how completely His greatness was beyond the reach of all her powers:—"Eye has not seen nor ear heard, nor has it entered into the heart of man." He had a work to do that she could not fathom; He called it simply "the Father's business" because no human word could fully express it. Thus Jesus stepped behind a veil of mystery into darkness far greater than the obscurity of the inner sanctuary with its shrouding veil of silk. The Evangelist describes it all so simply: "They did not understand the word that he spoke to them" (Luke 2:50).

Our Lady left the temple a changed woman. Her life with Jesus could never be the same again. She had always known that He was too wonderful to be comprehended even by her. But now His word opened a new depth of certainty in her soul, a calm yet thrilling certainty to breathe fresh ardor into her whole future life of adoration, love, and surrender. From now on, her spirit would echo with greater conviction the inspired writer's praise of God: "Whom has He made equal to describing His works, and who can probe His mighty deeds? Who can measure His majestic power, or exhaust the tale of His mercies? One cannot lessen, nor increase, nor *penetrate* the wonders of the Lord. When a man ends he is only beginning, and when he stops he is still bewildered" (Sir. 18:2-5). So it is: man thinks his best thoughts of God and dreams his best dreams; yet, when he is finished, he must say, "I have scarcely glimpsed how really wonderful He is!" Mary realized this now as never before.

Yet this very darkness was dearer to her than the garish light of all human thought, and more comforting than noonday's brightest glare. For the darkness was simply a new-felt certainty that God, her Son, was a treasure too rich for human thought to measure and too wonderful a lover for the heavens to hold. For was it not love that made God the little boy whom her heart and arms enclosed?

She never forgot this moment of change: "His mother kept all these things carefully in her heart" (Luke 2:51). We are grateful to St. Luke for this reminder; but the meek physician will pardon us if we tell him it was hardly necessary. No one is ever the same once God has opened up a new depth of faith in his soul. It was impossible for Mary to forget what she had heard that day in the temple. Her new insight into His ineffable greatness was too comforting ever to go back to her earlier thoughts about Him. Ever after she loved Him with more keen awareness of the mystery of His being. Thus the years that followed at Nazareth were happier and holier than the years that had gone before. Peace was deeper, joy was richer, her soul more tranquil, her adoration more worthy of God, her love more pleasing to Him. It had to be so; for that day in the temple, amid the teachers and their noisy human questionings, she "lost" Jesus and "found" Him again in the deep darkness of a richer faith.

No wonder our Lady permits her children to relive this dolor. She knows well what the suffering of loss achieved in her own life, and so she yearns to share this experience with all who are ready for it, especially with those who live in dependence upon her. St. Louis de Montfort (*The Secret of Mary*—Montfort Publications: Bay Shore, N. Y., 1950, pp. 21-22) states this clearly: "He who has found Mary by a true devotion will not be exempt from crosses and sufferings. Far from it; he is more besieged by them than others are, because Mary gives to all her children portions of the Tree of Life, which is the cross of Jesus." But to this warning the Saint adds a word of consolation: "If for a while her children feel the bitterness of the cup which one must needs drink in order to be the friend of God, the consolation and joy which this good mother sends after the trial encourage them exceedingly to carry still heavier and more painful crosses." Yes, the work of loss and gain is a lifelong process.

ST. CATHERINE OF SIENA

What does it mean practically in a human life—this exchange of one level of faith for another that is deeper and richer? St. Catherine of Siena offers a classic example. As a young girl she had learned the consoling truth that God dwells in our souls—the Father, the Son, and the Holy Spirit—as a devoted Brother and tender

Father. Life for her was glorious in the companionship of this divine Friend. She loved to spend days alone, locked up in her little room, enjoying the presence of the good God who dwelt in her heart. This was peace, joy, security. She had found a strong refuge, a fortress of impregnable strength: God, her God, was always with her. From now on, life would be a vision of peace. So she thought. . . .

But one day this comfortable existence exploded. Catherine lost the old feeling of secure possession. The Christ of her heart was gone. She lost the sense of His presence, and felt dead to His influence. The very memory of Him now seemed unreal, a wraith that had vanished into the air. Instead, evil loomed as the only thing that mattered. Impure images peopled her world of thought and desire; and every fiber of her being tingled in response. Catherine felt as though she had plunged into a pool of filth, where one lived simply to commit sin. There was no escape. She was powerless to snap the spell of the obsession. All she could do was to hold fixedly the last rampart of her will against consent. This she did—and suffered—and waited, even though it seemed she had lost forever her clean, joyous life with Christ.

This loss was the moment of grace. The whole scene recalls our Lady's experience in the temple. Of a sudden, Catherine found Christ again, in the very room where she had been so fiercely tempted. Her whole soul poured itself out in the loving complaint, "O Lord, where were You while these dread images filled my mind?" He answered with a word that opened a new depth of faith: "Daughter Catherine, all during these temptations I have remained with you, right in your heart. Otherwise you could not have overcome them."

Hearing this word, Catherine lost forever her old thoughts on the presence of God. It taught her that His presence in the soul is something deeper and holier than she could imagine or feel. In this life He must always be the hidden God; for His very transcendence cloaks His presence with darkness. Human feelings cannot touch Him; human thought cannot measure Him. Experience cannot heighten the certainty of His presence any more than fear of His absence can lessen it. God cannot be grasped by human powers; for He Himself is the very source of all their activity. As Job said, "Should he come near me, I see him not; should he pass by, I am not aware of him" (Job 9:11). One might lack all feeling of God's presence; one could be plunged, as Catherine was, into a sea of temptation; yet, as long as the soul remains in grace, Christ is always there, loving and helping with a tender goodness and all-wise power that surpass all human measure.

Catherine thrilled with the joy of this new awareness. She realized now as never before that nothing but sin could take Christ from her. Noise or bothersome people or temptation, success or failure, devout feelings or aridity—nothing but sin could separate her from Christ. He would always be there, in the quiet darkness of her own soul, just as He had once promised: "I will give you treasures hidden in darkness, hoards of secret places; that you may know that I am the Lord" (Isa. 45:3). She was ready now for anything, for the busy life of intense activity that He would soon give her. Her soul was strengthened forever with the joy and peace of certainty: God was always with her.

THE POOR MAN

St. Benedict Joseph Labré is another who knew this exchange of loss and gain. He tried time and again to become a religious; his poor heart craved the security of La Trappe or the silent peace of Carthusian solitude. For he was convinced he must become a monk in order to find God. Therefore, when poor health forced him to leave the first community of his choice, he bided time at home until he could try again. Once more, however, the oppressive melancholia settled down upon him, and again he had to seek peace of soul in the outside world. But the conviction still lingered: God was waiting for him in the only place that God could be found—La Trappe. And so back to La Trappe he went. This time, too, the sense of loss was unbearable. He found neither God nor peace of soul. Had he stayed on, he would also have lost his mind.

But this moment of loss was the moment of gain. God spoke to Benedict Joseph through the lips of a priest who told the poor sufferer of the beauty of God's will and the security of His mysterious providence. How that simple word freed his tortured soul. In accepting it, Benedict "lost" forever his narrow human thoughts of God to "gain" a broader and deeper awareness of God's real goodness. He could now throw away his old ideas that confined God to the cloister. For he saw more clearly than ever before that man's only security lies in the dark bosom of God's beautiful will and that the whole world becomes a cloister for the man who surrenders himself completely to the loving care of Him who pleaded, "Jerusalem, Jerusalem! . . . How often would I have gathered thy children, as a hen gathers her young under her wings" (Mt. 23:37).

Ever after Benedict Joseph Labré roamed the world as a carefree son of the great God. He was a lonely beggar in the eyes of men; but in his own soul he was at home with the heavenly Father. In the few years of life that yet remained, he lived constantly in the divine presence, full of joy and peace and confidence in his total dependence on the Father's loving care. He was one of those of whom the Psalmist sings: "Happy they who dwell in your house! continually they praise you. Happy the men whose strength you are! their hearts are set upon the pilgrimage: when they pass through the arid valley, they make a spring of it. . . . They go from strength to strength; they shall see the God of gods in Sion" (Ps. 83:5-8).

This free and happy spirit was born of the certainty that came to him through faith in God's word, in that dark moment when he suffered the loss of God only to find Him again in this new way. He surely needed this strong faith for the life God asked him to lead. No one understood him; hunger and cold and humiliation were his daily portion. But Benedict was at peace. He had accepted the word of God, directing him to the prayerful life of a perennial pilgrim; and he obeyed it, even unto death. That is why, even in appearance, this lovable beggar saint resembled the Man of Sorrows. Both lived and died in joyous obedience to a word of God that no one else could ever fully understand.

EVERYMAN

But ordinary folk, too, must often follow our Lady through the loss and gain of her third sorrow. Prayer often provides the occasion for it. In every life there are periods of fervor when one can almost touch the goodness of God. It is pleasant to think of Him, a comfort to speak to Him, and a joy to be in His presence. But all this may change: we "lose" Christ and fear He may never return. It is difficult to connect two thoughts about Him; all is artificial as faded tinsel. Every word spoken to Him becomes a forced word that rings hollow in an empty soul. Worse still, an oppressive feeling of guilt sharpens the sense of loss; somehow or other we have failed Him and have lost Him through our own fault. It is the experience of our Lady's loss all over again—with this great difference, of course, that we deserve the suffering, whereas she was sinless.

But the gain is never far away. Our Lord speaks a word that enables us to find Him anew. Something we read or hear makes us understand that He is beyond the reach of the ups and downs of our poor life: "O Lord, the earth and the heavens . . . shall perish, but you shall continue; and they shall all grow old as does a garment . . . but you are the same, and your years have no end" (Ps. 101:26-28). Yes, God's love and mercy are too great and too lasting to depend on the rise and fall of His frail creatures. The storm may rage beneath the clouds that shroud our soul in darkness; but, above it all, the sun shines brightly—God's mercy never fails. He who sees the real meaning of this truth finds Christ in a new way. The experience marks the beginning of a richer life wherein joy and peace flourish even in darkness; for they are rooted, not in superficial human feelings, but deep down in the dark certainty of faith that Jesus is always the same —"yesterday and today, yes, and forever" (Hebr. 13:8). Hence, the very inability to feel Him or to realize His goodness with feeble human thoughts becomes a help rather than a hindrance to true prayer. For this new-found certainty of God's unchangeableness strengthens the heart at prayer with tranquil stability. Joy or sorrow may play havoc with the feelings; but the man has learned that deep down beneath this shifting surface of his soul God dwells in darkness. It is there one must go to find Him; it is there one makes his prayer in peace, silent and lovingly attentive to Him who never changes.

The same loss and gain may occur also in the inevitable humiliations of life. Years pass in which a good man feels comfortably close to Christ, because life has been a success. He has made his mark; he has produced good work; he is loved and esteemed by all. It almost seems that his integrity gives him lasting claim to security. But one fine day our Lady takes mercy upon her poor, proud son and makes him lose what he thought he had to gain Christ in a new, real way.

"Loss" is the only word to describe the experience. The success of earlier years is suddenly seen as ephemeral and empty; it all vanishes like the dream of them that awake. Friendships and popularity wane;

and the onetime favorite grows conscious of distrust on the part of others and radical differences of view. He senses powerlessness in his will to accomplish and bitter frustration of his best desires. Sickness and inactivity may heighten the poignancy of these new insights. Self when viewed from a sickbed loses its attractiveness. Blessed Claude de la Colombière discovered this and wrote, "Since I have been ill, I have only learnt one thing and that is that we cling to ourselves by many imperceptible threads, and if God did not do it for us, we should never break them; we do not even recognize them." A siege of temptation may also reveal unsuspected and frightening weaknesses.

It is the hour of loss, when a man feels far from God and fears that a whole lifetime would not be long enough to find Him. He suspects that his life has been a disappointment to God, a disappointment which he is powerless to undo. He has lost Christ through the pride that blinded him and the selfishness that hardened his heart. He is convinced now that the rebuke of the divine judge in the Apocalypse was spoken with him in mind: "You say, 'I am rich and have grown wealthy and have need of nothing,' and dost not know that thou art the wretched and miserable and poor and blind and naked one" (Apoc. 3:17).

Everything seems lost. But it is the very moment when God opens a new depth of faith for the poor man to find Christ in a new way. Before, he had looked upon the merciful Lord as a friend who owed him good things in reward for his many virtues. Now he hears, as did Israel of old, that mercy is God's free gift of love to someone who is so miserable he deserves nothing: "It was not because you are the largest of all nations that the Lord set his heart on you and chose you, for you are really the smallest of all nations. It was because the Lord loved you" (Deut. 7:7-8).

What a change this word of God creates in the life of a man who believes it. It is a flaming torch that enables him to find Christ even in the darkness of his own misery. Indeed, instead of fearing the poverty of his soul, he loves it; instead of hiding it from God, he puts it forward, as a beggar would, because of its special claim on the mercy of the Master. Truly he has lost that union with Christ which he counted as his own hard-won possession; but he has gained a much better union through the humble surrender of his misery to the healing of that God whose glory is to show mercy to the wretched and whose mission on earth is "to call sinners, not the just" (Matt. 9:13).

Thus the sufferings of growth in faith spell loss for the life that has gone before but provide gain for the years that lie ahead. Our Lady was the first in Christ's kingdom to experience this sorrowful change to a deeper, richer life. For she too had to grow spiritually, by losing what is good to find what is better. How much more necessary this transition is for her children, who have spoiled the past with the sin that she has never known. That is why she often renews in their life the sorrow of her third dolor. The suffering of loss always hurts. But once the change has passed, a new life with Christ opens wide—a life tranquil in its new-found darkness, rich in its stronger certainty, and overflowing with a joy and peace that surpass all understanding.

17

"If We Endure with Him"

WILLIAM LAWSON, S.J.

Suffering is a fact of every human life. Pain of body, mind and heart have been with the human race from the beginning and will be with it to the end. Yet for all his centuries of experience man still cannot reconcile himself to suffering. He is shocked when it grips him. He has to think out his life afresh and make it admit an element which is foreign to it. Often he fails to find an acceptable meaning in pain, and he endures it hopelessly, or rails against fate, or charges God with cruelty and injustice.

Pain is a problem. Some small part of it can be explained as the warning of a sensitive nature that the body requires care. So, the pangs of hunger lead to nourishment of the body, and sensations of heat and cold to its protection. Physical excess brings fatigue, soreness, perhaps serious damage. But beyond the body's warning system, and its response to ill-treatment, there is pain that is unmerited yet unavoidable, pain that is crippling and intractable. We can all understand hunger and thirst, bruises, indigestion, and the disabilities of advancing years. We could see the reasonableness of great physical evils, were they an immediate result of wickedness. "Master, was this man guilty of sin, or was it his parents, that he should have been born blind?"[1] But the worst pains of life do not result from the sin of the sufferer. "Neither he nor his parents were guilty." Those pains have a meaning and purpose "that God's action might declare itself in him"; but if they are punishment why do they fall on the innocent rather than the guilty? "What of those eighteen men on whom the tower fell in Siloe, and killed them; do you suppose that there was a heavier account against them than against any others who then dwelt at Jerusalem? I tell you it was not so: you will all perish as they did, if you do not repent."[2] Is there carelessness in God so that he passes just judgement and then executes sentence haphazard? In the modern jargon, "victimisation" means taking revenge on offenders, or striking the innocent because of their "solidarity" with the guilty. By referring all evil back to original sin, do we not attribute to God the abhorred practice of victimisation?

But why should there be suffering at all? If there were no God, we might adopt a blindly optimistic theory of evolution and say that matter was gradually purging itself of imperfection, progressing steadily towards a state of faultless efficiency. The problem of pain would be one merely of ways and means. But the fact of God's existence, infinite in wisdom and love and mercy, makes pain a contradiction that is hard to resolve. It is because we know God's goodness that we have the problem of pain at its worst in the conflict between the human right to happiness and the seeming impossibility of reaching it.

The proper setting for a new-born child is a garden of Eden. Here is a work of God—perfect of its kind, you would be inclined to say. He comes into another work of God, also perfect of its kind. His goodness is progressive, the realization or actualization of his potentialities, both physical and spiritual. He is fully equipped in body and mind, and the world is there to supply all he needs for growth—air, space, light, food, knowledge, human relations in family and society. A complete present leads through continuous fulfilments into a future of boundless possibility and mounting achievement.

As a dream of a young married couple with their first baby, that would be smiled away as romanticism. But their dreams are like that; and they are not a mere reminiscence of a golden age, but a recognition that God made the world and mankind and saw that they were good. How else should human beings look at their future but with hope? And what is hope but the confident expectation of a satisfying conclusion to the desires of a nature created by God? Man is alive; ought not his life to be full? The very condition of human living is an inner demand for perfection, reached, from one stage of completeness to the next, by the satisfying of needs, the taking of opportunities, the transmuting of every new potential into actuality. It would be grossly unnatural not to have an insatiable appetite for life. Romanticism of that kind is genuine realism.

But there is a shock and a problem when that realism encounters reality.

The child is born to the hopeful parents. They expect the perfect baby; but doctors and midwives would not think the world had changed overnight if the baby were not fully human. Physical and mental defects are frequent enough for the birth of a good baby to be an occasion for sighs of relief.

Where should hope look when there is desire for life but no capacity of it? What is hope of health and vigour when the physically handicapped child can barely survive or can only drag himself painfully through successive stages of frustration? The lame, the blind, the deaf . . . it is only the senile defects which cannot be found in children. Can a natural and blameless romanticism survive in the presence of defect of mind, of children who should open eyes and spirit to all the promise of the world and of human relations and who must remain blank and lonely behind an impenetrable veil?

But would they be better off if they could see the world and if they had a full capacity for life? Of the nine hundred million children in the world, five hundred million will live and die in want. Half the children of black Africa will die of hunger or disease before they are fifteen. Is it any wonder if the rosiness of hope changes to the grey of resignation or the blackness of melancholy and despair? Life is not a secure possession from which man at his ease can enjoy a surrounding plenty, and grow to full stature. It is an imperfect reality, precariously held, beset with dangers and always on the defensive.

It needs defence against people. Man's inhumanity to man is an endless and gruesome story. Every year in England there are tens of thousands of new cases of cruelty to children, mostly by their parents. There is still slavery in the world, and sweated labour, and greed for wealth and power and security at the expense of people. Race hatred is in full fury in some countries, and in others it threatens to spread from sporadic outbreaks. The two halves of the world are irreconcilably opposed, and each possesses the means of destroying both.

What are ill-treated children to make of their natural need for happiness? You can see shock and bewilderment in their faces. Do they ever get beyond the recognition of an insoluble problem? Do they live and die in desperate puzzlement? What sense is there in hope for the inhabitants of a country admittedly insufficient for the good life? "In process of development" . . . how many millions will die before the process will be far enough advanced to provide the bare necessaries of life? All over the world what can parents depend on for themselves and their children? Safety and security are essentials of the good life, and they do not exist. Hope falters in face of so appalling a future; and with hope gone human nature is monstrous.

Something is terribly wrong with the world, or with human nature, or both.

Out-and-out evolutionists would say that we live at a stage in the development of matter which is a long way from perfection, but all we need is time. A state of complete happiness will inevitably be reached. Present unhappiness is not due to radical defects in human nature. The material for perfection is all there, but it must work itself out by its inner dialectic.

Milder versions of the doctrine are many. The present defects are admitted but they are attributed not to human nature but to the external conditions of human life. Human nature is thoroughly good, like, for example, a perfect seed. Give the seed everything it requires for perfect development—the right soil, fertilizers, weather and the rest—and it will come to perfect maturity. Put a human being into perfect material and social circumstances and he or she will arrive at a physical and spiritual completeness which will mean happiness for self and society. In the long run a united effort will free mankind from want, from the provocations to selfishness, from national and international unrest, and from the fears they breed.

There is a widespread reluctance to admit the presence in man of a spiritual, that is, a non-material element. Yet it is the spirit of man which makes him what everyone in practice expects him to be —self-possessed, free, responsible for his own acts.

It is the spirit in man which is the dominant element; and, when we find the conflict between rooted aspirations towards happiness and endless obstacles to their realization, it is in the spirit that we should seek for causes.

The revealed infallible teaching of the Church gives the full explanation. It is logical; it fits the facts of external history and of the inner history of every man, woman and child; and it shows why life is what we find it to be, and how we can make it what it ought to be. It reconciles the apparent contradiction between a natural desire for happiness and a natural inability to achieve it. It gives an acceptable solution to the problem of pain, and offers to everyone a way to happiness both present and future.

God made the world and all the creatures in it. It is an ordered world, where order depends on every creature being what it was made to be. That is understandable from our human affairs; a machine works when all its parts are what they should be and in their proper place; a play can be put on only if each actor takes his own part; life would be unlivable if nothing were according to its nature, if bread were stone, and fishes were serpents, and bricks were soluble in water. St. Augustine says "The will of the sublime creator makes itself known in the nature of every created being. According to God's law the poles of heaven turn and the stars follow their course, the sun lights up the day and the moon the night, and the great universe keeps its order through days, months, years, sun-years and star-years in the steady change of the seasons."[3]

Man, like all other creatures, has his nature from God, and his nature shows God's will for him. The will of God is that man should be what he was made to be. Man knows God's will, for he is rational and self-conscious.

> It is not above thy reach, it is not beyond thy compass, this duty which I am now enjoining upon thee. It is not a secret laid up in heaven, that thou must needs find someone to scale heaven and bring it down to thee before thou canst hear what it is, and obey it. It is not an art, practised far overseas, that thou must wait for someone to go voyaging and bring it back to thee before thou canst learn to live by it. No, this message of mine is close to thy side; it rises to thy lips, it is printed on thy memory; thou hast only to fulfil it.[4]

Man is in command of himself by free will, and he must make his will coincide with God's. He must obey the law of God, the law of his being, and so fulfill himself in an ordered universe.

At the root of all the disorder in the world is a disorder in the spirit of man, the only creature in the visible creation capable of refusing to accept the order in which he was set. The human spirit is free to accept the divine plan or to reject it for a plan of its own. At the beginning of human history stands the rejection by man of the will of his creator, and history unfolds itself consequently in disorder. "It was through one man that guilt came into the world; and, since death came owing to guilt, death was handed on to all mankind by one man."[5]

The good life for man cannot be other than the fulfillment of his

God-given nature. The first disobedience, in the allegory of the Tree of the Knowledge of Good and Evil, was to refuse the limits of nature, and to wish to establish codes of good and evil outside them, as though man were his own maker, and could say, regardless of God, what his purpose was and what his perfection.

By that disobedience man rejected God, and God's gift of supernatural life. His happiness is what it always was—to be himself. He has still that inner demand for full being, and he must respond to it. But because of the original disobedience he not only lacks sanctification, but he is uneasy within himself and out of balance. Having withdrawn himself from submission to God, which his nature requires, he has lost his bearings. Instead of having a sure direction of his life to God, and so, necessarily, to the people of God, he tends to turn inwards upon himself, to be ingrowing—selfish. Hope stays in man; it is part of his nature that he cannot lose. It becomes reasonable, because realizable, only when the Second Person of the Blessed Trinity takes on himself the leadership of the human race.

The fact of the "solidarity" of the human race is inescapable. The history which we are enduring and making today links all the centuries of the past with whatever remains of the future. Man's present achievements are built on the studies and inventions of earlier ages; his present troubles can be seen in the mistakes or malice of his forbears. Our very health, stature, energy and longevity can be traced to the habits and circumstances of ancestors. It is inevitable that we should feel the effects of man's most important decision, the rejection of God's will and of supernatural life. That is not just a theological proposition unrelated to human nature; it is a statement of a natural relationship admitted by everybody until there is mention of original sin. Hereditary diseases and deficiencies surprise nobody. Our lack of supernatural life, and our proneness to evil, are inherited defects.

The World of God, the second Person of the blessed Trinity, entered into human solidarity when he became man. He is like unto us in all things, except sin. Christ our Lord, the Son of God, must be not only one of us but our head. He draws all men to himself, by the force of his divine personality. His purpose in the Incarnation is to be our mediator with God, to represent us, to sum us all up in himself, to make us part of his mystical body, to bring back to all mankind the life which they lost in Adam. "Just as all have died with Adam, so with Christ all will be brought to life."[6] Instead of a solidarity with fallen man we now have a solidarity with the risen Christ.

Before our Lord's coming, every human being had the task that falls to every creature: to live according to his nature and so to do the will of God. Without the preserving and transforming power of sanctifying grace, man still had to use intelligence and will in an effort to know, love, and serve God. The effort had to be individual, against the direction given to humanity by its first head. With the Incarnation mankind is turned again in the right direction by Christ who is Head of the race. Man's personal obligation of fulfilling his nature by doing the will of God is met in solidarity with Christ and with all those who acknowledge him as their leader. The whole of life in co-operation with God's providence must now be "through him, and with him, and in him."

Christ is our Way. Not only does he show us how to live: he invites us to live with him, to share his purpose of doing the will of God, to join with him in love of God and of God's people.

Goodness and happiness begin, continue and end with obedience to the will of God. Man's whole purpose in living is to do God's will. Now especially obedience is necessary so that man may wipe out for himself and the race the disobedience which stands to man's account. The reparation is made first of all by Christ, but, as beings who possess themselves and are his members, we have to unite our obedience with his. "See then, I said, I am coming to fulfill what is written of me, where the book lies unrolled; to do thy will, O my God. First he says, Thou didst not demand victim or offering, the burnt sacrifice, the sacrifice for sin, nor hast thou found any pleasure in them; in anything that is, which the law has to offer, and then: —I said, See, my God, I am coming to do thy will."[7] What is true of Christ is true of ourselves: that we come to do the will of God. "Christ's mortal nature, then, has been crucified, and you must arm yourselves with the same intention; he whose mortal nature has been crucified is quit, now, of sin. The rest of your mortal life must be ordered by God's will, not by human appetites."[8] We should make his purpose ours, and by uniting ourselves with him who is our head we should achieve by obedience our own happiness and the healthiness of the whole world.

This also is true, that we owe obedience precisely in our own time and our own place. We are beings of history. Under the providence of God we have our historical setting. It is there and nowhere else that we can and must love and serve God. Let the circumstances be what they may, our obligation is always the same.

Our Lord came at his chosen moment into the world. But once the Incarnation was a fact he had to do God's will in the world as he found it and in a man-made history. He was born into a people prepared for his coming, and in the fullness of time, when there was an air of expectancy in the world. He gave his revelation of the restoration of hope to mankind, patiently, assiduously, skilfully, with all the warmth of his love. But "his own received him not." There were good ordinary people in his world, and bad ordinary people, "extortioners, unjust, adulterers" like the publican. There were also the ever-present rich and powerful, statesmen, politicians, bureaucrats, leaders of the people who had power and had been corrupted by it. They rejected Christ, and charity, and the will of God; and to make sure of their power they subjected Christ to torture and took his life.

The moment of our coming into the world is not of our choice; but as soon as we arrive we have the exact time in which we must make history which is pleasing to God. Nowadays the voices of the young are sometimes heard raised in protest at the chaos and terror into which they have been born—problems of hunger and disease on a world scale, racialism, the head-on collision of ideologies, nuclear warfare. If they think there ever was a golden age into which to be born they cannot have read their history. In any case, their task is no different from Our Lord's, to live and die for the will of God, and so to achieve their purpose and happiness and to help to recover happiness for the world. Die they must. What is important is to die doing God's will, whether they die worn out with charity or crushed by Mammon for opposing him. "Blessed are those who suffer persecution in the cause of right; the kingdom of heaven is theirs."[9] "As God's ministers, we must do everything to make ourselves acceptable. We have to show great patience, in times of affliction, of need, of difficulty; under the lash, in prison, in the midst of tumult; when we are tired out, sleepless, and fasting."[10]

We are historical persons in this age and no other. With the certainty that we shall suffer and die we should learn how to do both "through him, and with him, and in him."

We should make up our mind firstly whether or not we consider pain an unmitigated evil. After the fact of original sin it can be a blessing. The human race has had experience of a perfect existence which ended with man and woman so contented, so pleased with themselves, that they could not see God. Our own experience warns us that times of peace and prosperity are those when man feels he can do without God's kingdom easily. "And once again I tell you, it is easier for a camel to pass through a needle's eye than for a man to enter the kingdom of heaven when he is rich."[11] We can say "Out of the depths I have cried to thee, O Lord." If we were on top of the world, should we cry to him? Dependent as we are, we support ourselves on wealth, comfort, power, security, "happiness" in all its minor manifestations. It is a blessing to have these supports kicked away and to find that we depend solely on God. "As it is, the Lord judges us and chastises us, so that we may not incur, as this world incurs, damnation."[12] Sometimes the depths are so profound that the sufferer cries with Our Lord: "My God, my God, why hast thou forsaken me?" learning in his complete helplessness to cling to the strong, living God.

Pain, therefore, is not an unmixed evil in our present state. But it is not good in itself; and it is never an end in itself. Pain that can be avoided or removed has to justify its presence by the good resulting from it. If there is no good result, there is no justification for bearing pain. It is then a bad means to a bad end.

The Christian should base his decisions on the two purposes taught him by our Lord, obedience to the will of God, and charity. Suffering in others demands compassion. We are one people, naturally and supernaturally. We should suffer from the unsatisfied hunger and thirst of mankind, and have an appetite which will stimulate us to supply the necessaries of life to those in need. Our final examination is in the charity with which we responded to the sufferings of Christ and his people. "I was hungry and you gave me to eat: I was thirsty and you gave me to drink . . ."

To the sufferings of others the only satisfactory response is that of the good Samaritan. As we make our way through life we shall certainly see at the roadside the victims of injustice and cruelty, heredity and accident, sufferers in body and mind. They can be as near as our own home and as far as the unapproachable countries under communism; but whatever the distance, they are our neighbours. We are drawn and directed to them by membership of the one human family and by sharing with them the one condemnation our family disobedience, and also by a common hope in Christ who has come into the family as its head. Fellow-feeling, compassion and charity ought to be universal, as suffering is universal. The suffering of others is our responsibility, which we meet out of our union with Christ. "The sufferings of Christ, it is true, overflow into our lives; but there is overflowing comfort, too, which Christ brings to us. Have we trials to endure? It all makes for your encouragement, for your salvation. Are we comforted? It is so that you may be comforted. (Are we encouraged? It is for your encouragement, for your salvation.) And the effect of this appears in your willingness to undergo the sufferings we too undergo."[13]

The conclusion is the same if we describe the condition of mankind in terms of happiness. Christians can enjoy life, because in Christ their desire for completeness and fulfillment makes sense. It is reasonable because it is clearly satisfied in union with Christ from whom they have the more abundant life that meets their needs now and can continue into eternity. This fact in human history is the best news that the frustrated and the hopeless can hear. Christians should feel an irresistible impulse to pass on the good news, and to do it in the way our Lord brought it to them.

"The blind see, the lame walk, the lepers are cleansed, and the poor have the gospel preached to them."[14] Cries of suffering should be heard and answered.

This history of mankind, above all in Christian times, has endless examples of pity and compassion; but there are always Christians deaf to the call made on them by want and pain. It is only a small proportion of Christians who choose a career for its content of charity. The first consideration with most is the satisfaction of a selfish need for status, security, repute, power or wealth. Christian living should start from our Lord's teaching that the whole of Christian life is dedicated love and service of God and of God's family. Judgement on individual Christian lives is an examination of their content of charity. Any Christian life should be a response to Christ's insistent and urgent call to charity, and should therefore be a "vocation"—in religious life, or marriage, or a profession, or a way of making a living. Whether service of the needy is immediate or remote, it can and should be the conscious purpose of the Christian. It is that above all which will make a right distribution of the world's burden of suffering and privation.

The Christian's attitude to his own pain should be formed also on the example of our Lord and on the principles of obedience and charity which are to be found there.

The sufferings of our Lord, once he had undertaken the work of our salvation by entering into human history, were indeed sought, but within the historical pattern of his times. He accepted them under the Providence of God and for the benefit of mankind. There have always been Christians who added sufferings of their own choosing to those they could not avoid. But for them, as for everybody, it is the unavoidable hardships that most clearly indicate the will of God; and normally they make a full life of obedience and charity when they are borne in union with Christ. They are the essential of that painful progress towards unselfishness which is also the way to happiness for self and others.

Our Lord was always deliberately in the presence of God the Father, evaluating the events of his life from that point of view, and in all circumstances doing his Father's will. The Christian intent on doing God's will takes up the same position and tries in all situations to adopt divine values and to form his attitudes according to them. Martyrs, Thomas More for example, die because they will not purchase their life by disobedience to God. By keeping to Christian standards in spite of hardship the Christian submits himself to God's law. Like our Lord, he learns obedience by the things he suffers.

The simple-minded hope with which people enter into life and into states of life is always disappointed. The sort of happiness which just presents and unfolds itself belongs to fairy stories. In human history no-one lives happily ever after. The Christian has to build his life and his happiness on the performance of duty—the obligation of doing the will of God and of entering into a relationship of charity with God and his people. Return to paradise is by obedience, in company with Christ who is the way back to God and to happiness.

We should face life from a determination to do God's will. If the doing of God's will brings suffering and even death, we must endure as Christ endured. "He is led as a lamb to the slaughter, and as a sheep before his shearer he opens not his mouth." Instead of being disobediently a law unto ourselves we must obey the law of our nature. The Christian decision must be for poverty of spirit in a grossly materialistic world, for chastity in the midst of sensuality, for a loyal honouring of contract in spite of the betrayals and dishonesties of politics, commerce and industry, for selfless dedication to the partner in marriage though marriage may have disappointed hopes of happiness. We must make our life in this time, in a corrupt society, with inevitable pain, and by union with Christ in his life, death and resurrection, help him to purify ourselves and our race from man's original and continuous disobedience.

18

Childlike Spirituality and Infantilism

LOUIS BEIRNAERT, S.J.

Nowadays, everyone knows or thinks he knows that the spiritual childhood to which the gospel calls us is in no way to be confused with the infantilism modern psychologists discover under many pseudo-religious practices. Hearing some Christians speak or reading certain books, one realizes that the terms *childlike spirituality* and *infantilism* are not always used in their most precise sense by those who employ these terms. On the one hand, religious often use the term *childlike* in a way different from its New Testament meaning. *Infantilism* is often used in a way not justified by the psychological sciences. We must start by clarifying these concepts in such a way as to clearly distinguish the two above-mentioned attitudes.

After having clarified the meaning of these two concepts, we must go further and ask if childlike spirituality, far from obstructing psychological maturity, does not, rather, bring it to its full maturity, so that there is no antagonism between the spirit of childhood as proposed in the gospels, and mature adulthood as understood by modern-day psychology. It is extremely important to make these two points very clear, for believers are tempted to exalt childlike spirituality and pay little attention to psychological maturity, while those who are concerned with psychological maturity often confuse spiritual childhood with infantilism.

To attempt such a purification of ideas and show their relation would be beyond the scope of this paper. We will be content, then, with some reflections which may be an "approach" to the problem.

When we start searching for the exact meaning of *childlike spirituality* and *infantilism,* we touch on terms that today may have a confused meaning but are endowed with great affective importance.

It often happens that people will mistake childlike spirituality for a facility in accepting, not only the dogmas and directives of the Church, but also every bit of advice they receive from their pastors and confessors; a constant need to be lead and sustained; an existence with no problems and a way of life without critical judgment; in short, an attitude of total dependence which stretches to the point where any trace of personality is erased. Doesn't a child let those who are older and wiser guide and protect him?

To harbor such an opinion under the name of childlike spirituality, is to forget that it can be motivated by a fear of accepting responsibilities and by a need for a security that excludes any risks—even those required if one is to be fully human. Such an attitude of passivity is often fostered by those in authority. One can see how few difficulties there would be in governing such people. From this comes one of the worst interpretations of childlike spirituality, *i.e.,* an identification with the need for passive submission.

On the other hand, one can stretch the idea in the opposite direction and use the same term to cover a mythical innocence that is supposed to be that of a child. Such "childlikeness" would imply ignorance of evil, natural goodness, innocent eyes "which reflect heaven" and a pure heart, a sort of touching and disarming weakness. The child is a "little angel" in opposition to the evil and the degradation of adults. He then will be a "child" in the spiritual sense, who up till maturity has preserved himself free from the stains of the world. Childlike spirituality in this case would be nothing more than an extension into maturity of a primordial state that would most assuredly have existed at the beginning of life.

Without denying the truth contained in that picture, we must still notice that it shows an "angelism" which makes it hard to attain a true conception of reality. The child is not simply the little angel whom we like to praise and in contrast to whom the adult is a fallen creature. Without yet being capable of any moral good or evil, he still shows embryonic passions. It is true that some think we should turn away with horror from the depths the psychologists analyze in the child. Isn't it precisely this horror that clouds our vision of reality in a very subtle way? Why this need in an adult to "angelize" the child, except, as Guardini says, to furnish the former with "a cultural terrain for a sentimental idea that he has about a pretended innocence which was once his. This permits him to take pleasure in himself and to enjoy the power that he has over this touching creature."[1] There can be, therefore, in this basic exaltation of childhood, a narcissistic complacence and an avoidance of what is real, natural, historical.

Going to the opposite extreme, some label *infantile* every attitude of dependence, even if it be dependence on religious or moral authority. You can extol, in the name of psychological maturity, all sorts of dubious experiences. As if a truly adult man could go beyond every law and shake off all bonds. We could easily show the affective motivations that stand behind such a refusal of reality.

In order to know the precise meaning of either concept, *i.e.,* of "childlike spirituality" and of "infantilism," one has to return to the roots of both, to study the New Testament and psychology.

When Our Lord invites us to become as little children and says that the Kingdom of Heaven is for those who do this, He also shows us how they are to be our models.

This childlike approach is presented to us as opposing the thought of the disciples in regard to the Kingdom as found in Jesus. They argue among themselves as to which is the greatest among them (Mark 9:34). Their hearts, filled with ambition, make them desire the Kingdom as a good that should bring them consideration and honor, and they consider their part in the work of Jesus as an enterprise in which they can achieve a more or less brilliant career. They even go so far as to consider the little children brought to Jesus for His blessing as beyond this sphere. They waste His time. They aren't capable of playing a role in the business, nor are they able to keep up with the competition. They may even show a little jealousy insofar as they each consider Jesus to be their own personal possession.

It is precisely to this attitude that the Master opposes another, which the children help him to explain. The Kingdom of Heaven is not an object of possession or of competition. It is not won by following the usual norms of the world; it is not, furthermore, a place where consideration and honor will be given as happens to those who hold power and merit in an earthly kingdom. It is given to those who receive it "like children," *i.e.,* to those who accept it simply as a gift, which their importance does not justify. And as for greatness in the Kingdom, it is measured by the humility and service shown to the community, as the picture of the child shows, placed in the midst of the disciples as the least among them (Matt. 18:2-4).

Childlike spirituality has value only in relation to the Kingdom. It is a new area of thought, which depends on the Kingdom. If a child is used as a model of this new thinking, this is not to invite the disciples to return to a childish psychological state; on the contrary, it is to lead them to a way of coming to the Kingdom with an attitude analogous to the child's, who opens himself to reality as to a gift, and who lives and acts like the least in a service to all. There is no call to a childish innocence or to an angelic image; there is no teaching here about the actual psychology of a child. Rather Jesus notes that quality in children that is opposed to ambition, pretension and self-complacency. Father Lagrange judiciously notes:

> If children do have the same faults as adults, it is very rare that they have ambitions about the future. . . . Children, themselves, love to surpass and lord it over other children their own age. Yet they still feel very inferior to mature adults. When men begin to do for others without any thought of being rewarded, they then place themselves in the category of children. They become humble.[2]

It is, therefore, not a question of "reverting" to a childish position, whether real or imagined, but of adopting a specific attitude toward the Kingdom. The model for that attitude is the child.

The one with whom we must completely identify is Christ. We must adopt His filial attitude toward the Father, become one of His brothers by serving. *Now, in your midst I am as one who serves* (Luke 22:27). This is the childhood of the Spirit, the new childhood that the actions of our Lord set apart from any other; such an attitude has nothing to do with psychological infantilism, as a description of the latter will make clear.

While childlike spirituality takes shape in relation to the Kingdom of Heaven and to the Transcendant, infantilism is related to the evolutionary states through which the soul passes in the course of growth. A psychologically adult personality is characterized by certain traits: an integration of tendencies whose conscious play is under the control of the "Ego," the ability to adjust to social reality, an oblative attitude, etc. Such psychological maturity clearly requires that the individual has ceased to be ruled by any of the parental influences that once dominated his ego both internally as well as externally. He is no longer a slave to his emotions. When such an integration is defective, the individaul, at least in certain respects, remains static or even regresses to a prior stage of psychological development: He is more or less infantile.

We have a good example of infantilism in those whom Mrs. Guex calls, after Dr. Odier, the "totally abandoned."[3] This type of neurotic —or, in less severe cases, of nervous person—is characterized by a feeling of frustration and abandonment which is produced each time the facts of life go against his desires or threaten his security. This type of person has an insatiable affective avidity, "he never grows out of his longing for childish pleasures."[4] His attachment is exclusive and possessive. He not only must be understood, but his wishes foreseen. He demands constant proof that he is loved. Fixated at the receptive, demanding stage of childhood, he expects everything from others outside himself, and since he can never obtain satisfaction, he becomes extremely aggressive in many ways. At the bottom of this attitude is a deep-seated doubt about his own value as an object of human love and a painful feeling of exclusion. How does he show this fear? Such fear is shown by a refusal to accept risks, a fear of responsibility, etc. Such behavior in an adult shows the emotional state of a child who needs to be reassured of his worth by a parental love that is full of tender care. Such a person is truly infantile. He often transfers this infantilism into the religious sphere. He will experience there the same emotions and demand the same things of God and His representatives, from whom he will always expect complete satisfaction, just as does a child in his own insatiable quest. Childlike spirituality, too, considers God a Father, but unlike infantilism, which places before Him the demands of a frustrated emotion, it abandons itself completely to Him and gives Him a completely unconditional faith in the gift of a peace and joy that surpasses all emotion.

If this is so, we can conclude that childlike spirituality is not opposed to psychological maturity. Is it possible to go a step further and show that it is a condition for full maturity? Are not childlike spirituality and psychological maturity closely related?

It is evident that childlike spirituality can coexist in a Christian along with certain aspects of infantilism. But here we must clarify certain points.

We are often tempted to label infantilism religious behavior, or at least to so label religious practices in certain groups of traditionalists. In doing so we may be forgetting that the integration of personality is relative to the social and cultural norms of the society in which the individual finds himself. What can be termed infantilism in an adult who is a university professor is quite different from what would be called infantilism in a newly converted aborigine or a farmer from the West. We forget this too often. One's behavior is infantile in the strict sense of that word only when it is in contradiction with what is meant by psychological maturity in the cultural environment in which the individual is active.

There are certainly many Christians who have become children of the Kingdom and fully give of themselves and their trust, and yet whose conduct and emotions show definite infantile fixations: affective avidity, and unfounded feeling of inferiority, self-love, etc. Their fundamental attitude does not always succeed in dominating these traits. However, in spite of this persistent infantilism, they live, or try to live as children of the Spirit; even if their expressions betray them, they know that God is not that false paternal image where they are fixated, but a mystery of fatherhood, a new Love before which they have become a new creature.

Nevertheless, this break between the new spiritual childhood and the emotional situation is not normal. It tends to inhibit genuine confidence and authentic humility in everyday life. For childlike spirituality there is no more favorable atmosphere than psychological maturity. The person who is infantile tries to transfer his fixations to God and the religious sphere in general. On the contrary, the more one is adjusted to reality, open to others, self-confident, positive in attitude, the less he will try to find in religion a compensation for his infantile demands. Childlike spirituality will then be able to grow in him in all its authenticity.

This can seem disconcerting. Is it not common today to connect closely the unfolding of spiritual childhood with that openness to reality, that candor and sense of wonderment, that peaceful security and freshness, that is characteristic of childhood? Does not being grown up imply becoming hard, closing ourselves off, putting on a protective shield? Finally does not adulthood imply acting, calculating, reflecting, losing the possibility of immediate contact and spontaneity? This limpidity and simplicity seems to be the prerogative of childhood. Peguy has wonderfully illustrated this type of decay from childhood to "maturity."

We do not believe that the spiritual childhood of which we speak is contrary to psychological maturity. A candid and open acceptance of the world shows a good sense of reality. Whereas, the actor, the phony, the false-fronts, show a defense against an interior world apprehended externally as a threat. From this point of view, what we call a "grown up" may be still an infant. And just as one can meet some "grown ups" that are still children, so too one finds children who are already "grown up." In fact, this style of spiritual childhood is the product of psychological maturity. Far from being given once and for all, it grows, or rather it dies and is reborn at each stage of development, happily striving toward a still further stage of growth. When internal and external happenings that point the way to mature development of the young pose unforeseen problems, there is always a moment of confusion. Candor disappears in the face of anxiety. But if the novelty is combined with a deeper enrichment and a broader communion, the candor is reborn. Such a spiritual childhood is a perpetual creation, which is exactly the opposite of infantilism, which constantly reverts to past reactions. The gift of openness and wonder, when found in an adult, is a sure sign of a successful integration and adjustment.

Evidently it is in such spiritual childhood, which coincides with each stage of harmonious development, that childlike spirituality produces its best fruits. But in order for it to occur there are required such happy combinations of events and reactions, such harmony between nature and grace, that its achievement is a real event. It is at once a human and divine summit.

For most of us the effort to achieve childlike spirituality, of the type we discussed, which is nothing more than Christian maturity, will always coexist with certain infantile reactions. This childlike spirituality will help us to mature so that less and less will we ask God to keep us in an infantile existence. It may happen that all our efforts, guided by grace, do not succeed in breaking up our infantile reactions. Even then, at the deepest strata of our soul, we can reject these infantile manifestations and continue to try to live in the childhood of the Spirit. To live authentically the divine fatherhood is to know how to recognize Love and surrender ourselves to it at each encounter. This is the ultimate maturity toward which we must strive. It is given to some in its fullest, for the love of God meets in them a healthy maturity; but it is possible for all to touch it in the dark, for it is available to all men of good will.

19

Emotional Maturity: A Theological Outline

ALBERT PLÉ, O.P.

Moral theology does not usually study the processes, the stages and the criteria of moral maturity. Limiting itself to problems concerning moral conscience and the observance of law, it knows nothing about genetic perspectives. It scarcely ever studies Christian life in the process of maturing. This aspect is present, it is true, in the treatises on ascetic and mystical theology, which in accord with an ancient patristic tradition, note three stages or degrees[1] of progress toward perfection. But ascetical theology deals with the last stages, which are called mystical; and these assume that one has surpassed, at least for the most part, the preceding stages of moral and emotional maturity. We can only note with regret and amazement that moral theologians have been habitually silent about the earlier stages of affective maturity.[2]

I would have refused to write on a subject so alien to theologians had I not been able to rely heavily upon the thought of St. Thomas Aquinas. The *Summa Theologica* is certainly an analytical study—very definitely so. Its analyses are almost anatomical, but it also depends very heavily on dynamic and genetic principles. These will help us outline the basic lines of a theology of maturity.

Saint Thomas is a complete stranger to that mentality that is legalistic, nominalistic, and voluntaristic—a type of mentality widely accepted after his death,[3] and still present in contemporary secular and religious[4] thought. Likewise he knows nothing about the static and nominalistic conception of the "faculties" so dear to philosophers in the eighteenth and nineteenth centuries.

What we now call moral theology is present in three parts of the

Summa Theologica: God created man (first part), man returns to God (second part), in Christ (third part). These three parts are joined by prologues where St. Thomas outlines the general plan of the *Summa.* The prologue to the second part shows us his thinking on this matter and it will be useful to quote it here:

> Inasmuch as man is made in the image of God—and by this we mean, with St. John Damascene—that man is intelligent, free, and capable of self direction—we must, now that we have treated of the Exemplar, God, and of creatures who came from His power according to His choice, also treat man, His image, since man is also a free master of his own actions and responsible for his deeds.
>
> What first offers itself for our consideration is the last end of man's life; then we should consider the means by which man arrives at that goal or misses it, because we can only evaluate the means in reference to the end. Since everyone admits that man's final end is beatitude, we shall first discuss the final end in general and then discuss beatitude.

In the prologue to question 6 (I-II) St. Thomas continues:

> Since beatitude can only be attained through human acts we shall have first to analyze the human act to discover those which can aid man to attain beatitude and those which will lead him astray.

For St. Thomas morals are essentially an imitation of the "divine mores" and on the existential plan, they are nothing more than a progress to or return to God. This imitation and progress are, in effect, the actions of man, *i.e.,* the actions of one exercising purely human qualities: intelligence, freedom, self-rule, love of the ultimate good.

An animal (a superior one) can act by himself in view of an end, but he gets there passively, by instinct. He has no knowledge, reason, or love of the end as such. Man, however, can act on his own and move toward a goal that is known and loved for itself. Moral life (in the full sense of the word) is born with the first act by which man deliberately directs himself toward a "final"[5] end, which will give meaning and fruition to the secondary goals he chooses throughout his daily life.

It seems to me that St. Thomas has leaped forward several centuries in giving us this first principle of moral life. He has joined the modern existentialists and psychoanalysts who exalt the basic dynamism of man's "project."

This first principle of St. Thomas makes his moral theology one of freedom, love, and goodness. Taking man as he really is, we can see how this concept of morality touches his most intimate and free acts, recognizes a progress, a becoming, a definite progress from potency to act. By the very exercise of our human capacities, our capability to act humanly develops its force and its ease, along with its adaptability to reality, its orientation toward an end, and its effectiveness on its way to beatitude. Thus one acquires a sort of spiritual musculature, the whole ensemble of dynamic virtues, whose dynamic quality is indicated in the etymology of the word. In Latin *virtue* is *virtus,* and in Greek, *dunamis*—power or dynamism.

I cannot now explain all the characteristics of morality as expressed by St. Thomas;[6] but I must at least mention what would be pertinent for a theologian discussing emotional maturity.

AFFECTIVE MATURITY

First of all, what is affectivity? Classical philosophy (especially philosophy texts used in the schools) recognizes only one type of affectivity: that of emotion, sentiment, or passion. These texts fail to recognize the ability of *rational* intelligence to experience joy, love, or hate. To them reason is cold and rigid. It does not love; they cannot distinguish affectivity from sentiment. They even consider faith a "religious *feeling.*"

It is a plain fact that the mind can love. The mind is both light and heat at the same time. St. Thomas distinguishes two types of affectivity that correspond to our two types of learning: sensitive and intelligent. "Animal" knowledge, that of the internal and external senses, releases an appetite in us that is both emotional and passionate. Intellectual knowledge arouses another type of appetite, one that is affective but also intelligent and rational. This intellectual appetite is what St. Thomas calls the will. According to his definition, the will is quite another thing than what we usually mean by the word. To will, to St. Thomas, is to *love* what we know through the intellect.

We usually use the same words (love, pleasure, etc.) to speak about both types of affectivity. Yet the reality they express is quite different.[7]

Animal affectivity is passion. It has something submissive about it. It is passive. Whatever attracts it, exercises a physio-psychological attraction. It transforms the subject. Of course it is understood that passion is an emotional change (*i.e.*, a passage from potency to act). It is not *exclusively* passive, but still the passionate act is a reaction to an influence on the part of an external object.

Spiritual affectivity knows nothing of such passivity. It is not intimately connected to the bodily organs. It is act without passion:

> When we attribute love, joy, and other emotions to God, angels, or men, insofar as they are endowed with an intellectual appetite, what we mean is a simple act of will, whose effects resemble sensible affectivity but without passion.[8]

Human affectivity, then, has this double richness of being both animal and spiritual. Their unified unfolding allows us to measure one's emotional maturity. That is to say, for the theologian, emotional or affective maturity is nothing other than *moral* maturity.

In effect, progress in virtue consists in a specifically "human" growth in affectivity, for virtue is nothing more than strengthening our "muscles" to love. The virtues of justice and the infused virtues of charity and hope are virtues of the *will*. They allow the will (spiritual affectivity) to love well and to love others, as it befits man to do, especially a man who has the theological virtues and is endowed with God's grace.

The virtue of temperance helps us control our passionate desires, to *humanize* them. The same is true of man's irascible appetite. It is humanized by the qualities that the virtue of courage lends to it. Prudence, too, while it is a virtue of the practical intellect, points out to a well-orientated appetite the proper means to reach its ends. Prudence is intellect in the service of love.

The virtues, then, are nothing more than the "muscular growth" of our two fully human appetites, or our two types of affectivity. Affective maturity is moral maturity.

In order to delve deeper into moral maturity, we must distinguish —in order to synthesize—between the double affective maturity, the passionate, and the spiritual.

SPIRITUAL AFFECTIVITY

Spiritual affectivity is evidently the prime concern of the theologian. The most specifically human acts are those in which intelligence and will are completely joined in all their specific richness. The moral act is, for St. Thomas, a "human" act;[9] *i.e.,* an act determined by man toward an end he knows and loves as such. It is a free act. As soon as the will acts against the movement of the appetite, it loses all or part of its freedom and therefore of its nature. If it desires what is really good, but is misled by the influence of passion or evil habit, it acts like a slave. But man also acts *freely* when he willingly follows the passionate or spiritual desire of a false moral good. On the other hand, when he *refrains* from acting badly due only to a fear of the law, he acts like a slave.[10]

The voluntary, and therefore the moral act, is either indigenous or it is not. One can measure the growth of emotional maturity by the amount of liberty one possesses. One can also measure it by the reasonable character of conduct. The moral act is intelligent. This means that spiritual affectivity depends on an object known by the intellect. This type of affectivity, then, is objective, universal, and efficacious. It proceeds from a knowledge that uses science as its model (to see things as they really are), which attains laws and universal essences, and which is also a type of wisdom, because it accurately adapts the general principles of human conduct to every individual case in a human situation to find the most happy and efficacious solution.

Therefore, having all the characteristics of the intellect, of which it is only the appetite, spiritual affectivity possesses the most noble and most developed qualities of love. In psychoanalytic language, one could say it is "oblative." St. Thomas says that it is ecstatic, *i.e.,* it causes the subject to go out of himself to give him as an object of love, the reality of the person loved, and this in an explicit reference to that person's goodness.

St. Thomas speaks here of the "moral good." By that he means an object really loved for itself, for its moral beauty and not for its usefulness or for the pleasure it gives us. Of course the moral good is both enjoyable and useful, but it is not loved primarily for these advantages. It is a reality that is loved for itself, for its own qualities. This fact does not suppress any of the joy that results from such a love, but, to revert to a Freudian concept, we might say that the pleasure-principle yields to and becomes subordinate to the reality-principle. What is loved is reality: This is the primary and final goal of spiritual affectivity; the joy that comes from it is like an epiphenomenon, morally good as long as it is relative to the morally good reality, whose possession results in this joy.

It is not the same as sensual affectivity, which acts primarily to obtain pleasure:

> Perception does not reach the general notion of the good. Rather, it is directed to a particular good which is presented as pleasurable. That is why, in respect to the sensible life of animals, they only look for things that will give them pleasure. The intellect, on the other hand, grasps the universal idea of the good, the by-product of which is pleasure. That is why it seeks principally the Good, and not pleasure. . . . Now it is proper to the intellect to come to a decisive appreciation, not so much by basing itself on the sensible appetite, but rather on the intellectual appetite.[11]

Here we have a good criterion for moral maturity: What is our attitudes toward joy? Is it taken as our primary goal? Sensible affectivity and sin come together when spiritual affectivity subordinates itself in the service of joy. Does it exist relative to a reality that is loved for itself? Then spiritual affectivity is at play, acting according to its specific rules, and we can be sure we are on the path that leads to a full, moral maturity.

Spiritual affectivity is characterized by a quality of love that we can call affection or love of friendship. By that St. Thomas means a love based on a community of life among people living together in the same love of genuine values. The object of love is not a thing, but a person (or several people). The name reserved for this type of love is *dilectio*.[12] It supposes a choice, a judgment, an open, generous response toward people.

SENSITIVE AFFECTIVITY

Moral maturity also brings sense affectivity to a felicituos development.

Need we recall that for the theologian the passions are not necessarily evil? They become evil only when they are left to themselves and especially when the will becomes their servant. But they become good as soon as they are integrated into the human person, whose will carries them toward the good. The passions in man, once integrated, are raised to the capacity of being the seat of specifically "human" acts.[13] That is, sensitive affectivity is made human. It becomes reasonable and plays an indispensable role in the love of the moral good. It participates in the freedom of spiritual affectivity.[14] It escapes its instinctive fixation and knows a certain liberty, which allows it to go toward many and diverse objects:

> The forces of sensibiliy can be considered from two standpoints: according to whether they act by natural instinct, or under the control of reason.
>
> Natural instinct determines a unique way of acting according to nature itself [ordinantur ad unum sicut et natura]. That is why any natural act of sensibility, as long as it is naturally instinctive, cannot be habitual [*i.e.,* vice or virtue]. On the other hand, whatever acts under the control of reason can be orientated toward various goals [ad diversa ordinari possunt] and can be the center of habitual actions which are either good or bad.[15]

This control of reason (St. Thomas speaks of *imperium*) ought not to be violent. If violence is at times needed, this is due to a weakness of virtue or perhaps to an error in the ideal that is sought, the ideal of a "superego," which through a weakness in the ego or will, drives back instinct because it fears the censor, instead of assimilating it into spiritual emotion and making it serve reason.

When the passions undergo violence, with the will imposing its law contrary to them, there results (says St. Thomas) a violence which creates difficulties and sadness. It is not proper, he assures us, to call this type of control a perfect control of reason over the passions. On the contrary, when the will's control is from *within the passions,* giving them, as it were, a new nature, then they easily and willingly act in a reasonable manner, in moral rectitude. This situation, solidly established, is exactly what St. Thomas calls virtue.[16]

For example, he who has the virtue of temperance is a man of desire, but his concupiscence desires only what is fitting for man's specific nature and his particular state. He yearns for what is fitting.[17]

Thus integrated, the passions are not only good (morally) but they are also useful:

> Just as it is better for a man not only to want the good but to realize it in his acts, so too the perfection of the moral good requires that a man go to the good not only through his will, but also with his sensitive appetite; so say the words of the psalm (83:3): *My heart and my flesh have exulted in the living God,* the heart here being the intellectual appetite, and the flesh the sensitive appetite.[18]

The will, says St. Thomas, cannot bring itself fully to anything without the sensible appetite first having been excited.[19] Passion can be awakened in two ways, either by *redundantia, i.e.*, by the very dynamism of the will, which naturally carries with it the sensitive appetite, or by the reasonable decision of man who decides, for example, to satisfy the demands of justice by deliberately becoming angry. In the first case the awakening of passion is a witness to the intensity of the will and hence to a moral goodness that is even greater; in the second, passion adds to the moral goodness of the completed act.[20] In short, the more perfect the virtue, the more it awakens the passions.[21]

What if passion precedes spiritual affectivity? Then it runs the risk of degrading affectivity and falsifying judgement. If it does not do this, it can be less free and yet can still have a real moral goodness: It is better to perform an act of charity out of spiritual affectivity than from the emotion of pity,[22] but this emotion, if it is animated by charity, becomes the virtue of mercy, the greatest of all the virtues dealing with the neighbor.[23]

INTEGRATION

Much time would be needed to develop all the laws that govern this harmonization of our double affectivity. They are only a consequence of the Thomist hylemorphic concept, which sees the soul and the body as one and the same substance—that of man—and which explains to what extent the "soul needs the body to reach its end, for it is through the body that it attains perfection, both in knowledge and in virtue."[24]

The harmonization of affectivity is an integration, a gradual acquisition, on the level of acts, of that ontological unity that specifies the human person. It is facilitated by the acquisition of virtues whose connection one with another is such that "one cannot have one virtue without having all the others."[25]

Moral maturity consists in the optimum development of our spiritual affectivity, in itself, and in its potential integration with the sensitive emotions. It could be compared to an orchestra, where many instruments are playing in a unity imposed upon them by both the composer and the conductor. Without an orchestra the conductor remains expressionless. Without a conductor there is only cacaphony. Without the sensitive emotions, man is deprived of a means of expression; without spiritual affectivity there is nothing but anarchy. Maturity is the complete unification of our emotions, both spiritual and sensitive.

Finally, it is charity, "the form of very virtue," that by its presence in very act, fulfills and lifts this integration of affectivity to a higher level. Since charity constantly increases, maturity is not, especially for the Christian, a stable state, definitely acquired and fixed. It has a dynamic and evolving nature, never full and definitely acquired.

IMMATURITY

Never fully realized and entirely relative to the concrete possibilities of each man, in most men, emotional maturity exits alongside a certain amount of immaturity.

How can this immaturity be explained theologically? By taking seriously one consequence of Thomist metaphysics: in the *via generationis,* vegetative acts precede sensitive acts, which come before intellectual acts. They even do more than precede them, they prepare the body for the higher activities of the soul. *Prius enim animal generatur quam homo.*[26]

It often happens, then, that the awakening of higher activities in man are retarded, distorted, or blocked. Spiritual affectivity, while performing some particular activities well, has not yet reached its full growth and does not yet have total control over sensitive affectivity.

In a number of passages St. Thomas recognizes this immaturity and notes that, far from being the exception, it is the rule for the majority of men. Here, for example, is how he explains the "prophecies" of the astrologists:

> The sensible appetite is the act of a bodily organ; it is possible, then, that under the action of celestial bodies, certain men may be inclined to anger, to concupiscence or any other passion of this type; in light of their natural state, many men obey their passions, unlike the wise who resist them. That is why certain truisms about human conduct can be predicted about most men, after the heavenly bodies have been studied. But, as Ptolemy has witnessed, "the wise rule the stars," *i.e.,* resisting the passions through free will and independently of the movement of the heavenly bodies, he removes their effects.[27]

Whatever may be the influence of the stars or other cosmic or climatic conditions, we must agree with St. Thomas about the frequency of immaturity. This can come from two insufficiencies—more or less connected but not necessarily: a lack of quality or intensity in the spiritual emotions, and a lack of control or an unbalanced type of control by the spiritual emotions over the sensitive ones.

In the first case immaturity is due to the passivity of the intellect and the will; in the second, to a lack of integration. (It is in the second category that we would place neuroses.)

This double lack of specifically human action and integration seems to explain, among other things, how after the fervor of the seminary and the first few years of the priesthood (when youthful emotions give the illusion of fervor and quality to spiritual affectivity), so many priests slide into routine and mediocrity. Their theological life is not dead, but it vegetates and loses control over the sensitive emotions. Psychosomatic predispositions, habits and passions that are insufficiently motivated by spiritual affectivity, lose a certain quality that is specifically human. The person is certainly capable of human acts and performs some, but most of the time he lives on a level of action that might be called "subhuman," only analogously human acts.[28]

EXAMPLES OF IMMATURITY

Subhuman acts seem to point out a certain immaturity. Here are some examples:

St. Thomas recognizes a double type of contrition: that of spiritual affectivity which deals specifically with contrition. The sinner sees that he has done wrong and detests his sin because he loves God. The second is that of the sensitive emotions, which is a type of sorrow ordinarily produced by contrition, but which is not constant, is difficult to control, and wholly secondary.[29] There is moral guilt (pertaining to spiritual affectivity) and an emotional guilt (pertaining to the sensitive emotions)—not to mention what the psychologists call the unconscious feeling of guilt.

In the light of this distinction it is not too difficult to judge a good deal about the sorrow of a penitent. What dominates his conduct and the state of his soul: unconscious guilt? The feeling of guilt? The contrition of spiritual affectivity? If it is the first or the second, we can guess that he acts on a subhuman level and can trace the signs of immaturity.

So too with chastity. We can distinguish three degrees of decreasing perfection. The virtue of perfect chastity is realized when the bodily passions are totally and peacefully integrated with the spiritual emotions. When the passions are well orientated in their love but *not* integrated, there is the virtue of continence, but this virtue is imperfect precisely because there is a struggle: The sensible appetite is not ruled. Finally these passions can be thwarted (but not integrated) by the other passions, which are shame and fear; in this case conduct is ruled by shame and fear and not love. Such chaste conduct, ruled by the above two passions (shame and fear), manifests a subhuman level of action. This is immaturity.[30]

There is another criterion of immaturity which can be noted in man's attitude toward pleasure. If he constantly acts for his own pleasure, he shows, as I have already noted above, that he is following the law of the sensitive appetite. He is seriously immature. Spiritual affectivity directs pleasure to an ultimate goal. It first loves the person and not the pleasure received from his friendship.

I would like to point out here a more involved attitude of the "pleasure-seeker" which seems quite frequent in many people of "good will": many "men of duty" cannot stand pleasure. Pleasure, whether spiritual or sensible, carries an aura of guilt for them (consciously or not). It makes them afraid. It may also explain their false conception of merit. They will undergo anything—but not for charity. It would seem that to them virtue consists in being unhappy and suffering. For St. Thomas, on the contrary, the joy a man feels by acting virtuously is the best proof that he is really acting through virtue.[31] This inability to tolerate pleasure seems to me to be a sign of immaturity. It is moreover a terrible obstacle to maturity and a theological error. Once again, for St. Thomas at least, pleasure (morally good) is useful and necessary: It is the fruit of action. It gives joy. It intensifies action. It even gives the rest needed by both soul and body. "The remedy for a tired soul, as with the body, is rest. What gives the soul rest is pleasure."[32] How many times in the exercise of the ministry have I had to rectify this inability to tolerate pleasure? How many times have I wished there was some way to produce an emotional re-education, analogous to the method Vitoz used for sense perception, and by which one might learn the best use of spiritual and sensible pleasure?

We can even evaluate (probably in a crude way) the more or less specifically "human" quality of the religious attitude. I am particularly thinking of devotion to the Blessed Virgin. Likewise the attitude in regard to authority, the quality of apostolic zeal,[33] etc. The principle is the same: What dominates? Spiritual affectivity, capable of authentic "human acts," or the sensible emotions, not to mention unconscious motivations? The criteria of immaturity that can be drawn from the thought of St. Thomas seems to me sufficiently clear.

MATURITY AND CHILDLIKE SPIRITUALITY

I would not want to neglect the most specific character of the emotionally mature Christian, *i.e.,* his return to childlike spirituality.

This maturity is that of a child of God. And the spirit of childlikeness, which is the opposite of infantilism, seems to crown every authentically mature Christian. This truth only appears paradoxical. It is logical.

Dr. Charles Odier,[34] expanding Piaget in a Freudian light, discusses the last stages of maturity, which go from adolescence (twelve to twenty years) to full maturity. These consist, he says, "in a healthy passage from emotional realism to the acquisition and maintenance of the feeling of interior security (the process of indigenous security), to the feeling of interior worth (the process of indigenous value), to the feeling of autonomy (the process of indigenous autonomization)."

By their growing activity, the virtues, those capacities to place human acts and to go toward Happiness, place us in a situation of security, value, and autonomy. The theological virtues and their acts transcend, and in a sense, return to this human maturity. In effect, through faith, hope, charity, and the gifts of the Holy Spirit the Christian lives in a superhuman security. He has God for a Father. What would he fear? He knows by faith his infinite worth, because the only Son of the Father died and rose for him. The one who is Love itself loves him, and he loves him with a gratuitous and eternal love, an incessant love that is present and active in his life. As for his freedom, grace, the gift of God restores it to him. The grace of God, precisely because it comes from God, is indigenous and has a depth that we cannot imagine. It allows us to act on an interior level and by a personal autodetermination of which the sinner is incapable.

It is in this way that the emotionally mature Christian grows in childlike spirituality, which is nothing more than a "supermaturity," the work of grace.

In short, for the theologian, emotional maturity is nothing more than progress toward human and divine perfection. It is a continuous movement of actuation of what is specifically human, which grace transforms in the Son of God. This movement progresses from the biological level to the psychological, then to the human act, then to the virtues. In the Christian this grace, present since baptism, progressively exercises its power of integration to make the adult man a child of God. Distinct in their essence, these steps are one in the existential development of the person who acquires maturity.

20

Psychiatric Concepts of Emotional Maturity

ALFRED R. JOYCE, M.D., F.A.P.A.

Many attempts have been made to define emotional maturity but a complete description remains very elusive. Perhaps one reason is that the definition, if comprehensive, must of necessity be theoretical, since no one is emotionally mature in all facets of his personality. To a certain extent defenses established in early childhood remain unmodified by subsequent changes; to a certain extent behavior remains overly-determined by parental attitudes valid in childhood but invalid in adult life. To a certain extent everyone deals with reality as if it were an echo of childhood rather than a new experience.

In the attempt to describe maturity, the following criteria suggesting questions may be posited:

1. How successfully have the emotional responses of the different phases of childhood development been resolved?
2. What direction is given to the instinctual drives?
3. How successful is the capacity to integrate instinctual drives, reality, and the demands of the conscience?

If a person is to grow towards well-balanced maturity, he will find it helpful to have had secure developmental childhood foundations. He should not have to divert his energies into fighting childhood conflicts and nursing old hurts. Maturity can be built only on sound solid foundation. Without basic trust in himself and the environment, he cannot establish autonomy and the trust in himself that enables him to separate his identity from that of his parents and to stand on his own as an individual person.

The starting point of maturity is reached when the person is free to move about within the limits set by the legitimate demands of society. He no longer has to question repeatedly his identity, wishes, and aspirations. He no longer has to strive for freedom but he counts on freedom and uses it responsibly.

Many persons do survive and recover from early childhood injuries sometimes with help, and sometimes on their own. They somehow get beyond their childhood conflicts. Adversity, although hardly to be recommended, does sometimes have a strengthening effect. Growing out of childhood does not mean abolishing one's past. Having a solid foundation in childhood means that one can carry into adulthood those childhood qualities of freshness, enthusiasm, and emotional involvement that stand a person in good stead throughout life. When a person can live with his past without being hindered by it, he is adaptable and capable of change.

What kinds of changes are and are not possible in adulthood? At birth, the infant has before him many different developmental paths. Constitutionally, he is committed to a particular line by heredity but with many possible avenues of development. If he was born with blue eyes, he can never go back and start off with brown eyes. In a similar sense, as the effects and additions of each stage of childhood development are consolidated during childhood, certain doors are closed behind him and new doors are opened up ahead. The only way the adult can go back is by a pathological regression or a sick retreat from the world.

By the time the person has reached adulthood, individual choices are limited by where he has been and by what he intrinsically is capable of becoming. As the person matures, he has a greater say in what further lines of development he chooses to follow. The person's early development depends upon birth, environment, parents, and circumstances. As he moves towards maturity, he develops self-control, self-direction, self-assertion, self-determination, and a greater appreciation of his capacity of free-will. The mature person is able to accept or reject the choices offered to him and is able to invent new ways of development independent of his parents and the environment. He becomes, within certain obvious limits, the master of his own destiny.

WISDOM

Another aspect of maturity is the development of wisdom. The mature person is not only knowledgeable but he is also able to apply this knowledge practically. He learns to discriminate between what is worth knowing and the irrelevant. He learns to apply things at the level of generality and thus decreases in specificity. Children think in concrete, specific terms whereas mature adults think in abstract general terms and see the broad aspects of things. To the mature adult things are not white or black as they generally are in childhood. Maturity means the ability to see things in different shades of gray, that is, a mixture of black and white. Somewhere between the two extremes lies normality.

The mature individual is aware of gaps in his knowledge and is better able to see his own ignorance and learn what he needs to learn. His experience gives him new insight, understanding, and tolerance. Out of his total experience, he builds up a broad perspective. His emotions are established and his ego remains strong but is controlled and integrated. His enthusiasms are focused and less volatile. He can plan and act in long range terms. As he loses his infantile, childhood, and adolescent elasticity, he gains a mature flexibility. He is not bound by rigid habitual ways of thinking. He is willing to take a fresh look, to consider new evidence, and to have his principles challenged.

The mature person can change with the times. He outgrows old tastes and interests; he may even outgrow friendships and careers. He can make changes and still hold fast to such fundamental values as esteem for human feelings and integrity.

Wisdom means assuming the role of a philosopher. The mature person can be genteel, sweet or acid, jolly or glum. The important point is that he be alive with interests. He will find expression in humor. He is able to enjoy wit and is able to give his own original twists to his observations of the human comedy.

AT HOME WITH REALITY

Another important feature of the mature person is that he is at home with reality. This does not mean that all mature persons see reality in the same way. They share a common body of interpretations of reality based upon fixed principles; but they differ as to the meaning to attach to them, and what opinions to hold. The mature person has to accept the stubborn reality of things as they are without retreating from them or being overwhelmed by them. The mature person may dislike reality at times and may want to modify it, yet he acts within the limits of practical principles. The mature person has to give up the pleasure principles of childhood and face the reality principles of work before play.

The mature person does not try to transform reality by magic or wishful thinking. He respects other persons' integrity. He uses force only in self-defense. He knows the limits of his power. He is not impatient for all change to take place immediately, even though critical situations may call for emergency measures.

The more in touch with reality the person is, the more he is aware that life is full of ambiguities and questions to which there seem to be no precise and easy answers. He has to learn to tolerate such ambiguities without taking refuge in a groundless dogmatism.

AT HOME WITH ONE'S SELF

No one can look outer reality in the face unless he is prepared to look at himself. He has to be at home with himself. He has to be able to live comfortably with himself twenty-four hours a day. He should know his own weaknesses and limitations. He should be able to tolerate them and be able to laugh at them occasionally. The most important aspect of this part of maturity is the ability to know his inner needs, cravings, and impulses. He must be able to bring his feelings into conscious awareness, he must be able to master and control them, and then finally give them explicit shape. The alternative is to push feelings out of awareness and leave them to the mercy of the unconscious mind.

It is most important that a mature person have about his own feelings a knowledge which gives him an insight into the make-up of others. It should be made clear that the person headed for maturity is not immune to guilt and anxiety; but he keeps them within bounds, accepts them as part of his human nature, and even utilizes their motive power. It follows that the mature person must accept and live with his own body whether it be weak or strong, handsome or ugly, healthy or failing.

HUMAN RELATIONSHIPS

If the person's growth toward maturity is rooted in the positive emotional bonds of early infancy, human relationships will have a high priority for him. In his own life, he may be concerned either with the persons closest to him or persons en masse, but he cannot help having a sense of affiliation with humanity at large. He feels this way in full recognition of human weakness and evil. He will not esteem all persons equally. He recognizes gradations of affiliation from proud involvement with those closest to him to less acute feelings for those at a distance. But whether his existence is centered in family life or not, he needs and seeks close human attachment. He will be able to give and receive affection freely without embarrassment or fear for his own integrity. He learns to adapt to various kinds of human relationships and roles; friend to friend, student to teacher, lover to lover, spouse to spouse, and parent to child. He will find out that close relationships cost something in emotional wear and tear. Most important, in his relationships with others, he will become better able to react to persons themselves, not to some image of them formed out of his own inner needs.

When he can truly perceive others, he will develop a respect for their integrity as well as a compassion for them. He will not have to go looking for affection because he is at ease with himself. Because he respects himself, others respect him.

The person equipped with human sensitivities that make for maturity will usually have a powerful concern for social problems. This does not imply that he engages directly in working for a new order. There are approaches to advancing human welfare other than working in the field of social education or mental health.

MATURITY AND SOLITUDE

For all his social mindedness the maturing person is not dependent on always having companionship. He requires a certain amount of solitude in which to think his own thoughts and enjoy his own company. He likes to devote time to reading, listening to music, gardening —whatever his tastes dictate. This capacity for entertaining himself, drawing on his own resources, contributes to his social life, for he thus acquires something to offer others. Such a person with his sensitivity to the feelings of others is committed to a democratic code of conduct. He is democratic in a deeply personal sense. He has a sense of humility balanced by self-esteem. He knows that there are satisfactions to be gained and things to be learned from almost everyone. He is interested in what others have to say. A mature person is not impressed by high position or repelled by a low one, nor will he disdain the high and espouse the low.

It is apparent that the person who is becoming mature does not accept values ready made. He looks for a rational, consistent, and realistic value system. The consequent liberation is an important part of mature flexibility and creativity. Highly original ideas about values are likely to bring the individual person into conflict with his society. A mature person wants to live within society, even when some of its goals conflict with his. Thus, for example, he does not feel compelled to advertise his views or refuse to pay his taxes. He learns when to conform and when not to conform, when to speak out and when to remain silent. His values must be so structured and scaled that he distinguishes between what is fundamentally a matter of principle and what is not. He has to achieve a reasonable balance between his convictions and his natural wish to lead a quiet, comfortable life.

The mature person will by definition be committed to certain basic religious, political, ethical, and intellectual principles. In their everyday affairs mature persons are probably brave and timid in about the same proportion as everyone else, but they generally have in common a streak of stubborn moral courage that appears when the chips are down. To live realistically means to live in consciousness of one's moral responsibility. However, if this becomes a morbid preoccupation, it is no better than pretending that one will never face death. Held in perspective, the ability to face certain expectation of death, of a final limit to one's period of achievement, lends a valuable urgency and importance to what one does, and helps keep one's values in focus and proportion. In general, the mature person has a healthy respect for danger without fleeing in panic from commitments.

MATURITY AND HAPPINESS

The author has not been painting a design for happiness. There are built-in pain and penalties in becoming mature. The mature person knows that because certain things lie beyond his power of decision or influence, he has to tolerate them. As an active person, he prefers to make decisions whenever he can, instead of letting things happen to him. He knows he has to go on choosing between alternatives and that each alternative costs him something. He also knows that there are things that he will never be able to do and experience again.

In spite of these drawbacks, he knows that the only rewards of life come with growth. The person who has approached maturity can feel that he has loved and been loved, has done his work, has made his mark on others, and has made the most of what there was. The adult with a true capacity for maturity is one who has grown out of childhood without losing childhood's best traits. He has retained the basic emotional strengths of infancy, the stubborn autonomy of the toddler, the capacity for wonder and pleasure of the pre-school years, the capacity for affiliation and the curiosity of the school years, and the idealism and passion of adolescence. He has incorporated these into a new pattern of development dominated by adult stability, wisdom, knowledge, sensitivity to others, responsibility, and strength.

SUMMARY

The following is a simple list of feelings and actions that express emotional maturity:

1. *An ability to give and accept love and affection:* a. Ability to please one's self as well as others. b. Realistic appreciation of one's self. c. Freedom to accept enjoyment and pleasure. d. Ability to accept compliments and praise without feeling uncomfortable. e. Ability to take orders without feeling pushed around. f. Ability to express one's self appropriately in words as well as in actions without feeling guilty. g. Ability to give orders without fear of being disliked. h. Ability to risk the chance of failure. i. Confidence in one's ability to create one's own chances and accept them when they are present.

2. *Independence and adult behavior:* a. Ability to share one's loved ones and one's material possessions without feeling threatened. b. Realistic appraisal of one's self, one's life situation, and a belief in one's self. c. Realistic evaluation of family shortcomings, while still accepting them. d. Knowledge of one's capabilities without need of convincing others. e. Realistic selfesteem. f. Even disposition, calmness, with ability to express anger when necessary and to fight for one's just rights. g. Freedom from a need to dominate others. h. Acceptance of responsibility and a desire to grow up. i. Self-reliance and a feeling of being independent. j. Active participation in life. k.

A feeling of being accepted, of belonging. l. Ability to realize and accept the fact that not every person will like him. m. Realistic appreciation of one's individuality. n. Ability to make decisions without undue delay. o. Accepting differences in one's self and in others as being normal.

3. *Adult feelings:* a. Realistic awareness of emotional and physical health requirements. b. Ability to wait one's turn. c. Balance of work with play, enjoying the present and planning for the future. d. Ability to develop and enjoy new interests. e. Search for ethical and spiritual values. f. Ability to work in harmony with others.

4. *Constructiveness:* a. Moderation in saving and spending. b. Enjoyment of material things. c. Ability to show love towards others. d. Ability to accept criticism without feeling crushed. e. A willingness to accept the fact that "nothing is perfect."

5. *Acceptance of parents as persons:* a. Realistic love and devotion for both parents. b. Normal sex life—acceptance of one's sex as well as of the opposite sex.

6. *Ability to establish close emotional ties with others and still remain independent.*

A mature person believes in himself, in those that love him, and in those whom he loves. He has a capacity to deal with those who hate him and whom he tends to hate in turn. He approaches a disturbing situation with confidence that he can either modify it or adjust to it, knowing that he will not lose his own identity in the latter event because his own identity is so strongly established within himself. He is not anxious in a reality situation in which he is insecure. It is a challenge to him. He is not imprisoned and safe, but free and safe, or able to tolerate the lack of safety.

21

The Crisis in Christendom: A Sociological Perspective

THOMAS F. O'DEA

Perhaps the best way to move into this difficult and complicated subject is to comment for a moment upon the title. We have become accustomed to the word *crisis* in our time. In fact, we may be said to live out our lives in a prolonged and what has become a more or less normal state of crisis, and because of that to have lost the sense of crisis itself. Certain Protestant theologians, particularly sensitive to the realities of our condition in this respect, have called our attention to crisis—and to the crisis of our time—as revealing, albeit obscurely and ambiguously, the judgment of God upon our efforts and thus signifying a breakthrough of the Transcendent into our finite human world. Here, however, we are concerned with another aspect of crisis, the crisis that is not simply or even primarily, the crisis of the modern world, but rather the crisis of Christendom—a crisis of Christian consciousness and Christian institutions.

The word *crisis* implies some kind of separation, some sort of parting. It implies a time for decision, for choice, between what is in fact separated by the pressures of the crisis situation. It implies a time in which it has become—or is becoming, for crisis follows an etiology of its own—impossible to continue in the old way. It represents a situation that challenges the actors involved in it to a new creative response lest they perish, and it implies that this challenge is either not being met or is being met very inadequately.

Christendom is a term that implies that there is a genuine social and historical entity that is not simply the Roman Catholic Church, the Orthodox Churches of the East, or the Protestant communions of Europe and America and the Anglo-Saxon world, but that includes them, is affected by them, but also affects them. It implies that the problems of each are in some way the problems of all, though not of course in the same form or aspect. The existential reality of such an entity, divided in appearance and obscure to the observer, is nevertheless to be seen in the historical fact that the history of one part is quite unintelligible if removed from the context of the history of the whole. It is this great historic reality that has been both the center and the boundary of the historical existence of western man for so many centuries that is now in a state of grave crisis.

This crisis is seen most clearly when viewed from what we are calling the sociological perspective. Sociology is an empirical science concerned with uncovering two kinds of uniformities in human existence. There are in the first place coexisting uniformities of social interactions and solidarities, concerning the relations of men in societies at any given moment of observation. Secondly, there are the uniformities of process—of change, development, disintegration—of continuity and discontinuity, that can be discovered in the human record. It is when looked at from the first point of view that Christendom reveals itself as a real entity and as one struggling with great problems. When we turn from the examination of coexisting structures to look at the course of development that lies behind them, the nature of the struggle—its crisis nature—becomes quite clear.

First let us attempt to separate out and point up some important elements in that crisis. The most fundamental, of course, is the permanent element of crisis—of risk and decision—that lies at the very center of human existence. Human societies and human cultures, with their defined relations between and among men and their attempts to spell out some generally acceptable and customarily accepted answer to the meaning of life are man's responses to this basic crisis and its attendant insecurity. Malinowski has shown us the great importance among nonliterate peoples of religious and even of magical beliefs and rites in expressing and reinforcing hope and trust in those areas of life where the underlying uncertainty—what Sumner called "the aleatory element"—reveals itself. Without such trust—a kind of ontological *fides et fiducia*—human morale would falter. But the natural man always seems able to summon up that basic trust in being—except in the unusual case of the suicide—

though he often finds it threatened by the experiences of life itself. His beliefs—inherited from his culture—while enlarging his view of the human situation by assuring him that human effort and existence are indeed meaningful and worthwhile, often at the same time close his eyes to some of the more unpleasant and demoralizing aspects of that reality that he dare not face. Such is the natural man's attempt to purchase certainty and establish security. But beneath it lurk always the real and permanent crisis elements. Durkheim has shown that suicide is found precisely in those areas of life where cultures break down. When traditional value systems are undermined, and when the social securities that common agreement upon them made possible begin to crumble, life tends to lose its meaning for the individual and in that situation the rate of suicide increases.

Christianity looked at from one point of view reveals itself as a most frank—a disconcertingly frank, as a matter of fact—facing and acceptance of the crisis element in human existence. It offers in resolution of that element supernatural aid both in terms of cognitive and conative supplementation of human resources. Christianity represents the overcoming of the crisis of human existence by divinely proffered aid. In this sense too our faith overcomes the world.

Yet in order to make its supernaturally proffered answer to this fundamental human question permanently available to men in the real world of human activity and history, Christianity had of necessity to take on the forms of human social organization. It had to "reduce" so to speak its supernatural theme to a set of human orientations and stable relationships among men. To use sociological jargon, it had to become institutionalized. No theme, no great idea, no sublime motif, can be given permanent expression in human affairs without taking on the stable institutionalized context that involves the evolution of a set of stable reciprocal expectations and allegiences, specifying the rights, obligations, loyalties, and functions of the human beings who act in terms of it. If looked at from the point of view of theology, the Church is seen to be the continuation of the Incarnation, looked at from the perspective of sociology this fact is no less clearly seen, but it is seen from another angle of vision and other aspects are given salience.

The second set of problems to which we must turn then is that derived from the nature of human institutions and the difficulties necessarily involved in their functioning. For this process of giving a transcendent theme stable human social expression gives rise to certain paradoxes or dilemmas. These are revealed in some form in history of all institutions, whether governments, universities, trade unions, or what not. Since the Church is also a human organization—and it is this aspect that one sees from a sociological perspective—it also displays these dilemmas in its history. In fact, as the oldest social body in western civilization, the Church has exhibited and still exhibits these dilemmas in classical form. Five of these paradoxes seem to be of primary importance. Let us now examine these five as they are found in the history and structure of the Church.

The great virtue of social institutions from the point of view of the functioning of the social system is that they provide the stable points of reference and the established forms which permit ongoing human life and action. The brilliant performance of the hero, the genius, and the saint light up the record of human events with those illuminating flashes that provide beacons for future generations. But human activity would be an unsteady and incalculable universe indeed were it entirely or preponderantly dependent upon such unusual and unreliable phenomena. The great insights of mankind originate in the moments of charisma such unusual lives reveal, but the working out of those insights requires the prosaic context of stable institutionalized human activity. To achieve this necessary stability the basic motif must be brought within the operational scope of the ordinary everyday performance of men. Stability is purchased at the price of the prosaic and often less than mediocre quality of institutionalized performance. Religion is the response of man to some kind of vision of God, whether natural or supernatural, and as such it reveals a most profound element of human spontaneity and creativity of response. Christianity is the response of men to the historical revelation of God to men in the Incarnation of the Only Begotten Son. But in both natural and supernatural religion, the charismatic moment is prolonged in history within the context of social institutions.

THE DILEMMA OF MIXED MOTIVATION

In the preinstitutionalized stage of the development of a religious movement, the classical type of which is the circle of disciples gathered around a master, the attraction of the followers and the psychological motivation of devotees are characterized by single-mindedness. This is not to deny that the religious movement satisfies complex needs for the individual adherents, but it is to assert that the religious movement and its message, *as religious,* are the main focus of orientation with respect to such needs. The psychological motivation is structured by a response to the call of the charismatic leader and his ideals. Motivation, while not necessarily simple, is wholehearted.

With the emergence of a stable institutional matrix there arises a structure of statutes and roles—a set of offices—which become capable of eliciting another kind of motivation. The other kind of motivation must not be thought of as necessarily reprehensible—we are not making moral judgments, we are analyzing observable processes—but it differs in the way it relates itself to the basic *religious* message from the wholehearted content-centered *charismatic* response. It involves such things as fulfillment for abilities and talents—talents for leadership, for management, for governing, for teaching, and the like—it involves needs for self-expression for aesthetic talents, it involves the satisfaction of drives for power and control, and not to be underrated, the more prosaic desires for the security of a respectable and established position in the going professional structure of society.

This process may look very much like a simple declination from the high point of the charismatic moment, but it is in fact merely one side of the general process of embodying the ideal revealed in the charismatic moment in ongoing human activity. For one of the ways in which institutionalization brings stability is precisely by mobilizing a great variety of human motives behind its central thematic demands. The institution is stable precisely because it does not depend upon the unreliable and the heroic. Medicine in our society does not depend upon the pious, or heroic, or human desire of men to aid the sufferer, or upon the intellectual drive for pure knowledge. Both these factors are involved to be sure to one degree or another, but they are reinforced by all the human drives for prestige, well-being, and self-satisfaction which the successful practice of medicine rewards in our society. If that is so of the basic thematic core of medical practice, it is also true of many aspects of the religious life, secular or regular, lay or clerical.

Yet—and here comes the element of paradox—if it is the great strength of institutionalization that it is able to mobilize a great diversity of motives—self-interested as well as disinterested—behind its themes, it is at the same time its great weakness. It may in fact prove to be its Achilles' heel as Pareto recognized. Generally speaking the criteria for selection and promotion within an institution reflect functional and operational needs and do not in practice distinguish the two types of motivation involved. Thus it can happen within the context of institutional operation that the self-interested motives come to prevail. There will result a slow transformation of the original institutional aims and goals and in many cases this transformation may actually be a corruption. When the institution is suddenly confronted by severe threat or crisis the transformed motivation and outlook may reveal itself as impotence. Careerism of a type that is only formally involved with institutional goals, bureaucratic rigorism of the type that sacrifices institutional goals to the defense or pursuit of vested interests, and official conservatism and lethargy of the kind frequently referred to as "dead wood," are some of the more palpable evidences of the processes involved. I am sure that we are all sufficiently aware of the facts of Church history to make it unnecessary for me to point out the innumerable available examples of the sort of thing I have described. This must not, however, be interpreted to refer only to "corruption" in a moral sense or to spectacular scandal. Intellectual and spiritual hardening of the arteries as a result of bureaucratic behavior that is expressive of diverse motives and needs may in fact be combined with subjective piety on various levels of consciousness.

THE SYMBOLIC DILEMMA: OBJECTIFICATION VERSUS ALIENATION

Man's response to the holy, his apprehension of the sacred, finds expression in worship. In order to survive it charismatic moment worship must also become stabilized in established forms and procedures. Thus ritual develops, presenting to the participant an objectified order of attitude and response to which he relates himself and according to which he conforms his own interior disposition. Thus he participates in a collective and stabilized relationship to

God. Thus we see that cultus is very soon not a derivative of individual needs and motives, but rather is an objective reality imposing its own patterns of attitude and response upon the participants.

Such objectification is an obvious prerequisite for common worship, for without it prayer would be individual and ephemeral; it could hardly be shared by groups, and would be incapable of transmission from generation to generation. Yet here too the element of paradox—of dilemma—presents itself. For the process of objectification that makes of the cultus a genuine social and communal act, can proceed so far that symbolic and ritual elements become cut off from the subjective experience of the participants. The objective structure of cultus, instead of molding the attitudes of participants by the imposition of its own patterns upon them, becomes so separated and removed from them that it is entirely alienated from their interior dispositions and responses. Whereas the earlier processes of objectification evoked attitudes and responses and tended to mold personal religiosity after its own image and to affect the formation of personality itself, the overextension of such objectification of the cultus leads to routinization of performance, superficiality of participation and even ignorance of what is going on. This is a process to be seen in all religions, from that of primitive peoples to Christianity. The large area of liturgical blight in American Catholicism is something of which we are all painfully aware, although many priests in this country appear to take for granted that the laity will not really participate in cultus and resent any liturgical movement to the contrary as invasion of their own monopolized province. Such an attitude is of course an example of what we called, in terms of the first dilemma, bureaucratic vested interests. Thus we see that these dilemmas may and indeed often do interpenetrate one another in concrete life.

Yet this is not all that is involved in the symbolic dilemma. What has been said for cult could also be said with respect to graphic and musical symbolic expression as well. Symbols become counters, themes become cliches, and at times—more often perhaps than we might like to believe—such objectively manipulatable religious symbols, cut off and alienated from inner connection with religious responses, are degraded into a semimagical status. They become things to be used to gain ends.

Moreover the appropriateness of symbol to referent is lost from sight. I have found that by and large Catholic priests in this country, when compared to others of similar educational experience in terms of years and expense, have the most wretched aesthetic tastes imaginable. Most of them, were they to hear this remark, would dismiss it as unimportant, for in their pragmatic minds aesthetics as an ontological realm of real value fails to exist. They once learned that goodness and beauty were transcendentals but it had little practical import. For many of them the sacramental use of the aesthetic and symbolic medium is seen in terms of a most philistine and indeed "materialistic" world view. The natural symbol and its natural worth and dignity and the relation of that to its elevation to sacramental dignity is not well understood. Routinization of counter and cliche has resulted. I do not say this to condemn these unfortunate men, victims of an overinstitutionalized situation, but to point out a well-known example.

THE DILEMMA OF ADMINISTRATIVE ORDER: ELABORATION VERSUS EFFECTIVENESS

The process of institutionalization establishes a matrix of offices. One of the most important aspects of this process is the development of a certain distinction between the office and the incumbent. Moreover, such a matrix of bureaucratic structure tends to elaborate itself in the face of new problems, and this very elaboration while at first aiding the achievement of institutionalized goals, often leads to a further complication of difficulties. The fact, is, as Max Weber has noted, such a structure of offices tends to be the most effective instrument for rational purposeful management of human affairs. Yet at the same time its tendency to overelaborate itself and to overspecify its areas of competence and rules of operation in terms of *precedents,* tends to bog it down and transform what was originally an instrument of efficiency into an unwieldy mechanism with which it is difficult to accomplish anything. The problem of administrative reform or of any other reform that must be cleared through or implemented by the administrative bureaucracy becomes increasingly difficult.

This dilemma of the necessity to develop an administrative order and the danger of its overelaboration must be seen in the light of the first paradox. For the involvement of secondary motivations in bureaucratic vested interests complicates the picture. The history of the Church offers many examples but none perhaps more striking than those to be seen in the fourteenth and fifteenth centuries. As seen at that time when moulting becomes impossible, violent eruptions and conflict occur.

THE DILEMMA OF DELIMITATION: CONCRETE DEFINITION VERSUS SUBSTITUTION OF THE LETTER FOR THE SPIRIT

In order to affect the daily life of men, the import of a religious message must be translated and often transformed into terms that have relevance for the prosaic course of ordinary everyday lives. This translation is first of all a matter of concretization. Concretization involves the application of the religious ideals to the prosaic and in that process the content of the ideals themselves may appear to take on a limited prosaic significance. The process of concretization can in fact become a process of finitizing the religious message itself. Moral insights are translated into a set of rules. Since rules, however elaborate, cannot make explicit all that is implied in the original ethical epiphany, the process of establishing or evolving a set of rules becomes a process of delimiting the original message itself in terms of its implications. Moreover, the more elaborate the rules become in the attempt to meet real complexities and to render a profound and many-sided ethic tangible and concrete, the greater the chance of transforming the original insight into a complicated set of legalistic formulae and the development of legalistic rigorism. Then as St. Paul put it, the letter killeth, but the spirit giveth life.

Yet the fact is that the ethical insight and impulse must be given some institutionalized concretization or it will remain forever beyond the grasp of the ordinary man in the course of the ordinay events of life. In the process, however, the high call of the ethical message may well be reduced to petty, one might say pettifogging, conformity to rules. This fourth dilemma may be complicated and compounded by the third. The overelaboration of administrative order also tends toward complication of rules and a kind of legalism. Institutional regulations and moral norms can become involved in and obscured by professional casuistry in both cases. The results of this dilemma are certainly to be seen among us.

THE DILEMMA OF CONVERSION VERSUS COERCION: THE PROBLEM OF POWER

Since religion is a response of the whole man to realities that lie beyond him, it exercises an attraction upon its adherents. Its propogation involves an "invitation" or "call" to interior change. This interior turning or "conversion" is the classic beginning of the religious life. With the institutionalization of the religious theme such a conversion may in part be replaced by the socialization of the young, so that a slow process of educational and formation substitutes for the more dramatic conversion experience. Yet even here such a longer process often represents a propaedeutic to such an inner movement of the person. Christians all seem to agree that the act of acceptance of the religious view must be a voluntary one, although they often disagree on the theological definition of that vountary act.

However, as religion becomes institutionalized it comes to be a repository of many of the values from which the ongoing secular life of the society derives its meaning and its sense of legitimation. Thus the maintenance of the religious belief system becomes almost inextricably intertwined with the problems of political stability and public order. Moreover, since religion is dependent upon interior disposition, and since that disposition may in fact be weak among the merely nominally religious, there is always present the subtle temptation for religious leaders, defining their tasks in a way typical of institutional functionaries, to avail themselves of the close connection between religion and general cultural values, especially public order, to reinforce the position of religious belief with external props.

The punitive use of the secular arm, the various alliances between throne and altar, the curious combinations of religiosity and nationalism; these are some prominent examples. Even in cases where there is a separation of Church and state, such strange alliances can be seen although in more concealed form. The conduct of so many French Catholics in the Dreyfus incident, their identification with every reactionary force in the Third Republic, offers one example. We have had a recent painful example of this sort of thing in our own country in the enthusiasm for an unthinking loyalty that some Catholics have displayed in the past decade. Evidently they felt that by wrapping the Cross in the national flag, they could somehow denaturalize the threat that widespread unbelief appears to offer them. If we can make the unbeliever into a traitor and thereby make unbelief related to treason, we can strengthen religion—that is the strange and perverted logic of such behavior. Its unvoiced premise seems to be: We cannot convince, then we shall coerce. In this way sets in an important deviation from the fundamental religious orientation.

These five dilemmas or processes characteristic of social institutionalization offer an interesting context within which to view the problems of Christian history. I should like to examine three: the general problem of religion in relation to society; the particular problem of the Protestant Reformation; and the present Christian situation.

In terms of the first problem—the relation of religion to society—we have seen that in order to affect a culture the Church must enter it and become itself a part of it. It must devote itself within the given culture to the sanctification of the world. It enters a culture in order to lift men above that culture. But it may itself be brought down to the cultural level—may be enveloped and contained and indeed constrained within the culture. The process of sanctification of the world inevitably involves the secularization of the Church. The Church becomes involved in the fundamental social and cultural processes and important among these are the five paradoxes we have just discussed. To hold itself aloof from a given society and culture would be for the Church to desert its fundamental commission. To enter the society and culture in order to conduct its own mission is to face the tremendous risk of secularization. This dialectic is palpably unavoidable.

What we are really saying in effect is that the Church is always in a state of crisis. It is the institutional embodiment of the crisis involved in bringing together in an ongoing social structure, the holy and the secular, the sacred and the profane, the charismatic and the prosaic, the transcendent and human finitude. The five dilemmas we have analyzed are to be found in all human organizations, but because the Church is concerned with such a profound aspect of human life, it is therefore more deeply involved in these very dilemmas. The fundamental element of crisis in human life—the risk and choice at the heart of human existence—is profoundly involved—is most profoundly involved precisely in the religious response. Thus the Church cannot but be affected by this universal crisis element more deeply than organizations concerned with more peripheral human activities. Moreover, in the attempt to relate the transcendent to the finite human condition a second profound element of crisis is communicated to the Church's situation. These two crisis elements underlie and give a special weight and significance to the five dilemmas of institutionalization as they are experienced in the Church.

One might raise a question at this point as to why we have suffered so greatly from these five sociological processes? Is it not possible to restrain them, to control them, or in part at least to inhibit them? Perhaps one important reason why we have been much at their mercy, why their consequences have been unchecked to such an extent, why they have caused grave conflict and disorganization, is precisely because we have failed to recognize to what extent the Church, when viewed from a sociological perspective, is in such a permanent state of crisis. We have not therefore pursued a policy of fearless self-examination in this regard. Ecclesiastical leaders have fallen into the gaping pit that lies beneath the feet of all institutional functionaries—of allowing their loyalty to and identification with the institution to become a kind of uncritical self-congratulation. Thus have we tended at many times to substitute a type of institutional idolatry of a kind that covers up flaws with phraseology for rigorous and honest institutional analysis. Such ruthless intellectual analysis is often perceived by ecclesiastics as sacrilege. This is in part an unsophisticated and ingenuous response, understandable enough, but it is also in part the typical kind of bureaucratic behavior that we called above the defense of vested interests. There are two typical responses to this sort of situation. One is to take refuge in essentialist discussion and to neglect existential analysis of what is really happening. The other is to resort to legalistic obstruction.

In speaking of institutional idolatry, I do not simply refer to those adulatory demonstrations that clerics sometimes organize for their bureaucratic superiors, but these are symptomatic of the kind of deeper attitudes involved in this problem. It appears to be a matter of confusion of genuine religiosity with an uncritical acceptance of every piece of ecclesiastical behavior—however banal some cases. In our inability to face the perennial elements of crisis involved in the mission of the Church, we have run the great risk of blinding ourselves to those processes that devitalize Christian life with routinization and formalization.

The second problem illuminated by a consideration of these five dilemmas is that raised by the Reformation. The Protestant movement was in certain strategic sociological respects a protest against the results of these five processes we have analyzed. It was a revolt against the clerical bureaucratism, liturgical mechanization and degeneration, the transformation of so many areas of the ecclesiastical organization into a secular career structure, and the spiritual dispossession of so much of lay life. Its desire to return to a primitive Christianity—however misinformed its concrete attempts may in cases have been—was certainly a response to precisely the social processes we have been discussing. These processes had in fact proceeded so far and had so complicated themselves that protest and reform was unable to become effective and the result was revolution. A break occurred, and like all schismogenetic social processes, that break tended to carry protest increasingly to extremes. We can see this most clearly in two of the areas we described above. First, in reacting against the alienation of cult and the loss of interior resonance of symbolism, Protestantism tended toward the elimination of cult and symbol, some branches going to great extremes in this respect. Secondly, in its protest against the secularization of the Church, Protestantism in many respects surrendered the opportunity to enter society actively for the sanctification of the world. As a result it tended to become subsidiary to the state in Lutheran countries and to the secular society in others. Eventually Protestantism found itself progressively eliminated from vital areas of human action and shunted to the periphery of life in an increasingly secularized society.

To simplify the situation we may say that Protestantism's answer to the basic dilemmas of institutionalism was to proclaim by preaching the Transcendence of God, and to reject any definitive attempt to give worldly form to the relation between God and man. As a result the Protestant emphasized God's Transcendence, but lost the sense of His Presence in the midst of men. Protestantism thus contributed its own ironic twist to the paradoxes of institutionalization. It attempted to do nothing less than to institutionalize its anti-institutional protest.

The Catholic Counter-Reform facing two adversaries—the Protestant protest and the spread of secular humanism that was attracting the lay spirit that clericalism had left peripheral to the full spiritual life—developed another side of these dilemmas as characteristic of itself. Catholicism in that situation maintained the sense of Presence in the face of protest and unbelief. It did so by a combination of seventeenth century rationalism in intellectual matters with a rigorous reform of clerical abuses. Indeed there resulted a great blossoming of individual piety. The basic thematic core of Christianity—God's Incarnation and man's consequent call to divinization—was preserved. Yet it was constricted within the structure of an empirical Church mobilized for combat and from now on to be increasingly on the defensive in the face of the emerging modern world.

Protestantism had emphasized the complete Transcendence of the Holy above human finitude. It thereby eventually lost the sense of the immediateness of God to mundane life. God seemed to withdraw more and more from the world, and mere human existence tended to become all in all. Catholicism preserved the reality of Presence—the fundamental here and now quality in the relation between man and God. It was embodied and given timeless expression in the sacraments and the assembly of the people of God elaborated around them. But while conserving those primary characteristics, Catholicism tended to restrict their mystery and deeper implication in an elaborated rationalism and in the workings of a highly bureaucratized, highly rationalized, and highly legalistic structure. This structure of the empirical Church displayed, before all with eyes to see, its quite human deficiencies.

To simplify a complex process, we might say that Protestantism tried to solve the dilemmas of institutionalization by underinstitutionalization; Catholicism tried to do so by overinstitutionalization. Hence today the Protestant mind so often gropes for the Transcendent—often brilliantly—without any well-established points of reference, while the Catholic mind is literally hemmed in with authoritative statements, which while not *de fide,* must, we are told, always be listened to with respect, and only disagreed with for grave and weighty reasons. While the Protestant may be unsure in many instances of what answer to give to the question "What think ye of Christ?" the Catholic is told that he may pick up a diocesan newspaper in the rear of the church that contains an article defining *the* Catholic position on current entertainment. It seems that if it is nothing too little in one case, it is nothing too much in the other. This becomes among us an institutionalized culture pattern that in practice involves the infallibility of the parish priest of Kalamazoo or even of the first curate of Oshkosh!

This brings us to our third problem, the present Christian situation. While these developments were taking place within the Christian bodies, the world at large was losing sight of the Transcendent God proclaimed by Protestant preaching and was unable to perceive the Presence beneath the routinized and overinstitutionalized externals of Catholicism, not to mention its concealment by Catholic stupidities in too many instances. How much such things conceal that presence—what real scandal they offer—is often perceived by clerics only in a most faulty manner. I wonder how many priests really understand how difficult it would be for a sensible unbeliever—even for that strange abstraction, the rational animals of scholasticism—living in France in the nineteenth century, to believe it at all possible that He, "by Whom and in Whom and through Whom all things were made that were made" was really present on Catholic altars when the hierarchy and clergy and many laymen made asses of themselves in the Dreyfus incident. Or what about intelligent unbelievers at a neighboring university who see a Catholic chaplain denouncing, as the result of contemporary moral turpitude, the results of secular intellectual trends of several centuries' duration, and invoking patriotism and loyalty as part of the process in order to impart an element of coercion to his position? Do you think it would be very easy for them to believe that such a man is sufficiently intimate with Christ to call him down every morning upon our altars? We must not think of the rational motives for faith only in formal abstract terms. The tendency of many Catholics to do so is a result of that process of the alienation of symbols that we discussed above. We must see the problem of rational motives for faith in terms of the present situation and its generally accepted norms and criteria of knowledge and likelihood. From such a perspective the great scandal of our present situation becomes shockingly obvious.

The secular world turned from underinstitutionalized Protestantism and from overinstitutionalized Catholicism, and erected the magnificent ideal of the secular city of man, a place where men would dwell in increasing control over the forces of nature and without the blighting pessimism and ruinous fanaticism that attended so many of the efforts of their Christian ancestors. We must recognize what is truly valuable in that model, and we must recognize the situation that gave rise to it. We must not turn to rend that great vision as Christian fanatics still sometimes do. It is a great monument to the nobility of man's nature, and it has pointed the way to the accomplishment of many goods in our modern world. Modern science, whiggish moderation, democratic idealism, were in fact born of it, although they represent transformed elements of an earlier Christian tradition. We must not turn upon that vision to rend it as does the university chaplain to whom I alluded above. It is, I repeat, a great monument to the nobility of our nature, a nobility that Catholicism has always defended against Protestant pessimism. The failure of modern man to realize it also testifies to that human misery that Protestantism perhaps overemphasized and which Catholicism also portrayed in its definition of man.

Some years ago a Catholic sociologist in this country suggested that either Catholicism or Communism would organize the future community of mankind. He thereby meant to imply that the secular society had outlived its fundamental viability and was no longer capable of creative initiative. I should imagine that there have been times when many of us have been tempted to flirt with such notions. But in sober reflection we must all recognize that such ideas are nonsense. Secular society is devoid neither of great spiritual ideals nor of creative initiatives—and this is especially the case in the United States. Its hour is far from over. Reactionary outbreaks of our modern versions of witchcraft hysteria testify to illness but not to death. Moreover, it would be a great mistake to overestimate that illness. Secular society has not been able to show as yet the kind of spiritual creativity that would take the world initiative from Communism, but it is not for all that dead. While Christian initiatives—especially in France, Germany, and Italy—have certainly reinforced the secular society, modern secular society itself does in many respects appear to be far more capable of creative response than do either Catholic or Protestant bodies.

A sociologist surveying the situation is driven to conclude that despite a marked improvement of the status of Christianity in our time, Christians today are not inheriting the earth, and there is no indication whatever that they will inherit it without a drastic remaking and remolding of themselves. I do not pretend to know whether the defeats of Christianity before an advancing and enlightened secularism represent the judgment of God upon Christians for their sins and stupidities. That is a theological question, and I leave it to the theologians to answer. I cannot help but regret that so few of them show any genuine interest in attempting to answer it.

What in fact is offered today to the secular man by an underinstitutionalized Protestantism struggling hard to regain its basic religious insights and an over institutionalized Catholicism with its extreme—at times almost philistine—finitization of the Christian encounter? Looking at the problem from a sociological perspective, one is driven to conclude that the answer is very little. The secular scientific world has just made its first step in the conquest of space. Science still challenges man. Art still challenges man. And it is to science and aesthetics that modern man turns for spiritual energy and nourishment. Institutionalized religion is able to offer very little to the modern man. That is the brutal unvarnished fact, and we might as well face it. Moreover, we had better start thinking very hard about it, shouting it from street to street, even though it will certainly offend some ecclesiastical bureaucrats.

However, our picture of the modern world will not be complete until we recognize that there is abroad among secularized men a new interest in religion. Men are looking for deeper values—are searching for spiritual depth. The evidences of this are many and are to be seen in many fields as well as in the area of religious activity itself. The finitude and self-sufficiency of secular values are not enough for the modern secular man. The pursuit of secular values very often becomes a vestibule to the search for something more fundamental. Of course, there are hardened secular mentalities unconcerned with anything that transcends the world of the here and now. But they are not our primary concern at this time. What we must realize is that it is too often the searching man looking for God who cannot find Him among those who claim He dwells among them.

This then is the crisis of Christendom in our day. Having entered the world for its salvation, having assumed institutional form to keep among men the Presence of Christ, the Risen Lord, the One, Holy, Catholic and Apostolic Church became involved in the historic dilemmas we have explored. As a result it has been reduced to its present condition. Meanwhile the lay world, which seceded from it and built modern civilization, now begins to look for new and deeper spiritual roots. This presents the Church and the separated communions as well with a challenge that they do not meet.

NOTES

CHAPTER 2

1. X. Léon-Dufour, *Vocabulaire de Théologie Biblique,* p. 213; col. 368.
2. K. Rahner, *Mission et Grâce, trad. francaise,* vol. 1, p. 226: Mame, 1962, p. 48.

CHAPTER 7

1. *Documentation catholique* (hereafter referred to as *D.C.*), v. 60 (1963), col. 1584 and 1598. When we speak here of the *holiness* of the Church, it is not the moral aspect of holiness that is primarily envisioned by us. Without excluding this aspect, we are first of all stressing the transformation which Christ assures to humanity in the Church and the union with God in Christ which flows from her.
2. *D.C.*, v. 60 (1963), col. 1586–7. The Cardinal enunciated his position at that time in the name of all the bishops of Germany.
3. All the interventions can be found summarized in the December 1, 1963, issue of *D.C.*, col. 1582–1600. It is this issue that has been already referred to in the two preceding footnotes. On the discussion, see R. Laurentin, *L'enjeu du Concile. Bilan de la deuxième session* (hereafter referred to as Laurentin II) (Paris: Seuil, 1964), pp. 83–8; and A. Wenger, *Vatican II. Chronique de la deuxième session* (hereafter referred to as Wenger II) (Paris: Centurion, 1964), pp. 114–23.
4. Laurentin II, p. 84.
5. Wenger II, pp. 120–1.
6. On this matter see the enlightening explanations given by Father Schillebeeckx in a conference to the episcopate of Holland; his remarks are reported by Father Oechslin in the March, 1963, issue of *Vie spirituelle,* especially pp. 362–3.
7. See Ghislain Lafont, "Sainteté du peuple de Dieu," in M.-J. Le Guillou and G. Lafont, *L'Eglise en marche* (Bruges: Desclée de Brouwer, 1964), pp. 146–209.
8. Charles Journet, *L'Eglise du Verbe incarné,* v. 2 (Bruges: Desclée de Brouwer, 1951), pp. 1031–50.
9. Stanislas Jaki, O.S.B., *Les tendances nouvelle de l'ecclésiologie* (Rome: Herder, 1957).
10. Jean Daniélou, "The Place of Religious in the Structure of the Church," REVIEW FOR RELIGIOUS, v. 24 (1965), pp. 518–25.
11. *D.C.*, v. 60 (1963), col. 1584; Wenger II, p. 116.
12. E. Fogliasso, "Exemption des religieux," in*Dictionnaire de droit canonique,* v. 5, col. 646–65.

13. On the fundamental role of the abbot at the base of cenobitic life see Dom Adalbert de Vogüé, *La communauté et l'abbé dans la règle de saint Benoît* (Bruges: Desclée de Brouwer, 1961).
14. Y.-M. Congar, "De da communion dans l'Eglise à une ecclésiologie de l'Eglise universelle," in *L'épiscopat et l'Eglise universelle* (Paris: Cerf, 1962), p. 241.
15. This is the title of Volume 7 of the Fliche-Martin *Historie de l'Eglise* which deals with the period under discussion. On p. 220–42 there will be found a study of *episcopal feudalism* and on pp. 317–67 a study of the *monastic reform* and of the *emancipation of the monasteries.*
16. *Discourse to the Members of the Congress of the States of Perfection,* December 8, 1951, *Acta Apostolicae Sedis,* v. 43 (1951), pp. 28–9; an English translation of the relevant passage of the *Discourse* can be found in REVIEW FOR RELIGIOUS, v. 14 (1955), p. 172.
17. *Discourse on Religious Life,* May 23, 1964, *Acta Apostolicae Sedis,* v. 56 (1964), pp. 565–71; an English translation of this document can be found in REVIEW FOR RELIGIOUS, v. 23 (1964), pp. 698–704.
18. For example, Cardinal Ruffini, *D.C.*, v. 60 (1963), col. 1586.
19. Gustave Thils, *Les notes de l'Eglise dans l'apologétique catholique depuis la Réforme* (Gembloux: Duculot, 1937), pp. 121–53. See also Jaki, *Les tendances,* pp. 11 and 211–39.
20. Hans Küng, *Structures of the Church* (New York: Nelson, 1964), pp. 52–68.
21. And this was pointed out to the Council by Cardinal Cento (*D.C.*, v. 60 [1963], col. 1590) and by a number of superiors general of religious orders (*ibid.*, col. 1598–9).
22. It is well known that the Dominican school holds more for the existence of two powers: that of orders and that of jurisdiction, to the latter of which the power of teaching is connected. As Father Schillebeeckx explains (on p. 367 of the reference given above in footnote 6), the teaching of the Church would have no value if it did not have the power to "bind me"; and this power is that of jurisdiction. Jesuit theologians, on the contrary, (as we ourselves will), distinguish a triple power: for them, the power of teaching is not reductible to that of jurisdiction. So. J. B. Franzelin, *Theses de Ecclesia Christi* (Rome, Typographia Polyglotta S. C. de Prop. Fide, 1907), pp. 40–64; and L. Billot, *Tractatus de Ecclesia Christi* (Rome: Gregorian University, 1927), pp. 333–43. But the most important thing is to realize that these "powers" are "services" and that the "rights" they imply are all of them "ministerial."
23. Küng, *Structures of the Church,* pp. 43–9.
24. This is the point of view from which H. Küng (in the work cited in footnote 3) studies the council as a structure of the Church and as a work of the Spirit. See also Charles Journet, *L'Eglise du Verbe incarné,* v. 2, pp. 893–934, who shows very clearly that the instrumental holiness of means is completely controlled by the formal holiness of the term. On p. 925 he writes: "Light is thrown on the important question of the holiness of the Church by contrasting the merely *tendential and instrumental* holiness of the teaching Church (more exactly, of the Church as instrument of holiness) with the *formal and terminal* holiness which is the subject of holiness and on which depend all the faithful, not only lay people but priests, bishops, and popes as well. The first holiness is at the service of

the second: 'He established some persons as apostles, some as prophets, others again as preachers, and others still as pastors and teachers—*and all this for the perfecting of the saints . . .'* (Eph. 4:11–2)." This is the aspect we speak of in our analysis of what we call the holiness of response.

25. *Ecclesiam Suam, Acta Apostolicae Sedis,* v. 56 (1964), p. 622.
26. We have treated this question more methodically in "Horizon théologique de la deuxième session du Concile," *Nouvelle revue théologique,* v. 86 (1964), 449–68; and in "Les recontres oecuméniques des Dombes. Conclusion: point de vue catholique," *Verbum Caro,* v. 18, (1964), n. 70, pp. 62–75.
27. In 1937 C. Feckes issued a posthumous edition of the Mariology of Scheeben under the title of *Die bräutliche Gottesmutter. "Bräutliche"* is exactly what the word "spousehood" expresses; it denotes the fact that Mary is also "spouse." It should be noted, however, that Scheeben begins with the relationships of the Trinity and of Mary in the mystery of the Incarnation; in accord with the fifth chapter of Ephesians and with the general lines of patristic tradition we prefer (without necessarily denying Scheeben's mariological viewpoint) to attribute this spousehood directly to the Church herself in her relationship with Christ. But we are fully conscious that the *word* "spousehood" has come to us directly from the mariological reflection of Scheeben.
28. "Fit totus Christus, caput et corpus, et ex multis unus. . . . Sive autem caput loquatur, sive memzra loquantur, Christus loquitur: loquitur ex persona capitis, loquitur ex persona corporis. Sed quid dictum est? 'Erunt duo in carne una.' 'Sacramentum magnum est.' 'Ego,' inquit, 'dico in Christo et in ecclesia' (Gen. 2:24; Eph. 5:31–2). Et ipse in Evangelio: 'Igitur jam non duo sed una caro' (Matt. 19:16). Nam ut noveritis has duas quodammodo esse personas, et rursus unam copulatione conjugi tanquam unus loquitur apud Isaiam, et dicit: 'Sicut sponso alligavit mihi mitram et sicut sponsam induit me ornamento' (Is. 61:10). Sponsum se dixit ex capite, sponsam ex corpore" (*Enar. in Ps.,* 74, 4 [*P.L.,* v. 36, col. 948–9]).
29. "For since the Church is gathered together from the gentiles, that is from sinners, how can it be clean being composed of those who are unclean unless it was first washed by the grace of God?" "Nam cum Ecclesia ex gentibus, hoc est ex peccatoribus congregata sit, quomodo ex maculatic immaculata potest esse, nisi primo per Dei gratiam, quod abluta sit a delicto? . . ." (*Exp. Evan. sec. Lucam,* I. 17 [*P.L.,* v. 15, col. 1540]). Father Congar has insisted on the importance of this view in his *Vraie et fausse réforme dans l'Eglise* (Paris: Cerf, 1950). This formula of St. Ambrose forms a part of an entire ecclesiology to which Monsignor Battifol has devoted a special excursus in his *Le catholicisme de saint Augustin* (3rd ed.; Paris: Gabalda, 1920), pp. 118–24; in this excursus he calls to mind the very enlightening remark of the Bishop of Milan: "It is not in herself but in us that the Church is wounded. Let us take care then that our fall does not become the Church's wound" (*De virginitate,* 48 [*P.L.,* v. 16, col. 278]).
30. Georges Longhaye, S.J., "Les saints dans l'histoire. Programme d'un programme," *Etudes,* v. 118 (1909), pp. 33–53; the article is an overall view of a course, "L'histoire par les saints," which remained in duplicated form. Along the same line but more directly centered on the person of

Christ is L. de Grandmaison, "Witnesses to Jesus Christ in History," *Jesus Christ. His Person—His Message—His Credentials.* v. 3 (New York: Sheed and Ward, 1934), pp. 447–81.

31. There is no need for us to give here a justification of this point of view which, moreover, is a traditional one. For the necessary complementary notions, see our article, "Mariage, amour et sacrement," *Nouvelle revue théologique,* v. 85 (1963), pp. 577–97, where a basic bibliography on the subject is to be found; to this bibliography should be added the important work of Henri Crouzel, *Virginité et mariage selon Origène* (Bruges: Desclée de Brouwer, 1963).
32. This is the notion of a *ratum et consummatum* marriage, the first term designating the contract as such, the second its fulfillment in the conjugal union.
33. Lateran Council IV (1215), motivated by the Albigensian crisis which can be considered as a Western outgrowth of both Gnosticism and Mannichaeism, pointed out at the end of its confession of faith against the Cathars and the Albigensians: "It is not only the virgins and the continent but also the married who, by pleasing God through their upright faith and their good action, deserve to achieve eternal happiness" (Latin text in Denzinger-Schönmetzer, *Enchiridion symbolorum,* n. 802). An analogous statement had been made seven years previously against the Waldensians who were guilty of the same condemnation of marriage and of the flesh: "In accord with the Apostle (I Cor. 7), we do not deny that marriages according to the flesh are to be entered into; moreover, we completely forbid the breaking up of marriages that have been correctly contracted. We believe and we confess that the husband as well as his wife are saved, nor do we condemn second or even further marriages" (Latin text in Denzinger-Schönmetzer, n. 794). These declarations do not pretend to exhaust the spirituality of marriage—something that was not involved in the question of that time. But in their simplicity they go to the essential point by denying any incompatibility between marriage and the Christian life. For a better understanding of the Christian tradition on the question of marriage and to help avoid the facile remarks about the Manichaeism of the fathers in general and of St. Augustine in particular (accusations which are repeated more and more frequently in our time), it is very profitable to read L. Bouyer, *The Seat of Wisdom. An Essay on the Place of the Virgin Mary in Christian Theology* (New York: Pantheon, 1962), Chapter 4, "The Virgin Mother," pp. 49–71.
34. Bouyer, *Seat of Wisdom,* p. 89.
35. 3, Suppl., q. 42, a.1, ad 4.
36. Cited in J.-M. Perrin, *La virginité chrétienne* (Bruges: Descleé de Brouwer, 1955), p. 145. The matter is well known; and we do not pretend to make a new contribution but simply to recall what has been so excellently said on the matter by J.-M. Perrin (*Virginity* [Westminster: Newman, 1956]. pp. 25–34, before him by Father Camelot, *Virgines Christi. La virginité aux premiers siècles de l'Eglise* (Paris: Cerf, 1944), and in a more scriptural way by X. Léon-Dufour, "Marriage et continence selon saint Paul," in *La recontre de Dieu. Mémorial Albert Gelin* (Paris: Mappus, 1961), pp. 319–29 (except that consideration of marriage should not be limited to the Old Testament in order to safeguard virginity for the New Testament alone: both marriage and virginity are inseparable in the New

Testament, the first as the sacrament, the other as the spiritual manifestation of the one and only mystery of the New Testament: the union of Christ and the Church. See also (applying the same remark) Father Léon-Dufour's, "Marriage et virginité," *Christus,* v. 11 (1964), pp. 179–93. A study of all the scriptural data has been made in *The Biblical Notion of Virginity* (New York: Sheed and Ward, 1963) by Lucien Legrand who establishes the New Testament nature of virginity as well as the necessary complementarity of marriage and of virginity or continence in the New Testament—a point that Father Léon-Dufour had himself insisted on. For a viewpoint that is more directly concerned with the matter of education and training, see J. Laplace, *La femme et la vie consacrée* (Paris: Chalet, 1963).

37. "Nec illa quae virginitatem Deo vovent quanquam ampliorem gradum honoris et sanctitatis in Ecclesia teneant, sine nuptiis sunt; nam et ipsae pertinent ad nuptias cum tota Ecclesia, in quibus nuptiis sponsus est Christus" (*Tr. in Ioan.,* 9, 2 [*P.L.,* v. 35, col. 1458]).
38. "Cum ipso igitur universa Ecclesia virgo sit desponsata uni viro Christo, sicut dicit Apostolus (2 Cor. 11:2); quanto digna sunt honore membra eius, quae hoc custodiunt etiam in ipsa carne, quod tota custodit in fide?" (*De sancta virginitate,* c. 2 [*P.L.,* v. 40, col. 397]).
39. Maria corporaliter caput huius corporis peperit: Ecclesia spiritualiter membra illius capitis parit. In utraque virginitas fecunditatem non impedit: in utraque fecunditas virginitatem non adimit. Proinde cum Ecclesia universa sit sancta et corpore et spiritu, nec tamen universa sit corpore virgo, sed spiritu; quanto sanetior est in his membris, ubi virgo est et corpore et spiritu?" (*De sancta virginitate,* c. 2 [*P.L.,* v. 40, col. 397]).
40. Hugo Rahner, *Our Lady and the Church* (New York: Pantheon, 1961), pp. 1–12: "An Introduction: Mary Essentially a Symbol of the Church."
41. An enthusiastic analysis of the notion is to be found in Dom Garcia M. Colombas, *Paraíso y vida angélica. Sentido escatológico de la vocación cristiana* (Montserrat: Abbey of Monserrat, 1958). A balanced judgment concerning the notion is given by J. C. Didier, " 'Angélisme' ou perspectives eschatologiques," *Mélanges de science religieuse,* v. 11 (1954), pp. 30–48. "On close inspection," writes the last named author, "it seems that the angelic world first of all offers an equivalent expression for the life of heaven and the eschatological kingdom." But when the sense of eschatology diminishes, "the reference to angels, no longer being correctly understood, runs the risk of having no foundation. This explains the gradual shift by which the nature of an angel and not his supernatural vocation becomes the term of comparison and the ideal that is proposed" (p. 47). The article is richly documented. Father Congar makes the same reservations in "The Theology of Religious Women," REVIEW FOR RELIGIOUS, v. 19 (1960), pp. 28–31; he gives a bibliography, p. 28, footnote 29.
42. "Quod futuri sumus iam vos esse coepistic. Vos resurrectionis gloriam in isto saeculo iam tenetis, per saeculum sine saeculi contagione transitis" (*P.L.,* v. 4, col. 462 A).
43. "Quod nobis promittitur, vobis praesto est, votorumque nostrorum usus apud vos. De hoc mundo estis, et non estis in hoc mundo. Saeculum vos habere meruit, tenere non potuit" (*De virginibus,* 1, 8 [*P.L.,* v. 16, col. 203 A]).

44. We shall return to this relationship at the beginning of the next section.
45. Congar, "Theology of Religious Women," p. 32, footnote 43.
46. After having shown how messianism implied victory over the gentiles and their subjection to Israel, J. Bonsirven writes in his *Le Judaïsme palestinien au temps de Jésus-Christ,* v. 1 (2nd ed.; Paris: Beauchesne, 1934), p. 412: "Another impression that these passages leave is that the figure of the Messiah in them is a pale one and that his role is insignificant." What purpose does a Messiah serve when through him men devote themselves to their own triumph? The same can be said of a certain kind of Christian eschatology that is overly obsessed by concern for human success; the latter has no appearance of a hundredfold received by reason of love that has been given.
47. Marcel Viller, "Martyre et perfection," *Revue d'ascétique et de mystique,* v. 6 (1925), pp. 1–29; and the same author's "Le bartyre et l'ascèse," ibid., pp. 105–42.
48. "Per hunc viae limitem martyres pergunt, eunt virgines, iusti quoque gradiuntur" (*Liber de habitu virginum* [*P.L.*, v. 4, col. 460 A]).
49. See his *De sancta virginitate liber unus* (*P.L.*, v. 40, col. 397–429). A translation of this treatise is given as an appendix in Perrin, *La virginité chrétienner,* pp. 122–76.
50. "But what this difference in fruitfulness means we leave to those who understand these things better than we do: whether the virginal life is involved in the hundredfold of fruit, the widowed life in the sixtyfold, and the married life in the thirtyfold; or whether the hundredfold fruitfulness is to be assigned to martyrdom, the sixtyfold to continency, and the thirtyfold to marriage; or whether virginity combined with martyrdom yields the hundredfold of fruit, but by itself only sixtyfold while the married who bear the thirtyfold attain the sixtyfold if they become martyrs" (*P.L.*, v. 40, col. 423).
51. He died in 312 and was one of the strenuous opponents of Origen. The text is cited in Viller, "Le martyre et l'ascèse," p. 114, and can be found in *P.G.*, v. 18, col. 100 B. A little later St. Ambrose writes in the West: "Virginity is not praiseworthy because it is found in martyrs but because it itself makes martyrs." "Non ideo laudobilis virginitas, quia et in marytribus invenitur, sed quia ipsa martyres faciat" (*De virginibus,* 1, 10 [*P.L.*, v. 16, col. 191]).
52. See *Lettres d'Ignace d'Antioche et Polycarpe de Smyrne,* Th Camelto, ed. and tr. (2nd ed.; Paris, Cerf, 1951). The same volume includes the remarkable account of the martyrdom of St. Polycarp.
53. J. Pourrat, *Lettre des Eglise de Vinne et de Lyon sur la persécution de l'an 177* (Lyon: Vitte, 1926). Some fifteen years ago the publishing house of L'Orante issued a new edition.
54. *P.G.*, v. 14, col. 563–638.
55. *Life in Jesus Christ.* The text can be found in *P.G.*, v. 150, col. 493–726; French translation in Nicolas Cabasilas, *La vie en Jésus-Christ,* S. Broussaleux, tr. (Prieuré d'Amay-sur-Meuse, 1932). The passage we have cited is on pp. 70–1 of that translation.
56. S. Broussaleux, tr., *La vie en Jésus-Christ,* p. 73.
57. *Ibid.*, p. 75.
58. *Ibid.*, p. 73.
59. Viller, "Martyre et perfection," p. 14. Basically the same remarks are

given by L. Bouyer, *The Spirituality of the New Testament and the Fathers* (New York: Desclee, 1964), Chapter 8: "Martyrdom," pp. 190–210.

60. "Gaudium virginum Christi, de Christo, in Christo, cum Christo, post Christum, per Christum, propeter Christum. Gaudia propria virginum Christi non sunt eadem non virginum, quamvis, Christi. Nam sunt aliis alia, sed nullis talia." "The joy of the virgins of Christ is a joy with regard to Christ, a joy in Christ, a joy with Christ, a joy like Christ's, a joy through Christ, a joy on account of Christ. The joys that are characteristic of the virgins of Christ are not the same as the joys of those who are not virgins even though these latter belong to Christ. Other classes have other joys but no other class has joys such as these" (*De sancta virginitate,* 27 [*P.L.,* v. 40, col. 411]).

61. Notably in the liturgies for the consecration of virgins. An example is the prayer from the Gelasian Sacramentary (from the end of the sixth century) toward the conclusion of the veiling ceremony when the Church prays for the newly consecrated virgin: "We suppliantly pray to Your divine majesty for her that You may bid her to enter the ranks of the holy virgins so that with an inextinguishable lamp she may meet You her Spouse when You come and that, having entered into the heavenly kingdom, she may give thanks to You in company with the choirs of holy virgins." "Pro qua maiestati tuae supplices fundimus preces, ut in numero eam sanctarum virginum transire praecipias ut tibi sponso veniente cum lampade suo inextinguibili possit occurrere, atque intra regni caelestis claustra gratias tibi referat, choris sanctarum virginum sociata." The text of the prayer is given in René Metz, *Le consécration des vieregs dans l'Eglise romaine. Etude d'histoire de la liturgie* (Paris: Presses Universitaires de France, 1954), p. 153, footnotes 55. In his article, "Vierge, virginité" (*Dictionnaire d'archélogie chrétienne et de liturgie,* v. 15), Dom H. Leclercq gives a similar prayer from the Leonine Sacramentary (earlier than the Gelasian Sacramentary).

62. H. de Lubac, *The Splendour of the Church* (New York: Sheed and Ward, 1956), pp. 92 and 106.

63. On this point see Karl Delahaye, *Ecclesia mater chez les pères des trois premiers siècles,* P. Vergniette and E. Bouis, tr. (Paris: Cerf, 1964) with its beautiful preface by Father Congar, pp. 7–32.

CHAPTER 11

1. I John 3:11.
2. Clifford G. Kossel, S.J., presents St. Thomas's views on the ideas in God in his unpublished Ph.D. dissertation, *Relation in St. Thomas* (University of Toronto, 1944), pp. 271–276:

"It is precisely from the requirements of order that St. Thomas proves a multiplicity of ideas in God. The good of order as the optimum *in rebus existens* is the ultimate end (*finis operationis*) in creation; it is, not the result of chance, but is *per se* intended by God. The first requirement of order is distinction, and therefore, multiplicity of parts. But he says that the idea of the whole (*ideam ordinis universi*) cannot be had without the ideas of the parts which constitute it. A builder must know the nature of bricks and mortar of other material, and he must know the difference and proper relationship between bedroom, kitchen and parlour, if he is to have a proper idea of the house to be built. Lack of these ideas would result in chaos and confusion, not in order. So God must know the proper nature of the parts of the universe; there must be many ideas in the divine mind.

"Now these ideas are not separated exemplars, as Plato would have it; they are in God. The problem is: How can this multiplicity stand with the divine simplicity? St. Thomas answered here, as he had done when treating the divine will, that there is only one principal object of the divine intellect, that is the divine being itself of which God has a speculative, not a practical, knowledge. God's knowledge of Himself, as His love of himself, is a relation of reason, for in this there is complete identity between the intellect, the act of intellection, and the object. Yet in knowing Himself, He also knows all things in their proper natures, and this must somehow be through a reference to the principal object.

"In explaining this he uses an example. If light could know itself, it would know all colors, for as the universal cause of color it has in itself the virtue and similitude of all colors. However it would not know the colors in the *proper* nature but only in that which is common to them, *in communi.* And the reason for this is that light is not the cause of the diversity and distinction of colors, for these result from the different dispositions of the diaphorous medium which receives the light. But it is different with God. He contains in Himself in a more excellent way not only what is common to all creatures, being, but every perfection—life, knowledge, will, and every form by which creatures are distinguished from one another and constituted in their own proper species. He is compared to them, not as the common or undetermined to the proper or determined, but as the perfect act to the imperfect act.

"Now the imperfect can be known properly through the perfect as one who knows man also knows animal. Since every creature is a participation in the divine perfection, God would not know Himself if He did not know all the ways in which creatures could imitate His perfection, and He would not know perfectly the very nature of being (*naturam essendi*) if He did not know all the modes of being. God Himself is the total perfection of being, esse without potency, and every perfection is a perfection of being. As there is nothing outside of being, so there is nothing which is not contained in the divine being, in the intellect which comprehends the latter perfectly, and in the causal efficacy founded on it. For this reason He also knows singular material things, for He is the cause of matter as well as of form, and therefore it must be contained somehow in His being and power.

"In operating through intellect God produces all things in the likeness of His essence, not as such, but as understood in the idea of things. But since creatures do not imitate the divine essence perfectly, but deficiently and diversely, the divine essence considered *absolutely* cannot be the proper idea of things, but only as considered with a proportion to the thing to be made. Hence, St. Thomas says that the divine essence is one, but there are many ideas in so far as the one essence is understood diversely according to the different proportions of things to it. Thus the one first form to which all things, as deficient similitudes, are reduced is the divine essence considered in itself; and from a consideration of this essence the divine intellect discovers (*adinvenit*) the different modes in which it can be imitated, and in this consists the pluraity of ideas.

"If, then, we wish to distinguish the order of God's knowledge, it would be thus: He knows the divine essence, the principal object, perfectly; through this as the eminent similitude and cause, He knows the proper nature of all creatures; in knowing the divine essence as thus imitable by creatures, He knows the proper nature, *ratio,* of each creature and this is its idea. The ideas, then, are many as relations of reason "caused" by the divine intellect comparing the divine essence, the primary object, to thing, the secondary objects. They are not founded on the divine esse as such, he says, but on the divine intellect; they are relations understood by God. Finally, he says, that they are not a multiplicity of species informing the divine intellect and reducing it to act, but are a multiplicity of objects understood through one species, the divine intellect.

"Strictly speaking the *ratio* pertains to speculative knowledge, and the idea to practical knowledge. The first is the principle of the knowledge of things, and the latter the principle of their generation as the extrinsic form and exemplar. But these two coincide in God since His knowledge is the cause of things. What is added to the idea is not something strictly in the order of knowledge, but in the order of finality, the will to the end and of the things to the end. This determines both the order of the parts in the whole, disposition, and the order of the whole to the end, providence. Hence, although providence presupposes the will, it remains in the intellect as the *ratio ordinis rerum in finem.*

"There is another important difference between disposition, the work of productive art, and providence, the work of directive prudence. Art looks primarily to the good of the work, the *finis operationis,* which is the form of the thing consisting of its essential parts. Hence it looks to the proper collocation of the essential parts of the universe, the species and their proper accidents. But since providence looks to the order to the extrinsic end, the final perfection which is attained through particular operations, it must also include the knowledge of those individual accidents which are not contained in the idea of nature."

3. *Theological Studies,* March 1961.
4. I John 4:12–16.
5. Clifford G. Kossel, S.J., "St. Thomas's Theory of the Causes of Relation," in *The Modern Schoolman,* 25 (March 1948), pp. 171–172:

"From this interpretation of the Platonic relationship of forms through exemplary and efficient causality, it is easy to pass to the Aristotelian view of the order of the universe as one of finality. The order of the parts to one another (*coordinata*) depends on the order of the whole to an extrinsic principle; in this order lies the good and perfection of things. [*De Pot.,* 7. 9.]

"The conclusions from a study of these texts seem clear. First, in the mind of St. Thomas, the immediate foundations for relations in creatures are certain accidental forms in the subject. Secondly, each of these forms has a twofold function. It is an absolute perfection of its subject making it to be what it is in the order of intrinsic accidental act. It also carries the subject outside itself by a virtual relativity, attraction, or—perhaps best of all—a potentiality for communicating with others in perfection. These are distinct and conceptually irreducible functions or modes of being, but they do not constitute two physical entities in the motion with which they are identified. Both derive from one physical form. Finally, this second aspect of form is intimately linked to the tendency of things to the good and perfection attained through operation. The root of relativity is ultimately in the finalization of created beings; they are not for themselves alone but for the universal order of harmonious co-operation by which all and each somehow attain the absolute good, the extrinsic end of the universe and each of its parts."

6. The metaphysics of providence and fate (or "destiny" as it is sometimes called) in Thomistic philosophy has been well explained by Clifford G. KOSSEL, S.J., in *Relation in St. Thomas* (unpublished Ph.D. dissertation, University of Toronto, 1944), pp. 276–281:

"Providence, then, includes not only the intrinsic potencies for operation and perfection, but their actual exercise and realisation in action; it includes not only the internal tendency and virtual relativity of nature, but also the external relations, the various and temporal modes by which potency is actualized through the concurrence of causes. Providence reaches to anything which has *esse* in any way.

"Here again we touch upon necessity and contingency and their relation to the universal intelligibility of being. Each of the series of secondary causes which make up fate, acts from nature and the potencies which flow from it; they are determined to one type of operation. But that this agent and this patient should come together in the proper dispositions for action at this time, has no necessary cause within the whole order of nature.

"Thus the individual accidents which do not flow from nature, and therefore depend for their coming into being on extrinsic agents, are strictly *per accidens* and scientifically undeducible. We may hold eternally that "homo generat hominem, et sol" but blue-eyed musical Johnny Jones is not the result of *a* nature, a *per se* cause, and is not *a* nature. That combination is determined neither in the nature of his parents nor in his stars; it results from a convergence of causes. Hence such a composite is not really being nor really one, because it is not one essence or nature; its unity is existential, not essential.

"Nor has the convergence of causes any cause in nature. That a fiery comet should fall to earth, may have a cause in the power of some celestial body; and that there be a combustible object on earth may likewise have such a cause. But that this comet should fall here at this time and burn this object, has no proper natural cause; it is *per accidens*. The internal relativity of fire to heat and of the heatable to be heated is necessary and determined in nature, but the external relations, the temporal and particular fulfillment of these potentialities, is contingent and unknowable until after it *is*.

"But the *per accidens* is not entirely unintelligible although it is not truly one nature, it can be known as one by intellect in the unity of a judgment. The intellect can form the proposition: "One digging a grave finds a treasure." And St. Thomas adds, as the intellect is able to apprehend this, so it is able to bring it about. The *per accidens* can be reduced to the cause which orders things by acting through intellect, and this is providence on which the intelligibility of the contingent is based. And the actual course of events, considered as subordinate to providence and mediated by second causes we call fate. Thus fate includes the contingent, in fact, more truly applies to this than to the necessary.

"Indeed St. Thomas refers with approval to both Plato and Aristotle when they maintain that individual accidents have no final cause. But his approval is conditioned. There is no final cause (as there is no *per se* efficient cause) for these in the whole order of nature; the intention of nature looks to the species. But they have a transcendent cause which is outside the whole order of nature. In the divine intellect there is the idea not only of the species and its properties, but of the material individual, of the material dispositions, and of the motions and actions resulting from the concurrence of natures and material dispositions. Nothing happens by chance in a world which is ruled by Providence.

"Both in Plato's world of separated forms and in Aristotle's world of forms in matter, all intelligibility derives from form, and matter is the absolutely unintelligible. It is the uncaused and indeterminate cause of the *per accidens,* and the latter therefore partakes of the unintelligibility of its cause. For St. Thomas too the material individual as such is unintelligible *quoad nos* owing precisely to the indeterminacy of matter. But neither matter nor the *per accidens* are absolutely unintelligible in themselves. They are caused by God; they are intelligible in God since they have their idea in Him; they must come under the order of providence; and are therefore finalised to God ultimately.

"Providence and disposition are the *ratio ordinis rerum* in the divine mind. But the order itself, its esse, is in the series of second cause, which are natures and to which God has given the proper virtues to produce their effect. And these natures are ultimately applied by God to their operations as instruments for His end. This execution of things is fate. The universe and its events, then are not really one nature, one substance or one form; they are one only by order which is the form of the whole.

"This order is derived from an intellect joined with an efficacious will to the end and the active power to produce its object in their own being. They derive from an intellect, will and power which are identically being, and therefore comprehensive in their unity of every mode of being, even the being of order or relation, which is the least being and unity (*Minima unitatum*). The unity of the universe derives from the unity of the divine mind.

"St. Thomas says indifferently that the nature (*ratio*) of order is drawn either from the distinction of natures or from the end. The first refers to the order of parts in the whole, disposition, and the second to the order of the whole to the end, providence. But as the first is determined by the second, the two orders will actually correspond. The end is first in causality, but the form is first in being. This form, as nature ordered to its act through its potencies, is the foundation of relation; but the actuation of these potencies in operation, which is the end, is the fulness of relation, the union which completes the *ratio* of relation.

"The human mind because it is not the cause of nature or its order, and because it is bound to space, motion and time, can know the virtues, forms, and their hierarchy to some extent, through their actuations as actually observed; thus is known the internal relativity, the esse of relation. But for the further unfolding of the order of things, to know new relations in the externality and contingency, it must wait until they *are,* until the potencies of nature are actualised. The divine mind, however, does not know the history of the universe in its causes alone; providence, strictly speaking, is not *fore*knowledge, it is eternal knowledge in which there is no before and after. God knows what is before and after, but all is present to Him at once—*uno intuitu in sua præsentialitate.* As the transcendent artist of the universe and the planner of its history. He knows all its relations in their internality and externality, their necessity and contingence."

7. *Un Poète regarde la Croix,* Paris, Gallimard, 1938, p. 248.
8. *Contra Gent.,* 4, 42.
9. *Summa Theol.,* Iª, q. 8, a. 3, ad 3ᵐ.
10. *Summa Theol.,* Iª, q. 18, a. 14.
11. *Summa Theol.,* Iª, q. 14, a. 1, ad 2ᵐ.
12. Karl Jaspers would call this the "unauthentic man" (*Psychologie der Weltanschauungen,* Berlin, 1925).

In his evasion of personal responsibility, this man says, thinks and chooses what everyone else does, regardless of what he knows to be true or right. As opposed to the rejection of the absolutely inauthentic subject to be rational, there is the divergence of the relatively inauthentic subject from a determined doctrine, religion, culture or way of life. It is a divergence between what the subject really experiences, understands and judges to be true (according to which he lives, wills and acts) and the characteristic mold of the experience, understanding and judgment of the particular group or doctrine. It is not a complete divergence: there are areas of harmony, conformity and squaring in thought which allow the subject to think he is authentically Thomist, Hegelian, American, Christian and the like. He thinks of himself as authentically Thomist, for example, and is unaware of the divergence. He uses the same words, with a different meaning, with the result that a simplification, devaluation and deformation of the original doctrine takes place. The divergence is beyond his horizon. He is blind to the elements in his position, outlook, attitude, and way of life which clash with or fall short of the ideal. It is hard for him to be converted, because his deficiency is beyond his horizon. By horizon is meant the totality of objects which an individual can master, cope with and enjoy through his acquired habits. A person does not avert to or see whatever is beyond this field. The horizon defines the limits of his world. Reality is partly within and partly beyond our horizon. The horizon is not absolute, because the human intellect and will can know and love all reality; but this only occurs with learning, persuasion and practice. The broadening of a man's horizon occurs when he operates on new mediated objects, and deal with new immediate objects. New experiences, symbols, conversation and reading broaden the horizon, and enrichen the imagination by providing a man with something new to reflect on. A man's scope for activity is enlarged by the further development of his scientific and philosophical knowledge. This development results from a man's experience, understanding and reflection on new immediate and mediated objects. However, no one really enjoys scientific knowledge unless he knows what he is doing and what he is trying to do. Until he can answer these questions, he can never master anything.

The absolutely inauthentic man is at least aware of his failure to be true to his experience, understanding and judgment. The possibility of conversion is greater for him. The conversion of a subject is the reorganization upheaven of the subject, of his operations, of the world with which he is familiar. The source of this change is within the subject himself. The reorganization of the subject, his activities, attitudes and world not only broadens his horizons—the chief task—but also changes his own interiority.

Moral conversion is a change from object of desire and fear as ultimate and absolute motives of conduct, to what ought to be absolute, to what has value, really counts, whether it pleases or displeases.

Intellectual conversion is a shift from one's childhood view of reality to an ultimate reliance on rational criteria, from the real "out there" to what is rationally affirmed. A child's prerational criteria of reality remain a fundamental conviction unless revised and corrected through education, persuasion and effort.

Religious conversion is a shift from a natural, humanistic view of life to the Christian view, where the ultimate ceases to be one's self, but God, not naturally known, but as revealed in the Catholic faith. It is a shift from egocentricity to theocentricity.

In every conversion what was formerly on top ceases to be on top, or all-important in the newly established personal order of things (these observations are taken from an introductory talk on theological method by Bernard Lonergan, S.J.).

13. Jacques BARZUN, *Marflect Lectures,* delivered at the Convention Hall, University of Toronto, March 14, 1960.
14. Rom. 15, 9.
15. *Summa Theol.*, I-II^{ae}, q. 99, a. 1, ad 2^{m}.
16. Fr. Barnabas Ahern pointed out in a recent talk that man's basic relationship to God and neighbor as [*sic*] presented in St. Luke's Gospel. St. Luke's method of working in balanced paris offers the data for this observation. The story of the Good Samaritan (Lk. 10, 30 ff.) immediately precedes the Martha and Mary episode and should be considered with it. The Good Samaritan story teaches that our basic relationship with other men should be one of *giving*. The Martha and Mary episode suggests that our fundamental relationship to God is one of *receiving*. [Martha had wanted to do something for Christ, whereas Mary's listening was preferred.] Receptivity and faith should keynote our relationship with God; generosity and love should ground our relationships with our neighbor.
17. "Karl Bühler distingue, dans la parole, un triple aspect: i) La parole a un *contenu*. Elle signifie ou représeute quelque chose: elle nomme un objet, elle formule une pensée, un jugement, elle raconte un fait (*Darstellung*). ii) La parole est une *interpellation*. Elle s'adresse à quelqu'un et tend à provoquer chez lui une réponse, une réaction. Elle agit comme un appel, une provocation (*Appell, Auslösung*). iii) Enfin, la parole est *dévoilement* de la personne, manifestation de son attitude intérieure, de ses dispositions (*Ausdruck, Kundgabe*). En bref, nous pouvons définir la parole comme étant l'action par laquelle une personne *s'adresse et s'exprime* à une autre personne en vue d'une *communication.*

"La parole est d'abord recontre *interpersonnelle*. L'homme parle *du* monde, mais il ne parle pas *au* monde. La parole s'adresse à un autre. L'homme entretient avec les objets des relations de *je à cela;* mais la parole s'établit entre un *moi et* un *toi*. Toute parole vise autrui. Même chez les professionels du silence (Montaigne, Descartes, Vigny, Proust), la parole est encore la recherche d'une présence personnelle authentique.

"Au surplus, dès que nous quittons l'univers des choses matérielles pour accéder au niveau des *personnes,* nous quittons de plan de l'évidence pour entrer dans celui du témoignage. Au niveau de l'intersubjectivité, qui est celui des personnes, nous nous heurtons au mystère. Or les personnes ne sont des problèmes qui se lassent enfermer dans des formules et résoudre dans une équation. Les personnes ne peuvent être connues que par révélation. Nous n'avons d'accès à l'intimité personnelle que par le libre témoignage de la personne. Et les personnes no témoignent d'elles-mêmes que sous l'inspiration de l'amour. La connaissance par témoignage est donc une connaissance inférieure là où, par suite de la nature de l'objet, nous sommes capables d'arriver à une évidence directe et immédiate du réel; mais elle n'est pas inférieure lorsqu'il s'agit de ces réalitésf que sont les personnes, où le témoignage est la seule façon d'entrer en union avec la personne et de participer à son mystère (René LATOURELLE, s.j., *La Révélation comme Parole, Témoignage et Rencontre,* in *Gregorianum,* Vol. XLIII, No. 1, 1962).

18. An appreciation and tolerance for the individual is wanting in highly industrialized countries where a conformistic society progressively drives more individuals outside of its own bounds. The more tolerant Latin culture provide for a much wider range of responses from various types of personalities, and afford them a place and a recognition that they need. "There are Germans who hate Germany, Americans who are revolted by America, Swiss who feel stifled in Switzerland, Englishmen who say that England is impossible to live in; all these are marginal figures of an all-too-compact and well ordered society. But a Frenchman who is not in love with his country is hard to find. He may curse beyond redemption the French state and its institutions and the morals and manners of his fellow countrymen, he may dismiss the French Government as a gang of crooks and the French administrative system as a racket, the most commonplace article of foreign manufacture may cause him to break out into a tirade and declare that only foreign-made goods are worth having, but at the end of it all he will passionately announce that France is the only country in which it is possible to live and breathe freely. What do technical achievements and social progress, efficient plumbing and lifts that work, amount to in comparison with the pleasure of being an unhampered individualist" (*France Against Herself,* New York, Meridian Books, 1957, p. 75. The author, Herbert Luethy, is a Swiss political commentator).

    Americans, on the other hand, fear being different in a culture that demands certain responses: a type of anti-intellectualism, physical ruggedness, bravado, and a hard-fisted drive to get ahead. Most men are fortunately able to accommodae themselves to the culture into which they were born; however, increasing demands for conformity means that more men find difficulty in integrating themselves and begin to feel "abnormal." They feel rejected by a society that does not support their individuality, their particular responses. For these individuals, it is easy to make the inevitable transfer from feeling rejected by society to being rejected by God: from seeing the angry face of society, to seeing the angry face of God. Salvation for these "outcasts" and "outsider" may only come through the manifestation of loving face of God by the friends of God. This phenomenon is expressed in Scripture by the word "glory." Glory expresses the active and radiant presence of God by means of which He helps others. It was also the guide that led the way to the Promised

Land. It is, thirdly, the concrete means of God's self-revelation. God is totally present where He operates. When His love is operative in the person of the believer, a light shines in the darkness, and this light is the glory of God. Men learn what God is like by encountering men who are like God, through and in whom His glory is manifest. The glory of God is found where God reigns (Apoc. 21:10); it is characterized by the appearance of radiant light, signifying the nearness of God and His intervention (either directly or through an angelic intermediary: (Lk. 2:9:31; Apoc. 15:8; 18:1). God continually communicates to His friends, His life, excellence and glory. Whenever the friends of God do anything that manifests their union with God, they glorify God by manifesting His divine life, or glory, in their activity; and they are simultaneously glorified by God who is giving them this share in His life, or glory (John 5:23; 8:49; 12:26). The opposite of glory is the egocentricity whereby a man seeks to honor himself independently of God. His desire for an independent glory excludes all readiness to accept the borrowed glory of God in Jesus Christ, the concrete manifestation and offer of God's glory through whom we receive the power to become the sons of God.

19. I Cor. 1:24.
20. Col. 2:3.

CHAPTER 15

1. Gregorianum 35 (1954) 608–629.
   The article was re-edited in summary in *Digest Religioso* 2 (1956) n. 2, 6–11, and in *Theology Digest* 5 (1957), 34–38.
2. On the meaning of the words αἰών and κόσμος both in Holy Scripture and elsewhere, cf. G. Kittel, Theol. Wörterbuch zum Neuen Testament, I. 197–209; esp. 203 ff. ("αἰών as World": "κόσμος als Welt"); *ibid.,* III, 867–896.
   For its biblical usage, also F. Zorell, *Lexicon graecum Novi Testamenti,* Paris, 1931,[2] s.v. αἰών et κόσμος and *Lexikon für Theologie und Kirche,* s.v. Welt (X, 811–813). On the use of κόσμος in St. Paul, cf. also F. Prat, *La théologie de saint Paul,* II, Paris, 1949,[38] Note Q, 505–507.
   For the apocrypha, pseudoepigraphica, and rabbinical writings, cf. L. Strack-P. Billerbeck, *Kommentar zum NT aus Talmud und Midrasch,* IV/2, 799–976 ("29. Exkurs: Diese Welt, die Tage des Messias u. die zukünftige Welt").
3. Cf. J. Mouroux, *Thélogie de la Croix—Théologie de la gloire:* L'humanisme et la grâce. Semaine des intellectuels catholiques (1950). Paris, 1950, 150–166.
4. Cf. W. Dirks, *Der Welt verloren und aller Welt Freund:* Geist u. Leben 23 (1950) 288–298.
5. Cf. F. Olgiati, *Le tendenze umanistiche attuali e l'apostolato:* Apostolotato e vita interiore (5ª settimana di spiritualita, promossa dall' Università del S. Cuore, 1949), Milano, 1950, 122–152. F. Hermans, *Historie doctrinelle de l'humanisme chrétien,* IV, Tournai-Paris, 1948.
6. Cf. the conspectus in M. Flick-Z. Alszeghy, *Teologia della storia:* Gregorianum 35 (1954) 256–298.
7. S. Thomas, *ST* I, q. 18, a.4: "Utrum omnia sint vita in Deo" (whether all things are life in God).

8. S. Augustine, *De Gen, ad litt.*, 2,8,16; ML 34,269: ". . . illic non facta, sed genita; hic vero facta . . ." (Not made there—*i.e.,* in the Father—but begotten; but made here—*i.e.,* in this world). S. Anselm, *Monologium,* c 33–35; ML 158, 187–189. Cf. Patres S. I. in Hisp. Professores, *Sacrae Theologiae Summa,* III, Madrid, 1952, 493–497.
9. Cf. P. Heinisch, *Theologie des Alten Testamentes,* Bonn, 1940, § 14, 3, and 23, 1.
10. Sess. 3, cap. 1; Denz. 1783.
11. *Ibid.*
12. Paul is not speaking in any way of the last times; his mind is that evil is already present and is beginning to manifest itself; cf. I Tim. 6:19.
13. C. Spicq, *Saint Paul. Les Épîtres pastorales: Etudes Bibliques,* Paris, 1947, i, 1.
14. J. Knabenbauer, *Commentarius in Epist. ad Thess., ad Tim., ad Titum et ad Philem.:* Cursus Scripturae Sacrae, Paris, 1913, i. 1.
15. M. Meinertz, *Die Pastoralbriefe des hl. Paulus,* Bonn, 1823², i. 1.
16. Cf. also I Tim 5,14, on the duties of widows.
17. It is hard to refer these prescriptions to a determined heretical sect.
"They are found again under one form or another in more or less precise fashion in certain pagan philosophies (Pythagoreanism) as well as in magical practices . . . in certain oriental cults—Phrygian and Asiatic —in Orphism, in Jewish circles—the Essenes—and in the preparation of the initiate for the mysteries. In them may be seen the first manifestations of what the Gnosis properly so called will later establish, but which in the Church of Ephesus probably emanated from Jewish converts with syncretist tendencies, since the prohibition of marriage is inspired rather by pagan conceptions" (Spicq).
18. Eusebius, *Hist. Eccl.* V, 3, 2; MG 20,437; ed. Schwartz, II, 432:
"There was among those imprisoned for Christ one Alcibiades. He led a hard and austere life, refusing to take food but eating only bread, water, and salt. As he wished to continue this rigorous way of life even in prison, it was revealed to Attalus after his first witness borne in the amphitheatre that Alcibiades was not acting aright in refusing the use of God's creatures and in leaving a form of scandal to others. Alcibiades on learning of this began to eat everything with thanksgiving, because what the spirit had revealed to Attalus to teach he also persuaded Alcibiades to follow.
19. Eusebius, *Hist. eccl.*, IV, 23:7–8; MG 20:385; ed. Schwartz, II, 376.
20. *Adv. Haereses*, I, 28, 1; MG 7:690; in Greek, from Eusebius, *Hist. eccl.*, IV, 29:2; ed. Schwartz, II, 390.
21. For documents condemning "encratism" see J. de Guibert, *Documenta ecclesiastica christianae perfectionis studium spectantia,* Rome, 1931, n. 1–9.
22. *Ibid.*, n. 16–17.
23. *Ibid.*, n. 31–38.
24. *Ibid.*, n. 44–50.
25. *Ibid.*, n. 139 ss.
26. Denz., 54.
27. P. Charles, *Créateur des choses visibles:* NRT 67 (1940) 267.
28. *Ibid.*, 275.
29. R. Cornely, *Epistola ad Romanos:* Cursus Scr. S., Paris, 1896, i. 1.

30. *Exposito quarandam propositionum ex Epistola ad Rom., 53:* ML 35, 2074–2076. *De diversis quaestionibus octoginta tribus, 67;* ML 40, 66–70.
31. R. Cornely, *op. cit.,* on Rom. 8:19 cites Haymo of Halberstadt, Peter Abelard, Hervé of Bordeaux, Peter Lombard, Nicholas Lyranus, Denys the Carthusian, Cardinal Cajetan. One of the chief arguments in favor of this view is that expectation and hope, which the text attributes to creation, are applicable only to man. To this A. Viard, *Expectatio creaturae (Rom. 8:19–22)* Revue Biblique 59 (1952) 337–354, says: "Still, nothing kept St. Paul from lending, by a current figure of speech, irrational or inanimate creatures a voice and feelings."
32. *Loc. cit., note* 30.
33. Cornely considers the interpretation that takes irrational creation in an exclusive sense "the commoner, especially among the Greek Fathers"; to it "practically all" interpreters since the sixteenth century have returned, while "nowadays all" hold it.

Likewise M. J. Lagrange, *Épître aux Romains:* Études Bibliques, Paris, 1916, i. 1: "The moderns have all returned to the exegesis current among the ancients."

But as Viard observes (*art. cit.,* 341), this can no longer be maintained at the present. He favors the opinion that takes "creatura" as "irrational creation along with man." There are scarcely any Scriptural data favoring its restriction to irrational creation. He appeals to Wisdom 2:6 ("Come, then, and enjoy we the good things that exist; and use we creation as in youth hastily"); but in this passage "*κτίσις* does not necessarily exclude man; for even—or rather, especially—man can be an instrument of the delights meant in the text; cf. Wisdom 14:22–26 and Rom. 24–27. Nor, he continues, does the argument from context have any force: in vv. 19, 21, 23, men are opposed to creation; for irrational creation does not expect the sons of God, but the "revelation of the sons of God," *i.e.,* the full manifestation of glory in them, which they themselves while still on earth expect Cf. Col. 3:3–4. Else St. Paul could find neither in Scripture nor in Rabbinical literature the idea of a hope proper to irrational creation alone: in the O.T. of course the question is one of a paradisiacal renewal of the earth (Isa. 65:17–25), which yet is connected with men's deliverance, especially—not exclusively: cf. Isa. 25:6–8—that of the Chosen People: cf. Isa. 51:3; Jer. 31:9; Osee 11:1; Ezech. 47:12. These canonical books sufficiently point to a hope in the bosom of the Jewish People for a renewal of the world by a return to the state of the lost Paradise; yet this renewal is always presented as an element accessory to the People's prosperity. "Here too everything depends on a genuine 'revelation of the sons of God,' since God is then to show himself truly the God of his People (cf. Jer. 31,9). The renewal of nature for the profit of the tribes of Israel is only an aspect and, as it were, one of the conditions of the peaceable and joyous life promised them" (346).

Viard's exposition has a vigor that must be acknowledged, though it it is not easily applicable to v. 23: "And not only it, but we ourselves also who have the first-fruits of the Spirit—we ourselves groan within ourselves, waiting for the adoption as sons. . . ." This difficulty Père Viard attempts to solve thus: "Will it be asserted that 'the sons of God' are only meant in v. 23, where St. Paul speaks of the groans of those possessing the first-fruits of the Spirit and who await 'the redemption of their body'? Their being mentioned here personally by no means precludes the possibility of their being already included in the preceding description—Saint Paul passing from the general to the particular. His argumentation utilizes concepts with clearly defined outlines much less than an ensemble of concrete perceptions and living images, whereby he tries to translate a complex reality as fully as possible."

34. Cf. Cornely i. 1.
35. *Expositio quarundam propositionum ex Epist. ad Rom.*, 53; ML 35: 2075.
36. *Art. cit.*, 349–350.
37. M. J. Lagrange, *Épître aux Romains:* Études Bibliques, Paris, 1916, i. 1.
38. Cornely, i. 1., earlier on decided to maintain, with Chrystostom and "later interpreters and many moderns," the view—which still creates a difficulty for him in the phrase ἐπ'ἐλπίδι. This phrase in this view ought to mean, he thinks, that man set hope before creatures; but man's action, leading irrational creation along with him rather opposes hope. Therefore he considers that the verb *subiecit* is to be referred to God. But this opinion labors under another severe difficulty: it fails to preserve the normal meaning of διά with the accusative; this requires, rather, that the "one subjecting" be considered as the cause of evil. This cannot be true of God.

    Viard says: "Certainly in Genesis God pronounces a curse upon the soil; but he rather states a thing which is a consequence of sin than introduces anything new. The curse strikes the earth 'on account of man' (Gen. 3:17)—an expression that seems to be recalled in St. Paul's 'by reason of him who made it subject.' God had made man the head of creation (Gen. 1:28); he still remained its supreme master to the extent to which man remained subject to him. But on taking another master, man delivered to him not only his own person, but all the beings bound to, or dependent upon, himself—*i.e.*, all his descendants and all other earthly creatures—in a word, all creation" (351). To the difficulty created by ἐπ'ἐλπίδι, Père Viard replies: "'ἐπ'ἐλπίδι could be left more or less dangling: thus it might be joined not to ὑποτάξαντα but to ὑπετάγη. It is a simple statement of fact, not an indication of its origin or cause."
39. Cf. esp. St. Irenaeus, on whom E. Scharl, *Recapitulatio mundi. Der Rekapitulationsbegriff des hl. Irenaeus und seine Anwendung auf die Körperwelt.* Freiburg i. Br. 1941, cap. 4: "Rekapitulation der materiellen Welt" (68–85); in cap. 6 (94–110) is treated the concept of recapitulation in Sacred Scripture, and in cap. 7, in the Fathers before St. Irenaeus—the Apostolic Fathers and the second-century Apologists.
40. M. J. Scheeben, *Handbuch der kath. Dogmatik,* § 267.
41. *Id., Mysterien des Christentums,* § 96.
42. Cornely, i. 1., in text et note 1.
43. Viard, *art. cit.*, 353, with note 1.
44. *S. c. Gent.*, Book 4, ch. 56.
45. Cf. A. Brunner, *Eine neue Schöpfung. Ein Beitrag zur Theologie ddes christlichen Lebens.* Paderborn, 1952, 38–39.
46. Encyl. *Mediator Dei,* AAS 39 (1947) 532.

47. W. Voelker, *Der wahre Gnostiker nach Clemens Alexandrinus,* Berlin, 1952, 218.
48. *Contra Celsum,* 8:33; MG 11:1566 B; ed. Koetschau, II, 248.
49. *Contra Celsum,* 8:32; MG 11:1564C—1565A; ed. Koetschau, II, 247–248.
50. This we have set forth more at length in an article *De viribus naturae humanae in vita spirituali:* Gregorianum 35 (1954) 610 ss.
51. For bibliography, cf. *Dict. de Spit., art.* "corps (spiritualité et hygiène du)" (D. Gorce).
52. A. Usenicnik, *Iz psihologije milosti:* Bogoslovni Vestnik 2 (1922) 241–242.
53. *De virtutibus infusis,* Rome, 1928,[4] 44.
54. *Tractatus de vera intelligentia auxilii efficacis,* cap. XI; *Opera omnia,* Paris, 1858, tom. X, 359.
55. *Opera omnia,* X, 362–363.
56. On the bond between the supernatural life and works of sacred art, cf. the reply of Pastor Max Thurian of the Community of Taizé (Saône-et-Loire), based on Calvinist theology, in a recent "enquête" (inquiry) on sacred art.

    "Properly revelation and inspiration belong only to the Word of God and of His Holy Spirit, who alone reveal and inspire. So a work of art, beauty, will not reveal anything to us about the supernatural world or give us any inspiration about it. Only the Word, illustrated by the work of art, or the Spirit signified by it can act supernaturally upon the believer. A work of fine art, beauty, has toward faith and piety an 'assisting function': by itself it does not reveal or inspire anything; it only assists faith and piety. This assisting function of beauty does not lessen the eminence of its role and of its value in the service of piety. Quite the contrary. It shuts out all poor romanticism and sentimentality. . . . A work of fine art is there to assist the believer's piety and it does this on the plane of the senses and of the soul. It fixes and nourishes the senses in the same direction as the Word and the Spirit fix and nourish mind and heart. It has a purifying—a cathartic—role. It puts every function of our being in its place; it satisfies senses and soul in order to allow the Spirit to make our mind understand the Word better. It merely occupies senses and soul while the Spirit is at work within our spirit (mind: esprit), but assists Him by orientating our senses and our soul toward the same aspirations after piety and adoration as the Holy Spirit stirs up in our hearts. In the practice, then, of worship and piety beauty has a true ministry, distinct from, but joined to, the Word and to the Spirit. If, therefore, such is the function of a work of art in its relationship to piety, it is evident that it can paralyse piety if it is ugly, distract it if it is complicated, or deflect it if it be not pure" (*Problèmes de l'art sacre.* Presenté par V.-H. Debidour. Paris, 1951, 201–202).
57. M. Flick-Z. Alszeghy, *Teologia della storia:* Gregorianum 35 (1954) 296.
58. Cf. A. Viard, *Expectatio creaturae:* Revue Biblique 59 (1952) 345, note 2.
59. L. Strack-P. Billerbeck, *Kommentar zum NT aus Talmud und Midrach,* III, 840–847.
60. *Lexikon f. Theol. u. Kirche,* s.v. "Welt."
61. J. Bonsirven, *Théologie du Nouveau Testament,* Paris, 1951, 387. F. Zorell,

Lexicon graecum NT, gives the word *καινός* in this passage the meaning: "of a new, sublimer, or more perfect order or nature; it is also used of something that has been raised to a more perfect state: *κ. οὐρανός, γῆ* II Pet. 3:13 . . ." (s.v. *καινός*).

62. Cap. 42; ML 1:490B—491A.
63. Cap. 5–6; MG 2:1173B—1176C.
64. Cf. *Umanesimo e mondo cristiano,* Rome 1951, esp. the articles: M. Pellegrino, Umanita nella prima letteratura cristiana; G. Lazzati, Umanesimo della Cattedra d'Alessandria; L. Thiry, "Humanitas" benedettina; P. Brezzi, Presenza dell'umanesimo nella dialettica e mistica medioevale; U. Padovani, La scoperta di Aristotele e l'umanesimo cristiano. Also, F. Hermans, *Historie de l'humanisme chrétien,* 4 vol., Tournai, 1948.
65. Cf. Radio Address of Pope Pius XII on technological advances (AAS 46 [1954] 7–8).

    "The Church loves and supports human progress. It is undeniable that progress in technology somes from God, and so can and must lead to God. . . . [The believer] will find it natural to place alongside the gold, frankinsense, and myrrh which the Magi offered to the Divine Child the modern conquests of technology also—the machines and numbers, laboratories and inventions, power and resources. Besides, such an offering is like the presentation to him of the work that He himself once commanded and which is now being successfully executed though not finally completed. 'People the earth and bring it under subjection' (Gen. 1:28). Such was God's command to man when entrusting him with creation as his temporary inheritance. What a long way from that to the present time, when man can claim to have fulfilled in a certain measure the command of God! Technology indeed leads man today toward a perfection in the control of the material world never before reached. . . . Now it is clear that every research and discovery among the forces of nature affected by technology is reducible to research into and discovery of, the grandeur, the wisdom, the harmony of God. Who could disapprove of or condmen technology thus considered?
66. Cf. A. de Bovis, *Le sens catholique du travail et de la civilisation:* NRT 72 (1950) 471–472.
67. Cf. B. Martin, *Die Bedrohung des inneren Lebens durch die moderne Welt:* Geist u. Leben, 23 (1950) 161–171.
68. "Properly [luctatio is a] contest, a wrestling-match a *certamen* between two, of whom he is winner who flattens the other and presses him on the ground" (J.-M. Vosté, *Comment. in Epist. ad Ephesios,* Rome-Paris, 1932,[2] i. 1.
69. In II Cor. 4:4 the devil is called "the god of this world" [of this age ? *αἰῶνος* saeculi].
70. R. P. Medebielle: L. Pirot-A. Clamer, La Sainte Bible, i. 1. For the rest of the teaching about the devil in Sacred Scripture, cf. *Dict. de Spir.,* art. "démon" (vol. III, 142–152) (S. Lyonnet).
71. J. Daniélou in the same art. (vol. III, 174).
72. *De spectaculis* 8; ML 1:640.
73. *De spectaculis* 10; ML 1:643.
74. *De corona* 13; ML 2:97.
75. For more about the devil according to Tertullian, art. *Démon* (vol. III, 174–182) (J. Daniélou).

76. Origen erroneously admits the possibility of the conversion of some devils to Christ.
77. For more about the devil according to Origen, art. *Démon* (vol. III, 182–189) (Daniélou).
78. Cf. Rufinus, *In Ps.* 75:4; ML 21:679 D.
79. Cf. *De Civ. Dei* 14:18; ML 41:426–427. *Ibid.*, 21:1; ML 41:709.
80. More in art. *Démon* (vol. III, 216–217) (F. Vandenbroucke).
81. S. Lyonnet, *ibid.* (vol. III, 145, 152).
82. For the devil's influence upon the world, cf. besides *Dict. de Spir.* art. *Démon,* J. de Guibert, *Leçons de théologie spirituelle,* I, Toulouse, 1943, lect. 23 and 24; *Satan:* Études Carmelitaines 1948; Anima 4 (1949), fasc. 2 entire.
83. Not in every case. Sometimes the "world" is the whole, the universe, of material creation: Act 17:24—God made the world; Rom. 1:20—from the creation of the world; Eph. 1:4—before the foundation of the world. Sometimes it is the earth as men's dwelling place, or a more general thing, the environment in which mankind lives: I Tim. 6:7—man brings nothing into the world; Rom. 4:43—Abraham, heir of the world; Col. 1:6—the faith is preached in the whole world. Sometimes it is mankind, the inhabitants of earth: Rom. 3:6—God, judge of the world; Rom. 3:19—the world, debtor to divine justice; II Cor. 5:19—God reconciled to the world in Christ; Rom. 5:12—by one man sin entered the world; Phil. 2:15—the apostles, luminaries of the world.
    More in the lexica of Kittell and of Zorell s.v. *αἰών* and *κόσυος*.
    F. Prat, *La théologie de saint Paul,* II, Paris, 1949,[38] Note Q, 505–507.
    Lexikon f. Theol. u. Kirche, s.v. "Welt."
84. Furthermore, I Cor. 3:19; 5:10; Gal. 6:14; Iac. 4:4; II Pet. 1:4. Cf. above-quoted lexica; Also J. de Guibert, *Leçons,* lect. 28.
85. *Ad martyres,* c. 2; ML 1:621 B; M. J. Rouet de Journel-J. Dutilleul, *Enchiridium Asceticum* (abbreviated EA), n. 40; Cf. Tertullian, *De spectaculis,* c. 24; ML 1:655 C; Corpus Vindobonense (=CV) 20, 24 (ed. Reifferscheid and Wissowa); EA 43.
86. *Epistula ad Corinthios* II, c. 6, n. 3; MG 1:336 C; ed. Funk 2:190; EA n. 10.
87. Cf. further St. Cyril of Jerusalem, *Catecheses,* 19:6; MG 33:1069 C; EA 236.
    St. Jerome, Epistulae, 130:7; ML 22:1113; EA 552.
88. *De habitu virginum,* 18–20; ML 4,470 A—473 A; CV 3,1,200–201 (ed. Hartel); EA 155–156. Cf. St. Athanasius, *De virginitate,* 2; MG 28:253 C; EA 216.
89. *Examen cum declarationibus,* cap. 4:44.
90. J. de Guibert, *Leçons,* lect. 28:334–335.
91. Cf. Allocution of Pope Pius XII on technological progress [Cf. note 65: "radio address"]. After speaking of its goodness, he continues: "It seems undeniable however, that the technology, which has reached the apogee of splendor and efficiency in our age, is turning by force of circumstances into a grave spiritual peril. To the man of today, prostrate at its altar, it seems to communicate a feeling of self-sufficiency and a sense of the satisfaction of his aspirations for unlimited knowledge and power. Its manifold uses, the absolute trust it gives rise to, the inexhaustible possibilities it promises—these aspects of modern technology open up to con-

temporary man a vision so vast as to be confused by many with the Infinite himself. To it, consequently, man attributes an impossible autonomy, which in turn, in the thought of some, changes into an erroneous conception of life and of the world. This is designated 'the spirit of technology.' What exactly makes up this spirit? These notions: It considers the highest human value and the highest value in life to be the drawing of the greatest profit from the forces and elements of nature; in preference to all other human activities it sets up as its goal whatever is technically possible in mechanical production; and it sees in these technical possibilities the perfection of life and of human happiness."

This spirit restricts man's attention to matter alone and renders him blind so far as religious truths are concerned: AAS 46 (1954) 8–10. See also the exhortation dealing with the benefits and dangers of television: AAS 46 (1954) 18–24.

92. Cf. the second part of the article, *De viribus naturae humanae in vita spirituali:* Gregorianum 35 (1954) 619–629.
93. F. Zorell, *Lexicon graecum NT*, s.v.
94. Cf. the commentary of St. Gregory the Great, *Homiliae in Evangelia* 36: 12; ML 76:1273 B; EA 1255.

"For that man has a wife as if he had her not who knows how to pay the debts of the flesh in such wise as not to be compelled by the flesh to cling to the world with all his mind; He weeps, too, but as if he wept not, who suffers the affliction of temporal losses so as always to comfort his spirit with eternal gains. He rejoices, but as if he rejoiced not, who grows happy over temporal blessings in such a way as always to think upon the unremitting tortures, and who, while lifting up his soul in joy, presses it down with the uninterrupted weight of fear that looks to the future. He purchases, but as one not possessing, who acquires the things of earth, while with caution foreseeing that he is soon to leave them. He uses this world, but like one not using it, who reduces all needful exterior things to the service of his life without letting them have the mastery of his soul, so that outwardly they are subdued and wait on him nor ever crush the striving of his soul as it tends toward the heights."

95. St. Gregory the Great, *Moralia,* 8, 54, 92; ML 75:857 D; EA 1146.
96. *Ibid.*
97. As to the need of some external separation, cf. the pretty story in John Moschus, *Pratum spirituale,* 194; MG 87, 3, 3076 C; EA 1294.

"There used to dwell an old man in the desert of Skete. One day he came to Alexandria to sell his handiwork. There he saw a younger monk enter a tavern. He was violently cast down thereby and waited outside to speak to the young man when he would come out. As happened. As soon as the younger monk came out, the elder took him by the hand and said: 'My brother, don't you know that you are wearing the garb of angels? that you are young? Don't you know that our enemy's traps are numerous? that the eyes and ears of monks are harmed in cities by various shapes and garbs? But you go into the taverns without any fear, and hear and see what you would not, and in disreputable sort have the company even of women? Leave off this conduct, I beg you. Run away to the desert, where with God's help you can be saved.' The young monk replied: 'Go to, old man. All God looks for is a clean heart.' Then the elder lifted both hands heavenward and said, 'Glory to thee, O God! I have dwelt in Skete, lo! these fifty years and have not a clean heart; and this brother who spends time in taverns possesses cleanness of heart.' He turned to the brother and said, 'God keep both thee and me, and confound me not of my hope!' "

98. St. Cyprian, *De habitu virginum,* 7; ML 4:446 A; CV 3, 1, 192 (ed. Hartel); EA 150.
99. St. Clement of Rome, *Epistula ad Corinthios* II, 6, 6; MG 1:336 C; ed. Funk 2:190; EA 10.
100. St. John Chrysostom, *Homiliae de capto Eutropio,* 5; MG 52:401; EA 359.
    St. Augustine, *In Ioannis Evangelium* 39:10; ML 35:1680; EA 679.
    St. Eucherius, *De laude eremi* 43; ML 50:702 D; CV 31:178 (ed. Wotke); EA 904.
    St. Gregory the Great, *Moralia* 22, 2, 4; ML 76:214 A; EA 1184. *Id. Hom. in ev.,* 4, 2, 5; ML 76:1090 B; 1092 B; EA 1224–1225.
101. St. Augustine *De musica,* lib. 6. c. 16, n. 52; ML 32:1190; EA 612.
102. St. Cyprian, *Epistulae* 1:14; ML 4:220 A; CV 3, 1, 14 (ed. Hartel); EA 177.
103. *Ibid.*
104. St. Jerome, *Epistles* 14:10; ML 22:353; CV 54:59 (ed. Hilberg); EA 481.
105. AAS 46 (1954) 16.
106. Cf. K. Rahner, *Schriften zur Theologie,* III, Einsiedeln-Zürich-Köln 1956, 336–342; 340:
    "Thus Christianity is essentially *fuga saeculi,* because it is the acknowledgment of the personal God of grace who freely reveals himself in Christ. Grace is not the fulfillment of an impulse-to-perfection immanent in the world, although eschatologically it brings that perfection about."
107. *Homiliae in ev.* 17:14; ML 76:1146 B; EA 1234.
108. St. Augustine, *De musica,* lib. 6, c. 16, n. 52; ML 32:1190; EA 612.
109. Cf. St. Eucherius, *De laude eremi,* 3 ss; ML 50:702D ss; CV 31:178 ss. (ed. Wotke); EA 904:
    "I would rightly call the desert the unconfined temple of our God; for he certainly dwells in silence and we must believe that he rejoices in silence. There time and again he has shown himself to his holy ones, and because the place pleases him, he did not spurn the intercourse of men. It is in the desert that Moses beholds God with countenance glorified; it is in the desert that Elias covers his fare for fear of looking upon God. . . . Only by dwelling in the desert did the children of Israel reach their longed-for land. And that nation first possessed this dry and uncultivated land that afterwards it might possess the land that flowed with milk and honey. The whole path to the true country is opened up by the sojourns in the desert. Let him that would see the good things of the Lord in the land of the living dwell in the land not fit for dwelling. And let him there be a stranger who strives to be a citizen of yonder country. Why too did he than whom no greater rose among those born of women and who cried out in the desert—why did he dwell in the desert? In the desert he baptized and preached penance. There the kingdom of heaven was mentioned for the first time. . . . Our Lord and Saviour, as the Scripture tells, after his baptism is led straightway by the Spirit into the desert. What Spirit is this? Of course, the Holy Spirit, we at once answer. The Holy Spirit's drawing into the desert is a thing that he himself silently inspires and orders, and at the Spirit's suggestion, the desert becomes a worthy suggestion. . . .

This dwelling-place in the desert, therefore, I will quite deservedly call a dwelling, a residence of faith; an ark of virtue; a sacred closet of charity; a treasure-house of piety; a jewel-box of justice. In a great palace all precious articles are kept locked away in remote closets; likewise, the magnificence of the saints hidden in the desert, which nature has preserved because of its hardships, is buried in the earth in a kind of large chamber in the desert, lest by the custom of human converse it be destroyed."

Cf. also St. Basil, *Epistulae* 2:2; MG 32:224; EA 287.

St. Jerome, *Epistulae* 14:10; ML 22:353; CV 54:59 (ed. Hilberg); EA 481.

Pseudo-Macarius, *Homiliae* 9:10; MG 34:537; EA 740.

Id., *De custodia cordis* 13; MG 34:836; EA 763.

Apophthegmata patrum, De abb. Arsenio, 1 and 2; MG 65:88B; EA 1010:

"Abbat Arsenius, while yet dwelling in the palace, made this prayer to God: 'Lord, lead me by the way on which I will reach salvation.' This voice came down to him: 'Arsenius, avoid human beings and you will be safe.' He made the same prayer another time after he had withdrawn to the solitary life, and heard this voice: 'Arsenius, fly, be still, be quiet: these are the roots of sinlessness.' "

110. Cf. St. Jerome, *Contra Vigilantium,* 16; ML 23:351 C; EA 477.
St. Ambrose, *De bono mortis* c. 5, n. 16; ML 14:584A; EA 438.
St. Cyprian, *Epistulae,* 1; ML 4:220A; CV 3, 1, 14 (ed. Hartel); EA 177.
111. T. Camelot, *Initiation théologique,* III, Paris, 1952, 1115.
112. *Ibid.,* 1115–1119.
113. For the opposition here in question, pp. 44–62; 168–196.
114. For the opposition here in question, esp. pp. 126–154.
115. For the opposition here in question, esp. pp. 188–219; 549–559.
116. *Der wahre Gnostiker,* 610: "Our attempt to grasp Clement's spiritual life in its completeness and peculiarity has shown us that the distinction [between a primitive spirituality, which Ignatius and Irenaeus especially would represent, and another, which the Alexandrians and Evagrius would represent] is hardly tenable, at least in the case of our author. In reality, Clement does not stand in opposition to the piety and mysticism of the earliest Church, but strongly under their intellectual stimulus and has made their most important impulse his own."
117. *Das Vollkommenheitsideal,* 227: "A glance at the setting of Origen's concept of imitation makes it evident that his ideal of perfection is mirrored in him. Asceticism as training, the mystical ascent, work for the brethren, martyrdom—all these are imitation of Christ—and this confirms our investigation—what great significance the image of Christ had for Origen. If our earlier research failed to take sufficient note of this and far overstressed the philosophical as opposed to the Christian element in Origen, this was partially the consequence of a one-sided preference for *De principiis* 1 Ξπερὶ ἀρχῶν . . ."
118. *Gregor von Nyssa als Mystiker,* 283: "All along the line there is observable the embittered struggle with Greek philosophy, especially Platonico-Stoic views, which finally fail to make a decisive breach in Christian modes of thought at any point, but are filled with a new intellectual content. Sometimes, it is true, their terminology is allowed to predominate. Still it always is necessary to examine carefully into what other sort of context they are being incorporated. At the same time the facts cannot be

neglected that previously for more than two hundred years the change of meaning had been already in process, and that Gregory himself moved within a solidly molded tradition."

119. Cf. esp. I. Hausherr, *Les grand courants de la spiritualité orientale:* Orientalia Christ. Periodica 1 (1935) 114–138; esp. the chapters "Spiritualité primitive" and "Spiritualité intellectualiste."

    A. J. Festugière, *L'Enfant d'Agrigente,* Paris, 1950; esp. the chapters "Mystique païenne et Charité" (127–133) and "Ascèse et Contemplation" (134–148).

120. This we have set forth more at length in the book, *De experientia mystica,* Rome, 1951, n. 83–104; and in an article, *Die Teilnahme der ganzen Seele am mystischen Leben beim hl. Ignatius und in der klassischen Mystik:* Gregorianum 37 (1956) 542–556.

121. Cf. J. Daniélou, *La vision ignatienne du monde et de l'homme:* RAM 26 (1950) 5–17.

122. Cf. K. Rahner, *Schriften zur Theologie,* III, 343: "Supposing man once to have submitted himself to the claim of God revealing himself, God can use his service in the world which is his creature as a way to him who is beyond the world; so that man not only meets the absolute God in radical opposition to the world but also in the world."

123. Cf. Apostolic Constitution, "Umbratilem" of Pope Pius XI, approving the revised statutes of the Carthusian Order: in J. de Guibert, *Documenta,* n. 651.

124. Cf. R. Egenter, *Die Aszese des Christen in der Welt, Ettal,* (sine die) (1957) 124: "All the Christian's *watching* is penetrated by faith in our Redemption. We have the power to become Light and from this world to drive the shadows within the circumference of our Life; for the Light is stronger than darkness, and God's grace makes us victorious over sin."

125. About the synthesis, cf. L. de Grandmaison, *Direction sur l'oraison:* RAM 10 (1929) 225–258.

    Id., *Écrits spirituels,* I, Paris, 1933, 126–199.

    B. Baur, *Der Wandel in Gott in der praktischen Seelsorge und seine Schwierigkeiten,* Anima 3 (1948) 214–222.

    C. Truhlar, *La découverte de Dieu chez saint Ignace de Loyola pendant les dernières années de sa vie:* RAM 24 (1948) 313–337.

    M. Nicolau, *Jerónimo Nadal, S.J. Sus obras y doctrinas espirituales.* Madrid, 1949, 318–341.

    L. Verny, *"In actione contemplativus"* RAM 26 (1950) 60–78.

    M. Nicolau, *Notas de la espiritualidad jesuitica:* Manresa 25 (1953), esp. 274–279.

    E. Coreth, *"In actione contemplativus,"* Zeitschrift f. kath. Theol. 76 (1954) 55–82.

    Christus, Cahiers spirituels, n. 6 ("Prière et action"), Apr., 1955.

    J. F. Conwell, *Contemplation in Action. A Study in Ignatian prayer,* Spokane, Washington, 1957.

126. *Contra Vigilantium,* 16; ML 23:351 C; EA 477.

127. *Confessiones,* lib. 10, c. 43, n. 70; ML 32:808–809.

CHAPTER 17

1. John 9:2–3.
2. Luke 13:4–5.
3. *The City of God,* 21:8.

4. Deut. 30:11–14.
5. Rom. 5:12.
6. I Cor. 15:22.
7. Heb. 10:7–9.
8. I Pet. 4:1–2.
9. Matt. 5:10.
10. II Cor. 6:4–5.
11. Matt. 19:23–24.
12. II Cor. 11:32.
13. II Cor. 1:5–6.
14. Matt. 11:5.

CHAPTER 18

1. R. Guardini, *The Lord,* vol. I, p. 302.
2. Lagrange, *The Gospel according to St. Matthew,* 1923, p. 347.
3. G. Guex, *The Neurosis of Regression.*
4. *Op cit.,* p. 17.

CHAPTER 19

1. They make an allusion to the distinction among the beginners, intermediates and advanced, and to the purgative ways, illuminative and unitive. Cf. and N. B. Garrigou-Lagrange, O.P., *Les trois âges de la vie interieure;* J. deGuibert, S.J., *Theologia spiritualis ascetica et mystica,* question VI.
2. Some recent studies show that theologians such as Guardini, Father Liégé, Father Brien, etc., are beginning to discover the pastoral importance of this question. Much is said today about "adult faith," "adult Christian," etc.
3. Cf. Vereecke, C. ss. R., *L'obligation morale selon Guillaume d'Ockham,* in the *Supplément de La Vie Spirituelle,* No. 45, 2nd sem. 1958, pp. 123–143.
4. B. Olivier, *La morale des Manuels* in the *Supplément de La Vie Spirituelle,* No. 27, November, 1953, pp. 381–400.
5. Cf. what St. Thomas thinks about a child's first sin: I^a II^{ae}, 89, 6, c.
6. May I note some previously published articles in this review that deal with this point: *Saint Thomas d'Aquin et la Psychologie des profondeurs,* in the *Supplément de La Vie Spirituelle* No. 36, February, 1956; *L'Acte moral et la "pseudo-morale" de l'inconscient,* in the *Supplément de La Vie Spirituelle,* No. 40, 1st sem. 1957.
7. Cf. I^a, 82, 5, 1^m; I^a II^{ae}, 22, 3, 3^m; II^a, II^{ae}, 18, 1, C.
8. I^a II^{ae}, 22, 3^m: "Significant simplicem actum voluntatis cum similitudine effectus, absque passione." Cf. I^a, 82, 5^m; II^a II^{ae}, 18, 1, C.
9. Cf. I^a II^{ae}, 1, 3, C.
10. Cf. IV Contra Gent., 22.
11. I^a II^{ae}, 4, 2^m.
12. Cf. I^a II^{ae}, 26, 3, C. See *L'amour du prochain,* especially the second part, *Cahiers de La Vie Spirituelle,* Editions du Cerf, 1954.
13. I^a II^{ae}, 24, 74, 3^m, etc.
14. Cf. I^a II^{ae}, 26, 1, C.
15. Cf. I^a II^{ae}, 50, 3, c.
16. Cf. III Sent., 23, 1, 1, c; *Q. D. deVirt. in com.,* 9, 4, c.
17. Cf. I^a II^{ae}, 17, 4, c.
18. I^a II^{ae}, 25, 3, c.

19. I^{a} II^{ae}, 77, 6, c.
20. I^{a} II^{ae}, 24, 3^{m}; cf. II^{a} II^{ae}, 158, 8, c.
21. Cf. I^{a} II^{ae}, 59, 5, c.
22. Cf. I^{a} II^{ae}, 24, 3, 1^{m}.
23. Cf. II^{a} II^{ae}, 30, 3, and 4.
24. III Contra Gent., 144.
25. Cf. I^{a} II^{ae}, 65.
26. I^{a}, 77, 7, C; cf. I^{a}, 77, 4, c.
27. I^{a} II^{ae}, 9, 5^{m}; cf. I^{a}, 115, 4^{m}; II^{a} II^{ae}, 95, 5^{m}; III Contra Gent., 85.
28. Cf. *Supplément de La Vie Spirituelle,* No. 40, 1st sem. 1957, pp. 56 and following.
29. Cf. III Supp., 3, 1. C^{m}; 4, 1, c; 4, 2, c., etc.
30. Cf. *Supplément de La Vie Spirituelle* No. 36, February, 1956; pp. 5–43.
31. Cf. I^{a} II^{ae}, 34, 4, c. Cf. *Supplément de La Vie Spirituelle,* No. 19, November, 1951, pp. 418–421.
32. I^{a} II^{ae}, 168, 2, c.
33. A. Plé, *L'Action apostolique, École de perfection,* in *La Vie Spirituelle,* July, 1956, N.B. pp. 25–27.
34. Doctor Charles Odier, *L'angoisse et la pensée magique,* Delachaux and Niestlé, 1947, p. 22.